A
Modern
Archives
Reader

A Modern Archives Reader:

Basic Readings on Archival Theory and Practice

Edited by Maygene F. Daniels and Timothy Walch

National Archives and Records Service
U.S. General Services Administration
Washington, D.C.
1984

Published for
The National Archives and Records Service
by the
National Archives Trust Fund Board

Library of Congress Cataloging in Publication Data
Main entry under title:

A Modern archives reader.

Bibliography: p.
Includes index.
1. Archives — Administration — Addresses, essays,
lectures. I. Daniels, Maygene F., 1948-   . II. Walch,
Timothy, 1947-
CD972.M63   1984   025.17'14   84-8327
ISBN 0-911333-12-6 (Paperback)
ISBN 0-911333-11-8 (Hardcover)

Contents

CONTENTS

Foreword

The Modern Archives Institute is the oldest continuous archival training program in the United States. It was founded in 1945 by Ernst Posner, who directed the Institute for The American University in cooperation with the National Archives. Posner's goal was to provide sound basic training for archivists working in all types of public and private institutions. Today, under the aegis of the National Archives Trust Fund Board and with the cooperation of the Library of Congress, the Institute carries on Dr. Posner's work in service to the archival profession. Nineteen eighty-four marks the fiftieth anniversary of the National Archives and the thirty-ninth birthday of the Modern Archives Institute. Publication of this *Reader* by the National Archives Trust Fund Board provides an appropriate commemoration of the long and mutually beneficial relationship between these two institutions.

This *Reader* grows out of the needs of the Modern Archives Institute. Until now, many basic readings in archives administration have not been available in reprint form for study and reference. This volume is designed to fill this gap. Its primary goal is to serve as a useful and practical instructional tool, but I believe that it accomplishes more. By bringing together in a single volume essays that helped formulate archival theories and more recent writings that refine or reinterpret earlier concepts or provide guidance for the practicing archivist, the *Reader* demonstrates the substance, breadth, and increasing sophistication of writings on modern archives administration and assists in giving a conceptual unity to the varied processes that constitute archives administration. I believe that all archivists whether new to the profession or its most experienced practioners will find this volume a valuable and convenient resource of information for the practice of their profession.

ROBERT M. WARNER
Archivist of the United States

Introduction

Archives administration is part intellectual discipline and part applied science. Archivists base their actions and judgments on a framework of ideas, yet within this framework they apply concepts to an often disorderly assortment of historical documents. Because archival materials are byproducts of human activity with all the peculiarities, irregularities, and irrationalities of the people and institutions that produced them, archivists must adapt their theories to the practical reality of records creation and records-keeping. Archives administration, therefore, is a blend of the abstract and the concrete, the theoretical and the practical. The essays in this *Reader* reflect this duality.

The *Reader* is a collection of basic essays for students of archives administration, developed in response to the requirements of the Modern Archives Institute of the National Archives and Records Service. The *Reader* includes classics of archival literature that outline and define important theories. It also includes more recent essays that review basic archival concepts or that synthesize various approaches into a cohesive whole. In addition, the *Reader* includes essays that demonstrate the practical application of archival principles. These selections have been chosen not only because they convey important information but also because they serve as useful models.*

No selection can possibly include all the articles that could be valuable to students of archives administration. This *Reader* is no exception. It does not include articles on technical subjects such as preservation, microfilming, and automation of archives. It also does not cover in detail concepts in archives administration that are still evolving, such as archival sampling and automated management of archives. This is not to suggest that these topics are not of great significance to students of archives administration. Instead, essays on these subjects are not included because data and opinions concerning them are changing rapidly.

The *Reader* is intended to be used in conjunction with other readily available archival texts. The "Basic Manual Series" of the Society of American Archivists, for example, provides practical introductions to many archival functions. T.R. Schellenberg's books *Modern Archives* and *Management of Archives* provide well-balanced explanations of many facets of archives administration. The *Reader* is intended to supplement the

---

*Selections are printed here as originally published with the exception of rare changes for clarification or to correct minor inconsistencies. The asterisk (*) is reserved throughout for editorial notes.

information and interpretation found in these sources with readings that provide different perspectives on basic topics or that introduce the student to aspects of archives administration not covered in other texts.

Essays in the *Reader* reflect the interests and activities of archival organizations and institutions in the United States during an important developmental period. The archival profession in the United States is relatively young. Its roots can be found in the work of nineteenth-century historical societies and the first state archival programs, which were established in the South in the early twentieth century. The profession acquired national stature, however, only with the establishment in 1934 of the National Archives and the incorporation in 1937 of the Society of American Archivists. The earliest writings in this volume appeared after the establishment of the Society and reflect its influence.

Early in its existence, the Society of American Archivists decided that the communication of information about archives administration was among its most important duties. The Society immediately expressed its commitment by inaugurating its quarterly journal, *The American Archivist*, an impressive undertaking for an organization of fewer than 150 members. Many significant additions to archival theory were discussed first at the meetings of the Society and then published in the pages of *The American Archivist*. It is not surprising, therefore, that the largest group of articles in this *Reader* first appeared in its pages.

The National Archives also has played a role in the development of the archival profession and its literature in the United States. The record group concept and the records center, among other innovations, were developed in the National Archives, tested there, and later widely adopted by the archival profession. Archivists from the National Archives wrote about these developments in periodicals such as *The American Archivist* and in staff information papers and bulletins published by the National Archives for its own staff. This work is included among selections in the *Reader*.

The development during the last decade of regional archival organizations and special interest groups in the United States and Canada has led to a significant new force in the archival profession and in archival literature. Just as one of the first activities of the Society of American Archivists was to publish *The American Archivist*, so also several regional organizations early began the publication of journals and newsletters. These periodicals have broadened dramatically the variety of writings on archives administration and have made significant contributions to the archival profession. Articles first published in these periodicals make important additions to the *Reader*.

Significant essays in archives administration also have been published in recent years in a small but influential group of volumes devoted exclusively to new articles on a wide range of archival subjects. Notable among these are *A Manual of Archival Techniques*, edited by Roland Baumann and published by the Pennsylvania Historical and Museum Commission, and a special issue of the *Drexel Library Quarterly* (Volume 11, January 1975) edited by Richard Lytle. Articles from both of these sources make important contributions to the literature of archives administration and are included in the *Reader*.

The *Reader* has been developed to be of general interest to all students of archives administration. For this reason, it includes essays concerning both records and personal papers. Even though individual essays may focus on either records or personal papers, most of the selections are relevant to the administration of both types of material. A half century ago, the characteristics of personal papers and records could be distinguished clearly. Records of organizations and institutions tended to be large, well-ordered groups of materials susceptible to rigid application of archival principles. Personal papers produced by individuals and families were usually smaller in quantity, frequently had no discernible order, and often were not susceptible to regularized treatment. Because of these differences, archivists traditionally distinguished between materials in their custody on the basis of origin, and authors often considered administration of records and personal papers as separate topics. Now, however, these distinctions cannot be made so clearly. Personal papers may be both voluminous and carefully organized and records may be small in quantity and disordered. Furthermore, manuscript repositories are likely to hold some institutional records and archival institutions are likely to include personal papers. Equally important, both records and personal papers can be increasingly created and stored in computers. With this convergence of trends, archivists increasingly view their profession as a unified whole, without absolute distinction between records and personal papers. The *Reader* reflects these developments.

Essays in this *Reader* also have been selected because of their relevance to all archival institutions, whether large or small. Despite the radical differences between institutions that may range in size from small societies with specialized collections that can be counted in pages to the National Archives of the United States with its three and one quarter billion documents, most archival institutions share similar goals. Archivists in every institution, whether large or small, seek to preserve without essential change the documentary materials entrusted to them. Archivists also take all necessary actions to make materials fully available for appropriate use in the present and the future. Every essay in this volume concerned with these issues recognizes these goals and provides practical guidance for achieving them. Their essential elements are applicable to virtually every institution.

The organized archival profession in America is still less than half a century old. Essays in this volume reveal the profession's efforts to blend

INTRODUCTION

its intellectual and practical elements into a unified whole. They also reflect the dynamism of a profession that is still working to find new solutions for problems it faces. We hope that both the challenge and excitement of archives administration will be conveyed by these pages.

MAYGENE F. DANIELS
TIMOTHY WALCH

Acknowledgments

The editors gratefully acknowledge the advice and assistance of Shelby Bale, Frances X. Blouin, Arthur Breton, Robert Brookhart, Frank G. Burke, Katherine Coram, Gwen Cyrkiel, Jan S. Danis, Kevin Flood, Elsie T. Freeman, Margaret L. Haley, Kevin Hardwick, Lorraine Herbert, Brenda Jones, Starr Oaddams, James E. O'Neill, Trudy H. Peterson, Constance Potter, Virginia Purdy, Leonard Rapport, Mary Ryan, Nancy Sahli, George Scaboo, John Scroggins, Richard Smith, George Vogt, Victoria I. Walch, Robert M. Warner and Serene Feldman Werblood, as well as the many students in the Modern Archives Institute who have shared their opinions with us and provided encouragement for this project.

The editors also wish to thank the Society of Georgia Archivists, the Midwest Archives Conference, the Society of American Archivists, Contemporary Review Co. Ltd., the Pennsylvania Historical and Museum Commission, and *Drexel Library Quarterly* for permission to reprint articles included in this *Reader*.

Chapter 1

The European Tradition

During their efforts to formulate their own archival precepts, American archivists turned for assistance to theories of their European predecessors and colleagues. European work therefore provided the basis on which Americans developed principles and programs in response to the American situation.

Ernst Posner (1892-1980) played a critical role in bringing knowledge of the European archival tradition to America. Posner arrived in the United States in 1939, a refugee from Germany, and for twenty-two years thereafter taught archives administration at the American University in Washington, D.C. Posner established the Modern Archives Institute at the American University in 1945 and served as Institute director until 1961. "Some Aspects of Archival Development Since the French Revolution" (1940), which Posner based on his European studies and experience, presents a historical overview of the development in Europe of principles and concepts that provide the foundation for most contemporary archival theory and practice. In particular, this influential essay traces the developing role of archives in national administrations and

1

delineates the evolution of the basic archival principles of provenance and original order.

Sir Hilary Jenkinson (1882-1961), the most influential British archivist of his generation, is remembered as the author of *A Manual of Archives Administration*, the authoritative guide to archival practice in Great Britain. Most significantly for Americans, however, Jenkinson was a propagandist who worked to bring the importance of archives to public attention. "Reflections of an Archivist" (1944) was published in *Contemporary Review*, a British intellectual journal devoted to a wide range of subjects. In this essay, Jenkinson reviews the essential qualities of archives and the duties of the archivist for their care and preservation. His observations about the sanctity of evidence and the archivist's responsibility to maintain documents without alteration provide the foundation for much archival theory and express a profound understanding of the archivist's vocation that remains valid to the present day.

Some Aspects of Archival Development Since the French Revolution

Ernst Posner

After the courses at one of the European archives schools had been terminated the teachers and members of the school met at a modest banquet, for which the latter had prepared a number of humorous entertainments. One of them represented an interview between the chief archivist of the Assyrian state archives and a prying newspaper man. A load of bricks was brought in and the archivist explained how archives had to be stored and arranged according to the principle of provenance and other sacred axioms. This was meant to be an amiable satire on the course on archives administration, which had dwelt somewhat exhaustively on the archives of the Orient and of classical antiquity. I should not need this warning to remember that, in order to trace an outline of the archival development of modern times, it is not necessary to start from the professional achievements of our dead and gone colleagues in Assyria and Nineveh, which have only an antiquarian interest for us. Still we shall have to go back some centuries if we want to understand the tendencies that have underlain the history of archives since the French Revolution.

There is no doubt that it is possible to reconstruct the channels of communication connecting the archives of antiquity and those of our times.[1] Certain rules of keeping the incoming and registering the outgoing letters had been observed in the Roman and Byzantine empires and, from there, taken over by the bishoprics and monasteries in Greece and Italy. We have only to remember that the beginnings of the archives of the Vatican reach back to the third or fourth century, and practices similar to those used in Rome must have obtained in other countries of Western Europe. If we try to point out the characteristic features of the early mediaeval archives, ecclesiastical as well as secular, we find that, originally, they were nearly always restricted to the incoming materials and chiefly to the instruments that had some financial or legal bearing. Kings and princes who had no permanent residence used to preserve these documents, together with the treasury and precious relics of saints, in a safe place or to deposit them with the institutions of the church,

Reprinted with permission from *The American Archivist* 3 (July 1940): 159-172.

[1]E. Casanova, *Archivistica* (Second edition, Sienna, 1928), 295 ff., and S. Pistolese, "Développement et caractère des archives du onzième siècle à nos jours," *Archivi d'Italia*, Series II, I (1934), 251-298, and also in *Guide international des archives, Europe*, Supplément (Rome, 1934), under the title, "Les archives Européennes du onzième siècle à nos jours."

which were the first to develop a certain system in keeping records. As a rule these early accumulations of documents were not connected with the chanceries, which during the Middle Ages were the sole or main administrative agencies, but formed independent units. Gradually the practice of retaining copies of outgoing letters began to prevail again. Copies were usually preserved in books, the so-called registers, and the habit of registering outgoing materials spread slowly over Europe. The consequence of this is that, at the beginning, two separate sets of archives can generally be observed: the original documents, received in the course of a transaction, preserved in a safe place, and considered as a most precious possession; and the registers or similar types of copied outgoing materials kept by the agency that had issued the originals. Occasionally a combination of the two sets was brought about when the chancery deemed it necessary to acquire copies of the documents received in order to have them at hand in the dispatch of its business.

Towards the end of the Middle Ages different factors made for a steadily increasing consolidation and differentiation of official archives. The residence of the monarchs became fixed, the scope of their administration expanded, the communities, especially in Italy, began to establish a primitive kind of archival depository, and, finally, paper came into use, whereby greater masses of materials accumulated, which needed care and preservation. As early as 1284 A.D. an inventory and regulations were drawn up for the Anjou archives in Naples; in France, Pierre d'Etampes began to catalogue the chests and registers of the Trésor des Chartes in 1318; and in England, William Stapleton drew up the first inventory of the Exchequer in 1323. All over Europe existing archives collections were arranged and listed for administrative purposes. Gradually the chanceries and similar government agencies began to preserve the incoming letters as well as the copies of the outgoing ones, but, of course, a concentration of all existing archival materials in a central depository was neither contemplated nor achieved. As a rule, the old accumulations of charters and other documents, of which the Trésor des Chartes was typical, maintained their independent existence for a long time, while newer materials remained with the agencies that had received or created them—that is, every government office kept its own files of noncurrent records. There are a few instances where unification was attempted at a very early time. As early as 1713 the erection of a special building was begun in Hanover for the storage of the records of the different parts of the country, which had been united in 1705. In Austria the Haus-, Hof-, und Staatsarchiv received the older archival materials of the house of Habsburg from 1749 and from 1762 records on foreign policy from the Hof- und Staatskanzlei. The Scottish General Register House was ready for the reception of records in 1784. But, on the whole, decentralization of archives is the characteristic trait of archives administration before the French Revolution. According to Richou, not less than 405 depositories of archives existed in Paris in 1782, and the number for France was 1,225.[2] The conception of general archives establishments as places where records of the whole state administration, central as well as provincial, should be preserved did not and could not materialize until an external impulse was received and an entirely new attitude towards archives developed.

The French Revolution marks the beginning of a new era in archives administration. First of all, the framework of a nation-wide public archives administration was established. The Archives Nationales, originally founded in 1789 as a parliamentary archives office of the Assemblé Nationale, developed under the decree of June 24, 1794 (7 Messidor II), into a central archives establishment of the state, to which the then existing depositories in the provinces were subordinated. Although during the first years of the Revolution the possibility of an actual centralization of all records in the one national archives was considered, under a law of October 26, 1796 (5 Brumaire V), sectional and local depositories were finally organized as Archives Départementales. The result was that for the first time an organic administration of archives covering the whole extent of existent depositories of older materials and of record-producing public agencies was established.

The second main effect of the Revolutionary legislation seems to have been that the state acknowledged its responsibility respecting the care of the documentary heritage of the past. During the first years of the Revolution, masses of historical documents had been destroyed as monuments of the feudal régime of the country. Minister Garat gave to the archivist of Lille the following significant advice.[3] "All the old documents with gothic script are presumably there as elsewhere only legal titles of feudalism, of the subjection of the feeble to the strong"; they could, therefore, be burned without hesitation. Gradually a sounder view began to prevail. The Agence Temporaire des Titres, created by the decree of Messidor II and charged with the disposal of useless records, later replaced (April 24, 1796) by the Bureau du Triage des Titres and headed by the archivist of the republic, showed a steadily growing comprehension of the historical value of the documents that it had to handle. The state began to learn that not only products of art but also the written monuments of the past deserve preservation and care.

The third outstanding contribution of the archives legislation of the French Revolution was the principle of the accessibility of archives to the public, which was proclaimed by Article 37 of the Messidor decree: "Every citizen is entitled to ask in every depository . . . for the production

---

[2]G. C. M. Richou, *Traité théorique et pratique des archives publiques* (Paris, 1883), 25 ff.
[3]*Ibid.*, 28.

5

of the documents it contains." It was not so much the desire to create opportunities for scholarly research that caused this regulation as the wish to provide for the needs of persons who had acquired part of the national property. But still for the first time archives were legally opened and held subject to public use.

These ideas that originated during the French Revolution constitute the main currents underlying the archival development of the nineteenth and twentieth centuries. Their spread was facilitated as considerable parts of Europe came and stayed for some time under French control and experienced the influence of French institutions. Thus the idea of a specialized public archives service was gradually taken over by other European countries. The French had established a central archives depository for the noncurrent records of central agencies and Archives Départementales for such records of the administrative sections of the state. Most of the other countries found it convenient to imitate this organization. Yet certain differences are to be observed. In France the national archives had been established as an entirely new creation, and the same thing happened in other countries where, under the impetus of a revolutionary movement, immediate action was necessary in order to provide for the records of disestablished bodies politic. The Dutch Allgemeen Rijksarchief in The Hague and the Belgian Archives Générales du Royaume may be mentioned as central establishments of this type. Other countries where the administrative framework was not so completely shattered were able to develop their archives service in a more organic way. In most of these countries a central archives depository grew out of an existing ministerial archives office. The archives of one of the government departments served as the center around which the others crystalized and finally became the central archives of the state. In England, for instance, the origin of the Public Record Office and the office of Master of the Rolls is closely bound up with the history of the chancery department.[4] Similarly, in Sweden the central archives started from the chancery, the oldest and a still existing central agency of the country. Its records were preserved in the Riksarkiv, established in 1617, which after the middle of the nineteenth century became the central archives of the state by gradually absorbing the archives of the other departments and central agencies—a process that was completed as late as 1921 by the incorporation of the Kammerarkiv.[5] Where the development of a central archives has been retarded, revolutionary movements have in recent times supplied the necessary impulse toward concentration. Germany, which until 1918 had lacked an organized archives serv-

---

[4]V. H. Galbraith, *An Introduction to the Use of the Public Records* (Oxford, 1934), 3.

[5]H. Brulin, "Das schwedische Archivwesen," *Archivalische Zeitschrift*, XXXVIII (1929), 167.

ice, founded the Reichsarchiv in Potsdam for the preservation of World War and other records; and Russia, where the system of special departmental archives had never been dislocated and where the historian had to find his way through more than a dozen departmental establishments, introduced centralization in a very radical way.

In this connection a strange fact can be observed. It might be expected that France, where the idea of the central archives originated, would have carried out this concept with utmost resolution. The contrary has happened. For a short time under Napoleon the idea was followed up along the line of continental predominance and of the renewed empire of Charlemagne: From the conquered provinces, from Spain, Italy, the Netherlands, and Germany, the most precious documents were brought to Paris to be stored in a new archives building of gigantic dimensions. But this over-strained idea of a central archives vanished with the man who had contrived it. It seems as if these years of exaggerated activity exhausted the energies of the Archives Nationales for a long time, for the oldest and one of the most noted central archives of Europe has not been able to bring about the transfer of records from all the central agencies of the state and to prevent the maintenance and expansion of special archives establishments by the ministries and other central agencies. Georges Bourgin, telling the story of the Archives Nationales since the World War, makes the emphatic comment: "Yet the Archives Nationales is not in truth wholly national, and it falls far short of containing the entire body of documents that record in diverse forms the many-sided life of the country."[6] As late as 1936, the French government tried to provide for the regular transfer of records from the ministries to the Archives Nationales. But it has not dared to question the continuance of the separate ministerial archives, which so considerably affects all research work in the French archives.

The idea of centralizing the records of all the offices of a country, central as well as local, in one archives depository, as it was originally conceived in France, has been given up. For a short time the archives administration established in Russia after the Revolution planned to carry out such centralization, but very soon it was learned that this is impossible and undesirable. As a rule a framework of archives depositories corresponds to the administrative structure of the country, with provincial or similar archives taking over the records of the respective provincial offices. England has been very slow in building up an archives organization answering the needs of her peculiar administrative set-up. Only very recently have county archives been created, and most of them are connected with libraries and similar institutions.

---

[6]G. Bourgin, "Les Archives Nationales depuis la guerre," *Revue des Bibliothèques, 1926,* 382.

The question has been discussed as to which ministry should, and would best, supervise the archives service of a country. Various experiments have been tried and the results have been diverse. When archives appeared to be developing into preponderantly scholarly institutions, it seemed reasonable to put them under the direction of the Ministry of Education. Some countries thought it more advisable to have them administered by the Ministry of the Interior. The question was discussed at the Congress of Brussels in 1910. Prussia was probably the first country in which the archives were subordinated to the head of the ministry, and it seems as if this solution, or the similar one by which they are made responsible directly to the chief of the state, has proved most successful. The countries that have established archives services most recently have preferred not to attach them to one of the ministries: Russia formerly subordinated her archives to the Central Executive Committee, and in the United States the archivist is appointed by the president by and with the advice and consent of the Senate and reports directly to the Congress.* Where the archives administration has been made subordinate to one of the ministers the result has often been that it has not been able to obtain the transfer of records from the other ministers because of their inclination to hamper rather than to promote the work of their colleague in charge of the archives. It is very significant that in France, where the administration of archives is a function of the minister of national education, he and the president of the Council of Ministers together have been intrusted with the execution of the important decree of July 21, 1936.[7]

Besides establishing the archives administration as a specialized branch of the public service, the French Revolution may be credited with making archives accessible to private examination. There are some examples even before 1789 of scholars being admitted to the use of official records. We may think of Geronimo Zurita (1512-1580), whose *Annals of the Crown of Aragon* are largely based on archives materials and who was even given access to the Archives of Simancas, or of Samuel von Pufendorf (1632-1697), who as a Swedish and Brandenburg historiographer was allowed to examine the records of the two courts. Especially the Danish Rigsarkiv was as early as the eighteenth century a center of historical activities.[8] But, on the whole, scholars had been denied access to the archives and, where they were granted this favor, it was a favor, not a right. With the French Revolution the accessibility of archives was firmly

---

*Under the provisions of the Federal Property and Administrative Services Act of 1949, the United States National Archives became a part of the newly established General Services Administration. Since then, the Archivist of the United States has been appointed by the Administrator of General Services and reports to him.

[7]*Journal Officiel de la République Française*, July 23, 1936, 7711-7712, and separate issue, Melun, Imprimerie Administrative, 1936.

[8]A. Linvald, "Das Archivwesen Dänemarks," *Archivalische Zeitschrift*, XLI (1932), 246.

established, probably with a view primarily to serving persons who might want to consult documents for judicial or other legal purposes. Accessibility for use in learned studies was at the beginning a secondary aspect, and the vast imperial archives that Napoleon accumulated in Paris were by no means intended for the general use of the public. It seems that, even more than the principle of accessibility proclaimed by the Revolutionary legislation, it was another force that threw open the doors of archives, and this force was only indirectly connected with the French Revolution. As a result of the struggle against the leveling tendencies of the Revolution and against the foreign domination of Napoleon, the beginnings of nationalism developed. The peoples of Europe gradually became conscious of their national individuality and began to use national history as a source of encouragement in the time of national disaster. Romanticism began to glorify the past, its works of art, and its literary and documentary monuments. Publishing the documentary sources, making them available for the history of the country, and writing its history out of the newly discovered materials became the aim of a vigorous and enthusiastic movement in historiography.

First the mediaeval charters, then more and more other public records, acquired the dignity of national monuments and, as such, had to be intrusted to the care of competent custodians. During the first decades of the nineteenth century the scholar entered the archives establishments of most countries and began to replace in part the former officials who had been trained in governmental writing and registry work. The ability of these officials should not be underrated. Very often they had shown a thorough knowledge of the necessities of archives administration, and, for instance, at the Prussian Privy State Archives, which was then only the archives establishment of the Privy Council, they had practiced weeding of useless records in the most careful and exemplary way. When the scholar took over most of the positions in the new general archives establishments, his attitude toward the materials had to be, of necessity, entirely different from that of the former custodians. Archives became preponderantly scientific institutions and lost somewhat their character of government offices. Conforming to the general trend in historiography, the archivists devoted most of their time and work, their efforts and their interests, to arranging and cataloguing mediaeval documents. No doubt this was a useful and, moreover, a very necessary task since, as a result of the secularization of convents and other church institutions, masses of mediaeval charters, registers, and similar materials had been taken over by the state archives. Still the effect was that these archives developed to a certain degree along the line of manuscript collections of libraries. This appears from two facts. First, the regular transfer of government records to the archives was neglected. Modern governmental papers seemed to be materials of minor importance and even undesirable. The archives, therefore, did not endeavor to take them over at regular intervals, and they accepted them only as far as the government agencies wanted to get rid of cumbersome bulk and were good enough to remember the existence of a state archives that would receive and store it. Secondly, within the archives, records were often arranged according to points of view not consistent with their peculiar character. Many archivists had obtained their training in libraries and were able to think only in terms of librarianship, and, moreover, the needs of scholarly investigation and research work were held so preponderantly important that it seemed obvious that records should be arranged and catalogued in a manner that would facilitate every kind of scholarly use. For that reason special collections of biographica, topographica, militaria, ecclesiastica, and the like were set up; artificial systematic schemes were invented, often covering the whole contents of an archives establishment; and the records were pressed into these schemes regardless of their original connection. The idea of the French "classement" and especially the organization, or rather systematization, of records in the Archives Nationales is representative of this range of ideas. Another example will show the scholarly trend underlying the archival management of this period: In 1830 Belgium had separated from the Netherlands. When the first records of the Prussian Foreign Office concerning the new kingdom were transferred to the Privy State Archives, then almost exclusively the archives depository of the Foreign Office, no place was provided for them. Here was a problem. Finally it was decided that these records would be appropriately stored under the existing heading "Duchy of Burgundy." This shows how much historical or even antiquarian points of view were prevailing with the archivists.

A change was bound to come. The principle of *respect pour les fonds*, rising from the conviction that archives bodies correspond to a former or existing administrative unit and should be preserved accordingly, was proclaimed in Belgium and France about 1840 and made its way during the following decades. It received its last and most pointed expression in the Dutch-Prussian doctrine according to which records within the single *fonds* must be maintained in the order and with the marks that they had received in the course of the official activity of the agency concerned. The well-known manual of the Dutch archivists[9] gave the final sanction to this theory, and the change in theory brought about a change in the character of archives institutions and of the work of archivists. The archives establishments began to stress their administrative features, to re-establish and to maintain contact with the administrative bodies from

---

[9]This work was originally published in 1898 by S. Muller, J. A. Feith, and R. Fruin; an English translation by Arthur H. Leavitt of the second Dutch edition (1920) has just been published as *Manual for the Arrangement and Description of Archives* (New York, 1940).

which they were expected to take over records, to demand regular transfers, and to claim a part in deciding what records should be preserved. This system has been carried furthest in some of the Scandinavian countries, especially in Denmark, where records of very recent times, often only one or two years old, are transferred to the Rigsarkiv. V. A. Secher, who was at the head of the archives from 1903 to 1915, wanted it to be chiefly a government agency and, therefore, made it his purpose to bring the ministries and the Rigsarkiv as closely together as possible.[10] The result is that, in some aspects, the Rigsarkiv has become a second registry of the ministries and that in 1938 it had to deal with no less than 22,456 of their requests for service.[11] A special room is provided where records are delivered to the messengers of the ministeries, and this work presses heavily on the other duties of the Rigsarkiv.

In a similar manner the character of the work of the archivist was affected. Where formerly it had resembled that of librarians, it began now to resemble that of registry officials. The ideal was to reconstruct as deliberately and carefully as possible the original arrangement of the files of the different *fonds* and to assign its proper place to each document and to each binder, and when this reconstructive work was completed the task of the archivist seemed to be fulfilled. To be sure, the same kind of reconstructive work was applied to the older *fonds* that had been mixed and methodized, and it proved to very useful, re-establishing the original connection of the records and thus showing the functioning of discontinued offices and rendering possible the investigation of their history; but, as a rule, the flow of incoming modern records was so great and the staffs of the archives were so lacking in subordinate help that the archivists had to spend most of their office hours arranging modern records according to original registry schemes.

A reaction has made itself felt in recent decades. It was pointed out that the original arrangement of a body of archives might not be the most desirable for purposes of research; that registry schemes might be primitive and foolish and not worth being reconstructed, especially if only fragments of the *fonds* were preserved; that, on the other hand, something must be done to make archives easily accessible for answering questions formulated according to the needs of present-day inquiries; and that, therefore, the archivist should do something more than secondhand registry work in order to make his possessions available for the scholar. Ideas along this line were first formulated in Germany by Max Bär,[12] who showed very effectively that slavish preservation of the

---

[10]A. Linvald, *loc. cit.*, 265.

[11]From an official pamphlet, *Rigsarkiv* (Copenhagen, 1939).

[12]M. Bär, *Das königl. Staatsarchiv in Danzig seine Begründung, seine Einrichtung und Bestände*, 34 ff. (*Mitteilungen der königl. preussischen Archivverwaltung*, Heft 21, Leipzig, 1912.)

original arrangement of a *fonds* is often insufficient and that a more rational order might be set up without destroying the possibility of reconstructing the former connection of archival units. In recent years voice has been given to similar doubts and reflections by Karl Gustaf Weibull,[13] a Swedish archivist, and Johannes Schultze has tried very successfully[14] to show how far the applicability of the principle of provenance is subject to certain restrictions. The struggle of ideas will go on for some time. It seems as if the future will bring a midway solution: The files and records will be arranged on the shelves and will be inventoried according to their original order; then the archivist will try to establish a more sensible arrangement, consistent with modern needs and likely to meet the questions of modern research work, by cataloguing and indexing the records and by preparing accurate and exhaustive descriptions of the contents of the different *fonds* and indicating the possible historical significance of their different series. There is no doubt that it is impossible to anticipate the historical problems of the future, to surmise for what possible purpose of research records may be made serviceable in coming times, and to make catalogues and indexes that will remain satisfactory forever. The work will have to be revised, supplemented, or even done again in the future. But that is no reason to desist entirely from the attempt to adapt our finding media to the needs of our own times without destroying the original arrangement of records as is done when archives are classified according to the French system.

The phase of archival development in which archival institutions became aware of their administrative duties, sometimes even overemphasizing them, has doubtless been responsible for enormous professional progress. It has prepared them for the time after the World War, when masses of very modern materials began to stream into their custody. It has made the archivists conscious of being a living part of the administrative organization of their country and of constituting a specialized service. It has made them realize and impress on their superiors the facts that not everybody who is interested in old books or has some background of scholarship is likely to be a good archivist and that the efficient administration of archives requires specialized training. In this respect efforts have been made in numerous countries to supply such training either by establishing special schools or institutes or by providing opportunities to acquire the necessary abilities in the course of preparatory occupation.

Building up a special science of archival technique has been a supplementary task. It seems as if the different methods of dispatching busi-

---

[13]See his last article in *Archivalische Zeitschrift*, XLII-XLIII (1934), 52 ff.

[14]"Gedanken zum Provenienzgrundsatze," in *Archivstudien zum siebzigsten Geburtstage von Woldemar Lippert*, H. Beschorner, ed. (Dresden, 1931), 225 ff.

ness, of making and keeping records, will hamper the attempts to draw up a theory of archival economy that will cover the needs of every country. At least the textbooks that have been published are so closely linked to the peculiar situations familiar to their authors that they have only a limited use in other countries. It is obvious that, first of all, the history of the making and keeping of archives has to be searched and treated for each country individually. Once this is done it will be possible to point out the common traits and discuss the common problems in the form of a comprehensive primer of archives. Meanwhile archivists have found it useful to examine the methods of other archives, especially those connected with the physical care and preservation of records, and to adapt them to the situations in their own countries if they are efficient.

Co-operation of archives administrations on an international basis has achieved at least one remarkable result. A committee of archives experts set up by the International Institute for Intellectual Co-operation has published the valuable *Guide international*, offering for the first time exact data concerning the organization and the activities of all European governmental archives institutions. The political tension of the last years and the outbreak of the war have at least delayed the carrying out of other plans of the International Institute, among which a dictionary of archives terminology is one of the most urgent, for such a dictionary is an essential preliminary to the approach to archives problems on a general scale.

The years since the end of the first World War have seen some entirely new developments. The Russian archives legislation has created the concept of the unity of governmental archives, according to which all records that are kept in government offices or have been transferred to archives depositories constitute one undivided and unique *fonds*. The decree of January 30, 1922, empowered the Russian archives administration to examine the files of all government offices of its own accord and, if necessary, to apply to the Central Executive Committee for remedy of conditions. The American National Archives Act has made similar, although less radical, provisions. Legally much the same or even greater authority had been conferred on the Master of the Rolls by the English archives legislation. The *First Report of the Royal Commission on Public Records* points out "that by the combined operation of the very wide interpretation clause in the Principal Act and of the Order in Council made in 1852, the whole of the archives of our State departments in England are now, and have been ever since the last-mentioned date, in the charge and superintendence of the Master of the Rolls. It follows that he can at any moment assume custody of all or any of them by issuing warrants under his hand as provided by the Act; and this without any exception for documents in current use in their respective Departments, or of a specially confidential nature, and without any requirement of approval by the heads of Departments, or even any provision for consulting them. In other words, it is possible, as a matter of strict law, for the Master of the Rolls, by a stroke of the pen, to dislocate the whole executive machinery of the State."[15] It is hardly necessary to mention that prerogatives of this extent have never been claimed by the English archives administration, and I do not know whether or to what extent the Russian and the American archives legislation has been influenced by these merely theoretical antecedents in England. At any rate the regulations of the two countries portend an enormous increase in the power of archives administrations, and undoubtedly the restricted right to examine the files of certain ministries conferred upon the French Direction des Archives is due to such precedents.

It seems that this will not be the final stage of the development. The authority of archives administrations to examine records still in the custody of the government agencies will prove to be a first step that leads to even broader powers. If all the public records of a nation are one sole undivided *fonds*, the agencies that are destined to receive and keep them ultimately will be justified in claiming the right to give their advice as to how the files of government offices should be organized and kept from the beginning so as to insure a satisfactory original arrangement that will also be suitable for retention by the archives agencies. We may assume that gradually the archivists will become the nations' experts who must be consulted in all questions of public record making and record keeping and likewise become the trustees who will safeguard the written monuments of the past, of the present day, and of the future.

---

[15]Royal Commission on Public Records [1910], *First Report* (London, 1912), 3-4.

Reflections of an Archivist

Hilary Jenkinson

W hat exactly are Archives? and what, in consequence, the Archivist's duties? Are Archives
sufficiently numerous, and is the care of them sufficiently important,
and sufficiently difficult technically, to produce, in a World returned to
sanity, a comparatively large number of Archivists—a number so large,
at any rate, that they would count, would matter, as a section of the
community in the same way as (say) the Librarians? and, supposing they
did take rank in this way, is there anything in the nature of their employment which would give special interest and significance to their point of
view as being different from that of other people? My answer to the last
two questions is *Yes*: that is why I am writing this article: it is a profession
of faith. Though the Archivists themselves have propounded varying
definitions of the word *Archive*, all would agree that it covers those written documents—Correspondence (registered or original), Accounts,
Memoranda—which, ever since writing came to be used commonly to
extend the scope of business and administration, have tended increasingly to accumulate in offices large and small, public and private, for the
purposes of current reference; to be consigned thereafter to oblivion in
attics or cellars; and ultimately, provided that they escaped the consequences of accident or neglect, to emerge from these dubious cocoons in
new glory as historical evidences. The business of the Archivist, put in
the simplest terms, is to take over such documents, conserve them, and
make them available for study. The outstanding feature of the Archive,
putting this also at its simplest, is that it is by its nature unique, represents some measure of knowledge which does not exist in quite the same
form anywhere else.

The possibilities of Archives as evidence, as correctives of the more
or less *ex parte* statements of contemporary or later commentators on
events, were not, of course, appreciated for some time after the accumulations began to form; and in England, as is our custom, we came later to
the recognition of new possibilities than almost any other great Nation.[1]
France, by 1791, had already begun to put her Central Archives in order,

Reprinted with permission from *Contemporary Review* 165 (June 1944): 355-361. This article was written and published in England during World War II.

[1]America, curiously enough, is our only serious competitor for last place, if we except
Asiatic possibilities: it took more than fifty years and over forty abortive proposals to bring
into being in 1934 the National Archives at Washington. Naturally, American Archivists
will draw profit as well as loss from the delay, having before them for guidance all the

15

taken some control of the local ones and evolved, to govern all, an Archive theory (characteristically summarised in five words[2]) which has held the field ever since; England had to wait till 1838 for a Public Record Office Act, and to this day has done practically nothing officially to bring Local and Private Archives into relation with the Central Authority. The fact is the more striking because Local and Private as well as Central Archives have survived in England, despite many lamentable gaps, with a richness which is probably unparalleled in any other country. How many millions of individual documents there are in the Public Record Office no one has tried seriously to compute; but they weigh between 3,000 and 4,000 tons, fill thirty or forty miles of shelving, and are numbered as 700,000 "pieces" forming 3,000 "classes" in over seventy "Groups"; and outside these—our Central Archives—lie the formidable accumulations of Local Authorities, Ecclesiastical Authorities, Public and Semi-public Institutions of all kinds, Private Corporations and individuals. From over 10,000 ancient Parishes and probably an even greater number of Manors, from County Authorities new and old, from three or four hundred ancient Boroughs, from Dioceses and other divisions of Ecclesiastical Authority, from Colleges, Schools, Hospitals, Trading Corporations and a host of other institutions, and from families and other private owners whose number no one has yet ventured to estimate, there has survived to our day (may it survive also the perils of these evil times) a mass of documents and documentary series covering in extreme cases as much as seven hundred years and in very numerous instances going back so far as to the fifteenth, sixteenth or seventeenth century.

It must not be thought that we have failed entirely to recognise and utilise this wealth. From the time of Archbishop Parker we have produced an increasing band of Antiquaries, Historians and Lawyers-scholars (to name only for each century) of the distinction of Lambard, Dugdale, Madox, Maitland, and the Webbs—who have seen themselves, and showed by their publications, the way in which the particular fields in which they were interested might be opened up by the use of new instruments. Perhaps the most illuminating example of such results is to be found in the books of Mr. and Mrs. Sidney Webb on Local Administration. Their work, apart from its other great merits, had the particular value of establishing beyond question the fact that to be important it is not necessary for Archives either to be old or to result from the activities of highly placed people engaged in great affairs. Masses of small details laboriously extracted from such drab and petty Records as Vestry Min-

---

mistakes that have been made in Europe; and their equipment will long remain the envy of establishments which have grown up in more haphazard fashion.

[2]Le respect pour les fonds.

utes, and patiently sorted and combined, became in their hands the material for an historical revision which not only modifies profoundly our ideas of social administration in the past but furnishes (if they would study it) a sure guide for politicians and reformers of the present. It is going only one step further to add that the Office Files of to-day are the Archives of to-morrow: that from the Accounts and Correspondence and Minutes of our own time (if they survive) students of the future, pursuing very possibly lines of investigation and subjects of inquiry of which we have not even thought, may produce work as fundamentally important as that History of Parishes and Highways and Justices' Sessions which no one had thought of until Mr. and Mrs. Webb were inspired to write it.

While Maitland and the Webbs were engaged in affirming or demonstrating the value of detailed work and the possibility of larger synthesis, straight publication of Archives, in the form of complete transcripts or full "Calendars" of the text of important series conveniently printed, had been going on increasingly; private enterprise supplementing the start which had been made by various Royal Commissions and Committees in the late eighteenth and early nineteenth centuries and carried on in the great series issued by the Public Record Office and the Historical Manuscripts Commission. When in 1934 an Exhibition of publications by private and local bodies was organised in London,[3] though it covered only the issues of five years, space had to be found for over 350 volumes. All this activity, however, though it has stocked the Libraries with a mass of very useful material, has only touched the fringe of the problem, made accessible a tiny fraction of 1 per cent. of the existing wealth.[4] It has, in fact, shown clearly that as a definition of the whole duty of those who find themselves charged with the custody of Archives, all *ex hypothesi* unique and all potentially valuable to Students, publication is in general inadequate: the mass is too large already, and daily becoming larger. Students, then, all except a few lucky ones who can find what they need in the printed volumes, will always have to rely to some extent upon personal access to the documents: and this gives at once a much increased importance to the task of the Custodian, who has to facilitate and superintend their researches. It also means that the measure of the Custodian's success in that task must be not only the extent to which he is found to have provided facilities (by means of arrangement, indexing, photography, and what not) for the use of those of his Archives which are in

---

[3]By the British Records Association.
[4]It would be useless to try and give in a small space any detailed account, even any adequate illustration, of the masses of Archives which have *not* been published. One may perhaps make a beginning by saying that the Record Office alone contains numerous series of the first importance, numbering each hundreds if not thousands of rolls, packages, or volumes, and covering in some cases as long a period as 700 years, which have never been touched by way of publication of anything save occasional trifling extracts.

demand, but also *the extent to which he keeps all his Records in an unimpaired condition*—all: not merely those which are momentarily the popular ones—against the day when they may become vital for somebody's work.

What in the last analysis is that element in Archives which their custodian must at all costs preserve? The answer lies in a slightly more detailed investigation of some of the peculiarities which are common to all Archives; lay and ecclesiastical; public and private; early and late; important (if you like) and unimportant; financial, legal, social, scientific, professional—*all* Archives. I shall specify in particular five.

First: Archives came together by a natural process—like Topsy, they growed. They were not singled out for preservation (herein lies their distinction from the pieces in a Museum Collection) on account of their believed value for esthetic, historical or any other purposes, by the more or less fallible judgment of an expert for whose inevitable bias and possible ignorance we have to allow. They are there: a physical part of the facts which has happened to survive.

In the second place, Archives are normally used by posterity for purposes quite different from those which caused their compilation. A medieval accountant sets down the amounts of his Master's almsgiving and the modern scientist extracts evidence illustrating a point in pathology—touching for the King's evil. Even in exceptional cases, where a document (for instance) is expressly stated to be made *in perpetuam rei memoriam*, the result is the same: it is safe to say that most of the deductions which historians and lawyers have made from *Magna Carta* never entered the heads of King John who granted it, the Barons who extorted it, or the Chancery clerks who copied it.

My third point is that the fact and nature of Custody are all-important for the Archive: first, as affecting its authenticity and impartiality, and second, as affecting its interpretation. Obviously, if the persons who made and preserved it, and their successors, did so for reasons quite independent of our interests, of which they were, in fact, ignorant, we start with the enormous advantage of knowing that there can be no intention on the part of the document to deceive us. As to the effect of Custody on interpretation—I have in mind the relation of the particular custody in which a document is preserved to the nature of the evidence it offers. To take the simplest of examples, a letter from A to B, preserved in the custody of A or his successors in business, is evidence of writing, possibly of despatch: preserved in that of B it is evidence of receipt. In neither case, of course, does it evidence the truth of A's statements, and it will probably be used eventually to prove some fact mentioned in it only incidentally, or not mentioned at all.

In the fourth place, the ranks of professing Archivists include, or should include, a vast number of amateurs and of part-time devotees. We have indicated the existence in England of something like 30,000 accumulations of documents sufficiently permanent in character to be dignified by the name of Archives: and the number is growing. Obviously not all, perhaps not much more than 1 per cent. of these, can afford, or indeed have work for, a whole-time Archivist; but that does not mean that the private owner, or the Incumbent who is custodian of a Parish Chest, or the Official of a small Council who is detailed to spend part of his office hours in regulation of the office Archives, should not, within the limited amount of time he devotes to the task, apply to his charges the same care, govern his conduct by the same rules, as the Official whose whole time is devoted to the care of a large Repository.

Finally, I would stress the universality of Archives—the way in which, once writing has become general in use, they include potentially everybody in the world and, in consequence, every conceivable human interest. It is literally impossible in a modern state to be born or die, and practically impossible to go through a large number of other experiences almost equally common, without becoming a figure in Archives of some kind: indeed, there are, as things are organised at present, very few activities that do not either themselves produce writings, which may survive as Archives, or figure in similar writings made by other people. It is, therefore, no exaggeration to say that there is not and will not be, so long as writing continues commonly in use for the business of life, any line of inquiry which can afford to ignore the possibilities of research in Archives. Half a dozen casual illustrations which I have cut out at this point for reasons of space ranged from Literary History to Patent Law and from that to Cricket, from the *cire fondue* process to the language of Diplomacy, from English Wallpapers (and the reason why they are twenty-two inches wide) to the doctrine of Apostolic Succession in the Anglican Church.

Faced with this mass, so vast and yet so diverse, what are the duties and what the qualifications of the good Archivist? Obviously he must have certain technical knowledge: he must generally be a bit of a Linguist and more than a bit of a Paleographer; sometimes a bit of an Architect; almost always a bit of a Book-binder, Librarian, Mycologist, and Photographer: must have a specialised smattering of the knowledge of many specialists. Moreover, in order to sort and list, he must understand his charges, and this means that he must have some knowledge of the technique which produced them; if he is to take charge of the Archives of a Bank, or a Court of Law, or an Ice Cream Factory, he has got to have or acquire some knowledge of Double Entry, the Common Law, or Chemistry; and even more, perhaps, of the best approach to people who possess such knowledge more fully. But all this, though considerable in quantity, is only equipment. What is to be his personal attitude? the interest which will govern and inform his treatment of his charges? What is the one common duty of all Archivists? The perfect Archive is *ex hypothesi* an evidence which cannot lie to us: we may through laziness or other imperfection of our own misinterpret its statements or implications, but itself it makes no attempt to convince us of fact or error, to persuade or dissuade: it just tells us. That is, it does so *always provided that it has come to us in exactly the state in which its original creators left it.* Here, then, is the supreme and most difficult task of the Archivist—to hand on the documents as nearly as possible in the state in which he received them, without adding or taking away, physically or morally, anything: to preserve unviolated, without the possibility of a suspicion of violation, every element in them, every quality they possessed when they came to him, while at the same time permitting and facilitating handling and use.

It may sound an easy task, but it is in fact extremely difficult—sufficiently so to defeat sometimes even the most skilled and conscientious Archivist—for the reason that the qualities or elements in question may be not merely infinitesimal, as it might seem, in importance (the precise location, for instance, of the holes through which one sheet is sewn to another); they may be actually imperceptible to all ordinary forms of examination. There may be, for example, some moral relation between two documents which nothing save their preservation, apparently by accident, in the same box remains to testify: there may be some chemical constituent in the ink or paper, invisible to the eye, unknown, if you like, even to the analyst, the modification of which by a process innocently used in the course of examination or of necessary repair would deprive the future student of evidence which would have enabled him to date, identify or authenticate. The Archivist has so to govern his own and other people's conduct in relation to the Archives in his charge as to preclude to the greatest possible extent, short of locking them up and refusing all access to them, any such modification. Perhaps one of the most difficult parts of this task is the guarding against his own interest in anything except their safety. The Archivist must not turn Student, or may at most do so only as an occasional treat, and with the strictest precaution against his own possible malfeasance; for every Student has an axe to grind, a theory to establish, a statement to prove: and that form of interest is incompatible with dispassionate conduct in sorting, in arrangement, in presentation—in all those processes in which the tiniest modification may have the most far-reaching results. I do not mean, of course, that Students are invariably unscrupulous or that their work necessarily has regrettable effects upon the Archives they use; but merely that to the Student his own interest (quite properly) seems to be of the first importance; and that left to himself he would quite often effect, in that interest, modifications (re-arrangement, to take the most obvious instance) which might be against the interests of other people. It was a Cabinet Minister who wanted all existing Records between certain dates re-arranged (by sorters from the General Post Office) in order to further a search for the name of Shakespeare. This was not done; but in very numerous cases plans hardly less revolutionary, advanced in this or that interest, have been adopted with devastating results.

To describe in detail what the good Archivist must do, and what leave undone, would be to outline here, where it is not in place and would not be read, a whole technical treatise. I have reached my point in submitting to the reader three considerations—first, the enormous mass of Archives accumulated, and continually accumulating, in any modern country and their equally enormous possibilities for the extension of knowledge; second, the very large number of people who are custodians of such accumulations and have, or ought to have, the Archivist's point of view; and, finally, the fact that of all the persons who pay service to the cause of Truth the good Archivist is the most absolute, the most complete, the most selfless devotee. It is his duty and privilege not merely to be as truthful as he can himself, but to be the guardian for the benefit of others of countless truths of all kinds—truths which interest him personally and truths which do not; yes, and truths of which he himself does not perceive the existence. The whole of his professional labours, rightly understood, are directed to that one end. In an age which has allowed important people to publish important books describing and differentiating with nice precision the possible uses of lies; which conceals lies of every variety, from *suppressio* to *imitatio veri*, from the subtler garbling to the lie direct, lies of all degrees of magnitude and turpitude, under fine names, such as "Propaganda" and "Publicity" and "News Value"; an age which witnesses with complacency the daily perversion by journalists and others of every word descriptive of importance, quantity or value; an age which permits not merely the bad and ill-informed teaching but the deliberate misleading of children and childish persons; an age in which the *ersatz* is admired, and that not in Germany only; one which has called to the assistance of misrepresentation all the resources of science—in such an age the thoughtful Archivist cannot but reflect that his professional point of view seems to be one which distinguishes him sharply from a very large proportion of the population. He may, in an expansive moment, go so far as to suggest that had his doctrine of the sanctity of evidence (which in four words is the Archivists' creed) been generally accepted in the world, the world would not now be at war. He may even be tempted to wonder whether that lost ideal of which everyone is in search, that standard for the better conduct of life which seems so difficult to determine, may after all be nothing more out of the way than a general application of those which govern professionally his own imperfect endeavours—the ideal of mere truth, the standard of truthfulness pursued not occasionally, as a means, but invariably, as an end.

Chapter 2
Pre-Archival Functions

A rchivists long have recognized that the organization and maintenance of records during the period of their active use have a direct
connection to records appraisal and archives administration. In 1941,
Solon Buck, second Archivist of the United States, wrote about this relationship as it affected the National Archives:

> A prerequisite to the judicious selection of records . . . is an appraisal of their
> value, and this appraisal can be made more readily and with greater assur-
> ance if the records have been arranged and administered with their perma-
> nent preservation or their disposal in mind. Arrangement usually takes
> place, however, when the documents are filed, that is, when they are first
> consciously considered as record materials. From this chain of circum-
> stances, it becomes apparent that the National Archives must inevitably be
> concerned with the creation, arrangement, and administration, as well as
> with the appraisal, disposal, and preservation of Government records.[1]

---

[1]*Seventh Annual Report of the Archivist of the United States for the Fiscal Year Ending June 30,
1941.* (Washington: Government Printing Office, 1942) p. 1.

Modern records management grew out of archivists' concern for records before their transfer to archival custody. The goal of records management is to achieve economy and efficiency in the creation, use, and maintenance of current records. Frank Evans provides a comprehensive history of the development of records management as an offshoot of the archival profession in his essay "Archivists and Records Managers: Variations on a Theme" (1967). Evans emphasizes the essential bonds between archivists and records managers based on their common interests and the unity of the life history of records. He argues for an increasingly close and cooperative relationship between the two professions.

Today records managers are often specialists trained in technical fields such as files maintenance, forms design, mail management, and word processing. In some institutions, however, archivists themselves are responsible both for management of current records and for care of archives. "Records Management and the Walking Archivist" (1975), by Patricia Bartkowski, describes records management functions from the perspective of those archivists who have dual responsibilities. By so doing, Bartkowski vividly demonstrates the relationship of records management to administration of archives in any institution, whether large or small.

The records center is another concept that grew out of archivists' interest in pre-archival administration of records. In "Archival Janus: The Records Center" (1968), Herbert Angel describes this versatile and practical institution and suggests its value to assist the archivist in identification, appraisal, and maintenance of valuable records.

Archivists and Records Managers: Variations on a Theme

Frank B. Evans

"In today's situation we find ourselves with archivists and records managers," observed a Federal records officer in a paper delivered a few years ago at this Society's annual meeting. "I suppose," he continued, "that an archivist is a records manager who has specialized or that a records manager is an archivist who has become a general practitioner. Whatever the difference is, there is need for a closer relationship between the two."[1] Not all of us need agree with our colleague's differentiation between archivists and records managers, but we must emphatically endorse his proposal for a closer relationship between the two. This plea has been one of the basic themes in our professional literature for more than two decades, and, as a contribution toward that closer relationship we all seek, I should like to examine that theme and its variations. Certainly we "second generation" archivists and records managers have much to learn from what we too frequently dismiss as simply the "ancient history" of our profession.

Records management, as a professional activity of government archivists, received its first formal recognition by this Society in 1941 when the Society's existing Committee on Reduction of Archival Material was renamed the Committee on Record Administration. The then committee chairman, Emmett J. Leahy, continued to serve as chairman of the renamed committee.[2] Behind this development was the formal establishment by the National Archives, early in 1941, of a "records administration program" intended "to assist in developing throughout the Government principles and practices in the filing, selection, and segregation of records that will facilitate the disposal of or transfer to The National Archives of records as they become noncurrent."[3] The basic justification for this program was the need within the Government for planned programs of records disposal and for beginning as early as pos-

Reprinted with permission from *The American Archivist* 30 (January 1967): 45-58. This paper was presented at the 29th annual meeting of the Society of American Archivists in 1965.

[1] J. J. Hammitt, "Government Archives and Records Management," in *American Archivist* (hereafter cited as *AA*), 28:219 (Apr. 1965).

[2] *AA*, 4:136 (Apr. 1941); *cf. AA*, 3:123 (Apr. 1940). The following year the name of the committee was given as "Records Administration"; see *AA*, 5:59 (June 1942).

[3] Philip C. Brooks, "Current Aspects of Records Administration: The Archivist's Concern in Records Administration," in *AA*, 6:160 (July 1943).

sible in the life history of records the process of selection for preservation and elimination.[4]

The archivists who thus became involved, on however limited a scale, in the administration or management of current records did not regard themselves as creating a new profession, or even as adding a new dimension to an existing profession. In reviewing the situation late in 1942, Philip C. Brooks, one of the new archivist-record administrators, observed that "the present-day interest of archivists in records before they become archives represents the florescence of a phase of archival economy that has been manifested without such clear recognition for some time." Dr. Brooks refuted the "occasional implication of a skeptic that we [archivists] have no concern for the way in which government agencies currently make and file records" by referring to eight articles, written by leaders in the profession and published in earlier issues of the *American Archivist,* in which "some responsibility of the archivist for records before they reach his custody" had been recognized. He found further evidence of this responsibility in the provisions of several State laws dealing with the inspection and control of inks, paper, and filing equipment; in the uniform State Records Act proposed by the Society in 1940, under which the head of the State archival agency would have supervision over the "making, administration, and preservation" of "all public records" in a State; and in the National Archives Act of 1934, which empowered the Archivist of the United States to inspect records in Federal agencies.[5]

Addressing himself directly to the relationship between archives and records administration, Brooks noted that "records have usually been a concern of management engineers, even though they have not always taken archival interests into account." Nevertheless, "archivists have been equally prone to ignore the interests of current administration. Yet the two cannot help affecting each other," he concluded, "and they can work together to mutual advantage. . . . Certain basic tenets of archival faith are being developed in the meetings and publications of this Society through the years. I believe the legitimate interest of the archivist in records administration should become one of them."[6]

To overcome whatever skepticism still existed among his archival colleagues, Brooks added one final justification for his proposal and a warning:

> Current record administration is to the archivist of today what the study of diplomatics was to the archivist of earlier times—and more. Authorities on

---

[4]See particularly Emmett J. Leahy, "Reduction of Public Records," in *AA*, 3:31-38 (Jan. 1940); and Philip C. Brooks, "The Selection of Records for Preservation," in *AA*, 3:221-234 (Oct. 1940).

[5]Brooks, in *AA*, 6:158-159. The citations in Brooks' article are especially useful.

[6]Brooks, in *AA*, 6:161, 164.

the qualifications of archivists say that archivists, in order to apply the principle of provenance, should know the methods by which records in their custody are produced. The complexities of modern administrative documentation have so multiplied the technical facets of filing that many persons regard it as a mysterious cult to be either feared or blandly ignored. Neither attitude is consistent with the principle that the whole life history of records is an integrated continuous entity. No period in that history can be ignored. It is inevitable that the iniquity of omitting care for records as they accumulate shall be visited upon the third and fourth generations of later administrators, archivists, research students, and society as a whole.[7]

Evidence of the success of this appeal assumed a variety of forms. Sessions on current records administration became a regular feature of the Society's annual programs; studies of current records administration programs in various Government agencies were published in the *American Archivist*; books and manuals on current records administration were reviewed in the journal; and the section on "Filing Techniques and Administration of Current Records" in the journal's annual bibliography continued to expand. In 1944 Brooks succeeded Emmett Leahy as chairman of the Society's Committee on Records Administration,[8] and for the next several years this committee, convinced that the most urgent need of the profession was "to arouse the intelligent interest of administrators in the importance of economical records administration," devoted itself to the task of preparing a pamphlet on the subject based upon the experience of the Federal Government and intended for the use of State and local governments.[9] In reporting to the Society on the completion of this pamphlet in 1949, Committee Chairman Brooks explained that the purpose of the committee was "to state common denominators of guidance for public officials in any way concerned with or responsible for records" and that the "common interests of records officers and archivists" had been recognized throughout the pamphlet.[10] The product of these labors many of you will recognize as *Public Records Management*, by Philip C. Brooks, published by the Public Administration Service in 1949. In a very real sense this publication marked the close of one era and the beginning of another in the professional relations between archivists and records managers.

According to our records management colleagues in the National Archives and Records Service, records administration in the Federal Government during this period generally meant the beginnings of what we today call correspondence management, with the emphasis on form

---

[7]*Ibid.*, p. 164.
[8]*AA*, 8:160 (Apr. 1945).
[9]*AA*, 10:78 (Jan. 1947).
[10]*AA*, 13:67 (Jan. 1950).

letters, files management, mail management, records storage, documentation, and surveys and audits, but with the emphasis in all of these activities on records disposition.[11] State archivists were increasingly hard pressed to keep pace with this rapidly developing Federal example, but many of them continued to hold to the ideal of rendering "advice and assistance to other departments in meeting their current records problems. We will not, of course, understand in detail all the procedures of filing and records handling with which the different departments have to deal," admitted one State archivist, "but through our contacts with many departments, with varying functions and problems, we will be in a position to develop a broad point of view and perspective which . . . [may] prove valuable to each department in solving its own problems."[12]

The only dissenting voice in the pages of the *American Archivist* during this period is in a 1948 article, "The Archival Profession in Eclipse." Explaining that his was "an essay in de-emphasis, an attempt to show that the archival profession is moving away from fundamental objectives because of the excessive influence of the management specialists who have become increasingly involved in records work, particularly since World War II," the author maintained that the result of this "disproportionate emphasis on management activity" was the "exclusion of the pursuits that ultimately justify the archivist as a member of a true profession."[13] Recounting the circumstances that led to the development of records administration within the Federal Government and tracing that development during the World War II and post-war years, the author readily admitted the many practical, immediate, and tangible benefits of records administration. He professed alarm, however, at what he termed the "heavy price paid" for these benefits:

> Among American archivists the cost has been the abandonment of the tradition of scholarship and research, desertion of historiography, and renunciation of a broad intellectual comprehension of the records, particularly an understanding of how they relate to the world of reality beyond the walls of the repository. The professional archivist is atrophying. At one time, he was coming to be recognized, on a coequal status, as the research partner of the historian, the economist, the administrator and the scientist. It was considered of primary importance that the archivist should be able to render his documents, however complex and specialized, available and usable. Now it

---

[11]Lecture by Arthur J. McCarrick, Oct. 21, 1963, in National Archives and Records Service Workshop on Records Management Principles and Techniques. See also National Archives, *Disposition of Federal Records: How To Develop an Effective Program for the Preservation and the Disposal of Federal Records* (Washington, 1940).

[12]Christopher Crittenden, "The State Archivist Looks to the Future," in *AA*, 8:190-191 (July 1945); see also Henry Howard Eddy, "The Responsibility of the State Archivist to the Other Officers of His State Government," in *AA*, 11:28-35 (Jan. 1948).

[13]Irving P. Shiller, "The Archival Profession in Eclipse," in *AA*, II:227 (July 1948).

appears to be sufficient to house the records safely, to mechanize reference service on the documents, and to keep storage and maintenance costs down to a minimum by means of wholesale records destruction.[14]

Claiming to speak for "many others" who had "noticed and deplored" this tendency, the author admitted "that it would be folly to deny categorically the contributions of a records management program," and instead he advocated better training of archivists and greater "opportunity for advancement and for intellectually challenging work, commensurate with the training and talent demanded."[15] It had already become necessary to recall, in his judgment, "that the archivist has along with his obligations to save money for his institution, an intellectual mission of at least equal importance."[16]

The temptation to comment—at length—on these observations and recommendations is almost irresistible, but in the interest of concluding this survey I forgo the pleasure. At the time this critique of the evolution of archives administration in the United States made its appearance, the First Hoover Commission—the President's Commission on Organization of the Executive Branch of the Government—was already deeply involved in its studies, and it was particularly appropriate that the next statement of the relationship between archivists and records managers, as they had now come to be called,[17] was written by one of the leaders of this movement.

In an article on "Modern Records Management" Leahy acknowledged that "aggressive and wide-spread destruction of records" presented a "critical problem," and he maintained that "any destruction of records must provide maximum insurance that the essential core of recorded experience in the form of modern records is preserved." Such insurance he found adequate in the Federal Government and in some States, but inadequate in many States and totally lacking with regard to the essential records of American private enterprise. "Management must be prevailed upon," he insisted, "to utilize the archivist's experienced counsel and the historian's expert training." He advocated the establishment of records centers as "extraordinarily effective in making substantial savings" but added that without the counsel of the professional archivist and historian "there is no insurance that the essential core of

---

[14]*Ibid.*, p. 229-230.
[15]*Ibid.*, p. 231, 232.
[16]*Ibid.*, p. 227.
[17]In addition to the areas of activity previously indicated under "Records Administration," the Navy Department had developed programs in forms management and the management of office equipment and supplies. These were included under the new term "Records Management"; Lecture, Oct. 21, 1963, NARS Workshop on Records Management.

records will be preserved, made available, and the experience recorded therein put to work."

"It is not enough," he concluded, "that the archivist, the historian, and the analyst give their unsolicited *nihil obstat* to . . . attacks on unnecessary record making. It can be readily conceded that a record which need not be created for the purposes of management cannot legitimately be expected by the archivist, the historian or the analyst. There is little danger on this score, therefore, but there is a substantial loss in the degree of potential gain because there is not available to management the valuable help and guidance the archivist and the historian have to give."[18] The author of this manifesto on modern records management and of these observations on the essential relationships between archivists and records managers, Emmett J. Leahy, was director of the National Records Management Council, which had been established in 1947, and also director of the First Hoover Commission's "task force" reviewing records management in the Federal Government.[19]

At the Society's annual meeting in 1950 the Archivist of the United States, Wayne C. Grover, informed the profession regarding "Recent Developments in Federal Archival Activities." These included, in rapid chronological order, the publication of the Hoover Commission recommendations on records management; the transfer of the National Archives to the new General Services Administration; the passage and signing by the President of the Federal Records Act of 1950; the establishment of a Federal records management staff, "separate from the staff of the National Archives but within the single organizational entity now called the National Archives and Records Service"; and the establishment of a system of Federal Records Centers in various regional areas of the country.[20] In explaining the circumstances attending these developments, Grover, at least indirectly, addressed himself to those who feared the archival profession was "in eclipse." He cited "the increasing amount of time and energy and thought" the "most experienced and best qualified archivists in the professional custodial branches of the National Archives were having to give to records problems in other agencies of the Government, at the expense of archival work within the National Archives." While affirming his belief that archivists should not "retreat to the cloisters," he explained that the National Archives "was at the point where some balance and stability had to be achieved: Some turning back,

---

[18]Emmett J. Leahy, "Modern Records Management," in *AA*, 12:233-235 (July 1949).

[19]*Ibid.*, p. 242.

[20]Wayne C. Grover, "Recent Developments in Federal Archival Activities," in *AA*, 14:3 (Jan. 1951).

within the branches having custody of records, . . . toward the traditional functions that had had to be neglected during the war."[21]

As for the relationship between the new records management staff and the archival staff of NARS, Grover added:

> There is and always will be, I hope, much overlapping between current records management and archival activites. But each has a basically different emphasis and requires different qualifications, no matter how closely the activities and individuals involved are related to each other in common purpose.
>
> Speaking by and large, academic qualifications in history and the social sciences are essential for an archivist, if he is to develop subject-matter competence in the areas of documentation for which he is responsible. I believe he must develop such competence if he is to perform his professional chores intelligently. On the other hand, management outlook and experience are essential to the records management specialist, if he is to develop as a member of the management team—and it is only as a member of that team that he can ever hope to be effective in the long run. In a word, the whole field of dealing with records has progressed sufficiently to demand a certain amount of specialization.[22]

The president of the Society that year, 1950, was Philip C. Brooks, and he devoted his presidential address to the topic: "Archivists and Their Colleagues: Common Denominators." Admitting his hesitancy to address his audience as "fellow archivists" because of the "variety of professional activity" they represented, he nevertheless reminded his listeners that he had "argued strongly for years that variety is both stimulating and essential to our being an alert, useful organization," and that the membership clause of the Society's constitution had been carefully phrased to include a wide variety of specialists and activities.[23] "There must be a difference between the broad concept of an archivist as we use it in defining the membership of this Society and the more precise view that must apply in civil service categories," he insisted. "One is a matter of interest, the other of occupation. We all have a concern for the preservation and effective use of valuable evidence of human activity in the form of records. We should focus on that common denominator." Referring to the theme he had stated a decade earlier, Brooks again reminded us that archivists had "entered the records administration field because economical administration of records at all stages is closely akin to the specialized activities of archivists, and because the results of good or bad records administration affect the job that archivists can later do with the

---

[21]*Ibid.*, p. 6-7.

[22]*Ibid.*, p. 7-8.

[23]Philip C. Brooks, "Archivists and Their Colleagues: Common Denominators," in *AA*, 14:34-35 (Jan. 1951).

31

records."[24] His views on the other common denominators of archivists and their colleagues in the fields of librarianship and private papers lie beyond the scope of this paper, but I recommend his entire article to your rereading.

The Federal Records Act of 1950 defined records management in the Federal Government as including records creation, maintenance, and disposition. Forms management and the management of office equipment and supplies had already been added to the activities formerly encompassed by the term "record administration," and this rapidly developing field received further impetus as a result of the recommendations of the Second Hoover Commission, 1953-55. This Commission popularized the term "paperwork management" and the concept of solving paperwork problems in the Federal Government through the creation of still other specialists within the framework of a broad administrative control program. The result was the addition of new programs and the creation of new specialists in directives management, reports management, paperwork quality control, and clerical work measurement. In brief, records management had evolved rapidly into a specialized phase of general management dealing with the origin, use, and control of records.[25]

And the implications of these developments for our Society and profession? Dr. Grover in his 1954 presidential address replied directly to this question as follows:

> The disturbing issue of recent times in this Society and in the archival profession has been the proper relationship of archivists and archival agencies to what is variously called "records management," "records administration," or if you like, "record administration." What is involved is the extent of the archivist's interest, or lack of interest, in the administrative procedures and techniques that result in the creation and maintenance of records in current files.[26]

While admitting that "there is room for debate on this subject and even more room for misunderstanding," Grover made quite clear the view of the National Archives and Records Service and the situation in the Federal Government. The common link between records managers and archivists, he asserted, "is their interest in improving the quality and decreasing the quantity of an organization's records. But they [records managers] are not archivists. They are specialists in their own right, usually placed near the top in the organizational hierarchy and able to demand fair pay. Like archivists,

---

[24]*Ibid.*, p. 36, 39.

[25]Lecture, Oct. 21, 1963, NARS Workshop on Records Management.

[26]Wayne C. Grover, "Archives: Society and Profession," in *AA*, 18:3-4 (Jan. 1955).

they are intent upon raising their professional standards and improving their training." But, although these specialists are not archivists, "they were developed under the auspices of archivists" to fill an increasingly obvious and basic need: the need of administrators for "the continuous, intelligent, and practical day-to-day assistance of specialists on their own staffs." Records managers "contribute to and improve the administrative methods and actions out of which archives are formed. In the Federal Government they are becoming quite numerous," he added. "They are spreading into business organizations and into State Governments. The question is, then, is it time for the archivists and the records managers to part company?"[27] After reviewing the origin and history of the archival profession in the United States and the Society and its purposes, Grover concluded:

> My answer to the question of whether or not the time has come to part company—with anybody—is no. On the contrary, we need to bring more company into our ranks, to become imbued with the missionary fervor of the Public Archives Commission, and to combine it with fervor for good records management that is attracting the attention of administrators in Government and out. It is folly for archivists even to think of parting company, literally or psychologically, from the newly developed specialists in records management; and no less folly on the records management side than on the archival side. Our numbers are too few; our common interests too important.[28]

As you know, in the following year, 1955, both the Association of Records Executives and Administrators and the American Records Management Association were organized. That fall this Society's president, Morris L. Radoff, also chose for his address the theme of "What Should Bind Us Together." While agreeing in principle with Grover, he questioned Grover's reasons for his conclusion.

> We do not share *common interests*, we have only *one interest*; namely, the guardianship of records. And surely if we have one interest we belong together, and we should be called by the same name. There is nothing between heaven and earth to prevent an American records management specialist from being called an archivist or *vice versa*. . . . Why could not the same man be both archivist and records manager? Is the care of the written word so complex that no man has science enough to master it? Is

---

[27]*Ibid.*, 4-5. See also Robert H. Bahmer, "The National Archives After 20 Years," in *AA*, 18:202 (July 1955), in which Dr. Bahmer observed that "the farther records management has moved into the field of current records maintenance and handling and into the more uncertain field of record creation, the less the professional archivist, as an archivist, can contribute."

[28]Grover, in *AA*, 18:9-10.

it so abstruse that it requires the combined efforts of obstetrician, pediatrician, geriatrician? Or is the humble general practitioner all that is needed? Are we, in other words, creating specialists where specialties do not exist; are we thinking too much of the record as a living organism requiring special care at various stages of its life history, when in fact it is inanimate and of the same texture and form from beginning to end?[29]

Dr. Radoff's answers are implicit in the questions themselves. For the present, he advised, "Those of us, records management specialists and archivists alike, who trained ourselves in *our* fields must do what we can to understand the other. The archivist," he warned, "must not continue his stiff-necked aloofness, nor must the records management expert despise the deliberate approach of the archivist." He then turned to the problem of the preparation of new archivists entering the profession and proposed an education and training that would make them "masters of the whole records field." Above all, he concluded, "we should strive to give our profession the dignity, the unity, the opportunity for service that can come only from the mastery of a body of learning. And this body of learning should by all means include the whole art and mystery of records. This surely will bind us together."[30]

At the same annual meeting in 1955, Robert A. Shiff, president of the National Records Management Council, presented his views on "The Archivist's Role in Records Management." According to Shiff, "The functions of the archivist and records manager are not only closely related but, in many instances and to a growing extent, they are interchangeable." His organization, he maintained, had been unable "to maintain any viable distinction between archivists and records managers. We find it necessary to be both archivists and records managers at the same time." Because of the corporate name, however, his council preferred the terminology "records management" and "records manager."[31] After reviewing the situation with regard to business records Shiff concluded:

There are some who contend that because the archivist serves the scholar and the records manager serves the administrator, the two functions require different disciplines and therefore cannot be fulfilled by the same person. We do not believe that this is uniformly true. Certainly, if it is true, then most of the business world will remain outside the sphere of archival influence. Few companies, if any, can reasonably maintain two separate positions, one for an archivist and one for a records manager. If we are going to have a

[29]Morris L. Radoff, "What Should Bind Us Together," in *AA*, 19:4-5 (Jan. 1956).
[30]*Ibid.*, p. 7-9.
[31]Robert A. Shiff, "The Archivist's Role in Records Management," in *AA*, 19:111 (Apr. 1956).

general archival and records management consciousness in business it must be in conjunction with the ability of the archivist or the records manager to serve the combined need.[32]

During the next 2 years not one article—indeed, not even a passing reference that I could find—appeared in our journal on the subject of our theme. But by 1958 we find the beginning of a new quest for a solution to the basic problem. The manager of a records division of one corporation, speaking at our annual convention on "The Relation Between Archivists and Records Managers," asserted:

We record managers are primarily businessmen, who pursue efficiency and economy. . . . There are probably records of importance among those we throw away, but we have no way of knowing. Perhaps this is where the experience of archivists could help us.[33]

His appeal was that we "explore the possibility of a closer relation between the archivist and the record manager—coexistence, if you wish." Explaining that record managers "are subject to somewhat different pressures than archivists," he insisted that "the differences between us— and Heaven knows there are some—are almost all due to lack of communication between us."[34]

This appeal was echoed by the other speakers at the panel session in which he participated. A records manager at the State level, speaking on "Archivists and Records Managers—A Partnership," asserted:

If there is competition between . . . [the two groups] it is one between two branches of a common profession. If this emphasis on differences is pursued with vigor, the entire profession will be the loser; and the entire profession will bear the responsibility for the loss. . . . Take away one—records management—from its relationship to the other—archives administration—and you remove a vital link. Combine the two branches and you present a united front whose total impact toward professional betterment is many times greater than the sum of efforts separately pursued.[35]

Finally, a State archivist, later president of the Society, expressed her conviction that "archivists and records managers must resolve not to continue on divergent paths but rather to join together in fostering the objective of closer alignment, combining their knowledge and efforts to

---

[32]*Ibid.*, p. 120.

[33]Robert H. Darling, "The Relation Between Archivists and Record Managers," in *AA*, 22:214 (Apr. 1959).

[34]*Ibid.*, p. 211.

[35]LeRoy DePuy, "Archivists and Records Managers—A Partnership," in *AA*, 23:49 (Jan. 1960).

bring about an integration of interests."[36] Two years later, however, Mary Givens Bryan, in her presidential address to the Society, while disclaiming any intention of attempting to define the terms "archivist," "records manager," and "records administrator," rather pointedly reminded us that "far more has been said than done about our being one and the same." Her own views were indicated by her later reference to "the special area within archives administration called records management."[37] Here, for all practical purposes, the matter still stands.

What conclusions can be drawn from this survey, and of what value are they for the development of our one—or two—professions? At the outset I readily acknowledge the inadequacies of this historical reconstruction of a theme. Like all essays in contemporary history it suffers from a too heavy reliance upon the printed word, and will, I hope, someday be rewritten, corrected, and elaborated upon through the use of official and personal records and taped interviews not now available to the researcher. But with all its inadequacies, I believe we have much to learn and ponder as a result of this brief journey we have taken.

I shall not attempt simply to draw the logical conclusions. Instead, I would call to your attention the continuing fact of mutual misunderstandings. No one conversant with modern paperwork management as it exists in the Federal Government—it has now expanded still further to include source data automation, automatic and electronic data processing, and information storage and retrieval—can realistically expect the same staff to function effectively in conducting a fully developed records management and a fully developed archival program. Where archival programs have not developed much beyond accessioning records antedating the New Deal and beginning arrangement and description work, and where records management programs have progressed little beyond inventorying and scheduling records for disposal and operating records centers, the archivist-records manager can and does exist. The extent to which most archival and records management programs in our States fit this description is amply documented in Dr. Posner's valuable study of State archives.[38] And there is much evidence that a similar study of archi-

---

[36]Dolores C. Renze, "The State Archivist—3-D Public Servant," in *AA*, 23:275 (July 1960).

[37]Mary Givens Bryan, "Changing Times," in *AA*, 24:5, 8 (Jan. 1961). See also Robert W. Garrison, "Maximum Records Management," in *AA*, 23:415-417 (Oct. 1960). The latter article defines maximum records management as "the complete utilization of scientific techniques for records control, creation, reduction, and reference" (p. 416) and maintains: "The records management analyst researcher, thrown into a sea of business and/or non-business records the classification of which often demands knowledge of both library and archival sciences, knows that greater *camaraderie* must develop among the archival, library, and records management fraternities" (p. 417).

[38]Ernst Posner, *American State Archives* (Chicago, 1964). See particularly Chapter 3, "A Summary of Findings," and Chapter 4, "Standards for State Archival Agencies."

val and records management programs in our business, religious, and educational institutions would not reveal too many well developed programs in both these fields. All of us have too much to do in fully accepting our own responsibilities, and in learning from each other, to spend time arguing over our differences.

Theodore R. Schellenberg, writing nearly a decade ago, defined "Archival Interest in Records Management" largely in terms of the experience of the Federal Government. His point of reference was the archivist's interest and concern in the management of current records, but his observations are equally applicable to the creation of records and to records of private as well as of public origin. Records managers, he reminded us, determine the quality of our archives, quality in the sense of the completeness or adequacy of the documentation, its integrity (including its freedom from useless material), and its accessibility or serviceability for reference and research purposes. In a very real sense records managers also determine the nature of our work with archives, for upon the success of their efforts depends the ease or the difficulty with which records can be appraised for disposition and can be selected for preservation; the ease or difficulty with which they can be physically preserved; the ease or difficulty with which they can be arranged and described; and the ease or difficulty with which they can be made accessible and available for use.[39] The interest of the archivist in records management is therefore not only legitimate—it is essential. Conversely, it is the recognition and full acceptance of his responsibilities in these matters that distinguish the professional records manager. Like the archivist he too is ultimately responsible to society at large and thus to posterity.

Regardless of the particular routes we may travel in our need for professional betterment, we share the common problems of the need for education, training, and closer relations with all of our colleagues in the fields of information and documentation.[40] Our common interests and our common problems—these are our "common denominators," to use Brooks' characterization; these, to borrow from Radoff, are "what should bind us together"; and, finally, these are what constitute the foundation, to borrow Grover's phrase, of archives as a society and a profession.

---

[39]T. R. Schellenberg, *Modern Archives: Principles and Techniques*, p. 26-32 (Chicago, 1956).

[40]See particularly Thornton W. Mitchell, "The State of Records Management," in *AA*, 24:259-276 (July 1961).

Records Management and the Walking Archivist

Patricia Bartkowski

W illiam Benedon, Corporate Director of Lock- heed Aircraft Corporation for Records Man- agement, and former President of the American Records Management Association, defines "records management" as: "The direction of a pro- gram designed to provide economy and efficiency in the creation, organ- ization, maintenance, use and retrieval, and disposition of records, assuring that needless records will not be created or kept and valuable records will be preserved and available."[1] Implicit in this definition are concepts, functions, facilities, and materials ranging from correspon- dence, forms and reports management to equipment surveillance, filing system control, inventories, microform applications, records centers, records managers, retention and disposal schedules, screening, searches, storage density, and vital records control and audit.

A cursory glance at records management seems to indicate that it is not within the purview of the archivist. A closer examination, however, reveals otherwise. Today's current valuable records will be tomorrow's archives. The records manager's main concern with current records is economy and efficiency, whereas the archivist's is the identification and protection of valuable records before arrival at the archives. The archi- vist's involvement in records management also can help prevent the archives from being a dumping ground for unwanted records of ques- tionable value. As Frank B. Evans has written, "The interest of the archi- vist in records management is therefore not only legitimate—it is essential."[2]

Implementing a records management program consistent with Benedon's definition is not feasible for many institutions. Constructing, or even renovating, a building to make it suitable for a records center can be costly. Additional staff salaries also must be considered. A university

Reprinted with permission from *Georgia Archive* 3 (Summer, 1975): 125-134, with slight revisions by the author. *Georgia Archive,* the journal of the Society of Georgia Archivists, is now titled *Provenance*.

[1]William Benedon, *Records Management* (Englewood Cliffs: Prentice-Hall, Inc., 1969), 258.

[2]Frank B. Evans, "Archivists and Records Managers: Variations on a Theme," *American Archivist,* 30 (January, 1967), 58. See also Gerald F. Brown, "The Archivist and the Records Manager: A Records Manager's Viewpoint," *Records Management Quarterly,* 5 (January, 1971), 21-22, 38; and R. A. Shiff, "The Archivist's Role in Records Management," *American Archivist,* 19 (April, 1956), 111-120.

archives, like most archives, is faced with budget, staff, and space constraints. Its primary concern is collecting, arranging and preserving material, preparing finding aids and giving reference service. Within this framework, records management becomes one facet of the archives program.

Consider the case of two individuals in Macon who want to reach Atlanta, but for different reasons. Airplane, car and bus are the conventional means of transportation. Each has advantages and disadvantages, but each will allow the individuals to realize the goal of reaching Atlanta. Assume for whatever reason—lack of funds, expired driver's license— that one of the two cannot use these conventional methods. Does this necessarily mean that the goal must be sacrificed? No. One can walk to Atlanta. Admittedly more time and effort must be expended, but in taking the first step, no matter how small a step, progress has been made. This paper is intended for the walking archivist—that is to say, the archivist who must be both archivist and records manager, the archivist without the conventional records center, and the archivist, recalling Benedon's definition, who implements a program designed to assure that needless records will not be kept and valuable records will be preserved and available.

The walking archivist's first step can be to standardize transmittal of material to the archives. Records arriving in a variety of containers present an archives, expecially one where space is a critical factor, with several problems. Non-uniform containers prevent maximum storage density. Their size may prohibit their shelving and force stacking on floors. Boxes of different dimensions may not stack easily, or withstand the weight of other boxes, thus causing damage to records. Tall stacks may topple and cause injury to employees. Larger containers, such as transfile and bankers boxes, are usually too heavy for easy lifting by one person. To alleviate these problems, it is preferable to use the standard records center container, with dimensions of $10 \times 12 \times 15$ inches, which can be used for either letter or legal size files.[3] Further, if the archives will supply offices with records center containers, it will save itself from the time-consuming necessity of transferring records into appropriate boxes. This standardization of containers can increase storage density as well as save the archivist's back.

The next step is to answer the question: "What's in the box?" Anyone who has searched ten or fifteen linear feet of uninventoried records knows that answering this question can be tedious and frustrating. The recourse is to secure a folder title inventory. Of course it takes time to

---

[3]For a discussion of containers and shelving, see Patricia Bartkowski and William Saffady, "Shelving and Office Furniture for Archives Buildings," *American Archivist*, 37 (January, 1974), 55-66.

prepare an inventory—time that the archivist could put to better use for other activities. An alternative is to have the sending office prepare the inventory. The archivist can explain quite positively that the archives has thousands of files, and for the archives to give the office the type of reference service that it needs and expects, a folder title inventory is necessary. Convince the office of this fact, and most of the time the office will provide an inventory.

To increase the likelihood of receiving the desired inventory and transmittal information, the archives should provide offices with a combined transmittal inventory form (fig. 1). Such a form secures the name and address of the office, signature of administrative official, name and phone number of person preparing the shipment, folder titles keyed to box and folder numbers, and access restrictions. To this information the archivist adds an accession number, date of receipt, name of record group into which the material fits, if different from the name of the office, and, finally, destroy date where applicable. When completed, the original copy is maintained in the archives and the carbon forwarded to the office.

At times offices may need information from, copies of, or temporary physical return of, records. Requests for reference service may be made by telephone or in writing, but the archives should record the transaction on a request for reference service form (fig. 2). The form serves the archives by impressing upon offices the value of an inventory, while helping to establish a systematic reference procedure. It will indicate the type of service needed—copies of records, information from records or return of records—as well as accession, box and folder number, folder title, name and address of office, name and title of requester, date, any specific instructions, and the signature of a person in the office authorized to obtain the files. One copy of the reference service form should accompany the records from the archives to the requesting office and back. This ensures that upon their return the records will be replaced in their proper location with a minimum of time and effort expended by the archivist. The office copy should be dated and attached to the archives copy to indicate that the records have been returned. Reference service forms provide a record of telephone and written requests, document the types of services given, record which offices are using the archives and how often, and indicate which records are out and which have been returned to the archives. Consequently the forms can be a convenient tool when compiling annual reports and usage studies.

Standardized transmittal and reference procedures are basic to an archives' records management program. To comply with these procedures, however, offices need to know that such procedures exist. Too often the archivist overlooks or dismisses this need, as well as the educational function of communication. The archives can inform offices about

WAYNE STATE UNIVERSITY
ARCHIVES
RECORDS TRANSMITTAL AND INVENTORY SHEET

NOTE: PLEASE FILL OUT THIS FORM IN DUPLICATE. SEND THE ORIGINAL TO THE UNIVERSITY ARCHIVES. RETAIN THE DUPLICATE FOR YOUR OFFICE FILES.	FOR ARCHIVES OFFICE USE ONLY
	1. ACCESSION NUMBER
5. NAME OF TRANSMITTING OFFICE	2. DATE RECEIVED
6. ADDRESS OF TRANSMITTING OFFICE	3. RECORD GROUP
7. PERSON PREPARING SHIPMENT TELEPHONE	4. RECEIVED BY (SIGNATURE)

INVENTORY OF RECORDS

8. BOX NO.	9. FOLDER NO.	10. FILE FOLDER TITLE	11. DESTROY AFTER	12. DATE DESTROYED	
					COLLEGE
					DEPT./DIVISION

RESTRICTIONS ON USE OF RECORDS: (IF NO RESTRICTIONS, WRITE "NONE")

FORM 10-462 5C (12-72)

ARCHIVES COPY

Figure 1.

WAYNE STATE UNIVERSITY
ARCHIVES
REQUEST FOR REFERENCE SERVICE

TYPE OF SERVICE REQUESTED (PLEASE CHECK ONE ONLY)

☐ COPIES OF RECORDS   ☐ INFORMATION FROM RECORDS   ☐ RETURN OF RECORDS

RECORDS OF INFORMATION REQUESTED

ACCESSION NO.	BOX NO.	FOLDER NO.	FILE FOLDER TITLE OR DESCRIPTION	
				COLLEGE
				DEPT./DIVISION

REMARKS

NAME OF ORIGINATING OFFICE   ADDRESS OF ORIGINATING OFFICE

NAME OF AUTHORIZED REQUESTER   TITLE   DATE

RECEIPT FOR RECORDS RETURNED TO ORIGINATING OFFICE

IF RECORDS ARE TO BE RETURNED TO THE ORIGINATING OFFICE, PLEASE SIGN BELOW AND RETURN FORM TO THE UNIVERSITY ARCHIVES IMMEDIATELY.

AUTHORIZED SIGNATURE   TITLE   CAMPUS EXTENSION   DATE

FORM 10-464 1M (2-81)   ARCHIVES COPY

Figure 2.

records management activities through memos, flyers, presentations, brochures and pamphlets. Each has advantages. Memos and flyers are inexpensive; presentations allow personal contact; brochures and pamphlets are attractive and may be more detailed. Whatever format is used, the following points should be emphasized: 1) offices will realize monetary savings since space is money; 2) offices are assured of quick retrieval of records or information from records when needed; 3) not all inactive records belong in the archives; 4) records of permanent value will be preserved. Since most offices are not concerned that records of permanent value be preserved, major emphasis should be placed on space savings and reference services.

Approximately two and one half years ago, when shelving requirements were being drafted for the proposed Walter P. Reuther Library building, the staff of the Wayne State University Archives reviewed its transmittal and reference procedures. It found 1) a reference service often unnecessarily time consuming and inefficient, 2) a considerable backlog of uninventoried, odd-size boxes, and 3) storage space rapidly diminishing. Changes, the survey concluded, were required.

The archives set its first goal as having records inventoried and housed in records center containers before deposit in the repository. Under the new procedure, offices wishing to transfer records are supplied with appropriate boxes, and a newly-designed combined Records Transmittal and Inventory form. Secondly, to facilitate and document reference activities, a Request for Reference Service form was created. Both forms have proved highly serviceable.

At this point the archives decided that it was desirable not only to inform the university at large of our new procedures, but also to reiterate the archives' existence. Frankly, it was hoped offices could be enticed into becoming involved in the records management program rather than resorting to the indiscriminate destruction of records. After careful consideration of methods of communication, costs, and expected results, the repository chose to produce a handbook. The handbook,[4] along with a covering memorandum from the executive vice president, was mailed to all executive officers, deans, directors, and department chairmen. It generated interest, fostered cooperation and gave visibility to the archives. Surely the handbook did not solve all of the problems, but our experience with it confirms that publications play a vital role in the success or failure of an archives' records management program.

When record accumulations threaten to evict university office personnel, the archives usually is called. In this crisis situation the office's primary concern is to gain space by ridding itself of records. The archi-

---

[4]Patricia Bartkowski and William Saffady, *Managing Inactive Records* (Records Management Handbook 1; Detroit: Wayne State University Archives, 1973), 20 pp.

vist easily can remove those records which should be kept permanently and earmark for destruction those which should not. This crisis situation presents the archivist also with the opportunity to promote other records management activities. Adopting a systematic procedure for the disposition of inactive records helps prevent future chaos and similar crises, alleviates space and filing difficulties, and promotes efficiency. In short, sell the offices on the concept of records retention and disposal schedules.

To establish schedules, the archivist must first gather data. What is the function and organization of the office? Where is the office located in the organizational structure of the university? Which are the general administrative policy records, the operational records, and the housekeeping records? What is the quantity? Where and how are the files housed? Do other offices have similar records? Who is responsible for maintaining the records?

Directories, organizational charts, and consultations with office personnel are helpful in answering these questions. Professional literature such as *Records Management Quarterly, Information and Records Management* and *The American Archivist* provide necessary background information. Considering that there are approximately nine hundred state and federal regulations concerning the disposition of records,[5] it is essential to establish a good rapport with the university attorney.

Even within an institution that has a formal policy regarding the disposition of inactive records, an archives often must pursue a course of tactful diplomacy to elicit cooperation. Coercion to compel compliance may be political and fiscal suicide for an archives. Then too, acquisition of the personal papers of faculty members is dependent upon their cooperation and interest. Within a university, the business, student and personnel records offices are usually most receptive to records management activities, while departmental and administrative offices quite often are reluctant to accept them. From an archival perspective, records from the latter offices, in particular policy records, are generally the most valuable. Establishing retention and disposal schedules requires careful work with both records and office personnel. Where Teddy Roosevelt could "Speak softly and carry a big stick," the walking archivist must speak softly and carry a records center container.

Space is usually at a premium in an archives' records management facility, and priority should be given to records of an archival nature. To accept records routinely for temporary storage should be the exception

---

[5]Electric Wastebasket Corporation, *Records Retention Timetable* (145 West Street, New York, 10036, 1974), 8 pp. William F. Schmidt and Sarah F. Wilson, "A Practical Approach to University Records Management," *American Archivist*, 31 (July, 1968), 247-264, suggest retention and disposal guidelines for specific university records.

rather than the rule. Semi-inactive records, or those that have a high retrieval rate, should be retained in offices until they become inactive. One way of determining the status of records is to ask "How often have these records been referenced in the past year?" If the answer is once or twice, the records may be considered inactive. As a rule of thumb, most departmental and administrative records generally become inactive after three years.

The archivist is vitally concerned with ease of access and maximum efficiency in retrieving records and information from files in the archives. There should be a similar concern for records outside the archives. An institution runs on its files. Unless information can be retrieved, for all practical purposes it is lost. Yet filing is often relegated to the least experienced member of the office staff, without special instruction or even the simplest orientation to the work of the office. Although alphabetic files are the most common, some individuals create their own filing system. With two or three individuals filing and with turnover in clerical personnel, it is not unusual to have several systems operating at the same time. Retrieval becomes time-consuming, inefficient, and highly distasteful. To help alleviate these difficulties at Wayne State University, the archives staff designed and is gradually implementing a university-wide subject filing system. A handbook publication again is being used to disseminate the system.[6]

The archivist-records manager must realize that offices will participate in records management activities in varying degrees. Some will contact the archives only in a crisis situation. At the same time, they will reject retention and disposal schedules, files revision, and any other services available. Others desire all assistance that can be given. It must be realized also that archives differ and consequently will place emphasis on different records management activities. Because of staff, budget, and space constraints, most archives cannot have a sophisticated, well-developed records management program. But if the archivist is truly concerned with the preservation of records and the quality of records that are preserved, there must be an involvement in records management. It is only when the archivist takes the first step that he or she becomes the walking archivist.

---

[6]Patricia Bartkowski and William Saffady, *A University Filing System* (Records Management Handbook 2; Detroit: Wayne State University Archives, 1973), 32 pp.

Archival Janus: The Records Center

Herbert E. Angel

For a generation we archivists have been told that the Greeks had a word for it. The word was *archeion*. It originally meant government house, and from it was derived the word archives, which has since been applied successively and perhaps indiscriminately to the records of a governmental agency, to the accumulated files of all sorts of organizations (governmental and otherwise), to the institution responsible for managing the accumulated files, and to the structure housing them.

But the Greeks did not have a word for another kind of house that also manages accumulated files—the records center. This shortcoming is not surprising, for the records center as we know it is barely a quarter of a century old. If for reasons of prestige we should like to go to antiquity for a name, we might try the Romans. They had a name that fits the concept of a records center, even though it was never so applied. Janus, whose name was derived from a Latin word for "going" or "doors," was the most important of the native Italian deities. He is characterized as not only the god of gates and doors, or "material openings," but more truly of "beginnings"—especially of "good beginnings which insure good endings." He is represented as facing both ways, some say with two heads as well as two faces.

Janus might qualify as the patron of records centers, not because they are two faced or have two heads, but because they face in two directions: toward the offices from which the records come and toward the archives or the wastepaper dealer to which the records eventually go. The records centers, like Janus, serve as a door or a passageway connecting these places of beginning and ending, and if they perform their functions properly the centers can assure that records that begin well will end the same way.

The records centers I have in mind are intermediate records depositories, which receive, store, service, process, and provide security for records that are not sufficiently active to be retained in valuable office or operating space but are too active to be retired directly to the archives or are still too valuable to be sent to the wastepaper dealer. Most people grasp the functions of centers very quickly when we refer to them as purgatories—places where records go to wait out their time, after which the good records go to the heavenly archives and the bad ones go to the

Reprinted with permission from *The American Archivist* 31 (January 1968): 5-12.

flames. Curiously enough, our British colleagues, also going to theology, call their records centers limbo. These uses of the terms purgatory and limbo are both very bad theology, but I believe purgatory is a bit closer than limbo to what we have in mind. As I understand it, storage conditions for records may be better in limbo, but the records never get out. Purgatory seems a better figure for us because we expect records in our centers to turn over like merchandise in a store and in time to move along to their ultimate destination.

Unlike records centers, records storage depots have been with us for a long time. They undoubtedly date back to the first empty attics, cellars, or storerooms, all of which quickly filled with old records that could not tolerate a vacuum. The hall of records, which was often proposed but never built in the years before the movement for a national archives in this country, was basically planned as a collection of vaults or lockers for the storage of older records of Federal agencies, each of which would send its own staff members to rummage for documents as they were needed. Nowadays the records storage depot is a vanishing phenomenon. A few still exist as museum pieces or monuments to inertia, but most have been replaced by that newer and more dynamic institution, the records center.

Not until 1941, however, under severe wartime pressures for space, was the first records center established in this country or, so far as I have been able to determine, anywhere in the world although an organization of this type was suggested by C. J. Cuvelier, the Belgian archivist, in 1923. The founders of the first center were two American archivists, the late Emmett J. Leahy and Robert H. Bahmer, now Archivist of the United States, both alumni of the National Archives and then employed by the Department of the Navy. Considering the joint involvement of an Irishman, a German, and the Navy in the enterprise, it seems particularly fitting that this first center should have been housed near Washington in an abandoned brewery, which has long since been replaced by a slick, modern motel that unfortunately bears no commemorative plaque.

Bahmer soon moved along to the War Department, where he joined another Archives alumnus, Wayne C. Grover, in developing the Army's records management program, including, of course, records centers. By the end of World War II both the Army and the Navy had chains of flourishing records centers that extended across the country and, in the case of the Army, overseas. Independently, but likewise born of wartime pressures, records centers were concurrently being created in and around London by officials of the Public Record Office.

Some of our senior members may recall that our own Society, at its meeting 25 years ago in Richmond, Va., when records centers were in their infancy, heard four papers on the problem of field office records of the Federal Government in which the possibilities of regional or combined Federal-State depositories were discussed.

The merits of records centers were too numerous to be concealed. By 1949, when the First Hoover Commission's Task Force on Records Management reported, the Federal Government had over 100 identified records centers, plus more than 200 "substantial accumulations" of records. Today the Federal Government is served by 14 Federal Records Centers holding 9 million cubic feet of records.

The ripples continue to spread. Ernst Posner, in his *American State Archives,* reported records centers serving more than half of the 50 State governments. It is not by coincidence that the first three archives to win our Society's Distinguished Service Award—North Carolina, Maryland, and Wisconsin—all have active records centers. Among our largest cities, New York, Philadelphia, and Los Angeles have municipal records centers. William Benedon, in a 1967 survey of the 500 largest corporations in this country, found that over half had established their own records centers, with capacities ranging from 4,000 to 200,000 cubic feet. He also noted that more industry records centers had been built in the last 5 years than in the previous 25. To these captive centers, if we may call them that, should be added commercial records centers, which provide a variety of individual clients with a wide choice of assistance ranging from dead storage to full-scale records center services. Initiated by Leahy, these commercial records centers are now operated by many companies—frequently by those engaged in commercial storage or underground storage businesses—in numerous locations throughout the country.

Nor is the records center confined to this country. I have already mentioned those operated by our British cousins. To these must be added the equally effective centers to our north in Canada, two in New Zealand, the new "Intermediary Archives" of the Federal Republic of Germany, located just outside Bonn, and a prearchival depot, to be called the Interministerial Archives City, soon to be constructed a short distance from Paris at Fontainebleau. It is significant that all of the centers enumerated, whatever their names, serve all the agencies of their Governments and that all centers are managed by the national archives of the country involved.

It is fair to say that a large proportion of the Federal, State, municipal, corporate, and commercial records centers in this country evolved from the Army and Navy records centers of World War II and that many of those responsible for the present-day records centers either had experience in the early centers or were trained by others who did have such experience. Because of these factors that the centers have in common, they have naturally developed similar physical characteristics, similar professional processes, and even similar patterns of evolution.

Although records centers differ from each other in size, capacity, and contents, they have a remarkable number of physical similarities, as William Benedon explained in his paper at our Atlanta meeting in 1966 and in his article in the January 1967 issue of the *Records Management Quarterly.*

Records center buildings have come a long way from the brewery in Washington. Gradually they have worked their way upward through a maze of old garages, uneconomical turn-of-the-century multistory warehouses, and outdated industrial plants once used for the manufacture of radios, electronic equipment, torpedoes, and other ordnance. Only good fortune has protected them from [being in] firetraps, abandoned mines, and even discarded silos intended for launching missiles—all offered in the hope of a quick profit or on the assumption that any building unsuitable for anything else must surely be ideal for a records center. As new buildings have been erected specifically for records center use, they have generally followed the modern industrial practice of a single windowless level for active storage areas. Occasionally they have been built on two levels because of size or terrain or have employed library-type catwalks, but these are the exceptions.

Early centers stored records in any container available. Among these were battered filing cabinets; steel, wood, and even cardboard transfer cases; and military footlockers. The centers had also a bewildering collection of shelving of all sizes, heights, and materials. Although some filing cabinets and transfer cases are still in use for records frequently searched or filed into, most records are now stored in standard-size cardboard cartons on standard-size steel shelves. The cartons usually measure 12F ⅛⅝F ⅛?F, suitable for both letter-size and legal-size records, depending on how they are placed in the container. The standard shelf, geared to the size of the carton, measures 42F ⅜?F, just enough to hold six cartons comfortably. There are variations, of course. The cartons may or may not have separate lids, and they may or may not have handholds. The cartons may be stored 1 high on a shelf so that it holds 6 cartons, or they may be stored 2 high so that it holds 12. The shelving may be erected in a single row so that each carton faces an aisle, or it may be erected in a double row so that there are four boxes between aisles and only the outer two boxes face an aisle. Whatever the variations, the cartons and shelving are basically the same as those developed in the World War II military records centers.

With increased diversity in the types and sizes of records sent to records centers has come corresponding diversity in storage equipment to accommodate small punch cards and large engineering drawings, bound volumes and computer printouts, and microfilm and magnetic tapes. Filtered forced-air ventilation has replaced the dust and soot from grimy and leaky windows. Air conditioning is provided for archives, microfilm, and magnetic tape; and air-conditioned vaults accommodate security-classified records. Fluorescent lighting has superseded dingy warehouse lighting—one bare bulb to a bay supplemented by battery-powered miner's lamps. Centers are protected from fire by sprinklers or smoke detectors or both and from intrusion by guards and sophisticated alarm systems. In short, most records transferred to records centers "never had it so good." Yet, according to current Federal Government figures, all this luxury for records in a modest functional building costs only 29 a cubic foot each year as compared to $4.43 per cubic foot for storing records in office space and equipment.

Records centers, as distinguished from records storage depots, provide most of the usual services of an archival repository—accessioning, preservation, arrangement and description, reference service, and disposal. Not only are these services generally absent from records storage depots, but they are also performed only indifferently in many offices from which the records come. Archives properly limit themselves to permanent records, leaving it to records centers to accept any records not needed in expensive office space but not yet disposable. Centers likewise accept records that have no fixed disposal date or the extent of whose reference activity is unknown. Disposition periods can be worked out in time, but this time is less expensive when the records occupy low cost records center space. As for reference activity, most office files personnel honestly do not know how often their records are used, but they invariably give one of two answers, depending on what they conceive their interests to be: They report either that the records are never used or that they are used all the time. Both answers are wrong, of course. Some statistical guidelines have been adopted for accessioning records. Federal records center officials, for example, accept records referred to no more often than once per file drawer per month. They also strive to have 50 percent of all Federal records in center-type space. Both standards have proved practical in application.

Like archives, all records centers strive to provide responsible custody, which includes security from fire, theft, insects, and vermin; clean and orderly storage; and temperature and humidity controls when needed. In addition the centers serve as a staging area, where records can wait until they become sufficiently inactive for the next step in their life cycle to be taken. Centers identify records coming to them—no mean task considering the poor condition in which many are transferred. They arrange or rearrange records received in disorder and supply additional detail when documentation received with the records is not adequate for prompt and effective reference service. They prepare and often publish guides, inventories, indexes, and other finding aids for their holdings but of course not in the detail required by archives for permanent records.

Many outside the profession find it difficult to realize that records centers are not simply warehouses where records remain in dead storage. Records centers—because they hold large quantities of recent records that are frequently used—are "where the action is." Reference services are provided by the thousands every year—by the millions in a few larger centers—chiefly to those from whom the records were received. Some searching is done for scholars, of course, but not nearly to the same extent as in archives. The reference service process has been incorrectly renamed by some status seekers as information retrieval, though none has yet had the courage to call a hard-working staff searcher a retriever. Under whatever name, documents are found, copied, or returned, and information is furnished by telephone or letter, all in a matter of minutes or hours. Records center staffs are accustomed to being praised for providing better service than inquirers receive from their own file rooms.

For the archivist the real merit of the records center is measured by its accomplishments in records appraisal and disposal. With knowledge gained through identifying, arranging, and furnishing reference service on his records, the center archivist can help in determining their value. He can develop disposal schedules and apply existing ones. When permanent records are in proper order, he supervises their transfer to the archives or to an archives area within the center itself. When temporary records are eligible for disposal, he carefully reviews the boxes and their contents as they move on to the wastepaper dealer or to incineration or pulping often performed under his supervision.

Records centers are increasingly called upon to add new but related services. As part of close relations between archives and records centers, overcrowded archives have used the centers as annexes. Conversely, where centers exist and archives do not, centers have concentrated the cream of their records into archives areas awaiting the day when archives will be established. Some centers have areas set aside as depositories for vital records. Some offer microfilming services in conjunction with their documentary reproduction facilities. Still others assist their parent organizations by identifying and recommending improvements in poor recordkeeping practices. Center staffs are especially well situated to detect problems such as those caused by inadequate filing systems, piecemeal transfer of file series, careless packing and shipping of records, disposal schedules that cannot be matched with the records, and files retained long after their value and activity have ceased.

Just as records centers have archival characteristics and processes, so they likewise perform functions of the offices from which the records come, and often they perform those functions better. They store records economically and securely, releasing costly space and filing equipment as byproducts. They act as a sure memory, furnishing quick and accurate reference service from a huge data bank. They provide professional advice to management on recordkeeping practices. At the same time, through the application of such modern management techniques as program planning, performance budgeting, work measurement, and manpower utilization, they not only pay their own way but also make a modest profit for their sponsors. In the language of the investment market, records centers are not a glamour stock, promising rocketlike advances and subject to similar crashes. Rather, they are a blue chip, whose solid professional assets assure a steady income of security and service and a value that increases unfailingly through the years.

This brief review of the physical characteristics and professional processes of records centers demonstrates more than their great similarity one to another. It also shows that these characteristics and processes, although varying from those in offices and archives, have much in common with each. When we consider these similarities and overlappings, the appellation of Janus for records centers seems neither farfetched nor pedantic.

A concluding word must be said about similarities of the developmental patterns of records centers. It is axiomatic that records management has three parts, dealing with the creation, maintenance, and disposition of records. But it is also true that every good records program begins by concentrating on the disposition phase: the inventorying, appraising, and scheduling of records and the full use of records centers and archives. Only after these processes and facilities are fully operational can sound progress be made in the areas of records maintenance and records creation.

A corresponding three-part cycle in the establishment and development of records centers might be described as reluctance, acceptance, and overreliance. In the early days of any center—and the same can be said for any archives as well—its clients are suspicious of, if not hostile to, the new institution. Hardheaded officals seek the hidden motives of archivists who are willing, without charge, to take old records, preserve them well, and make them available for use. Cautiously the officials transfer to the center records that are old and worthless or records so neglected that their nature and value are unknown. When nothing catastrophic happens, younger and better records are transferred. Eventually it becomes evident that there is no sinister plot to harm either the records or those transferring them and that, though the archivist may not be "quite bright" in his willingness to perform this free service, he is really harmless.

With the passage of time officials learn the advantages of centers— the economies in storage, superiority in care, and excellence of service— and reluctance gives way to acceptance when it appears that all concerned will live happily ever after. The cycle has not truly run, however, until some official, convinced that the archivist is gullible, attempts to foist off on that unsuspecting individual active records that are in daily use, perhaps even the official's central files. When the archivist meets and rejects this temptation, when he insists that Caesar accept the responsibilities that are Caesar's, then the archivist has found his place in the bureaucracy and has really arrived.

Granted that Janus did well in Rome and is thriving in his present situation, what of the future? We sometimes hear that the records center is obsolescent if not obsolete, doomed to replacement by microfilm, computer, or some other form of miniaturization. We may come eventually to this end. But 40 years ago we were told that microfilm would replace paper records. Instead, microfilm has achieved an important and honorable place in documentation; it has supplemented paper records, but it has not replaced them. Today we hear the same claims for computers and other new inventions. These have yet to find their ultimate place in the scheme of things. Meanwhile the records centers keep rolling along, storing microfilm and magnetic tape with complete impartiality alongside paper records, looking both forward and backward, and providing a documentation door at which the past and the future can meet.

Chapter 3

Records Appraisal

Records appraisal is the process of determining which records created by an organization or institution should be accepted for preservation in an archives. Sound appraisal decisions have a direct effect on the holdings of an archival institution and therefore are at the foundation of its work.

Theodore R. Schellenberg (1903-1970) was the most influential American theoretician of archival appraisal. During his long career at the National Archives, Schellenberg came to recognize that available European archival theories were not adequate to meet the practical problems presented by the voluminous and loosely organized bodies of records created by modern institutions. In response to these problems, he developed and wrote about the concepts of "informational" and "evidential" values in records, concepts that offer a framework for the consideration of the research uses of records. In the excerpts from "The Appraisal of Modern Public Records" (1956) included here, Schellenberg provides a comprehensive overview of the theoretical basis for these concepts.

In his article "Appraising Machine-Readable Records" (1978), Charles Dollar applies the analytical framework developed by Schellenberg to machine-readable records. Dollar demonstrates how Schellenberg's theories can be applied to nontraditional records forms and provides a useful model that can be adapted for appraisal of other record media as well.

Even though Schellenberg's concepts are widely accepted by archivists, they are not exempt from review and revision. In "No Grandfather Clause: Reappraising Accessioned Records" (1981), Leonard Rapport provides a fundamental reconsideration of some of Schellenberg's arguments. Drawing heavily from the work of G. Philip Bauer, Rapport discusses what archivists should do with records in their institution that would not be accessioned under current appraisal policies or standards. He also questions Schellenberg's emphasis on accessioning records for their evidential value and emphasizes the importance of weighing the value of records against the cost of maintaining them.

Recent experience with modern records and the requirements of efficient archives administration also have led to the clarification and definition of certain concepts. "Intrinsic Value in Archival Materials" (1982), the report of a National Archives committee, establishes definitions and standards to be used in determining which archival materials should be retained in their original form regardless of the availability of archivally acceptable copies. The Committee also describes the tests for intrinsic value and identifies nine qualities and characteristics of intrinsically valuable records.

The Appraisal of Modern Public Records

T. R. Schellenberg

Modern public records are very voluminous. Their growth in volume corresponds closely to the increase in human population since the middle of the 18th century. This population increase has made necessary an expansion of governmental activity, and this expansion has had as one of its concomitants a tremendous increase in record production. As modern technological methods have come to be applied to the production of records, their growth, in the last several decades, has been in a geometric, rather than an arithmetic ratio.

A reduction in the quantity of such public records is essential to both the government and the scholar. A government cannot afford to keep all the records that are produced as a result of its multifarious activities. It cannot provide space to house them or staff to care for them. The costs of maintaining them are beyond the means of the most opulent nation. Nor are scholars served by maintaining all of them. Scholars cannot find their way through the huge quantities of modern public records. The records must be reduced in quantity to make them useful for scholarly research. "Even the most convinced advocates of conservation in the historical interest," according to a pamphlet issued by the British Public Record Office, "have begun to fear that *the Historian of the future dealing with our own period may be submerged in the flood of written evidences.*"[1] The scholarly interest in records, for that matter, is often in inverse ratio to their quantity: the more records on a subject, the less is the interest.

In the reduction of modern public records great care must be exercised to retain those that have value. In the long run the effectiveness of a record reduction program must be judged according to the correctness of its determinations. In such a program there is no substitute for careful analytical work. Techniques cannot be devised that will reduce the work of deciding upon values to a mechanical operation. Nor is there a cheap and easy way to dispose of records unless it is one of destroying everything that has been created, of literally wiping everything off the board. Such a drastic course would appeal only to the nihilist, who sees no good in social institutions or in the records pertaining to them. The difficulties

Excerpts reprinted from "The Appraisal of Modern Public Records" by T. R. Schellenberg. National Archives Bulletin 8. Washington: National Archives and Records Service, 1956.

[1] Great Britain. Public Record Office, *Principles governing the Elimination of Ephemeral or Unimportant Documents in Public or Private Archives* (London, n.d.), p. 1.

in appraising recent records are so great that it is small wonder some archivists were at one time inclined to shut their eyes to them and take no action at all. Like Louis XV before the French Revolution, they seemed to feel that "the old regime will last our time, and after us the deluge."

DISTINCTION BETWEEN PRIMARY AND SECONDARY VALUES

The values that inhere in modern public records are of two kinds: primary values for the originating agency itself and secondary values for other agencies and private users. Public records are created to accomplish the purposes for which an agency has been created—administrative, fiscal, legal, and operating. These uses are of course of first importance. But public records are preserved in an archival institution because they have values that will exist long after they cease to be of current use, and because their values will be for others than the current users. It is this lasting, secondary usefulness that will be considered in this bulletin.

DISTINCTION BETWEEN EVIDENTIAL AND INFORMATIONAL VALUES

The secondary values of public records can be ascertained most easily if they are considered in relation to two kinds of matters: (1) the evidence they contain of the organization and functioning of the Government body that produced them, and (2) the information they contain on persons, corporate bodies, things, problems, conditions, and the like, with which the Government body dealt.

For purposes of discussion, the values that attach to records because of the evidence they contain of organization and function will be called "evidential values." By this term I do not refer to the value that inheres in public records because of any special quality or merit they have as documentary evidence. I do not refer, in the sense of the English archivist Sir Hilary Jenkinson, to the sanctity of the evidence in archives that is derived from "unbroken custody,"[2] or from the way they came into the hands of the archivist. I refer rather, and quite arbitrarily, to the value that depends on the character and importance of the matter evidenced, i.e. the origin and the substantive programs of the agency that produced the records. The quality of the evidence *per se* is thus not the issue here, but the character of the matter evidenced.

For purposes of discussion, also, the values that attach to records because of the information they contain will be referred to as "informational values." The information may relate, in a general way, either to persons, or things, or phenomena. The term "persons" may include

---

[2]Great Britain. P.R.O., *Guide to the Public Records, Introductory* (London, 1949), pt. 1, p. 6. See also Hilary Jenkinson, *A Manual of Administration*, p. 11 (2d ed., London, 1937).

either individuals or corporate bodies. The term "things" may include places, buildings, physical objects, and other material things. The term "phenomena" relates to what happens to either persons or things—to conditions, problems, activities, programs, events, episodes, and the like.

It should be emphasized that the distinction between evidential and informational values is made solely for purposes of discussion. The two types of values are not mutually exclusive. A record may be useful for various reasons. The value that attaches to it because of its evidence of government organization and functioning may occasionally be the same as the value that is derived from its information on persons, things, and phenomena. A government's actions in the fields of diplomacy and war, for example, are the main objects of inquiry in regard to those fields. Here the evidential value coincides to a marked degree with the informational value, for the historian is as much interested in a government's actions in regard to diplomatic and military happenings as he is in the happenings themselves.

EVIDENTIAL VALUES

REASONS FOR TEST OF EVIDENTIAL VALUES

There are a number of reasons why we should consciously and deliberately apply the test of evidential value in the sense in which this term has been defined and why records having such value should be preserved regardless of whether there is an immediate or even a foreseeable specific use for them.

An accountable government should certainly preserve some minimum of evidence on how it was organized and how it functioned, in all its numerous and complex parts. All archivists assume that the minimum record to be kept is the record of organization and functioning and that beyond this minimum values become more debatable. By a judicious selection of various groups and series an archivist can capture in a relatively small body of records all significant facts on an agency's existence—its patterns of action, its policies in dealing with all classes of matters, its procedures, its gross achievement.

Records containing such facts are indispensable to the government itself and to students of government. For the government they are a storehouse of administrative wisdom and experience. They are needed to give consistency and continuity to its actions. They contain precedents for policies, procedures, and the like, and can be used as a guide to public administrators in solving problems of the present that are similar to others dealt with in the past or, equally important, in avoiding past mistakes. They contain the proof of each agency's faithful stewardship of the responsibilities delegated to it and the accounting that every important public official owes to the people whom he serves. For students of public

administration who wish to analyze the experiences of an agency in dealing with organizational, procedural, and policy matters, they provide the
most reliable source of what actually was done.

The test of evidential value is a practical one. It involves an objective
approach that the modern archivist is especially trained to take; for his
training in historical methodology has taught him to look into the origin,
development, and the working of human institutions and to use records
for the purpose. The test is not easy, but it is definite. It will bring to view
first the records on which judgments of value can be made with some
degree of assurance, the degree depending upon the thoroughness with
which the records have been analyzed. It can be applied by all archivists,
for no archivist is likely to question that evidence of every agency's
organization and functioning should be preserved. Differences of judgment will arise only as to the completeness with which such evidence
should be preserved. The test of research value, on the other hand,
brings to view records on which judgments are bound to differ widely.

The information obtained by an archivist in applying the test of
evidential value will also serve to evaluate the significance of records
from other points of view. The archivist must know how records came
into being if he is to judge their value for any purpose. Public records, or,
for that matter, records of any organic body, are the product of activity,
and much of their meaning is dependent on their relation to the activity.
If their source in an administrative unit of a government or in a particular activity is obscured, their identity and meaning are likely also to be
obscured. In this respect they are unlike private manuscripts, which
often have a meaning of their own without relation to their source or
reference to other manuscripts in a collection.

In applying the test of evidential value the archivist is likely to preserve records that have other values as well—records that are useful not
only for the public administrator and the students of public administration, but also for the economist, sociologist, historian, and scholars
generally.

APPLYING THE TEST OF EVIDENTIAL VALUES

At the outset it is important to emphasize that appraisals of evidential values should be made on the basis of a knowledge of the entire
documentation of an agency; they should not be made on a piecemeal
basis. The archivist must know the significance of particular groups of
records produced at various levels of organization in relation to major
programs or functions. In many Federal agencies, offices at various organizational levels build up their own files, which are usually related to and
often duplicate, in part at least, those of offices below or above. In the
central organizations of such agencies departmental records may be

related to bureau records, bureau records to divisional, and divisional to sectional. In field organizations records of regional offices may be related to those in State offices, and records of State offices to those in subordinate offices. The use of modern duplicating devices, moreover, may lead to an extensive proliferation of records in any particular office.

In reviewing the entire documentation of an agency, the archivist's decisions on which of its records he should preserve depends on a number of factors, the more important of which are embodied in the following questions:

1.   Which organizational units in the central office of an agency have primary responsibility for making decisions regarding its organization, programs, policies, and procedures? Which organizational units carry on activities that are auxiliary to making such decisions? Which field officers have discretion in making such decisions? Which record series are essential to reflect such decisions?

2.   To which functions of an agency do the records relate? Are they substantive functions? Which record series are essential to show how each substantive function was performed at each organizational level in both the central and field offices?

3.   What supervisory and management activities are involved in administering a given function? What are the successive transactions in its execution? Which records pertain to the executive direction, as distinct from the execution of the function? To what extent are such records physically duplicated at various organizational levels? Which records summarize the successive transactions performed under the function? Which records should be preserved in exemplary form to show the work processes at the lower organizational levels?

While an archivist dealing with modern public records will have great difficulty in reducing them to manageable proportions, he will nonetheless often find that the records he wants were not produced at all. The records on important matters with which he is concerned are often not so complete as records on unimportant matters. It is a curious anomaly that the more important a matter, the less likely is a complete documentation of it to be found. While modern technology has aided the making and keeping of records in many ways, it has also made unnecessary the production of many documents that once would have become part of the record of Government action. Much that influences the development of policies and programs never makes its way into formal records. Important matters may be handled orally in conferences or by telephone, an instrument that has been referred to as the "great robber of history."[3]

[3]Paul Hasluck, "Problems of Research on Contemporary Official Records," *Historical Studies: Australia and New Zealand*, vol. 5, No. 17, p. 5 (Nov. 1951).

Records on important matters are often handled much less carefully while in current use than are records on unimportant matters. This lack of care is not intentional. Policy documents cannot always be identified as such when they are first created. Policies usually arise in respect to particular transactions, and so the records pertaining to them may be interfiled with others of no lasting moment on the transactions with which they were initially associated. Records on policy and procedural matters—on general as distinct from specific matters—are difficult to assemble, to organize into recognizable file units, and to identify in such a way that their significance will be apparent. Records of routine operations, on the other hand, are easily managed in a routine way.

The important policy documents are also difficult to schedule for retirement. Important records on policy and procedure do not become obsolete, or noncurrent, as soon as the transactions in connection with which they may have been made are completed. The policies and procedures they establish often continue in effect. And even if those policies and procedures are superseded, the records of them serve to explain and give meaning to the change. Such records are thus difficult to retire because the period of their administrative utility is difficult to establish. Records evidencing only the execution of policies and procedures, on the other hand, usually become noncurrent when action on the particular case has been completed. The termination of routine actions is usually definite and clear. Important records, moreover, are difficult to assemble for preservation in an archival institution because many of them must first be segregated from the mass of trivia in which they may have been submerged. And at the present time this segregation commonly has to be made after the records have lost their significance for current operations and their identity has become obscured, although more effective management of current records could greatly improve this situation over the years.

INFORMATIONAL VALUES

Informational values derive, as is evident from the very term, from the information that is in public records on the matters with which public agencies deal; not from the information that is in such records on the public agencies themselves. The greater proportion of modern public records preserved in an archival institution are valued less for the evidence they contain of Government action than for the information they contain about particular persons, situations, events, conditions, problems, materials, and properties in relation to which the question of action comes up. Most of the larger series of records in the National Archives, for example, were accessioned primarily for the information they contain relating to other matters than the action of the Government itself. Among such series are the voluminous census schedules, military service records, pension files, passenger lists, land-entry papers, and various kinds of case files. In most instances such series shed light on the activity of Government agencies, but so little in proportion to their bulk that this is not an important factor in their selection for preservation; it is presumed that other records show the activity of the agencies more effectively.

TESTS OF INFORMATIONAL VALUES

In appraising the value of information in public records, the archivist is not greatly concerned with the source of the records—what agency created them, or what activities resulted in their creation. The concern here is with the information that is in them. There are a number of tests by which informational values of public records may be judged. These are (1) uniqueness, (2) form, and (3) importance.

Uniqueness

The test of uniqueness must be carefully defined if it is to be meaningful. In applying the test the archivist must consider both (1) the uniqueness of the information, and (2) the uniqueness of the records that contain the information.

The term "uniqueness," as applied to information, means that the information contained in particular public records is not to be found in other documentary sources in as complete and as usable a form. Information is obviously unique if it cannot be found elsewhere. But information in public records is seldom completely unique, for generally such records relate to matters that are also dealt with in other documentary sources, and the information they contain may be similar or approximately similar to that contained in the other sources. To be regarded as unique for appraisal purposes the information need not be completely dissimilar from all other information. But it should pertain to matters on which other documentary information does not exist as fully or as conveniently as in public records.

In applying the test of uniqueness to information in records, an archivist must bring into review all other sources of information on the matter under consideration. These sources encompass materials produced outside as well as within the Government. The materials produced outside may be published or unpublished: they may consist of private manuscripts, newspapers, books, nearprint materials, or any other form of documentation. The Government materials are the various record series relating to the matter under consideration. The archivist must understand the relation of such series to each other and must be able to identify the particular series that should be preserved. To determine if a body of records is the sole adequate source of information on a given matter, he needs to be a real expert in the subject—acquainted with all outside resources and the products of research as well as with the other records of the Government dealing with the subject in question. The Federal archivist should know of all the significant documentation that relates to his field of specialization; the State archivist should ordinarily know of all the significant documentation relating to the history of his State.

In applying the test of uniqueness to the form of the records rather than to the information contained in them, the matter to be considered by the archivist is the physical duplication of the public records. In the Federal Government of the United States, as is well known, there is a great and perhaps an unnecessary proliferation of records. Not only are records duplicated from one administrative level to another, but within a given Government office several copies of a particular record may exist. While records having informational values are not likely to be found in as many forms or as many series as are records having evidential values, it is nonetheless necessary to carefully compare records containing information on any particular matter to avoid retaining more than one copy of them. To illustrate: records containing economic data filed by various business firms with the Office of Price Administration to obtain price adjustments were physically duplicated, to a certain extent at least, in the regional and national offices, and within the national office in the Enforcement and Price Departments of the agency. A collation of the price adjustment records was necessary to avoid keeping duplicate copies.

Because of the greater technical difficulties our ancestors faced in publishing or duplicating information and because of the inevitable loss of many records through the centuries before archival care became general, records of the remote past are likely to be the only remaining source of information on many matters with which they deal. This fact led the German archivist Meissner to formulate a maxim that "old age is to be respected"[4] in records. Archivists of various countries have set chronological date lines before which they propose that all records shall be kept. In Germany the date is 1700, in England 1750, in France 1830, and in Italy 1861. The Italian date corresponds fairly closely, by historical coincidence, to that adopted by the National Archives of the United States, where almost all surviving records created before the Civil War, which began in 1861, are being preserved.

While public records are likely to be more valuable as a source of information when other kinds of documentary materials are scanty, the converse of this statement is also true. The proportion of public records

---

[4]Leesch-Brenneke, *Archivkunde*, p. 40.

requiring permanent retention diminishes as other kinds of documentary materials increase in quantity. It is doubtful if governments are justified, in the face of other forms of recent documentation, in keeping more than a small proportion of the voluminous contemporary public records. But an archivist's job of appraisal increases in difficulty as the documentation of society increases in quantity. He must apply standards of selection with constantly greater discrimination as he deals with more recent records; in particular, he must apply the test of uniqueness to them with great severity. For "of the making of many books"—and of many other types of documentary materials—"there is no end," to paraphrase the Preacher.

Form

In applying the test of form the archivist, again, must consider both (1) the form of the information in records and (2) the form of the records.

As applied to information, the term "form" relates mainly to the degree to which the information is concentrated. Information may be concentrated in records in the sense that (1) a few facts are presented in a given record about many persons, things, or phenomena, or (2) many facts are presented about a few persons, things, or phenomena, or (3) many facts are presented about diverse matters—persons, things, and phenomena. In the first case, the information may be said to be extensive, in the second intensive, and in the third diversified. Census schedules and passenger lists, for example, provide extensive information in the sense that each schedule or list pertains to many persons. Case files of various labor boards and other adjudicative, investigative, or regulatory bodies serve as examples of records containing intensive information about a limited number of particular matters. Reports of county agents of the Agricultural Extension Service and of the consular and diplomatic agents of the State Department serve as examples of records containing information about diverse matters. In their pamphlet the British archivists expressed their ideas about the concentration of record information in their criterion that business records should be preserved which "affect, name, or touch by inference *a large number of persons and/or things or topics*," and particularly "if both persons and things are involved in quantities." In general, records that represent concentrations of information are the most suitable for archival preservation, for archival institutions are almost always pressed for space to house records.

The term "form" as applied to the records rather than to the information contained in them relates to the physical condition of the public records. Physical condition is important, for if records are to be preserved in an archival institution, they should be in a form that will enable

65

others than those who created them to use them without difficulty and without resort to expensive mechanical or electronic equipment. Chemistry notebooks, for example, are not likely to be intelligible to others than the chemists who recorded the results of their experiments in them; while punchcards and tape recordings are commonly unusable without resort to expensive equipment.

Arrangement is also important. Certain record series may be preserved by the archivist simply because they are arranged in a particularly usable manner. If he has a choice among several series relating to a given matter, he will choose for preservation the series whose arrangement most facilitates the extracting of information. For example, reports of American agricultural agents and attachés, though duplicated in the files of the State Department, are being preserved as a separate series accumulated by the Foreign Agricultural Service of the Department of Agriculture because their arrangement makes it easier to use them than the copies of the reports embodied in the classified filing system of the State Department.

Importance

In applying the test of importance, the archivist is in the realm of the imponderable, for who can say definitely if a given body of records is important, and for what purpose, and to whom? An archivist assumes that his first obligation is to preserve records containing information that will satisfy the needs of the Government itself, and after that, however undefinable these needs may be, private scholars and the public generally. He should take into account the actual research methods of various classes of persons and the likelihood that they would under ordinary circumstances make effective use of archival materials. He will normally give priority to the needs of the historian and the other social scientists, but he obviously must also preserve records of vital interest to the genealogist, the student of local history, and the antiquarian. He should not, however, preserve records for very unlikely users, such as persons in highly specialized technical and scientific fields, who do not use records extensively in the normal exercise of their professions and are not likely to use archival materials relating to them.

Public records may have a collective, as well as an individual significance. Research values are usually derived from the importance of information in aggregates of records, not from information in single items. Records are collectively significant if the information they contain is useful for studies of social, economic, political, or other phenomena, as distinct from the phenomena relating to individual persons or things. Records of the General Land Office, for example, collectively show how the public domain passed into private hands and how the West was settled; individually, the land-entry papers also have value for biographical studies and for studies of family history. In his article on "The Selection of Records for Preservation" in *The American Archivist* for October 1940, Dr. Philip C. Brooks has correctly observed that " . . . most records having historical value possess it not as individual documents but as groups which, considered together, reflect the activities of some organization or person or portray everyday, rather than unique, events and conditions."

Records relating to persons and things may, of course, have an individual research value in relation to particular persons or things. Normally, the more important the person or thing, the more important is the record relating to it. Such records may also have sentimental value because of their association with heroes, dramatic episodes, or places where significant events took place. Usually such values are attached to single record items, such as the Emancipation Proclamation, though extreme sentimentalists sometimes attach them to all records relating to the objects of their reverence, no matter how voluminous or trifling they may be. Utility for determining significant facts is with such persons only a secondary consideration. But archivists must exercise their sense of proportion in judging sentimental value.

Before applying the test of importance, an archivist should be sure that records meet the tests of uniqueness and form. The test of importance relates, as has been noted, to imponderable matters—to matters that cannot be appraised with real certainty. The tests of uniqueness and form, in contrast, relate to ponderables—to matters that are capable of being appraised on the basis of ascertainable facts.

An archivist normally brings to his task a general knowledge of the resources and products of research, which he acquired during his academic training. In the discharge of his duties he normally acquires a specialized knowledge of subject-matter fields pertinent to the records with which he works. And while performing reference service he learns to know of genuine research needs. He will also acquire a knowledge of the documentation produced by the agencies with which he deals so that he can reduce to manageable proportions the quantity of records that must be used for research. But if he does not have such knowledge, he should deliberately seek it by searching out and comparing the documentation available on various matters; and if his investigation fails to yield an answer he should not hesitate to consult subject-matter specialists.

CONCLUSIONS

Several general observations may now be made regarding the appraisal of modern public records, to wit:

First, the considerations that should be borne in mind in ascertaining values in records cannot be reduced to exact standards. Our standards can be little more than general principles. They can never be made precise, though, of course, the series or types of records produced by a particular public agency that meet certain general standards may be precisely identified. The standards should never be regarded as absolute or final. At best they will serve merely as guidelines to steer the archivist through the treacherous shoals of appraisal.

Secondly, since appraisal standards cannot be made exact or precise, it follows that they need not be applied with absolute consistency. Archivists may use different criteria in evaluating records of different periods, for what is valuable for a past age may be valueless for the present. The American historian Justin H. Smith (1857-1930) observed that "a great deal is said by some people about 'rubbish,' but one investigator's 'rubbish' may be precious to another, and what appears valueless to-day may be found highly important tomorrow."[5] Archivists of different archival institutions may also use different criteria in evaluating similar types of records, for what is valuable to one archival institution may be valueless to another. Complete consistency in judging informational values is as undesirable as it is impossible of accomplishment. Diverse judgments may result in records on particular matters being preserved at particular places, although the records are not deserving of general preservation. Diverse judgments may also spread the burden of preserving the documentation of a country among its various archival institutions, making one preserve what another may discard. Certain Federal records may thus be more appropriately preserved in regional depositories than at the National Archives because the information they contain is in such detail that it can be preserved only in concentrated form at the national level or because the information they contain is predominantly of a local or regional rather than a national interest.

Thirdly, since appraisal standards cannot be made absolute or final, they should be applied with moderation and common sense. An archivist should keep neither too much nor too little. He should follow the Aristotelian precept of "moderation in everything, excess in nothing." This precept, for that matter, is similar to two of Meissner's standards, which are "extremes are to be avoided," and that "too great an abstraction is an evil."

Fourthly, appraisals of records should not be based on intuition or arbitrary suppositions of value; they should be based instead on thorough analyses of the documentation bearing on the matter to which the records pertain. Analysis is the essence of archival appraisal. While

---

[5]Proceedings of the Second Annual Conference of Archivists," American Historical Association, *Annual Report*, 1910, p. 312.

appraising the evidential values of records the archivist must take into account the entire documentation of the agency that produced them. He should not make his evaluations on a piecemeal basis or on the basis of individual organizational units within an agency. He should relate the particular group of records under consideration to other groups to understand its significance as evidence of organization and function. His appraisals, it is apparent, are dependable to the degree to which he has analyzed the origins and inter-relations of records. Similarly, while appraising the informational values of records, the archivist must take into account the entire documentation of society on the matter to which the information relates. He must determine if the particular group of records under consideration contains unique information and if it has a form that makes it valuable as a source of information, and only after he has done this should he enter into the realm of the imponderable—into questions of research importance. His appraisals of records, again, are dependable to the degree to which he has analyzed all other available documentary sources on the matter to which the records pertain.

Fifthly, if his analysis does not yield the information that is needed in the appraisal of records, the archivist should seek the help of experts. Obviously an archivist cannot be expected to know the research needs of all scholarly disciplines. Occasionally he will be called on to evaluate records that involve a knowledge beyond his sphere. In evaluating records needed for disciplines in which he is not trained he should, if necessary, seek the help of specialists in those disciplines. If the archival institution is a very large one, a number of subject-matter specialists are likely to be found on its staff whose special competencies can be brought to bear on the evaluation of special groups of modern public records. If the institution is small, the number of staff subject-matter specialists will be limited, and the need for outside help will be greater. In the National Archives a panel of experts was used to help evaluate the records of the General Accounting Office, an agency of the legislative branch of the Government that audits the fiscal operations of agencies of the executive branch.[6] The records offered by this office spanned the years 1776-1900 and comprised over 65,000 cubic feet. They obviously had very little value for the evidence they contained of organization and function; but since they covered the whole of the national history of the United States, they were likely to contain incidental or accidental information on important historical, economic, and social phenomena. Appraisal of these records was an onerous task that could not very well be accomplished by any one person, no matter how comprehensive his knowledge of research resources and research needs might be. After the records

---

[6]Lyle J. Holverstott, "The General Accounting Office Accession: Its History and Significance," *National Archives Accessions,* No. 52 (Feb. 1956), p. 1-11.

were reviewed by various subject-matter specialists on the staff of the National Archives, therefore, help was obtained from specialists in the fields of military history, western history, and public administration.

Sixthly, before seeking the help of experts the archivist should do the basic analytical work that is preliminary to the appraisal of records. He should first accumulate the data about the records in question that are essential in determining the uniqueness and form of the information contained in them. He should describe the various series to be appraised, indicating their form and volume, the types of information available in them, their relation to other groups or series that contain similar information, their relation to published sources, and the like, in order that the scholars consulted may more quickly get at the business of determining which particular series or groups contain information valuable for investigations of various matters and which contain this information in the most usable and condensed form.

Seventhly, while exploring the interest of scholars in particular groups of records, the archivist should assume the role of moderator. An archivist dealing with modern records realizes that not all of them can be preserved, that some of them have to be destroyed, and that, in fact, a discriminating destruction of a portion of them is a service to scholarship. He is therefore inclined to agree with the observation that "too great an abstraction" in the appraisal of records "is an evil," for he knows that any scholar with a little intellectual ingenuity can find a plausible justification for keeping almost every record that was ever produced. In evaluating certain of the large series of records that are useful for social and economic studies, therefore, he must take into account the practical difficulties in the way of their preservation and bring these to the attention of the scholars who are interested in preserving them. He must show that a careful selection of the documentation produced by a modern government is necessary if he is not to glut his stacks with insignificant materials that will literally submerge those that are valuable. He must call attention to the fact that a government has only a limited amount of funds for the preservation of its documentary resources and that these funds must be applied judiciously for the preservation of the most important of these resources.

Appraising Machine-Readable Records

Charles M. Dollar

Machine-readable records are defined as records created for processing by a computer. While this definition encompasses a wide variety of storage media including punched cards, magnetic discs, cassettes, and paper tape, the vast majority of machine-readable records are stored on magnetic computer tape. It is reasonable to anticipate that, over the next decade, on-line storage and retrieval devices with random access capability will replace magnetic tape as the primary storage medium. This suggests the possibility that new computer storage technology will radically alter the appraisal of machine-readable records.

Current appraisal practices of machine-readable records differ in significant ways from those for textual records; and as computer technology progresses these differences will become even more pronounced. Indeed, it is likely that current practices and standards will be obsolete and irrelevant with a decade. It is quite costly to accession and preserve properly a single reel of computer tape. The proliferation of on-line data base management systems will make this process even more expensive, and costs will receive even greater consideration in appraisal decisions. As a result, the consequences of the rationalization (in the British sense) of the records retention process will become more evident, to the discomfort of archivists and researchers.

These possibilities suggest or imply a number of points that merit consideration. The standards and practices now employed in the Machine-Readable Archives Division of the National Archives and Records Service, with attention to the changes likely to occur within the next decade, provide the context for this consideration.[1]

Since 1969 the staff of the National Archives has appraised machine-readable records and thereby contributed to the refinement of certain concepts and criteria that comprise the present "state of the art," as it were. A delineation of the sequence of decisions involved in the appraisal of machine-readable records can convey the current state of the art.

Reprinted with permission from *The American Archivist* 41 (October 1978): 423-430, with slight revisions by the author. The author wishes to thank Thomas E. Brown for his assistance.

[1] For an earlier study see Meyer Fishbein, "Appraising Information in Machine Language Form," *American Archivist* 35 (January 1972): 35-43.

The first decision—whether a file will be appraised—is left largely to agency records officers. A disposition schedule for machine-readable records identifies categories of disposable and non-disposable computer tape files.[2] The former, consisting of processing files that range from initial data input to update transactions, are automatically disposable without regard to subject matter. In most federal agencies at least 60 percent of computer tape files are disposable as "processing files." Most non-disposable files, which must be offered to the National Archives, are so-called master files—the definitive state of a data file in a system at a given time. Although they are defined as non-disposable, master files are accessioned only if they meet a number of stringent criteria. (See Decision Table, fig. 1.) Following is a full discussion of only the more salient of these criteria.

When a tape file is offered to the National Archives, it must be accompanied by adequate technical documentation which at minimum consists of a record layout and a codebook, and a description of what persons, places, or things are covered by the records. These are crucial since they provide the key to the exact location of each item of information on the tape and define the value the numeric characters represent. (Thus technical documentation may be seen as a "finding aid" at the item level.) If this essential documentation is missing or can not be reconstructed, the offer is rejected.

If it is intact, the tape is then physically checked for readability by mounting it on a tape drive to be read by a computer. Sometimes minute particles of dust or other material on a tape will prevent a computer from "reading" some portion of the tape. Usually, readability can be restored by passing the tape over a tape cleaner to eliminate these particles. Sometimes a tape can be physically damaged by a crimp or stretching of a portion of a tape so that magnetic signals cannot be read. When any portion of a tape cannot be read because of physical damage, a decision to proceed further depends on both the scope and the magnitude of the damage, as well as the basic value of the file.[3] (These problems are analogous to those involving deteriorating paper, film, or microfilm with poor resolution.) If the tape is readable, a record count and a partial printout are produced, as well as a duplicate copy of the tape for security storage, while the archival qualities of the file are evaluated.

As is the case for records in any form, the major archival consideration is the legal, evidential, and informational value of records. At the

---

[2]See General Records Schedule 20, Machine-Readable Records (GSA).

[3]The decision will vary, depending upon record length, block size, and the pattern of error distribution. The same error in every block would be handled differently from random errors. If only a few blocks are unreadable, the value of the file is not seriously diminished. On the other hand, if more than 5 percent of the blocks are unreadable, in most instances the file would be rejected.

state level, it appears that some machine-readable records are of permanent legal and evidential value.[4] For example, in the State of Illinois, nineteenth-century land sales records, which clearly are of legal value, are being converted into machine-readable form. At the federal level, informational value is often the basic concern. The concept of informational value refers to the residual value of records after agency needs and individual rights have been satisfied. To put it another way, the value of the records is such that the information can be analyzed in ways and for purposes other than those for which the agency originally collected them.

Generally, the informational value of computer-readable records is proportional to their level of aggregation. For example, a summary of census data at the enumeration district level is far more valuable to researchers than a summary of county level census data. Similarly, census information at the household level is more valuable than a summary at the enumeration district level. The rule is that while you can never disaggregate summarized data (down from group data to individual data), you can always aggregate micro-level data to the desired summary level. Thus, unaggregated micro-level data has the greatest potential for further computer processing.

A file's potential for linkage with other data is another consideration of informational value.[5] Usually, records arranged at the lowest reporting unit (individual person or individual business firm) have considerable linkage potential. Common attributes (if they share similar codes) such as place of residence, occupation, sex, age, and the like permit the linkage of groups with similar attributes. Personal identifiers such as name and social security number permit even more sophisticated data linkage.

The evaluation of a file's potential for further processing and data linkage is merged with an assessment of the importance of its subject matter. This is approached, just as in the case of textual records, in terms of the interests and concerns both of current researchers and those working fifty years from now. Obviously, this kind of evaluation requires an understanding of a wide variety of research trends. It also involves considerable luck, since accurate prediction of future research trends is at best an educated guess. It is necessary, then, to turn to established researchers or special interest groups for guidance. For example, the

---

[4]Records with informational value are being created in a number of states. For example, in Vermont longitudinal data on wildlife population size, habitat, and migration patterns dating back to the 1930s is in machine-readable form.

[5]In a review essay, Myron Guttman notes that accumulating life histories of individuals is not the only way to study social mobility. He points out that linking groups with shared characteristics is a viable alternative. See "The Future of Record Linkage in History," *Journal of Family History* 2 (Summer 1977): 155.

APPRAISAL OF ADP RECORDS

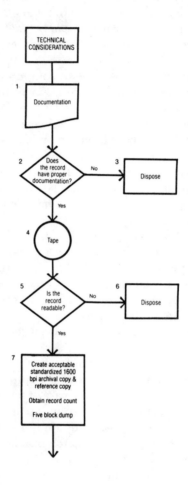

Figure 1. Decision table.

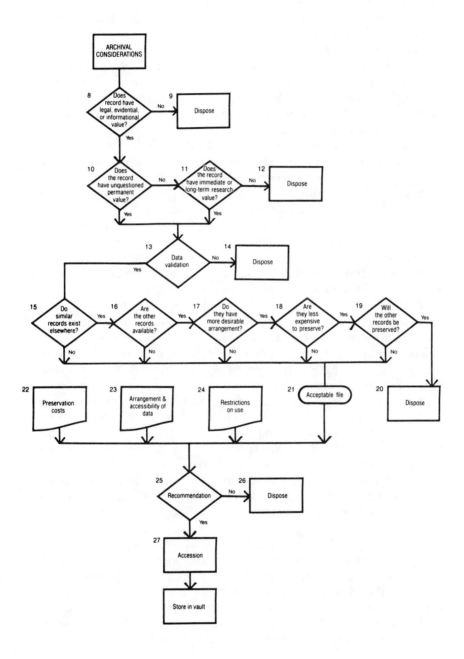

Figure 1. Decision Table (con.).

National Archives requested a subcommittee of the Social Science Research Council to review some preliminary retention guidelines for certain Bureau of the Census tape files.

If a tape survives the test of informational value, attention is turned to data validation. This involves a manual comparison of the codebook and record layout specifications with the partial printout made as evaluation began. If this comparison reveals any inconsistencies, values not noted in the codebook, or missing data, they are noted and included in the written appraisal report.

Data validation also involves consideration of the reliability and validity of the data. Since records of informational value probably will be used in ways and for purposes other than for which the agency collected the data, careful attention is paid to possible biases. This is particularly important with data collected for regulatory purposes. Frequently, data validation can reveal the existence of data imputation—cases in which estimates have been substituted for missing responses or incorrect figures. Unfortunately, in many instances there is no simple or inexpensive way to identify specific data imputation, even though the overall process can be documented.

Even when a tape file satisfies all of the appraisal criteria discussed above, arrangement and accessibility of the data and estimated preservation costs must be weighed against its value before its accession into the National Archives is recommended. Arrangement refers to the internal data structure of the file, while accessibility refers to whether or not the file is software dependent or is in some non-standard character code.

From the viewpoint of the National Archives, a file dependent on any system or package is termed "software dependent"; that is, it can only be processed in a computing environment that supports the system. Increasingly, at all levels of government and in the private sector, data base management systems, information retrieval systems, and special purpose statistical software packages are being used. Since the policy of the National Archives is to preserve files in a software independent state, this means that conversion is necessary. Such processing can be very time consuming and expensive.

The mounting costs of accessioning and preserving machine-readable records cannot be ignored in appraisal decisions. Thus far the experience of the National Archives is that it costs approximately $360 in staff time, computer time, and supplies to accession a single reel of tape and prepare it for dissemination when it is software independent, is in a standard code, and requires no data compaction.[6] While data compaction is not very costly for a single reel of tape, it can become quite expen-

---

[6]It should be noted that this cost includes appraisal, description, and validation of a finding aid at the item level. Also, a fully packed 1600 bpi tape can store the equivalent of

sive when hundreds of reels of tape are involved. It costs even more to convert data to standard character codes or unpack it from a data base management system or statistical analysis package. Currently, such conversion costs run between $400 and $600 per reel of tape. The long-term preservation costs using existing storage technology over the next twenty-five years would be about $5 per year for each reel of tape.[7]

Using these estimates, the approximately 1,500 reels of tape now in our holdings represent an investment of approximately $1 million, one-half of which consists of conversion and projected preservation costs. Since these 1,500 reels of tape comprise about one-half of 1 percent of the total volume of tapes we estimate are of sufficient value to warrant acceptance by the National Archives, it is clear that an enormous sum of money—probably on the order of $200 million—would be involved in accessioning, converting, and preserving the projected 300,000 reels of tape. Conversion and preservation costs are of such a magnitude— approximately $100 million—that they cannot be ignored in determining whether a file will be accessioned into the National Archives. Indeed, given our limited resources, increasing caution and care must be exercised in selecting files to be accessioned.

Since the application of a rapidly growing computer storage and retrieval technology seems inevitable, there are at least two consequences which are potentially very troublesome. The first concerns the development of mini-computers which are relatively inexpensive and powerful enough for many data processing tasks. Word processing is but one such task that now is on the threshold of enormous growth. It is too early to predict the impact word processing will have on the appraisal of machine-readable records. On the other hand, since more traditional data processing tasks will be performed without our having to rely on computer programmers and a central computer facility, mini-computers eventually could be as widespread as electrostatic copiers are today. This raises the possibility of an enormous proliferation of machine-readable records in a highly decentralized environment. The absence of any central control would make it more difficult to ensure the proper disposition of machine-readable records.

---

about 15 cubic feet of textual records. Thus, the cost corresponds to about $24 per cubic foot of textual records.

[7]This estimate is based on the use of 1600 bpi computer tape and assumes recopying tapes every ten years. When compared with the cost of storing an equivalent quantity of textual records, this is rather inexpensive. Use of a different record mode and storage medium (such as optical laser recording) could greatly reduced preservation costs. These figures are based on National Archives experience to 1977. Since that time, decreases in computer processing costs may have been offset by increases in the cost of materials and staff time.

A far more serious problem will be the increase in data base management systems. Such systems provide an on-line or interactive computer environment in which users may retrieve and analyze data while working at a desk-top typewriter-style terminal with a video display screen. A significant aspect of an on-line computer environment is that random access capability eliminates the necessity for the sequential or serial storage and retrieval common to magnetic tape files. In an on-line computer environment a user can retrieve information from a variety of storage areas instantaneously without needing to know where the data is physically located on a disk or disks. Because sequential storage and retrieval no longer constrain the arrangement of data, the computer itself decides where subsets of a data file will be stored, with the criterion being maximum utilization of the available storage capability.

Since the concepts of processing files and master files, crucial in the development of disposition instructions for machine-readable records, are based on the paradigm of magnetic tape files, it is possible that these concepts may no longer be viable in an on-line computer environment. This possibility becomes even more likely when data is merged from a variety of different files or created as a subset of a larger data file. Typically, an analyst would select the data elements needed for a particular study and then instruct the computer to create a temporary data set composed of these elements. His subsequent statistical analysis might be displayed on the video screen with results copied by hand or printed out by the computer. Once the analysis is completed, the temporary data set would be erased. The only evidence of the process would be the analyst's brief report which might include a copy of the summary of the statistics. And even its existence would depend upon the analyst's work habits. In this scenario there are no processing files in the usual sense of the term, and the automatic erasure of the temporary data set means there would be no master file. Furthermore, the problems of provenance could become insoluble, since there would be no record of data transactions to reveal the sources of data.

Earlier it was noted that preservation will become increasingly expensive in the future. The reason for this is rather simple. A 300 megabyte disk (the equivalent of about 7 reels of tape written at 1600 bpi) may contain a variety of data organized by a computer to maximize storage space on the disk. It is possible that one or two very valuable files may be dispersed throughout the disk in such a way that it would be most economical to accession all of the data, the garbage as well as the treasure, because the expense of having a computer assemble subsets of data that comprise the one or two valuable files may be prohibitive. An even greater problem is the cost of making these files accessible. Essentially, there are only two alternatives: to accession the files as they are embedded (formatted) in a data base management system along with the data base system itself, or to unpack the files so that they no longer are software dependent. Either alternative will be very expensive, although the latter may well be less costly in the long run since updating it to new technology will be relatively easy and inexpensive.

Even a modest increase in preservation costs could have the unfortunate consequence of requiring even more solidly demonstrable research potential as a justification for accessioning. Of course, the more closely a file relates to current research the easier it is to demonstrate its research potential. This could lead into the cul-de-sac where increased preservation costs result in less and less machine-readable material being preserved for fewer and fewer researchers. Given this situation, it is conceivable that social-science researchers fifty years from now will be in an era of data poverty because so little useful data will have been preserved. The irony could be that a great volume of data may in fact have been preserved. This rather bleak outlook for the social science researchers and the archivists of a half century from now could be compounded even further by the fact that the proportion of machine-readable to textual information is steadily increasing at both the state and federal levels.

Of course, this is not a problem confined to machine-readable records since these developments will affect all records. Some of the long range consequences of rationalizing the record disposition process begun in the 1940s are beginning to emerge, albeit not very clearly. The systematized process of records retention, along with severe economic constraints, may result in preserving fewer and fewer records of less and less long-range research value without regard to storage medium!

This rather gloomy assessment of the future may not set well with many archivists and researchers. Certainly, there is a positive side that should be noted. There is abundant evidence that changing computer technology eventually leads to greatly reduced computing costs. It is possible that, in the long run, computer storage technology will make it feasible to ignore preservation costs in appraising machine-readable records. This would be of no little consolation to a growing number of archivists who will appraise machine-readable records.

No Grandfather Clause:
Reappraising Accessioned Records

Leonard Rapport

Every repository of public records has on its shelves records which, if offered today, we would not accept. If we wouldn't accept them today, why should we permit these records to occupy shelf space? For such records there should be no grandfather clause.

Why do we have such records? Why do we tend to hold onto them? How can we go about getting rid of them?

If storage, preservation, and servicing of records cost nothing, if everything—space, material, energy, personnel—were free and in limitless supply I would advocate saving a record copy of every document, however trivial. Such complete retention would anticipate every conceivable future use, including those we don't dream of today. But space, material, and energy, instead of being free and limitless, are becoming scarcer and costlier; and people, if not scarcer, are becoming more expensive. So, more and more, we have to think of what records we are going to be able to afford to preserve.

If this sounds vaguely familiar, it may be that at some time you have read a 1944 paper by G. Philip Bauer, one of the National Archives early staff members. Bauer was writing about accessioning, not internal disposal; but what he said about the former, I believe applies to the latter. Bauer proposed that an appraiser should in every case ask whether the public benefit to be derived from saving public records is sufficient to offset the necessary expenditure of public money. "The question of what absolute quantity should be retained," he wrote, "depends in the last analysis upon how much money the Nation is willing to pay for the purpose."

A half-dozen years later, when I came to the National Archives, there were those who still thought of Bauer as something of a records burner. I sensed that Herman Kahn, in his comments that followed Bauer's paper, expressed the prevailing feeling. Bauer's theme, as Kahn understood it, was that public value in records was purely utilitarian; and he disagreed.

"I believe, on the contrary," said Kahn, "that we keep records for the same reason that we build schools, or rear our children, or support our aged parents. It is one of those things that we do without asking our-

Reprinted with permission from *The American Archivist* 44 (Spring 1981): 143-150.

selves whether or not it represents a profitable investment but simply because it is our innate assumption that civilized men can do nothing else. We know that because we are not barbarians we must keep records. In other words, the keeping of records in a civilized society is primarily an act of faith. We keep records because of our deep emotional and intellectual commitment to the values of the civilization of which we are a part, and to what our ancestors did and to what we hope our children will do. . . . We keep records because we are civilized men and therefore must do so."

As to whether I am a follower of Bauer's pragmatism or of Kahn's response you already have sufficient clues.

Although what follows is based on my experience with federal records in the National Archives, it should be applicable to public records in general, and particularly to state records. But whatever the level—federal, state, county, or town—we should keep in mind that what we are talking about are *public* records, instruments created for a purpose. The records are to serve the citizenry, not the reverse. The records do not belong to archivists, historians, genealogists, or to any special group or class of persons any more than they belong to all and to each of us as citizens. We have to keep this in mind because, in addition to our obligation as archivists to do our best, as servants of the people, to preserve for them records of value, we have, as Bauer implied, an obligation not to make the nation pay for preserving what isn't worth the cost of preserving.

Why do we continue to keep records of questionable value and how did we come to have them in the first place?

Taking the second question first: there are several obvious ways we got such records. One is that the original appraisal was faulty. The appraiser judged them worthy of accessioning when, in fact, by the standards of the time of appraisal they weren't. Or the appraiser judged them correctly by the appraisal standards of the time; but the standards have changed and by today's standards they are not worth keeping.

Also, the records may have been accessioned without any real appraisal. This was not uncommon in the early years of the National Archives. In those years the vacuum of the building's hollow interior sucked in records that, in later years, would have gone to records centers, with perhaps a small residue finding its way into the National Archives. Recently, in reappraising the records of two agencies established during World War I—the U.S. Shipping Board and the U.S. Railroad Administration—I found, in going through the accession dossiers, that evaluations of these record groups were the exception rather than the rule.

It is recognized that an intensive study of these records will show that a number of them have no value but this separation of good from bad cannot

81

adequately be made under existing circumstances at the White House Garage.

or

It was deemed advisable to transfer the entire group to the Archives even though it was known that considerable parts of the files had no administrative or historical value or were duplicated in other places. This was done primarily because space and time were not available for an appraisal of their value.

or

It is recommended that the entire collection be accepted by the Archivist and that the General Subject file of the General Counsel be studied . . . to determine which claims might be eliminated. This recommendation is made in view of the fact that the United States Railroad Administration is closing its office and is forced to move from its present quarters within a few weeks.

More than forty years after the last was written somebody—I—got around to making the recommended study of the 400 feet of the last-mentioned series of the General Counsel's records. I recommended what I thought they deserved: total destruction.[1]

When records such as these occupy for four decades the country's most expensive archival shelf space, time inevitably burnishes them with a patina of permanence.

There are other reasons for having such records, reasons that may apply more to records in repositories other than the National Archives. In a state capital, in a smaller bureaucracy, where the archives may be less insulated against agency pressures, the officials who created and nurtured the records may want, and be able to get their creations into that archives, whether or not they meet the accessioning criteria. Again, public archives that lack strong enabling legislation may feel they have to accept some records they don't want in order to assure getting others that they do want. (This happens more often in the private sector.)

It is easier to understand why we have these records than it is to understand our reluctance or inability to get rid of them. We won't find explanations in archival theory; no theory is going to justify keeping what clearly should not be kept. We have to look closer to home, to human nature, to ourselves. These records sit peacefully on our shelves, making no demands. The dust on their containers is evidence that the absence of disturbance is mutual. We seldom walk down an aisle, open at random a box or tray, examine its contents and ask ourselves, "Why are

---

[1]Many hours of seeking, by systematic sampling and by use of a subject index, failed to reveal a single file I judged worth preserving. I did find significant products of the General Counsel's office—but they were in the subject-classified file of the Director General.

we keeping these particular records?" Their inclusion in our published guides and inventories helps establish their credentials. In archival institutions one isn't likely to get in trouble by leaving on the shelves records that shouldn't be there; but the persistent archival memory is not kind to the archivist who misjudges and throws away what should have been kept. The human mind multiplies few things as much or as fast as the value of a series of records that a searcher (particularly a Ph.D. candidate) asks for and discovers no longer exists.

It is human nature also for persons who brought in records to be touchy about having their judgment reversed. Custodians having a long association with particular records may develop possessive feelings, regardless of the value of the objects of their affections. Unit heads may have bureaucratic misgivings about emptying (and possibly losing) stack areas, particularly if heads of neighboring units, less interested in internal disposal, keep their areas full. And if the official line of an archival institution is that it is bursting at the seams and is therefore in urgent need of more space, perhaps of a new building, then internal disposal is not apt to get top priority.

Finally, there is mystique. Consider, for example, records that have to do with ships, with the sea. Trains, trucks, buses, and airplanes haul cargo and passengers all over this country; but records of individual trains, trucks, buses, or planes, or of their crews, or of their individual trips, are generally not viewed as immortal documents. But when cargo or people move on bodies of water, the carriers and their crews take on a mystique, as anyone disposing of maritime records finds out. And when you combine the mystique of the sea with the mystique of the military, you have a double mystique that can be overwhelming. I don't know how anybody gets rid of any records relating to a warship, whether or not the vessel ever fired a round in anger. Perhaps it is fortunate for all concerned that my appraisal experience has been entirely with civil records.

And so, for various reasons, most of us have accessioned records we probably shouldn't have accessioned. And for various reasons we hold onto records we should get rid of. And though we do reappraise on an *ad hoc* basis, and get rid of, some accessioned records, none of us, as far as I know, reappraises holdings systematically and periodically. That is what I am proposing we do.

Under this proposed reappraisal procedure we would be obliged to make a case for continuing to retain records rather than for getting rid of them.

The interval of reappraisal could be almost any period; perhaps twenty, twenty-five, or thirty years. Such an interval would allow time for the repository to publish and circulate descriptions of these records, to prepare guide entries and inventories, and otherwise to serve notice of their existence and availability. It would allow time to analyze what uses, if any, are made of the records. Where samples or selections are periodically accessioned, this analysis would be particularly useful in determining whether the actual uses of these samples and selections were those on which the sampling or selection schemes and percentages were predicated.[2]

It usually isn't hard to identify series of records for reappraisal. In most published guides and inventories are series that, from their descriptions, are obvious candidates. For example, it required no particular perspicacity to suspect that the item in the National Archives inventory of the U.S. Railroad Administration records reading "Correspondence Relating to Unused Ticket Claims Filed Prior to the Expiration Date. . . ." may have been on the shelves too long; and indeed an examination failed to reveal any redeeming values (no pun intended).

An objection certain to be offered to periodic reappraisal of accessioned records is that no matter how often a series qualifies for continued retention, it would take only a single unfavorable reappraisal to wipe it out. This is true. It makes the survival of accessioned records subject to changing standards. But most public records are destroyed without ever seeing the inside of an archives; and they are destroyed in accordance with whatever standards apply at the time of their one and only appraisal. Archivists of the nineteenth century, if they could have foreseen what we routinely destroy in accordance with general schedules, might have been horrified; and, similarly, archivists of the twenty-first century may be. But unless we save, as I wish we could, a record copy of every document, there is no way of appraising except according to what we at the time believe to be the correct standards.

Since what we destroy we cannot retrieve, accessioned records that fail reappraisal deserve safeguards. There might be a staff review panel to consider reappraised records that seem to deserve a last look before they disappear forever. Such a panel might want to question the reappraiser and his reappraisal. There might be some sort of public defender of reappraised records, an ombudsman, who could, if it seemed necessary, check the facts and reasoning of the reappraisal by going to the records themselves. The panel could consider any protests or comments from staff members or interested outsiders.

Up to this point, everything I have argued has been based on the assumption that we will reappraise accessioned records in accordance with our present standards. Now I would like to suggest that we consider some rather drastic revisions in our way of thinking about what records

---

[2]Suggesting an initial interval of at least twenty years after accessioning doesn't mean an advocacy of an arbitrary period of immunity. An obviously bad accession could and should be reappraised as soon as possible, no matter how short a time it has been on the shelves.

we should keep and how long we should keep them. (This gets into accessioning policy; but if we avoid accessioning the wrong records we avoid having to get rid of them.) If these suggestions are valid, following them would undoubtedly permit much more internal disposal than is currently possible.

The first suggested revision has to do with records that we keep chiefly for their evidential value.

The guidelines I believe most public archives in this country follow derive from those that Theodore Schellenberg established in 1956 in a National Archives bulletin, *The Appraisal of Modern Public Records*.

The 1950 Federal Records Act authorized the Administrator of General Services to accession federal records that the Archivist of the United States determined to have sufficient historical or other value to warrant continued preservation. Since 1960 the successive Archivists of the United States, in delegating the appraisal function, have declared this bulletin the chief authority for determining these values. Schellenberg's discussion of evidential and informational values, as spelled out in this bulletin, reproduced in subsequent archival literature, and taught in archival courses, has become gospel throughout the land.

It isn't bad gospel. I know none better. Schellenberg valiantly and with some success spelled out what records are important and valuable and why, and how to identify them. There is the temptation to boil it all down to a simple solution: save the valuable and get rid of the valueless, as simple and as surefire as the stock market axiom, buy low and sell high. But determining what is important enough to accession and what isn't is not as simple as determining that it is profitable to sell for $50 a stock that cost $25. Evidential and informational values are useful concepts. But Schellenberg did not advocate accessioning records simply because they were evidential or informational. He was aware that there is not a record created that is totally devoid of such values, however minute. These values had to be important values; and it is against this adjective that we collide and sometimes founder. "Important" involves subjective judgments about which Schellenberg couldn't do much more than give us his own definitions and some examples.

I believe we should reexamine Schellenberg's views, particularly on records kept mainly for evidential values. These are values, said Schellenberg, "that attach to records because of the evidence they contain of organization and function." Such records "should be preserved regardless of whether there is an immediate or even a foreseeable specific use for them." No archivist, he believed, is likely to question that such records should be preserved. "Differences of judgment will arise only as to the completeness with which such evidence should be preserved." As in the case of "important," "completeness" involves subjective judgment. I believe Schellenberg tended to overvalue the evidential. As a result, those of us who follow him tend also, I believe, to keep too many records as evidential. We accession what he describes as "the proof of each agency's faithful stewardship of the responsibilities delegated to it and the accounting that every important public official owes to the people whom he serves." "Stewardship" somehow has overtones of Sir Hilary Jenkinson discussing the records of the Lord Steward of the King's Household rather than of Schellenberg contemplating what to keep of the U.S. Railroad Administration of World War I. In the United States in the last half century the functions of the federal, state, and local governments have multiplied and there have risen, flourished, and died hundreds of authorities, councils, boards, departments, services, administrations, agencies, offices, commissions, committees, panels, corporations, systems, missions, and whatever, administered by secretaries, under secretaries, deputy secretaries, assistant secretaries, administrators, directors, commissioners, and the like.[3] To look back through the last forty years of the annual issues of the *United States Government Manual* or to browse in the more than two thousand pages of the National Archives *Federal Records of World War II* will reveal how much potential proof of stewardship is involved. Much of this proof we accession doubting, in Schellenberg's words, "even a foreseeable specific use," almost assured in our own minds that nobody will ever look at these particular records. If we could audit the documents brought into the National Archives and, probably, into other public archives, with proof of stewardship as a justification, I venture to say that we would find that most—probably 90 percent or more—have since their arrival never been looked at by a human eye. Further, I would guess that no matter how long we retain these predominantly evidential records, most are never going to be looked at by anybody. This isn't as bad as it sounds. The same can be said about the pages of many of the books on any library shelf. But it is troublesome to see rows of containers which within our memory have never been disturbed and which our instinct tells us aren't going to be disturbed; and assuring ourselves that these are proof of faithful stewardship may not totally settle our unease. It is as if we have raised and are maintaining memorials to ancestors, sometimes of no particular distinction or accomplishments, out of some atavistic stirring of conscience or from a feeling that this is a valediction we owe them without being able to explain to ourselves exactly why. When looking at these evidential

---

[3]There were in 1980 about a thousand such officials appointed by the President and confirmed by the Senate (not including diplomatic and military appointees); and there were several hundred other presidential appointees who did not require Senate confirmation.

records of some minor, forgotten agency or official there is a temptation to wonder if perhaps a certified statement of "well done, good and faithful servant" might not be enough.

As an example of the evolution by which we arrive at the degree of completeness of such evidence, consider the Wage Adjustment Board of World War II. In 1946, while the board was still in existence, a competent archivist appraised its records. The appraisal, in accordance with the archival thinking of the time (and perhaps reflecting the stack space available), called for the accessioning by the National Archives of almost 700 feet of records, with more to come. These were of enduring value as "the basic record of the policies, procedures, and operations of the Board, and as the principal source of information regarding labor-management relationships and wage stabilization efforts in the key building and construction industry during World War II." But later there were, apparently, some second thoughts. By the time the records were accessioned the quantity had been reduced to 175 feet.

Thirty years ago, as a new archivist, I prepared an inventory of these records. This inventory was published in 1954. Twenty years later, while a member of the Records Appraisal Staff, I asked an archivist on rotation there to look at these records and, if she thought it called for, to reappraise them. She did, and reduced the 175 feet to 24 feet.

In the late 1940s, not long after the records came to the National Archives, two former public members of the board, one a Harvard economics professor who was later to become Secretary of Labor, the other a Harvard Law School graduate and labor lawyer, wrote a history of the board, which the Harvard University Press published in 1950. Only their service on the board and their intimate knowledge of it accounts for such a high-powered team writing a book about such an obscure agency. In the thirty years since its publication I doubt there has been a single scholar who has used the board's records. I am aware that a published history is not supposed to do away with the need to preserve original records; but as far as the Wage Adjustment Board is concerned, I don't anticipate revisionists.

A recent reexamination of the remaining twenty-four feet of the board's records convinces me that something less than half that amount would include whatever worthwhile evidence and information there is, and would constitute all the proof of stewarship that it is worth asking the taxpayers to burden themselves with.

My other main suggestion is that we take a close look at our use of the term "permanent." We in the archival profession like that word, and we in the National Archives exemplify that liking. "Permanent" is the adjective that National Archives regulations, finding aids, catalogs, and other issuances apply to accessioned records; and we instruct federal agencies to earmark, segregate, and schedule for transfer to the National

Archives their "permanent" records. "Permanent" is a convenient term for which no simple substitute comes to mind. It may seem semantic hairsplitting to make a to-do about it. But the Federal Records Act, as adopted in 1950, does not include the word. It refers instead to records that "have sufficient historical or other value to warrant their continued preservation."

Again, I don't want to go on about a word. But for those persons involved in internal disposal, "permanent," with its overtones of everlasting, to the last syllable of recorded time, is not an easy concept to get around. "Worthy of continued preservation," awkward though it is, implies that some accessionable records may be less than eternal. It permits us more easily to entertain the thought that appraisal standards can change, that an appraiser's evaluation may be less than infallible, and that we might entertain the idea of bringing into an archives records we believe will have use and value enough to justify their accessioning but not their endless retention. To put it another way, we now canonize our accessioned records, a state that to the faithful is definitive, infallible, and binding. If we might, instead, beatify them, we could, with an easier mind, periodically reassess them to see whether they continue to possess enough value to warrant the cost of their continued worshipful retention.

Returning to the 400 feet of records of the U.S. Railroad Administration's General Counsel, I was aware that to store them in the National Archives Building would involve a true cost of at least $4,000 a year; to store them in the General Archives Division at Suitland, where in fact they were, would be less. To microfilm them at present rates would cost an estimated quarter of a million dollars.[4] If they were to be kept in their original form I wasn't too worried; though entirely on wood pulp paper, they would last, untouched as they were, longer than any of us will. If we—that is, the National Archives—are determined to keep such records, I suggest dead-storing them in a salt mine. We could pay air fare to the mine for any once-in-a-generation inquirer, and still come out ahead.

Turning to more specific suggestions, I offer some for reconsidering accessioned records.

First, let us ask ourselves the questions already mentioned: would we accession these records if they were offered today? If we wouldn't, why should we continue to keep them?

Second, is there a reasonable expectation that anybody, with a serious purpose, will ever ask for these records? I stress, a *reasonable* expecta-

---

[4]I would, of course, oppose this microfilming. But if an agency had been so ill-advised as to have misspent public funds to microfilm such records. I would probably be inclined to accession the film simply because the deed had been done and the film requires a fraction of the space of the original records.

tion, not a conceivable expectation (anything is conceivable). A century from now, for reasons not now easy to guess, it is conceivable that somebody will want to see the correspondence relating to the unused ticket claims that I recommended for disposal. This is a conceivable expectation but not, to me, a reasonable expectation. And it is on reasonable, not conceivable, expectations that appraisers must base their decisions.

Third, what if, following this reasoning, we throw away records and the conceivable indeed occurs and we or our successors have a request for them from a serious researcher? To anticipate and to allow for this, the best we can do, once we decide there is no reasonable expectation of use, is to ask ourselves: if we are wrong and someday somebody does come along who wants these records, will the requester or will scholarship in general be badly hurt because these particular records no longer exist?

Appraising is at best an inexact science, perhaps more an art; and a conscientious appraiser, particularly an imaginative one with an awareness of research interests and trends, is apt to know nights of troubled soul searching. Such an appraiser realizes that every scrap of paper has values, perhaps unique values. When reappraising records of the U.S. Shipping Board, I more than once listed for disposal records containing information about a particular vessel or a particular voyage that was unique—information that couldn't be duplicated anywhere else. This has to be displeasing to persons who may be interested in particular vessels and want every iota of information about them. To these persons unique and important may be synonymous; but they are not necessarily synonymous to an appraiser. The interests of these ship buffs have to be weighed against the cost to the taxpayer of maintaining for these persons these records. I could not justify for such a reason such maintenance.

Having qualified, I imagine, in the eyes of at least some for a place in the pantheon of archival Attilas, let me clinch that honor with some final thoughts designed to ease the consciences of those reappraisers who go against the wisdom and judgment of their predecessors and declare disposable what those venerable persons had declared permanently valuable.

We who reappraise should consider carefully what we are doing, realizing that what we destroy we can never recover. But having done what we believe we have to do, as diligently and as conscientiously as we know how, and having done the best we can, we should be philosophical and of good cheer. We should lift our line of sight and view records and our decisions about them as they fit into the sweep of time. We might think back to the Metroon, the city archives of ancient Athens, which Ernst Posner tells us contained not only "records pertaining to budgetary and financial matters subject to the Council's supervision" and "contracts of the state with private individuals" but also official copies of the dramas of the great tragedians, Aeschylus, Sophocles, and Euripides. These last were probably kept in the Metroon "as a result of a motion of the orator Lycurgus" (an appraisal judgment that has stood the test of time). Of the contents of the Metroon, little more than the great dramas managed to survive. Though I do not ask that you subscribe to the theory of that archivist who thought saving only the poetry of a nation might perhaps be enough, through the ages there does seem to be almost such a law of selection and survival, a law that results in our inheriting from the golden age of Greece, Homer and Sappho, Socrates and Plato, rather than the official records. If there is such a law (which there probably isn't) then no matter how carefully and agonizingly we appraise and preserve, it is possible that 2,500 years from now something of Emily Dickinson and Faulkner may survive, and nothing at all—nothing evidential, nothing informational—of the U.S. Shipping Board, of the U.S. Railroad Administration, of the Wage Adjustment Board of World War II.

If that does not put a troubled appraiser in a more comfortable frame of mind, share with me two apocalyptic visions. In the first it suddenly becomes possible to keep a copy of every single document created, and, for these documents, a perfect, instantaneous retrieval system. In the second, and less blissful, vision the upper atmosphere fills with reverse neutron bombs, heading toward every records repository. These are bombs that destroy records only, not people. They come down and obliterate every record of any sort.

Keeping these two events in separate parts of your mind, project forward a century. How different would the two resultant worlds be? In the first would our descendants, having all the information that it is possible to derive from documents, have, therefore, all knowledge? And if they have all knowledge would they have, therefore, all wisdom?

In the second, lacking the records we have as of this moment, would our descendants wander in a world of anarchy, in a world in which they would be doomed to repeat the errors of the past?

I leave it to you to conjecture as you please. My own guess is that between these two worlds there wouldn't be all that much difference.

Intrinsic Value in Archival Materials

The term "intrinsic value" has long been used by archivists to describe historical materials that should be retained in their original form rather than as copies. In 1979 the term gained particular importance for the National Archives and Records Service (NARS) as it began to consider possible large-scale replacement of paper records with miniaturized or other copies. To meet the challenge of distinguishing between records that need not be retained in their original form after an acceptable copy has been created and those that require preservation in the original, NARS established the Committee on Intrinsic Value.[1] The Committee's work was three-fold: first, to write a comprehensive and broadly applicable definition of intrinsic value; second, to define the qualities and characteristics of records having intrinsic value; and third, to demonstrate application of the concept of intrinsic value in decisionmaking. The Committee completed a preliminary report in January 1980 and its final report in September of that year.

The Committee intended that its work should be useful for decisions relating to all physical types of records and manuscripts and should be relevant under varying and unforeseen circumstances. The Committee therefore sought first to establish the theoretical basis for the concept and then to be as specific as possible in identifying the qualities and characteristics of historical materials having intrinsic value. The Committee recognized that application of the concept of intrinsic value would be subjective and must always be dependent on trained archival judgment and professional debate.

REPORT OF THE COMMITTEE ON INTRINSIC VALUE

INTRINSIC VALUE IN ARCHIVAL MATERIALS

Intrinsic value is the archival term that is applied to permanently valuable records that have qualities and characteristics that make the records in their original physical form the only archivally acceptable form for preservation. Although all records in their original physical form have qualities and characteristics that would not be preserved in

Reprinted from National Archives and Records Service Staff Information Paper 21 (Washington: National Archives and Records Service, 1982).

[1]Committee members were Garry D. Ryan, chairman, Maygene F. Daniels, Milton O. Gustafson, Ronald L. Heise, Edward E. Hill, Trudy H. Peterson, David S. Van Tassel, and Leslie Waffen.

copies, records with intrinsic value have them to such a significant degree that the originals must be saved.

The qualities or characteristics that determine intrinsic value may be physical or intellectual; that is, they may relate to the physical base of the record and the means by which information is recorded on it or they may relate to the information contained in the record. Records with intrinsic value may be retained for either their evidential or informational value.

The archivist is responsible for determining which records have intrinsic value. Ordinarily this determination is made at the series level. As in all other archival appraisal activities, context is the key to making these determinations and context is normally best preserved by considering the entire series. The archivist, however, also may determine that certain individual record items within a series have intrinsic value, especially those items to be retained because of special physical characteristics.

QUALITIES AND CHARACTERISTICS OF RECORDS WITH INTRINSIC VALUE

All record materials having intrinsic value possess one or more of the following specific qualities or characteristics. These qualities or characteristics relate to the physical nature of the records, their prospective uses, and the information they contain.

1. *Physical form that may be the subject for study if the records provide meaningful documentation or significant examples of the form*
   Documents may be preserved in their original form as evidence of technological development. For example, a series of early press copies, glass-plate negatives, or wax-cylinder sound recordings may be retained. All records having a particular physical form would not be considered to have intrinsic value because of this characteristic; however, a selection broad enough to provide evidence of technological development would be considered to have some value.

2. *Aesthetic or artistic quality*
   Records having aesthetic or artistic quality may include photographs; pencil, ink, or watercolor sketches; maps; architectural drawings; frakturs; and engraved and/or printed forms, such as bounty-land warrants.

3. *Unique or curious physical features*
   Physical features that are unique or curious might include quality and texture of paper, color, wax seals, imprints and watermarks, inks, and unusual bindings. All records having a particular physical feature would not be considered to have

intrinsic value because of this feature; however, an exemplary selection of each type would be considered to have such value.

4. *Age that provides a quality of uniqueness*

Age is a relative rather than an absolute quality. Generally, records of earlier date are of more significance than records of later date. This can be because of a historical change in the functions and activities of the creator of the records, the scarcity of earlier records, a change in recordkeeping practices, or a combination of these. Age can be a factor even with comparatively recent records. The earliest records concerning, for example, the development of the radio industry or of nuclear power could have intrinsic value because of age.

5. *Value for use in exhibits*

Records used frequently for exhibits normally have several qualities and characteristics that give them intrinsic value. Records with exhibit value impressively convey the immediacy of an event, depict a significant issue, or impart a sense of the person who is the subject or originator of the record. In these cases, the impact of the original document cannot be equaled by a copy.

6. *Questionable authenticity, date, author, or other characteristic that is significant and ascertainable by physical examination*

Some records are of doubtful authenticity or have informational content that is open to question. Although it is impossible to foresee which documents will be questioned in the future, certain types of documents are well known to have the potential for controversy and, if the original records are extant, handwriting and signatures can be examined, paper age can be ascertained, and other physical tests can be performed. In some cases the controversy can be resolved by recourse to the original item (such as by an examination of the handwriting, the age of the paper, or the original negative of the photostatic print), while in other cases the item will not be conclusive but will provide the researcher with the best evidence from which to draw conclusions (original photographs of UFO's, for example).

7. *General and substantial public interest because of direct association with famous or historically significant people, places, things, issues, or events*

This criterion is not only the most difficult to apply, but also the most important in terms of the volume of records to which it could be applied. It could be used to justify preserving in original form almost all permanently valuable records because of their historical importance. On the other hand, if limited to records of unusual significance, it would be used to justify disposal of almost all original records. Archival judgment is the crucial factor in determining whether there is *general* and *substantial* public interest, whether the association is *direct*, and whether the subject is *famous* or *historically significant*. Generally, those series with a high concentration of such information should be preserved.

8. *Significance as documentation of the establishment or continuing legal basis of an agency or institution*

Agencies or institutions are founded and acquire or lose functions and responsibilities through the actions of the executive, legislative, and judicial branches of the Government. Records documenting these actions may be found concentrated in series or scattered in various series. They have in common the characteristic of documenting the shifts in function of the agency or institution at the highest level.

9. *Significance as documentation of the formulation of policy at the highest executive levels when the policy has significance and broad effect throughout or beyond the agency or institution*

Numerous records reflect policy decisions; however, most policy decisions have a relatively limited impact and reflect a relatively small area of authority. The characteristics that give policy records intrinsic value are the origin of the records at the highest executive levels, breadth of effect, and importance of subject matter.

APPLICATION OF THE CONCEPT OF INTRINSIC VALUE

Records that possess any characteristic or quality of intrinsic value should be retained in their original form if possible. The *concept* of intrinsic value, therefore, is not relative. However, *application* of the concept of intrinsic value is relative; opinions concerning whether records have intrinsic value may vary from archivist to archivist and from one generation of archivists to another. Professional archival judgment, therefore, must be exercised in all decisions concerning intrinsic value. Coordination between units holding records within an archival institution also may be necessary. For example, members of units holding similar records whose form may be the subject for study (quality 1) should consult one another to ensure that an adequate but not duplicative selection of records in that form is preserved. Although the concept of intrinsic value may be easier to apply to older records, decisions concerning intrinsic value can be made for all records determined to have sufficient value to warrant archival retention.

Copies of records having intrinsic value may be made for necessary archival purposes, including use by researchers. In fact, the fragility, rarity, or significance of the records may require that researchers normally work from reproductions.

Records that have intrinsic value should be considered for conservation or restoration; however, the determination that records have intrinsic value is only the first step in a decisionmaking continuum for preservation activities. Priorities and order of preservation activities should be guided by additional factors such as significance and frequency of use, rate of deterioration, seriousness of potential future preservation problems, and efficacy and expense of available treatments.

Although records with intrinsic value constitute the core of the holdings that archival institutions should maintain in original form, institutions also must retain records for which archivally acceptable copies cannot be made. This report does not attempt to establish comprehensive standards for archivally acceptable copies. At a minimum, however, such copies should have durability and utility for research use and for duplication equivalent to the records in their original form. If adequate copies of such records cannot be made, originals lacking intrinsic value may not be considered for disposition. For example, because, at present, reproductions made from duplicates of audiovisual records normally are of lower quality than reproductions made from the originals, most audiovisual records should be retained in their original form. When copies with equivalent or superior quality can be produced from reproductions, the originals could be considered for disposal.

Some records without intrinsic value also must be preserved in original physical form because such preservation is required by law.

Following are three examples of the use of the concept of intrinsic value in the decisionmaking process as applied to particular series of records in the National Archives. In these examples, archivists first reviewed the series in accordance with the intrinsic value criteria. Second, if the records lacked intrinsic value, archivists then determined whether any statute required retention of the records in their original form. Finally, if the responses to the first two inquiries were negative, archivists examined the archival adequacy of the copies of the records. While archivists may not prepare formal papers such as those that follow, similar questions should be asked and answered for any proposed disposition of original records.

I.   RG 33, Records of the Federal Extension Service. Farm Labor Program. Prisoner-of-War Program. 1943-46. 1 ft.

Arranged alphabetically by State.

Correspondence regarding the needs, placements, and status of prisoners of war employed in agriculture. The records reflect the relationship between the use of prisoner-of-war labor and migratory labor from Mexico and the Caribbean.

A. Intrinsic value criteria

  1. Example of physical form? No. These are records in the usual physical forms of mid-20th-century records.

  2. Aesthetic or artistic? No. These records are not visually interesting.

  3. Unique or curious physical features? No. There are no three-dimensional materials or unusual bindings, seals, papers, or inks.

  4. Age? No. These records are not unique in terms of age because there are many records from the World War II period, including records relating to POW's, among the permanent holdings.

  5. Exhibit potential? Unlikely.

  6. Authenticity? No. There are no doubts as to the authenticity of the records and no suggestion of forgery or other record tampering, There is no problem of signature or handwriting identification.

  7. General public interest? No. Although the records reflect a significant issue in U.S. history (i.e., the treatment of POW's in World War II), the records are not used frequently, no significant persons are named in the records, and no significant events are recorded.

  8. Legal basis of an agency or institution? No. These are records of implementation.

  9. Policy at high level of Government? No. These are operating level records.

Conclusion: This series of records does not have intrinsic value.

B. Are these records covered by a statute requiring retention in original physical form? No.

C. Can adequate copies be created? Yes. The records do not vary in size, there are no problems of scale or color coding, and the ease of reference is not impaired by use of a reproduction.

There is no privacy problem that would bar reproduction at this time.

Conclusion: The custodial unit can duplicate and request disposition of these records.

II.   RG 49, Records of the Bureau of Land Management. Public Land Disposals. Abandoned Military Reservations. 1818-1945. 60 ft.

Arranged chronologically by date of initial disposition or activity on the reservation land.

Executive orders, correspondence, title papers, plats, maps, blueprints, tracings, and printed items that document the General Land Office's role in the creation of military reservations from public lands and its responsibility for the disposal of reservations or portions of reservations abandoned by the War and Navy Departments. The records include information about goods and services available on the posts. Related records are found in other series of records of the General Land Office and among the general records of the Department of the Interior, the Office of the Chief of Engineers, the Office of the Quartermaster General, the Adjutant General's Office, United States Army commands, and the Office of the Judge Advocate General (Army).

A.   Intrinsic value criteria

1.   Example of physical form? No. These are routine types of records of the Government in the 19th and 20th centuries.

2.   Aesthetic or artistic? Occasionally. The cartographic and architectural items are usually utilitarian, although some have artistic embellishments.

3.   Unique or curious physical features? No. There are no three-dimensional materials or unusual bindings, seals, papers, or inks.

4.   Age? Yes. The pre-Civil War records concerning military reservations in the United States are small in quantity in comparison to the records of post-Civil War periods. In these files, pre- and post-Civil War materials are interfiled.

5.   Exhibit potential? Yes. These records could be used for exhibits on military posts, exploration of the West, organization of the frontier, surveying, land

disposition, military organization, and even autographs (William Tecumseh Sherman, Joel Poinsett).

6. Authenticity? No problem.

7. General public interest? Yes. Many military historians and enthusiasts use these materials; the Council on Abandoned Military Posts is particularly interested.

8. Legal basis of an agency or institution? No. These are records of the implementation of land acquisition and disposition policy, not the records of the establishment of the basis for the policy.

9. Policy at high level of Government? No. Although the records do contain significant correspondence from the Secretaries of War and the Interior regarding the implementation of land disposition policy, this correspondence does not document the making of policy.

Conclusion: The records have intrinsic value.

III. RG 341, Records of Headquarters U.S. Air Force. Air Technical Intelligence Center, Wright-Patterson AFB, Ohio. Aerial Phenomena Branch. Three related series of audiovisual records composed of photographs (7,280), sound recordings (23), and motion pictures (20) from "Project Blue Book." 1950-67. 7,323 items.

Arranged by case number.

Audiovisual records in different formats created, acquired, or collected by the U.S. Air Force during its official investigation into the existence of unidentified flying objects (UFO's). There are photographs (35 mm negatives) of 21 alleged sightings of UFO's, including some photos recorded on roll film that show timed radar responses of the observed phenomena. The motion pictures (8 mm and 16 mm) are composed mainly of original camera footage (unedited) filmed by military personnel and civilians. The sound recordings were recorded or acquired by the Air Force and contain interviews with individuals claiming to have seen UFO's as well as sound recordings made at the time of the alleged sightings. Related textual records are in accompanying series of case files and project files of "Project Blue Book."

A. Intrinsic value criteria

1. Example of physical form? No. The forms represented are standard, common forms of audiovisual reproductions.

2. Aesthetic or artistic value? No.

3. Unique or curious physical features? No.

4. Age? No.

5. Exhibit potential? Yes.

6. Authenticity? Yes. The entire phenomenon of the history of UFO's and the controversy surrounding their existence, as well as questions concerning the purpose and function of "Project Blue Book," require that the original records created or acquired by the Air Force and deposited with NARS be preserved and available for research scrutiny, testing and examination, and verification. This is especially a consideration because audiovisual documents are highly susceptible to tampering and manipulation. There is continued speculation and public doubt about the adequacy of the "evidence" and the conduct and conclusions of the official investigation.

7. General public interest? Yes. The history of UFO's, although a specialized research topic, does have a wide-ranging and emotional interest and fascination to the public.

8. Legal basis of agency or institution? No.

9. Policy at high level of Government? No. These are operating level records.

Conclusion: The records have intrinsic value.

Chapter 4
Archival Acquisition

A rchival acquisition is the process of identifying and obtaining by donation or purchase historical materials to add to the holdings of an archival institution. Manuscript repositories customarily acquire historical materials through the acquisition process. Many archives also acquire historical materials from outside their institutions to supplement their holdings of institutional records.

Acquisition can be seen as a series of interrelated decisions and actions. First, an institution must define its collecting policy based on an analysis of its interests and resources and identification of the users it wishes to serve. "Good Sense and Good Judgment: Defining Collections and Collecting" (1975), by Mary Lynn McCree, describes the elements of this procedure and its importance. Next, manuscript repositories must implement collecting policies by attracting donations through an organized program of public information and personal contacts, as Richard Kesner explains in "Archival Collection Development: Building a Successful Acquisitions Program" (1981). A strong acquisitions program also depends on effective field work to identify, locate, and secure appropri-

101

ate materials. Virginia Stewart gives practical guidance for this important function in her essay "A Primer on Manuscript Field Work" (1976). Finally, the transfer of the legal title to acquisitions must be documented to effectively complete the transaction. Trudy H. Peterson succinctly outlines the elements needed to document acquisition through transfer of legal title in "The Gift and the Deed" (1979).

Good Sense and Good Judgment: Defining Collections and Collecting

Mary Lynn McCree

There is a small four-year women's college located in a middle western town of 50,000. Originally settled in 1830, the town is now the county seat of government. It is served by train, bus and interstate highways from a major metropolitan area located 50 miles away, containing several major colleges and universities. The private liberal arts college, founded in 1882, has an enrollment of 450 students, 80 percent of whom continue on to graduate school. In its almost 100 years of existence, it has counted among its graduates some famous and influential American women.

Quite suddenly and unexpectedly a member of the college's class of 1945 died. For the past 10 years she had served in the U.S. Congress, representing the district in which the college was located. She was also a member of the board of trustees of the college. Prior to being elected to Congress, she had been one of the first practicing women lawyers in the district, active in the civic affairs of the area, and an early proponent of women's rights. In her spare time she wrote poetry. One of her collections of poems won a Pulitzer prize.

During her lifetime she had accumulated a sizable personal archive. Her husband felt it should be preserved. After all, other congressional representatives preserved their papers by presenting them to an educational institution of their choice. He believed a fitting place for her papers would be her alma mater. Accordingly, he approached the president of the college offering, not only the congresswoman's archives, but a $20,000 scholarship fund in her name as well.

The college president knew her institution had no manuscript collection, yet primarily because of the scholarship proposal, she convinced herself that perhaps it should have one, and without hesitating, she accepted the gift, informing the college librarian of the new acquisition. The gift was made with the understanding that the college would add other appropriate collections to that of the congresswoman to create a prestigious and recognized manuscript repository.

As soon as announcement of the gift was made in the local newspaper, the librarian began to receive calls from individuals offering a variety of material to add to the manuscript collection being organized at the college. Was the library interested in the family correspondence of a

Reprinted with permission from the *Drexel Library Quarterly* 11 (January 1975): 21-33.

pioneer settler of the town? Would it be appropriate to present the archives of the local women's club? A professor inquired as to whether the college was going to gather its own archives, for she had some papers she felt should be deposited. Clearly, the librarian, or someone, had to come to terms with what kind of collection the college was going to create.

ESTABLISHING A COLLECTING POLICY

The librarian was confronted with the same issue all other archivists and librarians face or should try to face when they initiate and create a collection of primary source materials to be used for scholarly inquiry and research. Too many institutions refuse to address the problem of adopting a collecting focus and their manuscript collections grow higgily-piggily, with little prestige or recognition from the scholarly world.

The librarian realized that the congresswoman's papers could provide the impetus to building a variety of manuscript collections, each with a different focus. After some consideration, the librarian singled out five separate ideas that she felt should be explored further for possible development as a collecting policy:

1. Papers of individuals and organizations revealing the growth and development of the town and county;

2. Papers of influential women and women's organizations in the town, county, state, or perhaps in the Middle West for a given time period;

3. Papers of political figures from an as yet undefined geographic area to include the town in a specific time period;

4. The papers and writings of literary figures of the state or the Middle West for a specific time period;

5. Development of the college's own archives.

Let us consider which of these topics is most appropriate for the college to adopt as its collecting policy. Almost all of these topics are defined by subject, geographic area and time period. While it is important to have some definition in any collecting policy that is developed, it is equally important to create a guideline with some flexibility so that the collection has some room to grow and evolve.

Many manuscript collections in America today were started, like the one at this midwestern women's college, because an individual or an organization presented its papers to a library, historical society, college or university. By accepting those papers, the institution signals its willingness and ability to assume responsibility for the maintenance of that gift for the benefit of the larger scholarly community. It also implies an intent to create a manuscript collection composed of the papers of individuals and organizations who have participated in or observed a series of activities relating to the focus that the institution has elected to establish.

In this regard, an institutional collection is far different from a collection of manuscripts and related items gathered by an individual. The private collector may select a person, event, or subject around which to build his collection, e.g., Franklin Delano Roosevelt, the American Civil War, American women novelists of the nineteenth century. He is interested in individual items for their uniqueness or autograph more than for their informational value. He is often content if he can boast complete "sets" of the autographs, for instance, the Northern generals who saw action during the American Civil War or a signed F.D.R. note or letter on letterhead stationery from each of the offices F.D.R. held. The private collector builds his collection almost entirely through purchase.

An institution, on the other hand, is not interested just in the unique item, but rather in complementary, interrelated bodies of consecutive files of manuscripts that provide detailed information on a person, event, organization, period of time or subject. These manuscripts when viewed together tell a story; the content of the documents is more important than the autograph value. This does not mean that institutions with manuscript collections would turn down unique and autographically valuable manuscripts. They wouldn't. But their primary responsibility is to create a focused body of materials that informs the scholar.

Does an institution know when it receives an initial gift what additional materials it should seek in order to develop a unified collection? Usually, no. Neither has it considered what such a commitment means in terms of personnel, facilities and money. The extent and focus of the collection have a direct bearing on the personnel, facilities and funding necessary to maintain it, and vice versa. Therefore, it seems logical that one of the first prerequisites for establishing a manuscript collection is defining a collecting policy. This should be done before any additional manuscript materials are added to the initial gift collection. How does the institution develop its collecting policy? What are some of the considerations?

Whether the manuscript collection begins with a gift collection or with nothing but an idea of what the institution might like to collect, a consideration of the course the development of a manuscript collection should take depends on an assessment of the following: the institution's resources, resources available for use from other area institutions, and the public the institution thinks it serves now and wants to attract in the future.

Manuscripts are not used in a vacuum. Scholars and students usually turn to primary resources only after they are familiar with the published works or secondary sources in their chosen field of inquiry. So, to begin with, survey your institution's scholarly resources to determine what secondary and other primary research tools it has that support the kind of manuscript collection you are considering. Look at your library's books, periodicals, newspapers, public documents, microfilm, record, tape and film collection, pamphlets, prints, maps, etc., to see if and how these holdings complement your intended collection focus. Then consider the resources available in other institutions in your immediate geographic area to discover if there are materials that would enhance and complement your projected manuscript collection. It usually makes very little sense to create a manuscript collection that has a focus completely alien to the interests of your institution and/or neighboring institutions, as expressed in secondary resources they have already gathered.

After you have assessed the depth of supporting resources, you will have some idea of how much material is already on hand. If you discover there is little or no material of a secondary nature in close proximity, then you will have to consider either discarding the collecting focus you were considering or acquiring at least a basic bibliography of secondary resources as one of the costs of starting the collection.

It is equally important to consider the economic consequences of creating a manuscript collection. Assess your institution's financial position, not only to determine if it can support the collection by acquiring or continuing to acquire secondary resources complementary to the collection, but also to ascertain whether it can provide the funds necessary to maintain staff to administer, process and service the collection, acquire the collection, and house it. Remember, it takes money to secure collections by purchase *or* by gift. If you believe that the necessary funding is available at present, ask yourself if it will be there in the future. Try to judge if there is a good possibility that the funding necessary to support a manuscript collection will be there in the increasing amounts required to maintain the initial collection or to build a growing collection.

For instance, a collection that you anticipate will be built largely through purchase will probably require more funding than one created through gifts. Yet if the collection you intend to build through gifts has a broad geographic focus, more funds will be required for identification of prospective collections, for deposit, travel and communications, than if you were creating a collection with a local focus.

Next, take a look at your staff. Manuscripts and archives are not processed into a collection or made available to the public in the same manner as printed library material. They require special handling by individuals trained in the theory and techniques of managing manuscript and archival resources. It is vital that you find and maintain well-qualified staff to support your collection, for it is worth little to the prestige of your institution, to students, scholars and researchers who wish to use it, if materials in the collection are inaccessible to them for lack of proper professional care.

Last, but certainly not least, you must consider the physical facilities required to maintain a manuscript collection. To begin with, there is simply a matter of having adequate space in which to store, process and service collections you anticipate receiving immediately. It should be a self-contained area to which you can limit access; it should be fireproof and waterproof. Controls to provide proper temperature, humidity and lighting are desirable.

But can your institution provide adequate long-term permanent space to process, house and service the manuscripts you anticipate receiving, given the collecting policy you are considering? How does the space your institution agrees to make available to you affect the kind of manuscript collection you can develop? If the space is small and there is absolutely no hope of enlarging the allotment you should be certain that the collection you plan can be contained in it. For example, you will probably require more space to preserve the papers of political figures and organizations which tend to create and maintain large correspondences than you would require for the manuscripts of a poet. Seeking and accepting papers when you have no means of preserving and protecting them is irresponsible and reflects discredit on your institution.

Once you have assessed these aspects—the supporting secondary and primary holdings, funding, personnel, physical facilities—of your institution's ability to maintain a collection, you should consider at least three other major issues: your institution's public, other institutions' collecting policies, and problems related to institutional archives.

When your institution commits itself to create and maintain a manuscript collection it is with the clear understanding that it is doing so for the benefit of the entire scholarly world. Your institution cannot in good conscience limit access to the collection it is creating to its own members, students or scholars. A manuscript collection should be open to qualified researchers who are willing to abide by the rules of use your institution establishes. So it becomes a matter of deciding which public you would most like to appeal to or to serve.

Usually, your first concern is to create a collection that will be useful to your most immediate constituency. A college or a university may wish to collect materials that will be useful to its own students or faculty, secondarily to the students and faculty of other institutions, free-lance writers and researchers, and amateurs. On the other hand an historical society might feel obliged to consider the interests of its membership, often times history buffs and leisure time scholars, as co-equal or more important than those of students and scholars. A collection with a local history flavor or focusing on some popular event, person or time will attract many more amateur scholars than the papers of less romantic, stellar subjects.

It is also important to remember that there are pitfalls in attempting to tailor a collection to the interests of one group of faculty or students, or one small pressure group. For example, there may be a faculty member doing research on the Japanese who have settled in your community since 1900. Though no one else has shown any interest in that topic and there are no secondary resources to support that interest, you accede to the faculty member's wishes and direct all your resources—staff time and funds—to collecting material for her. As soon as you begin to acquire some of the collections in which she is interested, she accepts a job offer on the West Coast. Faculty and students leave institutions, and pressure groups who are successful lose their *raison d'être* and fade to nothing. Then where is the public for whom you have developed your collection? It is your responsibility to create a collection that holds a continuing interest and relevance for scholars as a research and teaching tool. Hopefully, the manuscripts you select to preserve will be used over and over again for a variety of topics and points of view. Be sure that your public is broad enough to be continually supportive and interested.

Another major consideration in determining a collection development policy is knowledge of the established collecting policies of other institutions, particularly those in the area in which your institution is located. It would appear to be bad judgment to create and implement a manuscript collection policy that duplicates one already functioning successfully within the geographic area that you propose to serve. Competition with an established, recognized collection is costly in terms of time, staff and funds. It leads to feelings of ill will between institutions. The scholarly world is better served and your own institution's reputation benefited by building a unique collection of resources formerly unavailable to scholarship. For instance, why should your institution collect local history materials if there is a historical society that already has an established collection consisting of papers that you have determined are central to a creditable collection. Strike off on a new direction, but try to be sure that what you are spending time, effort and money on has relevance for more than the immediate future, for more than a limited public.

It is wise for institutions to cooperate with one another, especially if they are located in the same geographic area. Be sure to know what other institutions are collecting so that should someone offer your institution papers which do not fall within the scope of your collection you might suggest another institution that would be a more appropriate home for the materials. For the same reason, communicate your collecting interests to other area institutions or appropriate repositories outside your locale. Perhaps they will send some collections your way.

A thorough knowledge of the collections of other institutions with collections development policies that overlap yours will save you the expense of pursuing a collection of papers already located in a repository. It will also help you provide better reference service to students and scholars using your collections, for you will be able to suggest other repositories near your institution which have materials that might be helpful.

A third major consideration is the existence of many institutional archives—archives of colleges, museums and the like—which preserve the documentation of their own institutions. Should you attempt to collect official records of other institutions which pertain to your subject area? The answer is "no" in virtually every case where an institutional archives is functioning effectively. What about the papers of individuals prominently associated with an organization which has an effective archives program? This is a more complex problem (the professor may be determined to destroy his papers before turning them over to his college), but those directing subject collections should not attempt to lure personal papers away from institutional archives. The pot of gold at the end of the rainbow—a complete archival subject collection—is chimerical anyhow; important, unique segments of documentation in your subject area will always remain outside your grasp. Better techniques for achieving comprehensiveness are exchange of information about collections, and exchange of microfilm copies of closely related collections.

Now let us return to the problem faced by the librarian of the midwestern women's college. After considering the five prospective collection development policies in light of the foregoing criteria, she made her decision. The first possibility—developing a local history collection—was discarded when she discovered that the county historical society had been collecting local manuscript materials for the past 10 years. It had an established collection used mostly by genealogists and local history buffs, a clientele she had decided she did not wish to cater to. Likewise she discarded the third suggestion—collecting the papers of prominent political figures from her state—and the fourth—collecting the papers and manuscripts of leading literary figures from the Middle West. In both cases she discovered another institution with a well established reputation for collections it had developed in these two areas. The state historical society collected political materials; one of the universities located in the nearby metropolitan area had been collecting the papers and manuscripts of midwestern literary figures for about 50 years.

That left two options: to focus on collecting the papers of women and women's organizations in the Middle West or to establish a college archive. A survey of her institution and those in the surrounding area revealed a sizable holding of secondary and primary resources on women and the woman's movement. She knew that her own institution had

109

some courses that stressed the contributions women had made to life in the United States. She also discovered that two universities in the large city had programs and courses at both the graduate and undergraduate levels to explore the problems, experiences, and contributions of American women. After a discussion with her institution's president, the librarian was reassured that adequate funds would be available on a continuing basis to create a sizable and noteworthy collection. The president seemed eager to gather and preserve a unique collection of materials which might bring her institution to national prominence, for the librarian had discovered only two similar collections in existence in America—one on the East Coast and one on the West. Both women reasoned that developing and preserving such a collection for the Middle West would not only support the research and teaching needs of their own institution but attract scholars, students, writers and journalists from throughout the Midwest. It would appeal to the kind of public the institution wanted to support. The librarian and the president were convinced that this was the focus they should adopt for their manuscript collection. But what of the college archives? They decided to consider the development of the archives as a facet of the broader collecting focus on women of the Midwest. The college was an organization which for nearly 100 years had educated influential women who made contributions in America.

IMPLEMENTING THE POLICY

Now the institution had a collecting policy that it believed to be feasible; one it hoped would make a contribution to scholarly knowledge. How should it be implemented and how might that action affect the collection scope? There are two major ways to acquire manuscripts, by purchase or by gift. Most collections are created by relying on both dealer and donor. These two individuals are instrumental in giving definition to a collecting policy.

Before you approach either of them it is necessary that your institution have considerable knowledge about the field it has chosen as a focus for its collection. Not only should the archivist or librarian activating the program be familiar with the major published secondary sources but also he or she should identify the individuals and organizations which have been signally involved in the events, movements and time periods with which the collection is concerned. It is imperative that an institution identify the resources it wishes to collect. The published interpretations of historians may help you make some of the judgments regarding records that should compose the collection; however, in many cases you will have to decide on the basis of your own knowledge of the subject, the papers you should seek. Do not hesitate to enlist the advice and help of scholars with special knowledge or experience doing research on subjects that fall within the scope of your collection.

Be sure you understand the type of documentation you are seeking in collections you acquire. Original and unique documents consisting of correspondence, diaries, memoranda, manuscripts of articles, books, speeches, notes, etc., are some of the types of documents that should compose most collections. Generally, do not concentrate on gathering numerous duplicates of published or copied items. Do not seek types of materials already part of a library collection, e.g., newspaper clippings, reprints and offprints of articles. Be familiar with the kind of materials that provide good meaty information that will make the papers you acquire so beneficial to scholars. Once you are certain that you have a good understanding of the information available on the subject matter of the collection, as well as an idea of the types of papers you want to acquire, you are ready to approach dealers and donors.

DEALERS

An experienced manuscript dealer can be a tremendous help to an institution building a scholarly collection. Explain your collecting focus to the dealer. Let him know the kind of material you are looking for; let him know that you have funds from which you can draw to purchase appropriate items for your collection. The dealer's daily business includes his familiarization with all American autograph markets and many in other countries. If he knows what the boundaries of your collection are, he can become your eyes, not only prepared to note if, when and where an item or items are offered, but to track down *any* rumor that some particularly attractive morsel may come upon the market. Frequently, the dealer becomes the clearinghouse between seller and purchaser, receiving an agreed-upon commission on the successful transaction. He is also prepared to offer advice about appropriate items that you may not be aware of.

For all of these reasons, it is important that the dealer with whom you work is familiar with your growing collection. He is equipped and alert to channel items to particular customers, and this he normally does in a personal communication without waiting for the publication of his catalogs. He is customarily willing to submit material on approval if an institution well-known to him requests that it be mailed for inspection. The request is not made, it is generally understood, unless the institution is fairly certain that it wishes to purchase the offering. The material, if not bought, must be returned at once, since delay may result in the loss of its sale to someone else. The librarian is bound to observe fully the well-defined ethics of approval shipments (no copying of any kind; recognition that having an item temporarily in your possession does not allow you any rights to its contents.)

A dealer guarantees the authenticity of any item you purchase through him. If at any time the authenticity of an item can be authoritatively challenged, it may at once be returned to the dealer. Dealing with a reputable dealer is the best protection from the risk of either being unmercifully taken by deliberately unscrupulous persons or purchasing either stolen material or facsimilies or forgeries. A dealer's reputation rests on his ability to guarantee his stock. Often, manuscripts you would like to own come up for sale on the auction market. Here a friendly dealer can be a help, too, for the dealer who frequently secures materials in the auction market is much more familiar with peculiarities of the market than the librarian. You will have a better chance of securing materials you want that are to be offered at auction if you engage a reliable and experienced dealer. This does not mean that the librarian should not be in attendance at the sale. Obviously, when the dealer is to represent an institution, the two should confer in advance to determine the maximum amount the latter is willing to pay. And always, if the dealer is able to buy below the maximum set, he will do so and save his customer.

No reputable dealer will ever represent two clients in bidding for the same item. It may occasionally happen that both a client and the dealer are interested in acquiring the same item. In such cases, if the client's declared maximum is higher than that of the dealer, the latter, accepting his client's bid, will not compete. And should he, representing his client, find it possible to obtain the item at less money than he himself would have paid, he would still turn over the item to his client. If, on the other hand, the dealer's intended bid exceeds that of the client, the client is expected to withdraw his bid, permitting the dealer to obtain it.

The dealer's fee, as the institution's representative, is customarily 10 percent of the sales price. He has earned this fee by guaranteeing the purchase's authenticity as a document and as the document described for sale by the auction house. He has also provided his expertise and experience with regard to current market values and the delicacies of buying at an auction. American auction houses now usually provide an approximate valuation of items to be sold in advance of their sale. Unfortunately, these estimates are often low—someone bidding the recommended fair market price often loses out on the item. Again, rely on an experienced dealer to give you a better idea of what the items you are interested in should cost. Dealers, when they buy at such sales, are permitted a limited period of credit, but other buyers are requested to pay at the time of purchase.

A word of caution, however. Remember, dealers are in business to sell manuscripts. You must be the ultimate judge of whether or not you can afford an item or whether it is what you need in the collection you are building. Know your collection, be honest and firm about your needs, pay your bills promptly, and you and the dealer with whom you work should have a long and respectful relationship.

DONORS

While many institutions rely on dealers for individual specific items to highlight or fill in their collections, many try to acquire the bulk of their collections through gifts. Just as dealers help an institution develop a collecting policy, so do donors. Not only do they present their papers, which may provide important and hitherto unknown information, they also provide suggestions and leads to new prospective donors who usually have created collections which are complementary to theirs. So it is vital that you achieve a good continuing relationship with an individual or organization who places papers in your collection.

As with the dealer, honesty is always the best policy. Establish the credibility of your institution and your collection with a donor. Explain the scope of your collection, why his papers are important to it. Tell him the kinds of people who will seek access to his papers and the probable uses to which they will be put. If it is appropriate, provide information on copyright, literary rights and appraisal. Let him know that your institution accepts responsibility for the preservation of the papers it believes to be of value to scholars. If he is interested, explain some of the procedures of arrangement and description, some of the methods used to guarantee their safety, including physical facilities, that your institution provides.

A donor who respects you and your institution will willingly provide information on his collection that will be helpful, not only as you prepare his papers for use by scholars, but also as you seek leads to other collections. He may even be willing to vouch for your collection personally to those other prospective donors, thus providing the person-to-person contact, usually a more persuasive method of establishing the donor relations than a phone call or a letter from an unknown source.

CONCLUSION

Establishing a collecting policy is a multifaceted activity. It requires knowledge of your institution and its public, of manuscript collections and how they operate, and of the subject you select as the focus for your collection. After you have the collections development policy you feel you can live with, write it down, abide by it as you go about creating a manuscript collection, and review it frequently. Good luck!

Archival Collection Development: Building a Successful Acquisitions Program

Richard M. Kesner

A rchival programs have three primary objectives. The first entails identifying and selecting or collecting appropriate papers or records for permanent preservation; the second involves arranging and preserving them; and the final objective is to insure their accessibility by preparing finding aids and providing reference service. While many archivists, especially those responsible for the administration of large programs, spend a significant portion of their time preparing grant applications, raising funds, and training staff, all of these activities ultimately contribute to an archives' primary responsibilities—the acquisition, preservation, and dissemination of documentary information.[1]

Certain aspects of archival administration, however, have received less attention than others in the archival literature. In particular, "collection development," the process by which materials of historical or otherwise enduring value are selected and acquired by an archives, requires a more thorough and systematic consideration.[2] Current literature pertaining to collecting can be divided into three distinct categories according to its main focus or concern. There are works that deal with specific legal questions, such as literary property rights, copyright law, and physical ownership of papers and records. One also finds articles that deal with such financial aspects of manuscript acquisition as the determination of fair market value, tax appraisal, and gift policies. Finally, a

---

Reprinted with permission from *The Midwestern Archivist* 5 (2, 1981): 101-112.

[1]The author would like to acknowledge the generous financial support provided by the Archives of Appalachia Fund and the East Tennessee State University Foundation; the assistance of Susan Nayer Kesner and Katherine Wilson in the preparation of previous drafts of this article; and the professional guidance of Philip P. Mason and George Tselos.

[2]Frank B. Evans' bibliography includes only a few references concerning collection development in the sub-section, "Administration of Personal Papers and Manuscripts," *Modern Archives and Manuscripts: A Select Bibliography* (Chicago: Society of American Archivists, 1975). His more recent UNESCO bibliography includes no references to literature dealing specifically with collecting practices in archives: *The History of Archives Administration: A Select Bibliography* (Paris: UNESCO, 1979). Neither of Paul V. Guite's two bibliographic updates published in *The American Archivist* included references pertaining to collection development: "Writings on Archives, Historical Manuscripts, and Current Records, 1976," *American Archivist* 41 (July 1978): 307-327; and "Writings on Archives, Historical Manuscripts, and Current Records, 1977," *American Archivist* 42 (July 1979): 321-343.

number of archivists have written brief histories of their respective programs in which they chronicle their experiences as collectors. All of these
works are to a certain extent both useful and relevant, but only a few take
a broad view of the collecting process.[3] However, in a period when the
archival profession is promoting institutional cooperation and a reevalu-
ation of archival ethics and educational practices, there is a demonstrable
need to re-examine collection development procedures.

Similarly, there is a need for a basic manual dealing with all aspects
of the acquisition of archives and manuscripts. This article can do little
more within its limited context than suggest the direction that such a
manual ought to take. While the recommendations it includes are
couched in general terms, they are based upon the experience of establishing an archives program at East Tennessee State University. In many
respects, the Archives of Appalachia, which opened in 1978 on the
ETSU campus in Johnson City, Tennessee, is a typical special-subject
archives.[4] As a didactic model, the Archives is also of some interest
because it was given a broad mandate by the University "to collect" without the encumbrance of any further instructions. Thus, it began without
a specific collecting focus or policy. The collecting strategies that developed during the first year of the Archives' operation illustrate many of
the broader concerns of this article. While some of the suggestions and
observations that follow may prove applicable in other archival settings,
the wide diversity among institutions—ranging from government and

[3]Works dealing with legal questions include: Marie C. Malaro, "A Lawyer Advises on
Collecting Policy," *History News* 35 (October 1980): 13-14; Trudy Huskamp Peterson, "The
Gift and the Deed," *American Archivist* 42 (January 1979): 61-66; and Marie P.G. Christine,
"A Note on Deposit Agreement Forms," *SLA Bulletin* 8 (December 1951): 21-22. Studies
concerning the financial aspects of manuscript acquisition include: Winston Broadfoot,
"How Inflation Affects Institutional Collecting," *Manuscripts* 31 (Fall 1979): 293-296; Wil-
fred I. Smith and John H. Archer, "Donors, Taxmen and Archives," *Canadian Archivist* 2
(1971): 25-31; and Charles L.B. Loundes, "Tax Advantages of Charitable Gifts," *Virginia
Law Review* 46 (April 1968): 409-412. Among the histories of specific collecting programs
one finds: Harley P. Holden, "Collecting Faculty Papers," *Harvard Library Bulletin* 19 (April
1971): 187-193; Robert L. Brubaker, "Clio's Midwife: Collecting Manuscripts at a State
Historical Society," *Illinois Libraries* 47 (June 1965): 495-501; and Lewis E. Atherton, "Western Historical Manuscript Collection: A Case Study of a Collecting Program," *American
Archivist* 26 (January 1963): 41-49. Recent publication of more general works dealing with
collecting archival materials include Edward C. Kemp, *Manuscript Solicitation for Libraries,
Special Collections, Museums and Archives* (Littleton, Colorado: Libraries Unlimited, Inc.,
1978); Bruce W. Dearstyne, "Local Historical Records: Programs for Historical Agencies,"
AASLH Technical Leaflet No. 121 as published in *History News* 34 (November 1979); Mary
Lynn McCree, "Good Sense and Good Judgment: Defining Collections and Collecting,"
Drexel Library Quarterly 11 (January 1975): 21-33; and Kenneth W. Duckett *Modern Manu-
scripts* (Nashville: American Association for State and Local History, 1975), pp. 56-86.

[4]Linda J. Henry, "Collecting Policies of Special Subject Repositories," *American Archivist* 43 (Winter 1980): 57-63. See also Dorothy L. Heinrich, "Establishing an Ethnic Collection in a Small Institution," *The Midwestern Archivist* II, No. 1 (1977): 41-48.

organizational archives to specialized manuscript repositories—makes it very difficult to establish universal truths. This particular case study is intended to furnish a critical framework for the evaluation of collection development policies in other institutions.

All archives should have a collecting focus that can be employed to appraise the relevance of each prospective acquisition. Potential accessions must, of course, meet other criteria as well, involving the quality or character of their evidential or informational value. A collecting focus is also essential to an archives program because it gives meaning and direction to staff field work. If successful, such a focus can bring together collections that complement one another, thereby making the archives a more attractive and valuable resource for its user constituency.

How does one select a focus? In many instances there is no choice. Universities, government agencies, and corporations, for example, engage archivists to manage their non-current records. The collecting focus of these types of repositories is usually confined to the official records of the respective host institution. While this type of situation may limit the scope of many archives' collecting activities, it is possible to exercise a more expansive interpretation of an official mandate through the use of oral history and the collection of the private papers of important individuals connected with the organization or institution.[5]

Other archives, however, do not start out with such inherent limitations. While it is not difficult to fill one's archives with paper, it is much more difficult to ensure that one's holdings individually and collectively justify the cost and effort of preserving them. A collecting focus can help by requiring the archivist to evaluate each potential acquisition in light of the institution's larger mission and objectives. In selecting a focus for a collecting program, three questions should be asked: what is available? what is needed? and what are other pertinent repositories collecting? No matter how specific one may choose to be in defining an archives' mission, there is invariably more material in existence than one could or would want to acquire. If time and resources allow, an archivist might conduct a survey of extant records or papers in a given geographical location or in a particular subject area, such as labor history, civil rights, or railroad development. Such a survey could reveal what records are in the field, who holds them, and whether they might be available for accessioning. Various state archival programs and special subject repositories have employed surveys to help develop or refine their collecting focuses.[6]

---

[5]See Nicholas C. Burckel, "The Expanding Role of a College or University Archives," *The Midwestern Archivist* I, No. 1 (1976): 3-15; David B. Gracy II, "Starting in Archives," *Georgia Archive* I (Fall 1972): 20-29; and Dorothy L. Heinrich and Linda J. Henry (note no. 4).

[6]For a number of illustrative examples of records surveys and their usefulness to archivists, see the articles by John Fleckner, George Mariz, and Michael Stephen Hindus in the *American*

Surveys need not be massive undertakings. In the case of the Archives of Appalachia, the staff circulated a form letter to scholars in the field of Appalachian studies, to community organizations, companies, and labor unions active in southern Appalachia, and to civic leaders and public officials. The Archives was assisted in this regard by the timely publication of a special issue of the *Appalachian Journal* (Vol. 5, no. 1, Autumn 1977) devoted to Appalachian studies programs. Since the Archives was dealing largely with people who were totally unaware of the needs of archives, its survey instrument began with an explanation of the basic aims of the Archives—to collect and preserve significant historical and research materials in southern Appalachia. It then queried those to whom it was addressed about the availability and physical condition of the papers and records in their custody and solicited their knowledge of other holdings in the community. The rather limited number of responses received from this survey nonetheless contributed to the development of a useful profile of what was available in the region.

Having thus identified, even in vague terms, a number of possible collecting themes, the archivist must choose a single focus or perhaps several focuses. To make this final determination, one must be aware of both what is "needed" by the research community and how well other repositories have already addressed these needs. In carrying out its survey, the Archives of Appalachia staff discovered that there were other archival programs in the region. Information of this sort may also be obtained from organizational directories published by the National Historical Publications and Records Commission and the American Association for State and Local History. Subsequent inquiries addressed to other repositories in the region should provide some idea of the nature and scope of their collecting efforts. Since there are more records worthy of preservation available than all of the archives in the country together could possibly accommodate, in most instances it is unnecessary and counter-productive for archives to compete for the same materials. By choosing a collecting focus wisely, one can avoid such wasteful competition.

To complete the delineation of a collecting focus, the archivist must establish a set of priorities governing the acquisition of collections based upon their value and the needs of potential users. This should be seen as part of the appraisal process.[7] Scholars actively engaged in research involving the use of the types of documentation under consideration for

Archivist 42 (July, 1979). See also Francis X. Blouin, Mary Pearson, Andrea Hinding, and John A. Fleckner, "Survey of Historical Records," *American Archivist* 40 (July 1977): 301-306; and John A. Fleckner, *Archives and Manuscripts: Surveys* (Chicago: Society of American Archivists, 1977).

[7]Maynard J. Brichford, *Archives and Manuscripts: Appraisal and Accessioning* (Chicago: Society of American Archivists, 1977). For an example of systematic appraisal strategy, see

accessioning can be very helpful by suggesting areas in which more papers or records are needed. Also, they often may provide useful leads as to where one might go in search of these materials, and may even be able to assist the archivist in sensitive negotiations with potential donors.

Some collections will have obvious research value, but many others may not appear attractive until their relevance to a user constituency has been established. Here again the advice of outside specialists should be solicited. One ought to always keep potential users in mind when developing a collecting focus. Failure to do so may result in the acquisition of collections that are of little interest or value to the archives' clientele. The implications of such a mistake for the future of a repository are quite apparent.

If selected wisely, a collecting focus should be able to help identify valuable records available in a community, region, or subject area and provide an archives with a clearly defined set of acquisition objectives. As an archives develops, it will succeed in attracting more users as well as additional donors because it will have created an identity that is distinct from that of other institutions in the region. The greater the effort made by new repositories to define and adhere to their collecting focuses, the better able archivists will be to serve their user constituencies and work together to preserve the documentation of our nation's past.[8]

In establishing a collecting focus for the Archives of Appalachia, the aforementioned methodology was employed. In the first place, it was discovered that very few archives existed in central southern Appalachia. Archives such as the ones at Berea College in Kentucky and at West Virginia University, that had operated in Appalachia for some time, had not collected in the immediate five-state region of east Tennessee, eastern Kentucky, southwest Virginia, southwest West Virginia, and western North Carolina that lies within one hundred miles of Johnson City, Tennessee. Furthermore, only one of these institutions was actively engaged in the collection of economic records; and no archives in the region appeared interested in the records of the grassroots and self-help organizations that abound in southern Appalachia. This, then, became the focus of the Archives—to collect the papers and records of persons and organizations active in the economic and social development of the region, especially in the twentieth century.

Despite this carefully selected focus, the Archives was criticized for encroaching upon the preserves of other repositories in the area. These

Richard M. Kesner, "Labor Union Grievance Records: An Appraisal Strategy," *Archivaria* 8 (Summer 1979): 102-114.

[8]Philip P. Mason, "The Ethics of Collecting," *Georgia Archive* V (Winter 1977): 36-50 remains the single most definitive statement pertaining to the ethical aspects of collecting practices.

charges stemmed primarily from the fact that the Archives chose a regional instead of a state or local collecting focus. Some colleagues in Kentucky did not like the thought of "Kentucky" records going to Tennessee! Even with these initial problems the Archives of Appalachia has successfully attracted the records of organizations with a regional focus, such as the Congress for Appalachian Development, as well as other collections from its immediate five-state area. Now that the Archives has firmly established its identity and collecting focus, these criticisms have subsided.

Having established an archival program with a collecting focus, the archivist's next task is to implement the program. As a first step, the archivist must begin to publicize the archives. In initiating a publicity campaign, the archivist should draft a clear statement of purpose. This document, which ordinarily should not exceed one letter-size page (no more than five hundred words, single spaced), should include a brief history of the archives, a summary of its general purpose and services, a roster of its personnel, a list of the types of records (e.g., diaries, correspondence, business files, photographs) that it seeks, and most importantly a clear, succinct paragraph articulating the archives' collection focus. It is important to keep in mind that to most people the term "archives" conjures up images of dusty books and old newspapers. A prospective donor is apt to dismiss his or her letters and photographs as being of no consequence compared to an "old" newspaper or periodical. The archives' statement of purpose should alert members of the archives' potential constituency to its activities and suggest ways in which they might participate in these activities—either as donors or as users.

A carefully drafted statement can be used with great effect in any number of ways. It can serve as the basis for a promotional pamphlet on the archives program or it might constitute the core of news releases prepared for newspapers, radio, and television. Individual letters to potential donors might also be based on the statement. In this case it is better to personalize such messages by having them typed individually, but the basic intention is always the same: to create a greater awareness of the program's existence and needs. Some donors mainly read newspapers; others only watch television; and still others attend public lectures. Hence, some might be reached through an effective newspaper campaign, while many others will be missed if publicity efforts fail to use all of the mass media. Mail campaigns promise only a marginal return and then only if they maintain at least the appearance of a personalized approach. Some programs may wish to employ a newsletter similar to the one published quarterly by the Archives of Appalachia to communicate with its user constituency. However, such an approach is often inefficient and ineffective as a fund raising or collection solicitation tool, since it is too generalized in its approach to impress individual donors. Nonetheless, one may enclose newsletters with personalized letters or leave them with potential donors after personal interviews. Used in this manner, newsletters appear to have a more lasting effect.

If the archives' publicity campaign is successful, it may result in the receipt of a few collections, but more often than not the most tangible return from such promotional efforts will be a series of leads and perhaps a number of invitations to speak before various organizations. The only way to acquire collections on a systematic basis is through actual field work, and this means personal contact with prospective donors.[9] In following up leads, one must meet people face-to-face. During these meetings, it will be necessary to carry on some of the same educational activities mentioned above, detailing what an archives is, describing the nature of its collecting focus, and informing a prospective donor how he or she might "participate in the program" by contributing papers or records to the archives. Community meetings may also be an extremely effective means of alerting people to an archives' activities. Communication with an audience is enhanced by the use of slides and a brief, formal presentation about the archives' program, what it collects, and how its collections are used. A few descriptive slides with an appropriate accompanying narrative can save many valuable minutes that could more profitably be used otherwise in soliciting new collections.

A business card or brochure that includes the archivist's name together with the archives' address, phone number, and hours is an important aid for archivists in the field. One will always need to provide potential donors and patrons with this information. Successful collection development is very much a matter of image. Brochures, newsletters, and business cards all demonstrate that the archivist represents a professional, "permanent" organization. This sense of permanence is absolutely essential if one plans to instill a degree of confidence in potential donors to the extent that they are willing to donate their treasured private papers or records to the archives. Similarly, it is important that the archivist conveys to audiences a commitment both to the preservation of materials left in the archives' care and to the dissemination to researchers of information concerning the availability of these collections. Beyond establishing the proper professional demeanor with potential donors, these practices should serve to strengthen one's standing both with the user community and among colleagues.

A well conceived collecting focus and an effectively executed publicity campaign can help provide the basis for a sound collecting program. But to be successful, the archives must also establish a series of procedures to insure that the program is properly administered. At the heart

---

[9]The literature dealing with field work is very limited. See Virginia R. Stewart, "A Primer on Manuscript Field Work," *The Midwestern Archivist* I, No. 2 (1976): 3-20.

of this system ought to be some type of lead file mechanism. Some archives use formatted index cards for leads. Others use elaborate file structures. The Archives of Appalachia employs a three-component lead file system. A "lead file" is established showing the lead's name followed by the word "LEAD" in capital letters (e.g., "Gordon Ebersole LEAD"). This step is taken to avoid misfiling lead files with other administrative files, such as those set up for accessioned collections which are referred to as "case files." All information pertaining to the lead is then placed in the file, including newspaper clippings, correspondence, resumes, and photographs. These files are arranged according to the name of the person to be contacted, even though the purpose of the lead may be to track down a collection with another name. This procedure is used to minimize confusion in corresponding with donors, a practice which has proven particularly useful in situations where a donor has custody of more than one possible acquisition.

After establishing a lead file, the Archives director writes a letter to the potential donor explaining the Archives' program and enclosing a brochure and one or more issues of the *Newsletter*. This letter will always include a specific reference to the collection(s) in the lead's possession. Unless the director has already met the lead, this letter is followed a week later by a phone call. This contact serves to further familiarize the potential donor with the Archives' program and sometimes to arrange a meeting between the lead and a member of the Archives staff. The most common way to obtain collections is through this final stage of person-to-person negotiations, although other archivists with differing temperaments and styles will approach collection solicitation differently.

To keep track of the status of each lead, the Archives maintains a series of "lead file log sheets." The log lists in chronological order letters sent, replies received, and the status of each lead. While this is time consuming, it insures that the Archives staff will follow every lead to its conclusion and serves as a permanent record of the nature and scope of the Archives' collecting activities. The third and final component of the lead-file system is a "lead locator file." This file of three-by-five index cards lists each lead by geographical location (by state and thereunder alphabetically by town). When a member of the field staff plans a collecting trip or arranges to visit a prospective donor, he or she will search the locator file for other leads in the general vicinity. Through the use of this simple file, the field representative can make the best possible use of each trip.

Lead files prepare the field worker to negotiate knowledgeably with potential donors; log sheets systematize communications; and locater files render field trips more economical. At the end of this process, the archivist will also need a series of legal forms through which the donor transfers physical custody and literary property rights for his or her papers or records to the archives.[10] Without a clear line of provenance from the creator of donated documents to the archives, no archivist can claim ownership of these documents for his or her institution with any degree of confidence. Failure to immediately obtain some type of formal deed of transfer may haunt the archives at a later date. If the donor for some reason refuses to sign such a document, the particulars of that refusal should be noted in the collection's case file for future reference.

However, in most instances a donor who has agreed to transfer his or her papers to the archives is quite willing to sign a deed of gift. Indeed, many may willingly sign over to the archives rights that they do not even own, such as the literary property rights to *all* materials in their respective collections. It is not necessary to explain the distinction between literary and physical property rights in this article, but both the archivist and the donor ought to be aware of the limitations on the latter's legal rights to transfer physical materials and their intellectual contents to an archives.

It is advisable to employ different forms for different types of donations. The Archives of Appalachia uses a release form for oral history interviews, a deed of gift form for archives, manuscripts, and photographs, and a deposit agreement form for collections placed in the Archives on permanent loan. While both oral history releases and deed of gift forms are widely used, the deposit agreement is less common and is usually employed as a contract between an institutional donor and an archives. In the case of the Archives of Appalachia, this document formalizes the transfer of large bodies of records to the Archives and obligates it to provide specific services to the creating organization but does not alter ownership of the files; thus they remain the property of the donor. In return for providing reference services to organizations and offering secure, permanent storage for their records, the Archives receives the right to make them available for research use.

Any archives employing a deposit agreement should be careful, however, to include a clause requiring that depositing individuals, institutions, or organizations agree to reimburse the repository for the entire cost of processing and storing their records should the depositor decide at a later date to withdraw them from the archives. In this manner the archives' investment of staff time, supplies, and other resources will be recovered even if the collection itself is lost. It might be argued that such a clause could frighten away prospective donors. While this may be true on occasion, it is better to risk losing a few collections than to jeopardize substantial investments made in processing and servicing large collections of institutional records.

---

[10]See Trudy Huskamp Peterson, Marie C. Malaro, and Marie P.G. Christine (note no. 3).

When drafting legal documents to finalize the transfer of a collection from a private individual or institution to an archives, archivists would do well to seek legal counsel. A deed of gift or deposit agreement is a contract that carries with it obligations for both parties. The document should be simple enough so that both the prospective donor and the archives staff understand it. A complicated legal document may intimidate potential donors. If one is obliged by one's institution to use lengthy contracts, sufficient time should be taken to explain the document to donors in order to eliminate problems and misunderstandings that might otherwise arise.

The final stage in any collection development program should always include a means of self-evaluation. One obvious measure of an archives' success will be a demonstrated ability to acquire numerous important collections. But the accumulation of linear feet of paper is perhaps the least critical measure of a program's accomplishments. Do the collections acquired by the archives accurately reflect its collecting theme(s) or focus? Does the focus encompass documentation of importance to the archives' user constituency? Is the archives unnecessarily duplicating the efforts of other archives? Have the archives' collecting activities been kept in balance with processing and storage capabilities? Have members of the archives' staff honestly represented themselves and the archives' program to donors and have they adequately documented the archives' right to its holdings? Finally, has a sincere effort been made to publicize the availability of collections for research use?

The theory and method of archival collection development is not a simple matter. Collecting is part of the larger fabric of archival administration. The professional and ethical considerations of collecting spill over into many other aspects of an archivist's job. Few archives, even those serving a specific parent institution, can afford to ignore changes in the ways records are produced, stored, and used. As technology and research interests change, so too should the focus of collecting programs. Through a critical awareness of changing environments and a systematic approach to their dynamics, well established programs can gain new vigor and new archives can construct solid foundations upon which to grow.

A Primer on Manuscript Field Work

Virginia R. Stewart

The process of acquiring manuscripts for institutional collections has received little systematic attention in the professional literature, most of which has focused on manuscript administration, definition of collecting policy, and competition between repositories.[1] Discussions of collecting manuscripts tend to be anecdotal, rich in illustrative example and lacking in analysis.[2] When the acquisition function is treated as an adventure story, two features are common to most accounts: a focus on the collector's personality, particularly traits such as curiosity, empathy, and perseverance; and an emphasis on the role of chance in the discovery of major collections. Neither of these elements is readily translated into guidelines for developing an institutional manuscript program, and the beginning collector may be thrown back on his own judgment and experience. If he has had an opportunity to work with more experienced field archivist, his judgment may be sufficient for good acquisition decision-making. However, not every archivist or curator with acquisition responsibilities has had an apprenticeship in field work; and a field work program can rapidly become too complex for common-sense approaches. Clear descriptions in the literature of the activities and controlling concepts of field work would obviously be of benefit to the beginner. They might also enable seasoned field archivists to compare their modes of work and develop generalizations about procedures, productivity, and costs of manuscript acquisition. Perhaps certain working assumptions could be formulated about the factors which make a negotiation relatively easy or difficult, or

Reprinted with permission from *The Midwestern Archivist* 1 (2, 1976):3-20

[1]The most useful references on manuscript acquisition are Kenneth W. Duckett, *Modern Manuscripts* (Nashville: American Association for State and Local History, 1975): Chapter 3; and Ruth B. Bordin and Robert M. Warner, *The Modern Manuscript Library* (New York and London: The Scarecrow Press, Inc., 1966): Chapters 1 and 2. A scenario on collection development is portrayed in Mary Lynn McCree's article, "Good Sense and Good Judgment: Defining Collections and Collecting," *Drexel Library Quarterly* 11 (January, 1975): 21-33. For a review of the literature, see *Modern Archives and Manuscripts: A Select Bibliography*, comp. ([Washington D.C.] Society of American Archivists, 1975): Section 23.1-23.6.

[2]See Robert M. Warner, "History in Your Attic," *Journal of Mississippi History* 26 (1964): 283-98; and Lucile M. Kane, "Manuscript Collecting," *In Support of Clio: Essays in Memory of Herbert A. Kellar*, William B. Hesseltine and Donald R. McNeil, eds. (Madison: State Historical Society of Wisconsin, 1958): 29-48. Both authors place their examples in the larger context of developing a program, but the acquisitions processes receive comparatively little attention in their discussions.

about the survival rate of certain kinds of manuscript materials. In any event, it is certain that archivists do not need to hear another disclaimer that collecting is, after all, more art than science. Even an art form demands rigor, attention to detail, and some rationale for the technique.

Although attempts have been made to standardize terminology for archival and manuscript functions,[3] acquisition work lacks a professional vocabulary. The following definitions are supplied to clarify subsequent usage. Manuscript repositories acquire material from many sources, by gift or purchase, according to some concept of desirable subject areas, time periods, and formats. These parameters make up the *collecting policy* of the repository. The collecting policy is also influenced by institutional factors such as the amount of space, staff, and budget allocated to the manuscript program. A repository may acquire individual manuscripts, but more commonly it seeks *collections*, bodies of unpublished materials which originate from a common source or have a common theme or format. In dealing with modern manuscripts, these collections usually are personal or family papers, literary remains, organizational records, or collections organized around a past event such as the suffrage movement.

Field work refers to the activities involved in identifying, locating, and negotiating for and securing manuscripts for an institutional collection. These tasks are carried out by a *field agent* or *representative* employed by the repository to develop its collection. Depending on the size, institutional history, and staffing patterns of the repository, the field work role may be performed in various ways. In a small institution, the manuscript curator may conduct field work as one of many responsibilities. A larger repository may support one or more fulltime field personnel. Some directors consider field work their exclusive province. Whatever the administrative hierarchy, however, the field agent should have some input into developing the collecting policy for the repository, and some measure of autonomy in negotiating on its behalf. Decisions made during field work operations largely determine the quality and completeness of collections accessioned, and the field agent is generally the person best acquainted with the problems and potential of any contemplated acquisition.

The field agent has the responsibility of translating the repository's acquisitions goals into reality by developing strong holdings in which the individual collections are significant and the total collection shows depth, interrelatedness, and a perceptible relationship to the universe of data.

---

[3]Frank B. Evans et al., "A Basic Glossary for Archivists, Manuscript Curators, and Records Managers," *American Archivist* 37 (July 1974): 415-33. This article, available as a reprint, does not include any definition of terms such as field work, lead, donor, acquisition, negotiation, etc.

The activities and tasks which make up field work operations can be grouped into six stages: data-gathering, preliminary contact, appraisal, negotiation, transport and receiving, and follow-up. For the purposes of discussion, these stages will be described sequentially, although they do not always occur in sequence.

DATA-GATHERING

Usually a field agent begins with a lead, a reference to a person or organization whose records might be valuable. Leads come from many sources: newspaper articles, collections being processed in the repository, research requests for material not held, and referral by donors, colleagues, and friends of the collection. The initial step is to flesh out the lead with information which will enable the field agent to determine whether the collection falls within his repository's collecting scope or possibly merits a shift in the policy. If the field agent decides to pursue the lead, he needs considerable data about the collection subject: for individuals, extensive biographical information; for organizations, founding date and personnel, current officers and administrative structure, and organizational affiliations. The data can be assembled from local directories, biographical dictionaries, obituaries and newspaper backfiles, annual reports, and similar sources. The field agent should also exploit related collections in his repository as sources of information about potential acquisitions, and cultivate scholarly and community contacts who can serve as informants in the anthropological sense.

If the collection subject is not a living person or a continuing organization, the field agent will have to bring his information up to date in order to locate a potential donor. If, for example, records are sought of a settlement house founded in 1900 but not currently operating, he will have to discover whether the organization merged at some earlier period with another settlement. If he cannot trace an organizational survivor, he must attempt to locate former staff members or trustees. When researching deceased individuals, the field agent may undertake considerable genealogical inquiry in the attempt to find descendants or collateral family members.

The field agent also needs information about the prospective donor, particularly the relationship between the donor and the manuscripts. This information can ensure a productive approach to a collection or terminate a fruitless negotiation at an early date. The prospective donor may not have the authority to dispose of the manuscripts even though he has custody of them. The field agent should assemble whatever data he can about the provenance of the manuscripts, being particularly alert to changes in custody which may have implications for transfer of legal title to the materials. If an organizational collection is being sought, the field representative needs to determine who has the power to commit the records to a repository under the constitution and bylaws of the organization.

Another important piece of information is whether any portion of the manuscripts in question has been deposited in or committed to another repository. Split collections do not seem nearly so undesirable to the general public as they do to scholars and archivists. Field agents must be alert to donors' practice of sending materials from a single collection to several repositories according to some notion of their subject specialty. Learning just what other repositories have in their holdings can be difficult. Repository guides, catalogues, and announcements are always out of date, and accession lists are selective and irregularly issued. Despite frequent appeals for the compilation and publication of collecting policies of major repositories, little progress has been made in this area.[4] There is no substitute for personal familiarity with the holdings and collecting policies of local institutions and those regional or national institutions which collect in the field agent's locality. If there are reasonable grounds to believe that another repository may already have a portion of the manuscripts being researched—or a commitment to them— the best thing to do is to ask the appropriate staff member of that repository. Depending on the response, the field agent must decide whether to pursue the collection. The risk that the inquiry will stimulate a competing offer to the potential donor is minimal and balanced by the reduction in time spent pursuing leads to unavailable collections. (While one cannot always depend on professional courtesy among archival colleagues, one can at least hope for it.)

Finally, the field agent should review the document types which he expects to encounter in the collection under consideration. If possible, similar collections in his own repository should be examined to determine what items, formats, and records series are characteristic. This prepares the field archivist with a specific answer to the inevitable donor question, "What are you interested in?" A detailed and informed response helps establish the field agent's credibility to the donor, and the familiarity with the records makes the ensuing appraisal considerably easier.

Throughout field work operations, careful record-keeping is essential. The field representative will undoubtedly have many negotiations in

---

[4]The National Historical Publications and Records Commission's project to update and revise the 1961 *Guide to Archives and Manuscripts in the United States* has requested information on the collecting policies of reporting institutions ("current subject areas of solicitation" and "other materials accepted"). The NHPRC plans to include this data in its forthcoming publication. [The first edition of NHPRC's Directory of Archives and Manuscript Repositories in the United States was published in 1978. The data is included under "Materials Solicited."]

progress simultaneously since individual collection negotiations can extend over years. One cannot rely on memory to keep these straight. A lead form is the first of several documents which will eventually comprise the repository's files on a particular collection. The lead form should be standardized and include space for the following information: collection name and significance; source of the lead; name, address, and telephone number of the prospective donor; relationship of the donor to the manuscripts; location and provenance of the manuscripts, date of initial compilation of the form; and the history of the negotiation. This amount of detail is necessary for leads which the field agent wishes to actively pursue; lower priority leads should be briefly noted with the date and source of information and maintained in a back-up lead file.

PRELIMINARY CONTACT

The data-gathering stage prepares the field agent for productive interaction with the donor. If the repository is soliciting materials, the field agent must convince the prospective donor that a consideration of "old papers" is worth his time. The field agent must establish his credentials and make his institution's program and merits intelligible to the donor. Communication difficulties often occur at this stage if the archivist is not careful to avoid jargon. One cannot assume that the donor has any concept of the organic unity of records, provenance, or the value of preserving historical materials. Without patronizing the donor, the archivist must convey his concerns in terms which are meaningful to a nonprofessional. Drawing on the information previously researched, the field agent should indicate briefly the kinds of material being sought and the reasons for the repository's interest. He should then request an opportunity to meet with the donor and examine the manuscripts.

The mechanism for making this initial contact varies according to the source of the lead, the nature of the entity which created the records, and the level of personal acquaintance between the field agent and the donor. A formal letter enclosing the repository's descriptive brochures may be an appropriate first approach to a bureaucratic organization such as a welfare agency, while a phone call or visit may accomplish more in dealing with a labor leader, an artist, or a political collective. A social lunch, arranged by a mutual acquaintance, may be the only way of meeting a prominent politician or businessman. The field agent must tailor his approach to the donor based on his assessment of the situation in which the donor will be most comfortable.

The initial overture to a donor may produce no response, and the field agent should be prepared to follow up the inquiry. This follow-up may take the form of a telephone call, a second letter, or a contact made by a mutual acquaintance. Securing the opportunity to meet with the donor is often the single most difficult step in a negotiation. Obviously some discretion must be used in the process to avoid harassment of the donor. This process can be prolonged, and the field representative must be sensitive to nuances of communication, evaluating the reasons for delay and the most effective means of prodding a stalled negotiation. Careful dated notes should be made of any contact with the donor, and telephone memoranda and copies of correspondence should be entered in the repository's collection file.

Once an appointment has been secured with the prospective donor, the field agent has a complex agenda. He is seeking concrete data about the manuscripts in order to determine whether they represent a desirable addition to his repository's holdings. He also wants information about the provenance of the materials and the locus of authority to dispose of them. Finally, he must ascertain under what conditions the donor would be willing to place the materials in a repository. The two tasks, appraisal and negotiation, generally proceed simultaneously.

APPRAISAL

Appraisal involves assessing the nature, informational content, and completeness of a manuscript collection and its relevance to an institution's collecting policy and goals. The format of the records and their physical condition must be evaluated in terms of costs and prospects for long-term preservation, and the administrative demands in processing and servicing the collection must be estimated. Optimally, the field agent formulates these judgments as a result of a thorough survey of the records on-site. During the preliminary research the field agent will have developed a hypothesis about the document types and subjects which "ought" to exist in any particular group of manuscripts. By comparing this outline to the actual materials, he can begin to determine whether there are gaps in the chronology or missing document types.

Surveying records on-site involves a feedback process. The field agent compares what he *sees* with what he *thinks* should be there, and asks questions. The materials which are initially shown to the field agent often represent only a small fraction of the extant manuscripts, since organizations are frequently unaware of the extent of their backfiles. Both organizational and personal donors are usually uncertain just what the field agent wants to see, and frequently think that the published reports or writings are essential and the unpublished material trivial. The field agent should routinely inquire about additional storage areas and examine them if possible, while educating the donor about the types of material he is seeking. For organizational records, or papers of professional people kept in office files, the field representative needs to learn what the actual practice has been in keeping files, as opposed to the formal procedures. Longtime clerical employees are frequently the best source of this information. Once they accept the legitimacy of the field agent's access to the files, they may be able to locate materials in dead storage as well as account for losses by natural disaster or records destroyed by former employees. Eliciting this kind of data requires patience and discretion; the field agent must also avoid being drawn into office politics. The survey is not a substitute for an accession record and the field agent should not become mired in detail. Essential information to be gathered about the records includes: inclusive dates, footage or number of pieces, document types, physical condition, and general arrangement. Unusual items such as rare periodicals, autographs, iconographic items, and artifacts should be noted. Large collections may require a survey of only a sample of the records series rather than examination of the entire collection, but in any event, the survey should not occupy more than a single working day.

The field agent's role in appraisal is not to determine the market value of records or their abstract merit as historic evidence but, rather, their value to his repository. Obviously, factors such as high monetary value and unique informational content will influence the assessment of desirability, but the field agent must also consider the relationship of the proposed acquisition to the repository's collecting policy and the costs and problems of housing, processing, and servicing the materials. Seeking to acquire any and every collection which is potentially available is not routinely the best decision; the field agent may recommend another repository as more suitable or may suggest that the donor consider establishing an in-house archive.

Frequently it is thought that a subject background in a particular area is the single most helpful tool in appraisal; but that emphasis leads to problems for the field agent who cannot be a specialist in all areas in which he collects. If the field agent relies exclusively on subject specialists for leads to collections, his collecting strategy may be skewed by the research interests of the advisors or current research fads. Furthermore, researchers who are not archivists are of little or no help in appraising potential acquisitions, since they are ill-equipped by training or experience to deal with voluminous collections of modern manuscripts. Most field representatives can tell horror stories about the prolonged negotiations required to correct problems with truncated collections which were solicited for repositories by subject specialists who were not archivists. The essential element in appraisal is the ability to perceive a collection as a whole, based on a brief examination of its component parts which are frequently disorganized and scattered.

Once that perception is gained, the archivist can proceed to evaluate the utility of the collection for research purposes and its suitability to the repository's program. The archivist should acquaint himself with research subjects and techniques in a number of fields so as to be able to gauge the information content of records. He should also study formats and techniques of record-keeping characteristic of the historic periods in which he collects, and the changes in such practices up to the present. Ultimately the archivist will have to make the determination of which materials are of enduring value and should be housed in his repository.

NEGOTIATION

The field agent's objective is to obtain both physical custody and legal title to the manuscripts being sought. Why a donor chooses to place materials in one repository rather than another is conjectural. Factors quite separate from a dispassionate evaluation of the merits of a repository may intrude upon the negotiation. Yet the field agent needs to keep in mind certain modes of decision-making behavior which frequently occur when dealing with donors.

For example, solicitation of organizational records usually involves preparation of a formal proposal submitted to the chief executive officer of the organization. The proposal summarizes the nature of the records sought, their historic significance, and the suitability of the soliciting repository for their deposit. Usually a draft copy of the proposed deed of gift is included, incorporating whatever restrictions or special provisions have been discussed in the preliminary stages. In a covering letter the archivist reviews the negotiation, outlines a sequence for implementation of the proposal, and requests an early decision.

The field agent must be aware of the effect of the donor's personal or institutional calendar on his willingness to make a decision about the records. Some administrators regard records disposition as a pre-retirement decision. Others will take action only when imminent disaster threatens the storage area or when the volume of non-current records being maintained in the office files becomes unmanageable. Even when the executive is convinced of the worth of an archival disposition, his ability to give priority to historic records will be influenced by such seasonal demands in the organization as budget preparation, reviews by a licensing or accrediting agency, or an annual meeting or fund-raising event. Unless the field agent gets a point-blank refusal to proceed with discussions, he should interpret delays as caused by internal factors. Sometimes a discreet inquiry about a more appropriate future date will produce the information that clarifies the source of the delay. In any event, the strategy with stalled negotiations is to maintain amicable personal contact with the executive. Forcing the issue will almost certainly be counterproductive—at all costs one wants to avoid a formal decision to refuse the repository's offer or to destroy the records.

Usually the final decision-making authority will be vested in a governing board with which the field agent may have to interact. The board may invite the archivist to address a monthly meeting or attend some social event. The field agent must adapt himself to the board schedule and have enough flexibility in his own working hours to meet over lunch, during the evening, or on weekends. Social invitations, particularly benefits, must be handled delicately. The field agent cannot be put in the position of financially supporting the organization in order to obtain the records, but he must realize that board members' responsiveness to a proposal may be conditioned by their personal acquaintanceship with the field agent.

Occasionally the field agent will pursue a collection to the final negotiating stage only to find that educating the board about the value of the records has precipitated their choice of another repository for their deposit. Although frustration at this kind of eventuality is natural, the archivist should take a long range view of the situation and conclude that the records are better housed in a repository—even though it is a competitor—than lost.

When dealing with donors of personal or family papers or collections assembled by a collector, the field agent has some different problems. Transactions between such donors and the field representative are likely to be considerably more personalized. The field agent will probably not be allowed unsupervised access to the manuscripts, and may have to proceed under the direct scrutiny of the donor and his lawyer. The donor may have an intense emotional reaction to the memorabilia of a spouse or parent and the field agent will need to exercise tact in meeting these feelings while getting his job done. The negotiations are very frequently conducted during quasi-social occasions, where discussion of business must be muted.

Personal privacy as an issue can often surface as donors attempt to avoid future embarrassment from disclosure of the papers. Donors may attempt to withhold certain materials they consider damaging to their reputation or that of their family. They may also attempt to draw the field agent into long-standing family disagreements, particularly if questions of the monetary value of the papers become involved. The field agent must be adept at diplomacy and prepared to suggest appropriate restrictions which will preserve the integrity of the collection without exposing the donors to casual scrutiny.

The timing of the decision to place papers in a repository can be quite different between institutional and personal donors. While dealing with a board may involve months of negotiation, a personal donor may offer papers on the spot—most frequently when a home or office is being vacated following a death. The field agent must be prepared to make a quick decision about the collection and to implement that decision. While a formal proposal is rarely employed in soliciting personal papers, the drawing of a deed of gift is frequently accomplished only after prolonged negotiation with family members and their attorneys.

Personal donors or collectors may also be interested either in selling the manuscripts or in having them appraised for purposes of obtaining a tax deduction. This situation is fraught with difficulties for both novice and experienced field agents. Purchasing manuscripts involves making an estimate of their fair market value—or having them professionally appraised. The field agent who does not regularly purchase manuscripts from dealers may be totally unprepared to make an offer to a donor without considerable research into auction catalogues and other price sources. Under the new tax law, donors of self-created materials will still be prevented from claiming tax deductions of the market value of their works.[5] Furthermore, donors of assembled collections have had the valuation of their gifts increasingly challenged by the Internal Revenue Service. The field agent should familiarize himself with the extensive literature on these issues and the names of qualified appraisers in his locality.[6] No one should attempt to offer tax advice to donors without a legal opinion.

Once the decision has been made to place material in his repository, the field agent's objective is securing transfer of title and literary property rights to the collection. The need for the repository to control access to and copying and publication of manuscripts in its holdings has been extensively discussed in the literature, and samples of deeds of gifts incorporating the basic provisions are available. A repository should have its own set of standard forms, approved by legal counsel, which can be modified to suit particular collections. Since most donors will refer this document to their lawyer, the deed of gift should be drawn in conformance with the relevant statutes governing contracts in a given locality.

If the early negotiations have been well thought out, this concluding transaction should present few problems. The deed of gift will have been prepared to reflect the negotiated terms between the donor and the repository. The final document should be prepared in at least two copies and signed by the donor and the representative of the repository. The field agent may have the authority to execute such deeds, but a higher-level signature may be more appropriate for major gifts, especially if the initial deposit signals a continuing relationship between the donor and

---

[5]Tax Reform Act of 1976, P.L. 94-455, approved October 4, 1976.

[6]The Society of American Archivists' Committee on Collecting Personal Papers and Manuscripts has compiled a list of appraisers which is available in mimeograph form from the committee.

ARCHIVAL ACQUISITION

the repository. The deed of gift becomes part of the repository's permanent files on the collection; the donor also retains a copy.

TRANSPORT AND RECEIVING

The field agent's goal is to deliver all the manuscripts designated for deposit from the donor to the repository with a minimum of disturbance of the original order and no physical damage. The field agent should arrange transport with the lowest expenditure of repository resources consonant with these objectives. Depending on the size and condition of the collection, and access to and distance of the storage areas from the repository, the field agent may become involved in packing, hauling, and supervising transport.

When collections are shipped to a repository from some distance, the reliability of the carrier and the storage conditions in transit are of paramount importance. If the donor is assuming responsibility for packing and shipping, the archivist should recommend packing techniques and the preferred carrier: air freight, bus, United Parcel Service, registered mail, etc. The packer must supply a detailed description of the number of items and containers, shipping date and point of departure, and shipping numbers and expected date of arrival. All of this information will be essential in tracing a shipment which fails to arrive, and a packing list will speed the inventory of the collection when received. In recommending a carrier, the field agent needs to be familiar with the experience of local repositories and weigh the relative importance of speed, reliability, and costs in transporting any particular collection.

If the field agent is to arrange transportation on-site, he has considerably more control over protection of the materials and maintenance of the original order. The field agent will decide whether part or all of the manuscripts must be repacked—in containers which he supplies. Delivery to the repository depends on the size of the collection, the distance, and the transportation available. If one is collecting out of the immediate vicinity of the repository, the material will probably have to be placed with a commercial carrier. Local collecting depends largely on the volume of the materials. Small collections (one to six records center boxes) can be carried in a taxi, and two persons can transport ten to fifteen such boxes in a station wagon. Anything larger may require a van or truck. Some institutions have their own truck and crews, others will have to hire them or rely on volunteer assistance. In dealing with unionized labor, the field agent must be aware of the conditions which govern working hours, breaks, and performance of specific tasks. A working acquaintance with the foreman or supervisor of whatever trucking crew is being employed will prove immensely beneficial.

134

Mechanics of packing are not complicated, although they can be exhausting. Some system of identifying the sequence of containers as they are packed must be established, the containers marked in at least two places, and a packing list prepared. Exceptionally fragile items will require special care.[7] If file cabinets are to be transported intact, drawers must be secured, and the filing labels noted. All repacking should be done by the archival staff or under the direct supervision of the field agent. There are many possibilities for misunderstandings during these activities, and the field agent must be available to answer questions, enforce the packing specifications, and generally mediate between the donor and the laborers. One cannot rely on the donor to supervise pickups on-site without risking missing containers and misdirected shipments. In the repository receiving room the field agent must leave instructions about the unloading order and the storage arrangements. The delivery must be verified against the packing list. Time spent at these tasks will not only guarantee the integrity of the collection as received, but will also immensely simplify the accessioning.

Optimally, every repository should have a receiving area isolated from the rest of the manuscript quarters. In practice this is not always the case, and the field agent has the responsibility of preventing contamination by incoming collections. If the materials have been stored in a basement, attic, or other location where presence of mold and insects is a reasonable assumption, the collection should be fumigated before it is brought into the repository. Commercial fumigators are often inexperienced in treating paper, and the field agent should seek advice from a conservator before proceeding. Once the collection has been accessioned, the materials are no longer the direct concern of the field agent.

FOLLOW-UP

Maintaining good donor/repository relations requires follow-up activities. Donors should be recognized for their contributions to manuscript collections. This recognition can take many forms: thank-you letters, listing of donors in the repository newsletter or annual report, social events, exhibits, and the like. In many cases a donor will have additional materials to give; either supplementary additions to the original collection, different collections, or leads to other potential donors. In some instances, donors may even support the establishment of a collection with a financial gift. They should be cultivated. If the institution has an organized group of friends and benefactors, much of the public relations work can be performed by them. Otherwise, the field agent will probably

---

[7]Caroline K. Keck's volume, *Safeguarding Your Collection in Travel* (Nashville: American Association for State and Local History, 1970) although addressed principally to curators of museum objects, contains useful suggestions on packing and shipping.

have the major role in continuing relations with donors. He may give advice on records management and microfilm projects, consult on exhibits and anniversary celebrations, and assist with special projects. The possibilities are endless and time-consuming, but a necessary part of the field operation.

In practice, of course, field work operations do not fit neatly into the sequence described; various stages are telescoped or elongated. The field agent is not always in the position of soliciting materials; sometimes collections are offered which he cannot appraise and must accept or reject on the significance of the subject or the reputation of the donor. Sometimes a supplementary accession proves more significant than the original, due to the discovery of missing materials or a more receptive attitude by the donor. Negotiations for transfer of title may continue long after materials are accessioned. In cases of defunct organizations, it may be difficult to determine who has the authority to transfer title. In some cases a personal donor may wish to place materials on indefinite deposit, perhaps awaiting a more favorable tax situation. Occasionally a donor may be willing to part with his entire collection at one time, but more often the field agent is involved in repeated dealings with the same donor as material is parcelled out to the repository over a period of years. It may not always be possible for the field agent to conclude a collection negotiation with all questions of ownership resolved. He must, however, make an effort to determine the ownership of materials in his repository's custody, even if he cannot secure transfer of these rights to the repository.

CONCLUSION

This discussion of the technical operations of field work would be incomplete without some consideration of the overall approach which characterizes a successful operation. In a sense, the field agent tries to create within his repository a microcosm of a past world, the boundaries of which are defined by the collecting policy. Collections accessioned are perceived as a part of a universe of data which once existed, only portions of which survive. The field agent strengthens his collection by acquiring materials which fill in gaps in that universe or make clearer the significance of previously acquired manuscripts. Thus, one of the most important characteristics of a field representative is the ability to perceive linkages between the present and the past, and among elements of that past.

The field agent must develop a sensitivity to various types of connectors, persons and geographic location in particular. It is a commonplace observation that individuals in modern society perform in many roles and that interest groups form around issues. The field agent tries to discover the connecting links among persons, organizations, issues, and events in the past in order to determine what materials to seek out for his collection. As one becomes more familiar with a historic period, certain individuals take on pivotal significance; all their associations, personal and professional, become potential acquisition targets. When such individuals cluster in an organization, it becomes a high priority collection subject. As the field agent researches a potential acquisition, he will undoubtedly turn up considerable data on these related entities which he should exploit as sources for additional manuscripts.

Like the historian, the field agent tries to develop an empathy for the past, a sense of the relationships which once existed. One of the most useful tools is a grasp of locality. In a metropolitan area, for example, one can identify residential, commercial, and industrial areas, and similar types of organizations which tend to cluster in certain areas, often in the same office building. This contiguity not only provides leads to current organizations, but also suggests the value of familiarity with the geography and man-made landscape of the area in which the field agent collects. Urban geography undergoes many changes, but scattered buildings, street names, and familiar colloquialisms may identify a former ethnic settlement or occupational district. The ability to pinpoint the physical location of a collection subject may enable the field agent to find long-forgotten manuscripts by walking the streets, looking at the buildings, and talking with local people. This technique may well be at the root of the discovery stories so dear to the hearts of raconteurs and journalists.

Planning and systematic allocation of resources are essential to the development of a repository's holdings. The field agent must have a concept of the specific areas in which he wants to build collections and strategy for their acquisition. Components of this strategy are both conceptual and pragmatic, since the field agent has limits on both time and money. If the field agent has funds with which to purchase manuscripts, the costs of acquisition are obvious, but gifts also involve costs in salary, mail or phone solicitation and entertainment of donors, and travel and transport of material. The field agent must attempt to rationally allocate his own time, devoting the major portion to tasks which he alone can perform (negotiation and appraisal in particular) and delegating others to trained staff. To achieve efficiency in acquisitions, the field agent must ensure that all tasks are performed in accordance with accepted professional standards, while resisting the temptation to do them all himself.

Finally, a successful field operation is characterized by meticulous attention to detail supported by careful record-keeping. Thorough research on a collection subject may turn up the essential fact which enables the field agent to make a productive approach to the donor. Assimilation of the details of the field survey may make the difference between accessioning a complete collection or a truncated one. Record-keeping is essential because acquisitions often run a tortuous course. Frequently, negotiations have to be deferred and resumed after months, even years, elapse. In the course of negotiations, manuscripts may be moved from their original location, suffer damage, or be lost. Challenges to already completed negotiations may arise subsequently due to changes in personnel in the donating organization or claims to ownership by a previously unknown person. The field agent must prepare for the unexpected by documenting the nature of the collection and the course of negotiations with carefully dated notes and copies of all relevant communications between repository and donor.

Completion of the tedious details of negotiating collections is a hallmark of a well-run program. One further quality deserves mention—the effort to make accessible to the repository the information about acquisitions which the field agent carries in his head. It is obvious that no two field representatives will have the same personal style or contacts, and thus no field agent is ever truly replaceable. However, it is unlikely that a field agent will devote his entire professional career to building the collection of a single repository, and therefore naive to assume that he will always be available to clarify the terms of the negotiation, the peculiarities of the donor, or the schedule for future accessions of supplementary material. It is his obligation to keep records of such facts so that his successor can carry on the program without re-inventing it. The ability to take a disinterested view of one's successes and failures in field work and to convey that experience to others is the *sine qua non* of a professional field agent.

The Gift and the Deed

Trudy Huskamp Peterson

F ew archivists believe that it is better to give than to receive. Archivists customarily depend upon gifts to increase the holdings of their institutions. These gifts may be eagerly sought or entirely unsolicited, but all of them involve the transfer of certain property. In legal terms, a gift means that title to the property passes from the giver to the recipient, i.e., from the donor to the archives. The common legal characteristics of a gift are a clear offer, acceptance, and delivery.

As most people know, when one buys a house a title search is made to insure that there are no claimants to the property other than the seller and that there are no outstanding restrictions on the use of the property other than those agreed to by the buyer. In other words, the seller must give to the buyer a clear title to the house. Many of the same considerations are important in the transfer of archival materials from a donor to an archives. A receiving institution must make sure that the title is clear and that the prospective donor is competent. Take as an example a case in which an heir offered to donate some papers but investigation by the archives revealed that he was not the sole heir. The other heirs were not agreeable to the donation, and the negotiations therefore foundered because the prospective donor did not have the capacity to convey a clear title. In another case, a very elderly woman signed a deed, but after her death the heirs claimed that she had not been competent at the time of signing; thus the deed was void. This does not mean that the archivist must hire a private detective to investigate prospective donors; but it does mean that some tactful questions should be asked early in the negotiating process.

All transfers of personal property to an archives should be documented in a clear, unambiguous fashion. As archival materials have both a physical and an intellectual component (i.e., a medium and a message), it is important that the transfer document record the disposition of both the physical and the intellectual property. A number of instruments can be used to record the transfer of property; the three most common are letter, will, and deed.[1]

Reprinted with permission from *The American Archivist* 42 (January 1979): 61-66.

[1]It is likely that some materials will always be transferred to an archives through simple oral statement and delivery. For example, a senior citizen comes to the local historical society with an armload of local newspapers from the 1920s and says, "I've been cleaning out the attic, and if you want these you can have them and if you don't want them, just

An exchange of letters is probably the easiest of the written instruments to execute, and many important archival holdings have been acquired with an exchange of letters documenting the transfer of the title. (The *exchange* of letters is not just common courtesy; the exchange serves also to indicate acceptance by the recipient, one of the keys to determining title.) Exchange of letters does not solve all the problems. The archives often does not have the opportunity to advise the donor or to obtain from the donor the elements of information that are or will be needed, such as the restrictions to be applied (if any), whether the archives has disposal authority, and many other such matters. The lack of this information may require protracted correspondence, or it may lead to legal difficulties in the future. ("I know I didn't say you should withhold my correspondence with X, but I thought you would have known better.")

Transfer of property by will is also common. Because a will is usually prepared by a lawyer, some of the elements such as restrictions, access, and disposition may be clearly defined, although the conditions may be more stringent than the archives would like. It is also likely that the donor and the archives will have discussed the gift before the provisions of the will are drawn up, giving the archives the opportunity to provide suggested language to use in the will's provision about the prospective donation. There are, of course, a few cases in which an archivist opens the morning mail to find that the archives has been left the Jane Doe papers, papers which are entirely inappropriate to its holdings and which have severe restrictions on them; but such cases are probably rare.

Deeds are the third common written instrument used to transfer property to an archives. A deed is an instrument in writing, purporting to effect some legal disposition, and sealed and delivered by the disposing party or parties. It is usually prepared after consultation between the donor and the recipient and is usually signed by both to indicate offer and acceptance.

There are a number of important or desirable elements in instruments of gift. Not all of these will be appropriate for every donation, but they are worth considering during the negotiations. Because the archivist generally has the most influence on preparation of deeds, the elements are discussed in terms of deeds. The elements include clear answers to the following questions:

---

throw them away." Such oral transactions may be perfectly sound, for they usually meet the three common legal tests for a gift: a clear offer ("you can have them"); acceptance ("we'd be delighted to have them"); and delivery ("here they are"). Presumably the conversation marking this transfer could be reconstructed at a later time if the question of legal title arose, and it would be buttressed by internal archives documents indicating that the material was received from the donor on a certain date, that the material was processed and made available on the assumption that it was the property of the archives, and so forth.

Who is the donor? The creator of the materials? The heirs of the creator? A purchaser? A corporation? This information should appear twice, once in the opening paragraph of the deed and again in the signature block at the end. If the relationship between the creator and the donor is complex and not self-evident (a child with power of attorney donating property of a living parent, an executive officer acting on behalf of a corporation), it should be spelled out in the deed. A cautious archivist may request that the donor have his or her signature notarized.

Who is the recipient? If, for example, the archives is part of a state university, is the formal recipient the state, the university, or the university archives? If the state is the recipient, the state may be able to remove the materials from the university archives and place them in the state archives; if the legal formalities require donation to the state (the university lawyer can provide that information), the donor may wish to specify that the donation is to the state *for purposes of deposit* in the archives of the state university. The same considerations would apply to a church-diocese-diocesan archives, conglomerate-corporation-corporate archives, or any archives in a multi-level bureaucracy.

What is the date of the transfer of title? This is important primarily for tax purposes. The deed should bear both the date when the donor signed it and the date when the recipient accepted it.

What is the material conveyed by the deed? Who created or collected the material? What is the volume? What are the inclusive dates? For small donations this information can be incorporated into the introductory paragraphs of the deed (for example, "seven typed letters signed by Franklin D. Roosevelt, dated October 4, 8, 9, 14, and 22, and November 6 and 12, 1919, concerning the possible purchase of a sloop from the Mariner Boatworks"). For most donations, however, it is useful to attach an appendix containing a detailed archival description of the material donated. This is especially important in instances in which the donor plans to give, for example, a large collection of autographs but wants to spread the donation out over a period of years to take as much advantage of the tax deductions as possible. The donor may physically transfer the entire collection at one time, but donate the items over a period of years. In such cases, detailed descriptions appended to the deed are crucial to determining what of the materials are the property of the archives and what are still the property of the donor.

Who holds the copyright? Here is where the distinction between physical property and intellectual property becomes important. It is entirely possible to transfer the physical property to the archives while reserving

141

the copyright in the material for the donor. It is desirable to write into the deed the transfer of the copyright from the donor to the archives; failing that, the deed should clearly specify who holds the copyright and for how long. Of course, a donor cannot transfer copyright to intellectual property unless the donor has created it or has had it legally transferred to him; consequently, most deeds will convey only such copyright as the donor holds in the materials donated.

What are the restrictions on use? Broadly speaking, restrictions normally specify either time or content, or both. For example, a restriction might specify that the entire donation remain closed for twenty-five years or until the death of the donor (time). Or, a deed might require that materials relating to the donor's service on the ministerial commission for the review of candidates for the clergy be restricted (content). Or, the deed might restrict correspondence between the donor and her husband until both are deceased (content and time).

While some archivists favor restrictions worded narrowly ("my correspondence with Jacqueline Kennedy") and others favor restrictions specifying general categories ("information that would be an unwarranted invasion of personal privacy"), both should strive for statements of restriction that are clear and unambiguous.

Who can impose restrictions? Here there are normally three options: the donor, the donor's designee, or the archivist. The donor usually establishes the restrictions through the deed, often in great detail, and the donor may also amend the deed with the concurrence of the archives if the archives suggests to the donor that further categories of materials should be restricted. In other instances the donor frames the restrictions in general terms and then either gives the archivist the authority to determine what materials fall within the restriction categories or names a person to review the files and establish what can be made available at various times. In the latter case, the archives should make sure that the duration of review by the designee is limited (the designee could take a decade with the papers completely closed during that time; the designee could die with the papers unreviewed) and that after such time the archives has the authority to make the access determinations.

To whom do the restrictions apply? Although it seems unlikely that problems would arise, it may be wise to indicate in the deed that the restrictions will not prevent the staff of the archives from performing normal archival work on the restricted materials and that any necessary preservation measures may be taken. Without a formal statement, it is possible that such steps could be barred by heirs.

Who can lift restrictions? There are two issues here, temporary waivers and permanent openings. In the category of temporary waivers, some donors want to be able to authorize select researchers to use restricted materials if the researchers obtain the permission of the donor or the donor's designee. Because this results in unequal access, archivists are usually reluctant to accept such conditions unless there is no other way to obtain the materials. If the archives will agree to such temporary waivers, it should be clearly stated in the deed. In the category of permanent openings, restrictions that have a specific time period are relatively easy to administer, but if restrictions have no fixed time, trouble can arise. It is advisable to state clearly in the deed that all materials will eventually be opened and that the archivist has the authority to open the materials at his or her discretion. Some donors want to review and approve or have a designee review and approve materials selected by the archivist for opening; this is cumbersome but workable as long as it is understood that all materials will eventually be open. A fixed duration for such review is preferable, the deed should specify the procedure in the event of the death of the donor or designee during the review period, and the deed should state the archivist's authority to open material after the time period for donor or designee review has expired. An archives should establish a policy on the length of time that donors, heirs, and designees can control access. Deeds have been proposed that would pass control from a donor to children and, at their deaths, to grandchildren. Such provisions could restrict materials for nearly a hundred years; this is almost always unacceptable.

Who has disposal authority? Donations often contain a certain amount of ephemera: multiple copies of donor's Christmas cards from 1958, a broken transistor radio, boxes of duplicate copies of congressional hearings. The deed should indicate whether the archivist can dispose of such materials in any way seemly, whether the materials must be offered to the heirs first before other means of disposal are used (in such cases, there should be a time limit), and what the criteria for disposal are ("no significant historical value," "inappropriate to the collections of the State Historical Society," etc.). In designing this part of the deed, the archivist should also consider whether the archives wants to obtain authority to dispose of the entire collection, not just those parts without historical value. For example, the donation might contain a collection of Confederate money which clearly has historical value; but the archives subsequently obtains an outstanding set of Confederate currency. Consequently, the archives wants to sell the money from the first collection or trade it to another institution in return for Confederate bonds. Legally, once the archives has title to the property, if the deed is silent on the matter of disposition the archives can do what it wants; but it may be neater to have a clause authorizing the disposition of any materials which, in the judgment of the archivist, are not required by the archives.

What provisions cover subsequent gifts? The nature of the highly competitive collecting business is such that young people who come to prominence are often asked to donate their materials to an archival institution. (Woodward and Bernstein, for example, were approached shortly after their Watergate book came out.) This means that the institution can look forward to acquiring increments of materials over a long period of time. Rather than write a new deed each time, it may be possible to include in the initial deed a provision saying that all subsequent donations will be made in accordance with the provisions of that deed. Then, at the transfer of each increment, the donor and the archives can sign a statement that the materials are transferred in accordance with that deed, and the archives can prepare a description of the material transferred and append to the deed both the statement and the description.

While developing a deed of gift, it is useful to remember that it is a contract in which both parties promise certain things: the donor to give, the archives to respect the conditions stipulated by the donor in the deed. And once the conditions are agreed upon, if the archives fails to meet its obligations (for instance, not restricting one category of restricted materials) the contract could be determined to be void and the donor could reclaim the property; alternatively, the donor could sue the archives for damages which resulted from the breach of the contract. Neither course, however, is likely to occur in the normal relations between donor and archives.

Finally, it is worth mentioning one other legal instrument common in archival circles: the deposit agreement. A deposit agreement is a statement of intent to transfer title at some future date, usually unspecified; but in the meantime the prospective donor deposits the physical property with the archives for safekeeping. Here many of the same elements must be incorporated as in a deed, but the deposit agreement should contain also a statement of the intent to donate, a statement regarding the archives' liability for accidental damage to the property, and a statement regarding the types of archival and preservation work that may be undertaken on the collection. In some cases, materials may even be made available for research use under deposit agreement; but the archives should consider very carefully how certain the donation is before agreeing to spend the money not only to store but also to process and provide reference on materials that could be withdrawn.

There is, of course, no one formula, no one instrument of gift, that will work for every archives every time. But with careful consideration of the gift and the giver, of obligations and potential legal hazards that may lie ahead, the archivist can help the donor construct a legal instrument to transfer title that will meet the needs of both donor and recipient.

Chapter 5
Arrangement

A rrangement of records and personal papers is the process of placing each record unit in an archival repository in its appropriate organizational order. Arrangement is therefore the means of achieving physical control over groups of archival materials, and its successful accomplishment is essential to every archival repository.

In his classic explanation of this function, "Archival Principles of Arrangement" (1961), Theodore R. Schellenberg describes the two basic principles that govern archival arrangement: provenance and original order. Schellenberg evaluates these concepts against the twin goals of preserving the evidential value of records and making them accessible for use. His observations and conclusions, which apply to both records and personal papers, remain sound and widely accepted to the present.

"Archival Arrangement—Five Different Operations at Five Different Levels" (1964), by Oliver Wendell Holmes, offers a major contribution to the archivist's understanding of arrangement by analyzing the complex of activities involved in arrangement at each level in an archival repository. This article is particularly noteworthy for its definition and

147

analysis of the important archival concepts of the record group and series. Although Holmes acknowledges his debt to Schellenberg's work, his perspective differs in important ways, particularly in his adherence to the principle of original order, a principle that Schellenberg viewed with some flexibility.

"Organizing Photo Collections: An Introspective Approach" (1981), by Nancy Malan, addresses another aspect of archival arrangement, the problem of arranging a type of material for which source and original arrangement sometimes have only limited importance. Malan shows the variety of options available to archival institutions for arrangement and control in such circumstances. The principle of provenance is only one of several options that Malan offers for consideration.

Ralph E. Ehrenberg analyzes distinctive qualities and considerations for administration of several nontextual media. In his essay "Aural and Graphic Archives and Manuscripts" (1975), Ehrenberg describes a variety of systems for arrangement of these materials. His discussion also extends to practical observations concerning storage and handling of nontextual materials—important considerations that are logical extensions of physical arrangement.

Archival Principles of Arrangement

T. R. Schellenberg

A ll classification or arrangement work involves a breakdown of a whole into its parts. This can easily be illustrated by looking at what is done while classifying in the physical sciences. In biology, for example, a specimen is dissected in order to classify it; in chemistry a compound substance is separated into its constituents in order to identify it; and the same method is followed in all other physical sciences. The very process of analysis is one of separating anything, whether an object of the senses or of the intellect, into its parts. By this process it is possible to distinguish each of the parts, separately, and to understand their relation to each other and to the whole. The same is also true in the social sciences and in the professions dealing with the materials of social sciences.

In arranging a group or collection an archivist should obtain a general knowledge of its meaning or essential nature and its structure before proceeding to deal with its parts. The arrangement, in a word, should proceed from an understanding of the whole group or collection; it should not be separated on a piecemeal basis. This fact has been ably stressed by Ellen Jackson in an excellent article on "Manuscript Collections in the General Library" in the April 1942 issue of the *Library Quarterly*:

> It is worse than useless—it is extremely dangerous—to try to arrange any portion of a collection without a considerable familiarity with the whole. Even if the papers appear to be completely disordered, breaking up an old file may destroy a clue vital to the nature and original condition of the whole collection. The librarian or assistant who is to handle it can do no better at the start of work than to sit down and begin exploring, like an archaeologist digging in a prehistoric rubbish heap, not looking for anything in particular, but alert for whatever significant items may meet his eye, always aware that the arrangement of materials may be as significant as the materials themselves.

Three levels of record units may be distinguished: (1) the very large, consisting of either groups of public papers or collections of private papers; (2) the intermediate, consisting of subgroups and series; and (3) the small, consisting of record units composed of individual documents

Reprinted with permission from *The American Archivist* 24 (January 1961): 11-24.

or aggregations of documents fastened together into folders, binders, volumes, and the like.

In this article we are concerned with the principles that should be followed in dealing with record units. There are two basic principles of arrangement that have been developed through years of experience. The first, which is generally known as the principle of provenance, is that archives should be kept according to their source. The second is that archives should be kept in the order originally imposed on them. These principles relate, in a word, to two distinct matters: (a) provenance and (b) original order.

Two things should be accomplished by arranging records. The first is to preserve their evidential values. Such values should be preserved, it should be underscored, in private as well as public papers.

An archivist normally deals with records that have an organic character. This is the case with respect to all records of public bodies, such as governmental agencies; all records of private corporate bodies, such as businesses, churches, learned institutions, and the like; and many records produced by individuals who engaged in extended activities of one kind or another. Perhaps the only records that do not reflect organic activity are artificial collections of private papers brought together by collectors or by archivists themselves.

Records that are the product of organic activity have a value that derives from the way they were produced. Since they were created in consequence of the actions to which they relate, they often contain an unconscious and therefore impartial record of the action. Thus the evidence they contain of the actions they record has a peculiar value. It is the *quality* of this evidence that is our concern here. Records, however, also have a value for the evidence they contain of the actions that resulted in their production. It is the *content* of the evidence that is our concern here.

These added values—values because of their production during action and their evidence of action—will be referred to as evidential values. Let us examine these values a bit further.

The character of the evidence in archives has been stressed for many years. As early as 1632 Baldassare Bonifacio referred to it in his essay "De Archivis." He wrote that "so great is the respect for archives that credence is obviously to be given to instruments produced from a public archives, and they make, as the jurisconsults say, 'full faith.'"

In England, the English archivist Sir Hilary Jenkinson refers to this quality as the "evidential value of records." Public records, according to Jenkinson, have a quality that is derived from the way they came into being, a quality that makes their evidence on the matters to which they pertain unusually valuable. In commenting on Jenkinson's views Ian Maclean, the Chief Archives Officer of the Commonwealth of Australia, observes, "The archivist's whole methodology is based on the sanctity of his Archives as evidence. Being records of transactions of which they themselves formed a part, Archives are, in a particular sense, authentic and impartial."

Archives also have an obvious value as evidence of the actions that resulted in their production. One of the basic approaches in evaluating records produced by public bodies is to select for retention those that show the functioning of such bodies. Every governmental archivist, for that reason, will preserve records containing evidence of the actions of the government he serves; every archivist dealing with records of private corporate bodies will preserve evidence of the actions of such bodies.

Records of organic bodies are normally arranged in relation to the actions that resulted in their production. The way they were brought together is therefore significant. According to Jenkinson, "they have . . . a structure, an articulation and a natural relationship between parts, which are essential to their significance . . . Archive quality only survives unimpaired so long as their natural form and relationship are maintained."

The second thing to accomplish by arranging records is to make them accessible for use. In order to do this it is necessary to arrange them so they can be described effectively. Arrangement, then, should also facilitate the description of records.

In analyzing the application of the two basic principles of arrangement I will try to show the extent to which they preserve the evidential values of records, make records accessible for use, and facilitate their description. They should be applied only insofar as something can be achieved by their application.

PROVENANCE

The principle of provenance stems from the French principle of *respect pour les fonds* first enunciated in regulations issued by Guizot, French Minister of Public Instruction, in 1839. The principle, which was first applied to the records of the *départements* in the Archives Nationales, simply provides that records should be grouped according to the nature of the institution that has accumulated them. As originally formulated, the principle was not precise in its definition of the kind of organic body, for records from similar types of institutions could be grouped into a *fonds*, nor was it consistently applied after it was formulated.

The principle was made more precise by the Prussian archivists, who in 1881 issued regulations for arrangement work at the Prussian State Archives that provided that public records should be grouped according to their origins in public administrative bodies. The Prussian principle was called *Provenienzprinzip*, or the principle of provenance.

151

ARRANGEMENT

Let us see, first, what bearing the principle of provenance has on evidential values. And let us consider this matter in relation to (1) groups and subgroups and (2) series.

GROUPS AND SUBGROUPS

The principle of provenance means that records should be kept in separate units that correspond to their sources in organic bodies. Each unit should be treated as an integral unit. Each unit should be kept intact. Records from one source should not be merged with those from another.

Before the formulation of the principle, archivists often tried to arrange records on a subject basis. They thus arranged in relation to subjects records that were originally brought together in relation to action. In doing this they had to impose an entirely different order on the innumerable single documents that are created in the course of organic activity by any office, no matter how small.

A subject arrangement not only obscures the source of records in organic bodies and organic activities; it also destroys the original order imposed on them. It is thus a violation of both the principle of provenance and the principle of original order.

While the principle of provenance is now generally observed by archivists, it is often violated before records reach the archival institution. This often happens when records within an agency are rearranged after they have served their current uses. Normally they should be kept, insofar as possible, in the order given them by the agency in the course of its official business. If they are rearranged, care should be exercised that their organizational origins will not be obscured. In a word, the evidence of their source in an organizational unit should be preserved; thus records of one office of an agency should not be merged with those of another, nor should records of various offices be reorganized into a new file.

In the Federal Government of the United States such rearrangements are often undertaken at the hands of official historians, who should be most concerned about the value of the evidence in records. While working with noncurrent records they often rearrange them by the subjects or topics in relation to which they are writing historical accounts. To the extent that they have an influence in regard to such rearrangement projects, archivists should counsel against them, for they seriously impair the quality of the evidence on organization and function.

If historians fail to preserve the evidential values of records by insisting on a violation of the principle of provenance, their action may be attributed to their ignorance of the archival profession, about which they are expected to know very little, and may for this reason be excused. But there is no justification, other than that of professional immaturity or ignorance, for an archivist to sanction or to participate in rearrangement projects that will destroy the evidential value of records.

While working with research materials historians may discover the organic relations that were destroyed by the dispersal of public records. They may find a map, for example, the identity of which was obscured by being buried in a geographic file that was once one of a series of maps pertaining to the Lewis and Clark Expedition (1803-6). Or they may find a letter embodied in a strictly chronological file that was once part of the files of some committee of the House of Representatives. While historians may derive a great deal of pleasure from fitting together the pieces of evidence, just as a child does in fitting together the pieces of a jigsaw puzzle, it is not the function of an archivist to create a jigsaw puzzle out of the research materials of his nation. It is his function to preserve them in such a way and at such places that their significance will be apparent and that the evidence they contain will be preserved.

Admittedly also, the arrangement of records is affected when an archivist retains part of the records of an agency and discards the rest. The retained records are obviously placed in a different relation to each other from the one they had in their current life. But this does not mean that the archivist while selecting records for retention should merge those of various offices with each other, or those of various activities with each other. If sound archival principles are followed the selected records are retained office by office and activity by activity, and there will thus be no fusion of files, no creation of new files excepting by archivists who do not understand or who have no regard for archival principles.

The value of public records may also be destroyed by improperly removing them from public custody. Such records often lose their significance when they are taken from the record groups in which they belong. They lose their organic character, their meaning in relation to activities of a particular office. They should not be removed from the record groups in which they were embodied and scattered among various repositories. They should not be made truck in the public market to be hawked about by dealers and collectors.

SERIES

While I do not wish to discuss here the factors that are taken into account in creating record series, I must refer to them to make clear one essential fact. It is that, regardless of what factor led to the creation of a series, it is likely that the series was created in the course of performing a particular kind of action.

153

If, for example, the series was established because a group of records was arranged according to a particular filing system, such a series is likely to embody records resulting from the actions of a particular office. Or a series consisting of a particular physical type of records is likely to denote a particular class of actions, for physical types are created in relation to classes of actions—reports for reporting, questionnaires for questioning, and so forth. Or a series established in relation to a subject is likely to reflect action in relation to the particular subject of concern to an office or an officer.

Let us, then, see how archival series should be dealt with.

Since series generally reflect action they should be preserved intact as a record of action. They should not be torn apart to create new series. While the arrangement of the particular record items within a series may not significantly reflect action, the series as a whole does. Each record item in it is thus a part of an organic whole. To separate it from the series in which it is embodied will impair its meaning, for the series as a whole has a meaning greater than its parts, that is, than the individual record items.

Series, just as archival groups and subgroups, should be treated as integral units. They should be kept apart from each other, for to arbitrarily combine series on different kinds of action into one file will confuse the record of action and vitiate the evidence that derives from the way records were brought together in the course of action.

Let me illustrate why series should be kept intact and separate from each other. In the case of the series within an archival group created by some bureau of the Federal Government, for example, one would normally find several kinds of series.

The most important of such series is the correspondence that is organized into a central file containing letters received or sent by bureau officials, copies of memoranda, reports, forms, and other adminstrative issuances. Taken as a whole the file contains records on every activity of the bureau and has a significance because it contains such records and no others; it contains no records of other bureaus except as they relate to its activities. Its value as a record of the activities of the bureau would be vitiated if it were merged with the central file of another bureau, or, for that matter, if records unrelated to the activities of the bureau were interfiled in it.

Or the series of a bureau may consist of the office files of its chief. Such a series has a significance as a record of his administrative actions, and this significance is obscured the moment the series, as such, is torn apart and the record items within it are merged with another file.

The series within a manuscript collection containing records of some noteworthy individual are similar in character to those in an archival group. If the individual, perchance, was a noted writer he doubtless accumulated a separate file pertaining to his literary activities, including manuscripts of his writings, correspondence relating to them, reviews of them, and other similar documents. If he also engaged in politics he doubtless accumulated an office file, which he removed on retiring from office, pertaining to his service on a legislative body. If he was actively interested in a business he doubtless kept records on his financial transactions if for no other reason than that of tax accountability. He probably also kept his personal and family papers apart from those relating to his other activities. His collection then falls into several natural series, each relating to a particular activity. These series have a value as a record of the activities to which they pertain; this value is lost the moment the series are not kept intact—the moment, for example, the various series are merged with each other into a chronological file—and once this value is lost it cannot be recaptured.

This value is something apart from the value of information in individual record items. It is a value derived from the arrangement of the collection into series, and this arrangement normally is one suited to the needs of the researcher, who is likely to be interested in the activities for which the individual was noteworthy and in relation to which he created the series.

Let us see, next, what bearing the principle of provenance has on accessibility.

Before the principle was formulated archivists, as we have seen, rearranged in relation to subjects records that were originally brought together in relation to actions. Such rearrangement work was very involved, no matter how small the holdings of an archival institution. It was so time-consuming that it normally absorbed all the time of an archivist forever and a day. It was also very difficult work, for the subjects in relation to which the records of any agency should be reorganized varied from one agency to another. The subjects, moreover, could not actually be chosen with finality until a fairly thorough analysis had been made of all the records to be reorganized. Any faulty choice of subjects led to faulty arrangement. And any list of subjects, no matter how carefully chosen, was not likely to cover all the records to be reorganized, with the result that a miscellany was usually left over—a residue of unclassified records.

The principle of provenance supplanted the procedure of arranging records according to subjects. It thus supplanted a completely impractical method of arrangement by a practical one, for arbitrary systems of arrangement cannot be applied to records without infinitely complicating the task of the archivist. It provided the archivist with a workable and economical guide in arranging, describing, and servicing records in his custody.

ORIGINAL ORDER

The second principle of arrangement to which archivists attach importance is that records should be kept in the order imposed on them during their current life. This principle is an outgrowth of the *Registraturprinzip* formulated by the Prussian archivists in 1881 to regulate arrangement work in the Prussian State Archives. The principle stated that "Official papers are to be maintained in the order and with the designations which they received in the course of the official activity of the agency concerned." This principle, which can be applied whenever records are properly arranged in a government agency before their release to the archival institution (as they are in German registry offices), has been the subject of a great deal of discussion among archivists in various countries.

Let us see what bearing the principle of original order has on evidential values. Does it provide evidence on how an organic body was organized or how it conducted its activities? Or on some other matter?

Let us consider this question in relation to (1) the arrangement of series within groups and (2) the arrangement of record items within series.

SERIES WITHIN GROUPS

Here we are considering the relation of series to each other, not to their source. Obviously all series from a given source should be kept together, but in what order should they be placed?

The question to be answered here is the extent to which the arrangement of a series within a record group—whether a manuscript collection or an archival group—has a significance other than that of making the records accessible for use. I believe a careful examination of all aspects of this question will indicate that the arrangement of series in relation to each other is important mainly from the point of view of their usability, not from the point of view of their integrity as evidence of organization and function. The main consideration in preserving the integrity of records is that groups, subgroups, and series should be kept intact and treated as integral units. They should not be merged with one another: one group with another, one subgroup with another, or one series with another.

But the order in which series within a group or subgroup are placed normally has little effect on their evidential values or on the integrity of the group or subgroup of which they are a part.

Let us examine typical series within an archival group produced by a bureau of the Federal Government to illustrate this point. Such a record group usually includes the following series:

A series of general correspondence of the bureau as a whole.
A series of the bureau chief's correspondence.
Several series of divisional correspondence.
Series of questionnaires, reports, and other forms created to perform classes of actions.
Series of technical and fiscal records, and so forth.

The above series may be placed in any conceivable relation to each other without affecting the integrity of each of them or of the group as a whole. The arrangement, whatever it is, should be one that will contribute to an understanding of the significance of the records and make them intelligible to the user.

ITEMS WITHIN SERIES

The order in which individual record items within a series should be arranged in an archival institution depends on two considerations: (a) the possible value of the arrangement in revealing the organic activity that resulted in the creation of the series, and (b) the value of the arrangement in revealing the information that is contained in the series.

ORGANIC VALUES

The question here is: does the arrangement of the items in the series show how things were done? If so, to what extent is this the case?

While the original order of record items in a series is not a sacrosanct thing—something to be preserved at all costs—it may nonetheless be one that reveals the significance of records and makes them usable. Lester J. Cappon, Director of the Institute of Early American History and Culture, states that "a *corpus* of manuscript papers, being something more than the sum of its parts, is not susceptible to regimented arrangement without loss of character." A collection of manuscripts, he adds, is more than "the sum of its parts," so that the mathematical formula known to every schoolboy that "the whole is equal to the sum of its parts" does not apply. The added meaning which a manuscript collection or archival group has is presumably derived from the arrangement of its parts, the context in which they were kept, and the way in which, in general, the collection or group was organized during its creation.

The original order imposed on items within a series may show time sequences, personal relationships, or even organic activity. If read in chronological order, for example, the individual item may show how things actually happened, how an idea budded and blossomed into action, or how the thinking of a person developed. Similarly, if read in relation to particular persons under an alphabetical arrangement, the individual items may reveal in a striking way how a friendship developed, or how views were interchanged on sundry matters between two persons who corresponded with each other. If read in relation to an activity, the items may throw light on how an organization was started, on what work it performed, or on what resulted from its work. But normally such facts are obtained because the series, as such, was kept intact, not because of the order given the items within it.

Usually the order in which individual record items within a series are arranged does not significantly reveal how things were done. The order seldom has a presumptive value and usually must be judged strictly on its merits. As a rule it is important only to the extent that it makes the records usable. The single record items usually derive no added meaning from their position among other record items, though a good arrangement may make their meaning more apparent.

To illustrate the validity of this point of view, let us examine how record items are arranged within series.

In current use are various filing systems, in accordance with which record items are arranged as they are accumulated. In accordance with them the individual record items may be arranged alphabetically, chronologically, numerically, or by subject, or under a combination of these various systems of arrangement. From an archivist's point of view, most of these systems are notoriously bad because they do not show how records were accumulated in relation to the activities to which they pertain. A file organized according to the Dewey-decimal system of notation, for example, may be broken down into ten main subject classes that may have little relation to the activities of the government body that produced the file. Nor are the divisions of the main classes likely to bear a relation to activity. While some filing systems are to be preferred to others from an archival point of view, no modern system reflects fully the activities of the body that produced the records organized under it. In a word, the arrangement of the individual record items does not contribute to an understanding of the activity that is reflected in the series as a whole.

Occasionally, however, the order imposed on items may reveal administrative processes. It may show, for example, how a given fiscal or technical operation was performed. Or it may show the sequence of action, or other organic connections. If the original order of the items within a series has any value in showing organic activity it should, by all means, be preserved.

Occasionally, also, the order imposed on items within a series may reflect how things were done in an office. The disorder of files is often characteristic of disorder in administration. And logically, therefore, an archivist, to preserve evidence of how things were actually done, should preserve records in the condition of disorder in which they were maintained during their current life. But this is obviously carrying logic too far.

Occasionally, also, the order imposed on items within a series may show the idiosyncrasies of an individual in filing, but these idiosyncrasies are important only if the individual who did the filing is important. When Thomas Jefferson, for example, who was accustomed to cataloging his library systematically, placed William Wirt's biography of Patrick Henry under the head of fiction it revealed Jefferson's estimate of the merits of the biography, and his classification therefore had an added significance. But the idiosyncrasies of a file clerk in filing papers are not as a rule significant. Usually they are attributable to a lack of understanding of the techniques of filing and the principles of classification rather than to personal idiosyncrasies.

INFORMATIONAL VALUES

An exception to the rule of preserving records in their original order should be made when records are preserved solely for their informational content—without reference to their value as evidence of organization and function. Many modern records are preserved solely for the information they contain on persons or places or on sociological, economic, scientific, or other matters. Such records should be arranged solely with a view to facilitating their exploitation by scholars, scientists, and others without regard to how they were arranged in the agency that created them.

An example of such records is the climatological reports that were received by the National Archives from the Weather Bureau. Under the original arrangement of these reports it was impossible to ascertain what climatological data existed for a given place. They were, therefore, rearranged. The series created by each of the agencies that originally produced the records—the Surgeon General's Office, the Smithsonian Institution, the Signal Office, and the Weather Bureau—were kept intact, but the volumes containing the reports were unbound and the individual reports within them were rearranged by places (States and localities) and thereunder in chronological sequence.

Another exception to the rule of preserving records in their original order should be made when the original order is not ascertainable or is manifestly bad. While most records developed by European governments are organized in registry offices before their release to archival institutions, many records of the Federal Government of the United States are left in a disorganized state. Several attempts have been made to bring uniformity on a national scale in the recordkeeping procedures of Government agencies, but the only result has been the adoption of systems that have tended to complicate rather than to simplify the organization of the records of any particular agency. Few records, even at the present time, are organized with the consideration in mind that they may eventually be transferred to an archival institution. And in the past, when no such institution existed, records were simply allowed to accumulate and, having served their current purposes, were relegated to out-of-the-way storerooms. The basic condition is generally lacking by which the principles of the German and Dutch archivists concerning the preservation of the original order established in a registry office can be made to apply. The reconstruction of the original order, therefore, is often very difficult and occasionally undesirable. The original order—to use the words of the Director of the Prussian State Archives in describing older registries—is "without system, foolish, and impractical." In such cases, the arrangement to be imposed on the records should be determined by the archivist.

Let us now see what bearing the principle of original order had on accessibility.

The significance of records must, of course, be made known in finding aids, and the way records may be described depends on the way they were arranged. If the records were arranged in a chronological sequence the only descriptive data provided by their arrangement are dates; if they were arranged in an alphabetical sequence the descriptive data are somewhat more complete in that information is provided on the correspondents involved; if they were arranged by subject the descriptive data are still more complete. The production of finding aids is also an important consideration in making records available for use, and the arrangement of individual record items to facilitate their description thus also indirectly facilitates their use.

SUMMARY

In recapitulation, then, there are two basic archival principles to be observed. While the principle of provenance is basic and inflexible and relates to a matter of the highest importance to the archival profession, the principle relating to the original order of records involves mainly matters of convenience or use.

The principle of provenance relates to the integrity of archives—the preservation of the values that inhere in them because of their organic character. While arranging records there are two things that will seriously affect their evidential values. One is anything that is done to obscure the source of records in a particular body; the other, anything that is done to obscure their source in a particular activity. Both of these actions involve origins—one, origins of records in an organic body; the other, origins in an organic activity.

The principle of original order relates mainly to use or convenience. Normally an archivist should preserve the order given series within record groups and record items within series during their current life, if it is one that permits him to find records when they are wanted and to describe records effectively. Normally he should try to understand the system of arrangement that was imposed on the records originally rather than to impose one of his preference. But he should have no compunction about rearranging series in relation to each other or single record items within them if by so doing he can make the records more intelligible and more serviceable. The test here is a very practical one of usability.

Archival Arrangement—
Five Different Operations at Five Different Levels

Oliver W. Holmes

A rchives are already arranged—supposedly. That is to say, an arrangement was given them by the agency of origin while it built them up day after day, year after year, as a systematic record of its activities and as part of its operations. This arrangement the archivist is expected to respect and maintain. Arrangement is built into archives; it is one of the inherent characteristics of "archives," differentiating them from nonarchival material.

Theoretically in the archives of an agency of government, or of any organization—and therefore in the archival depository that has custody of such archives—each document has its place, a natural place, so that its association and relation with all other documents produced or received by the creating agency remain clear. The archivist preserves and uses the arrangement given the records by the agency of origin on the theory that this arrangement had logic and meaning to the agency and that if the agency's employees could find and use the records when they were active, in connection with the multitudinous daily transactions of the agency, the archivist surely can do the same, using the contemporary registers, indexes, and other finding aids that came with the records as part of them. Thus artificial finding aids that the archival establishment must create are reduced to a minimum. The filing system used by the agency may not have been the best that could have been devised to start with, or it may not have been effectively carried out. It may even have broken down badly because of inefficient filing, sudden expansion or shifting of programs without adequate assistance in the file room, or for other reasons. Still, no major archival establishment will ever be given money to revise filing systems. It will have to get along with what it inherits, making minor adjustments at most.

Beyond such practical considerations as lack of time and money to create new systems, however, is the more important truth that, if the archival agency could reorganize the records, to try to do this would be unwise and undesirable. Perhaps no two archivists could agree on the arrangement concept to be built into any new system. Furthermore, what an agency has created in the past no man today can completely tear asunder. One cannot, for example, tear volumes apart. This author has seen such a process actually tried with press copy letter books, but with

Reprinted with permission from *The American Archivist* 27 (January 1964): 21-41.

minute books or account books it becomes impossible. To the degree that it could be done with loose papers, the original groupings, which have meaning in themselves, would be lost; the sequences of operations and events would be difficult, or almost impossible, to reconstruct; the efficiency or inefficiency of the agency itself would be obscured; and all the registers, indexes, and other finding aids created over the years by the agency, at great cost in manpower and money, would be rendered useless. (We are here considering physical rearrangement, not rearrangement on paper, which the archivist is free to do to his heart's content if he can find time and money for it. Paper rearrangements by the archivist may usefully supplement the physical arrangement established by the agency of origin; they cannot supplant it.)

To the energetic novitiate, who usually wants to start classifying and cataloging documents all over in some schematic arrangement of his own, these observations must sound strange—like the lazy man's way out. But every professional archivist knows these things. He has learned them from experience or from archivists who have had experience. These lessons have been expounded frequently in archival literature. The classic expression of them is in the 1898 manual of the Dutch archivists, Samuel Muller, J. A. Feith, and R. Fruin, translated into English by Arthur H. Leavitt (*Manual for the Arrangement and Description of Archives*; 1940). They are embodied also in the well-known treatises in English by Sir Hilary Jenkinson (*A Manual of Archive Administration*; rev. ed., 1937) and T. R. Schellenberg (*Modern Archives: Principles and Techniques*; 1956). They have been written into the instructional material of the National Archives, notably *Staff Information Papers* nos. 15 and 18, entitled respectively *The Control of Records at the Record Group Level* and *Principles of Arrangement*.

The overall principle discussed above is, of course, what archivists call the "principle of provenance." This is signified on an upper level by the French expression *respect des fonds* (maintaining the natural archival bodies of creating agencies or offices separately from each other) and on a lower level, that is, within the *fonds*, by the phrase *respect pour l'ordre primitif* (respect for the original order). Arrangement becomes then, for the records of any one agency, the task of determining and verifying the original order, filling and labeling of the archives containers to reflect it, and shelving of the containers in the established order.

But if this is all there is to arrangement, it would seem to be relatively easy and even somewhat routine—perhaps chiefly a physical operation. A first answer to such an observation would be that, although in theory arrangement is simple, in practice it always presents many problems. Almost the whole of the Muller, Feith, and Fruin manual is devoted to the exposition of these problems and suggested solutions to them. A second answer is that these authors treat only part of the

arrangement function, the arrangement of the records of an agency—
any agency—whereas archivists in the National Archives and in most
State archival establishments have custody of the records of hundreds of
agencies, more or less related to each other. There must be, first, overall
arrangement policies involving the grouping of these agency records
and, second, controls to implement the policies. In other words, there
are in any large depository many decisions that must be made above the
level of the *fonds*.

Much confusion that arises in discussing the arrangement function
could be avoided, this author believes, if it could be recognized at the
start that the term "arrangement" covers several different types of operations, of varying degrees of difficulty, depending in large part on the
level at which they are being carried out. An identification of these levels
and some analysis of the operations at each level, beginning at the top
level and moving down—the order in which control should be established—may lead to a better understanding of this function by archivist
and layman alike. In attempting this analysis, the author has had in mind
as audience chiefly would-be archivists (and position classifiers), but he
hopes what is written will also make sense and ring true to those who
have often dirtied their hands by actually doing arrangement work.

THE LEVELS OF ARRANGEMENT

In all large archival depositories there can be distinguished, usually,
at least five levels of arrangement:

1. *Arrangement at the depository level*—the breakdown of the depository's complete holdings into a few major divisions on the broadest common denominator possible and the physical placement of holdings of each such major
division to best advantage in the building's stack areas. This major division of
holdings is usually reflected in parallel administrative units (divisions or
branches in the depository organization that are given responsibility for
these major groupings).

2. *Arrangement at the record group and subgroup levels*—the breakdown of the
holdings of an administrative division or branch (as these may have been
established on the first level) into record groups and the physical placement
of these in some logical pattern in stack areas assigned to the division or
branch. This level should include the identification of natural subgroups
and their allocation to established record groups.

3. *Arrangement at the series level*—the breakdown of the record group into
natural series and the physical placement of each series in relation to other
series in some logical pattern.

4. *Arrangement at the filing unit level*—the breakdown of the series into its
filing unit components and the physical placement of each component in
relation to other components in some logical sequence, a sequence usually

already established by the agency so that the archivist merely verifies and accepts it.

5. *Arrangement at the document level*—the checking and arranging, within each filing unit, of the individual documents, enclosures and annexes, and individual pieces of paper that together comprise the filing unit and the physical placement of each document in relation to other documents in some accepted, consistent order.

The above five steps refer to the arrangement of the records themselves, independently of their containers. They establish the order or sequence in which records ought to be placed in containers and in which the containers ought to be labeled and shelved.

When all these steps have been completed the archival holdings of a depository may be said to be under control. This control may never be established completely (sometimes arrangement at the filing unit or document level may never be fully carried out), but it must be established to an acceptable degree before records description work is possible because finding aids have to refer to specified units in an established arrangement.

ARRANGEMENT AT THE DEPOSITORY LEVEL

A large archival depository, holding the records of hundreds of different agencies, each considered a record group, requires a first division of its holdings above the record group level, chiefly for administrative purposes. Each such division thus holds a number of record groups. This division may be:

(1) on a chronological basis, the breaks often coming at major changes in the organization of government (as in Latin American countries, where one usually finds at least a colonial section and a national-period section, with sometimes an independence-period section sandwiched between);

(2) on a hierarchical basis, according to major organizational divisions of government (as in the National Archives, where administrative divisions were first organized around the records of one or two major departments along with the records of related independent agencies, although through the years these boundaries keep changing);

(3) on the basis of levels of government (as central and local); or

(4) some combination of the above.

In the National Archives there is also a tendency to consider broad subject areas as a guide at this arrangement level, but this may be more apparent than real. Government organization itself normally follows subject areas to a considerable degree. Subject areas can hardly be a controlling guide but they may be an auxiliary consideration. So also are such important matters as the size and arrangement of storage areas, the physical nature of the records themselves (often necessitating special areas in the case of technical records such as maps, pictures, and film), the reference activity of the records, the degree of security to be given them, and the number and caliber of personnel needed to work with them. Because of all these considerations, this first division of the records is usually made at the highest level of administration and embodied in issuances approved by the head of the agency. Personnel of lower grade usually have no part in the decisions and no responsibility for them. Small archival depositories may not feel the need of dividing their holdings at this level; but over the years, as transfers continue from an increasing number of agencies and offices, the need to consider such a division will almost certainly arise.

<h2 style="text-align:center">ARRANGEMENT AT THE RECORD GROUP LEVEL</h2>

The basic principle of *respect des fonds* requires that the records of different creating agencies and offices be kept separate and never mixed. Under this principle an archival establishment must (1) decide what creating agencies and offices are represented by records and (2) identify all records as belonging to one agency or another. In the early years of the archival establishment concern for these matters may seem a bit academic, for the agencies represented are generally known to the staff and the identification of records with particular agencies is fairly obvious. Sooner or later, however, arguments will arise and decisions will be called for. How long an archival establishment may "get by" without carefully dividing its holdings into sharply delimited "record groups"—to use the term coined in the National Archives in 1941—will depend on how far back in time and through how many agency reorganizations its holdings extend and on how many attics and basements filled with accumulations of these records, confused by many movings over the years, it has cleaned out.

Before the National Archives began using the term "record group" the Public Record Office in Great Britain was using the term "archive group" to designate the records of an entire agency, no matter how large, including the records of entire ministries. The British practice, we believed, if applied in the National Archives, could lead sometimes to groupings too large for administrative convenience. We thought it better to divide the records of such large "agencies" as departments into a number of separate record groups, usually reflecting the bureaus within departments and of "convenient size" for administration.

On the Continent the French term *"fonds d'archives"*—meaning the body or stock of records of a record-creating unit—was widely known in archival literature and accepted as the basis of arrangement work. (The

Dutch term *"archief"* also had wide usage because of the influence of the Dutch manual.) As applied in practice, the records of any subordinate office that kept records, no matter how small the office, were considered a *"fonds."* This was going to the other extreme of "convenient size," and the "record group" principle as defined in the National Archives united the records of subordinate offices under their superior offices, usually up to the bureau level. Also the records of small though essentially independent satellite agencies were often included with the records of major agencies to which they were related. Many smaller *fonds*, such as the records of claims commissions or arbitration boards, were grouped together into what became known as "collective record groups," of which a number were established. There would otherwise be thousands of *fonds*. Thus, the National Archives, partly for administrative convenience, has aimed at the intermediate level in establishing its record groups. It established 206 such record groups in 1943 for its then existing holdings. Additional record groups have since been established and the number, considering the entire holdings of the National Archives and Records Service, now approaches 350.*

Although the term "record group" has never seemed to this author a happy one for the concept, no one has suggested a better, and both the term and the concept seem to be spreading in use to other archival depositories in the United States and Canada. It is not certain that the term is always defined exactly as it is in the National Archives, and perhaps it need not be—so long as the definition is applied consistently throughout the establishment. Some such concept is needed in all archival depositories having the care of records created by many different agencies and organizations. Once established, record groups are usually the basic units for administrative control; that is, for arrangement, description, reference service, and statistical accounting and reporting.

Inasmuch as the records of each record group are to be kept separate from those of all other record groups, any unit of records—whether bound volume, series of loose papers, single paper or map, or whatever—has to be identified as constituting a part of one record group and no other. There can be no overlapping, for records cannot be placed physically in two different places. Each new accession must be allocated to its proper record group; if none exists, a new record group must be established and a proper location in the depository found for it. So far as possible, all the contents of a record group should be kept together in one place in the stacks. Exceptions will often have to be made for technical records. Because decisions at the highest level are governed more by administrative than professional considerations, the establishment of a record group with the delimitation of its boundaries is the first real pro-

---

*As of 1984, the National Archives had established 465 record groups.

fessional operation as one moves downward in the arrangement function. It is impossible to discuss here all of the many considerations governing decisions about allocation of records to one group or another. They are set forth clearly and in detail, so far as the National Archives is concerned, in its *Staff Information Paper* no. 15, *The Control of Records at the Record Group Level.*

Recommendations for the establishment of new record groups and for their delimitation are made usually by branch or division chiefs of senior archivist level and require the approval of the head of the archival agency or a specially designated assistant. Topmost officials must also decide which division or branch is to be assigned responsibility for the record group. The division or branch chief, or a higher official in some cases, must decide where in the branch areas the record group is to be physically located. The amount of use the records may have, the quantity of additional records to be expected in the record group, and other considerations may affect the decision on the area in which the record group is to be shelved. Physical limitations of stack areas and equipment may not permit an ideal arrangement to be fully carried out and compromises then must be made.

All natural subgroups should also be recognized at this level of arrangement, accounted for in the registration statement prepared for the record group, and kept separate physically as subdivisions of the record group when it is arranged in the stacks. Subgroups must be identified and their affiliation determined when the boundaries of the record group are established; otherwise, the determination of subgroups could amount to a separate level in arrangement.

In many simpler record groups, some of which may be sizable, there are no subgroups. The subgroup determination can be made quickly except in cases of collective record groups or of records of an agency that has undergone frequent reorganizations and numerous changes of field offices, for the records of each field office ought properly to be considered a subgroup. Moreover, if the records over the years have become badly disarranged, the determination of existing subgroups can be most difficult. The untangling of the records themselves may have to be postponed to the next level of arrangement, the identification and allocation of series. The identification of subgroups and recommendations for the order of their arrangement within a record group is work of middle-professional grade or higher and is approved by the chief of the division or branch that has custody of the record group.

Although many difficult problems enter into decisions with respect to record groups and the decisions are of major importance, the time spent in arrangement at the record group level is so little as to be an almost negligible part of the total time an archival agency must devote to the arrangement function.

ARRANGEMENT OF SERIES WITHIN THE RECORD GROUP

It is arrangement at the three levels within the record group that represents the time-consuming work. Record groups in the National Archives average nearly 3,000 cubic feet each (the contents of nearly 500 4-drawer file cabinets). In other archival depositories the average may be smaller. Some record groups are so large and complicated that they contain thousands of series in many subgroups. These series must be identified and arranged in some logical order in relation to each other, so that the whole record group is given an orderly sequence on the shelves.

Although through classification schemes and filing practices an agency may have given a definitive arrangement to documents and filing units within each series, it almost never established a sequential arrangement for the many different series it created. It never dictated that a certain series was to come first, a certain other series last, and that each of the others was to have its place at some definite point in between. This larger classification sequence is what the archivist must establish for each record group. It is an operation that requires a full knowledge of the principles of archival arrangement and a knowledge of the administrative history of the agency or agencies whose records are involved. In many ways this is the heart of archival work, because the inventory and all other finding aids merely reflect this level of arrangement and are keyed into it.

The person to whom the work is assigned should be well trained and experienced and should prepare himself for his specific assignment by reading laws and regulations governing the organization and programs of the agency in question; its annual reports, special reports, and other publications; and all serious historical and analytical studies of its work and accomplishments. He must pay special attention to changes in its function and organization: these are usually reflected in the records and over a long period of years will be considerable. He must know the history of predecessor agencies whose records may have been inherited and of successor or liquidating agencies that have had custody of the records and that may have disposed of some, reorganized others, absorbed some into their own record bodies, or otherwise complicated the picture. He must study particularly the agency's way of keeping its records. If he studies also the records themselves he will learn much from them that is not in print or otherwise available. By putting together the knowledge gained from all sources, he will be in a position to identify and interpret the many series and to give them an arrangement that is not only logical but revealing of an agency's history and accomplishments. His arrangement scheme should have two dimensions. It should not only present the series maintained by the agency at any given time but through time, whether it existed 10 years or 150 years.

This arrangement process is much easier to carry out if the archivist has seen the records in the agency before they are accessioned. Ideally, records should be taken directly from an agency's file room by the archivist as soon as they become inactive enough for transfer to the archives depository. Perhaps the agency has had a central file, but certain important exceptions to centralization have been allowed. Perhaps the agency has had a number of file rooms or filing stations reflecting major functions or organizational units. Perhaps general decentralization has been the practice if not the rule. Knowing how the agency grouped its records is always helpful because the original groupings should be reflected in the final arrangement. It is less possible in these days of intermediate records centers for the archivist to see this picture. Nor is it possible to any extent with respect to the older records of agencies that existed for decades before the archival depository was established. These agencies may have moved their inactive records from building to building innumerable times before relinquishing them to the archives depository, each time further confusing any arrangement the records may have had when they were active and growing files. Even so, however, the archivist's opportunity to inspect the older records in attics or other places of storage, especially if they were still in their original containers with original labels, may have taught him much about them. In this sense arrangement begins before accessioning, and knowledge gained at this stage should be reflected so far as possible in the inventory prepared at the time of accessioning. The archivist who has had a share in the accessioning process always has a head start in arrangement if he can carry through in an advisory or supervisory capacity until the records are on the shelves.

The next step is the identification of the different series that must be assigned an order. This brings us to the definition of the word "series," one of the basic technical terms in the archivist's vocabulary. Until an archivist understands this term and is able to recognize a series, he should not undertake arrangement work on this level.

A true series is composed of similar filing units arranged in a consistent pattern within which each of the filing units has its proper place. The series has a beginning and it has an end, and everything between has a certain relationship. The pattern may be a simple one—alphabetical, numerical, or chronological—or a complex one, as, for example, annual reports arranged first by years, then by States, and then by counties within States. This may be complicated further by an agency's practice of filing reports of State officials in a certain order at the State level and of county officials in a like established order under each county. Such a filing pattern may be followed year after year until the records fill several thousand feet of shelving, but no matter how complex the pattern, so long as that pattern is being repeated, we still have a single series.

Another series may consist of only a few feet of reports relating to Territories in a somewhat different arrangement. The boundaries of these true series are never difficult to determine; gaps and disarrangements are easily recognized.

There will occasionally be a series made up of only one file unit. Perhaps this is more often true of book records, as when some special record has been maintained in a single volume that has no successor. "Series" may not seem to be the proper word in such cases unless one thinks of the item as the beginning of an intended series that did not advance beyond the first unit. In a short-lived agency there may be many such series. It might seem that a number of these one-volume series could be brought together at the end of the record group, but this would be the equivalent of giving up in determining their proper location. They would not belong together unless they had a common provenance. Instead they might belong properly in widely separated parts of the record group, some of them perhaps between series of unbound papers that they might help to elucidate.

There will also be cases where no discernible pattern seems to exist for certain groupings of documents although a subject or transaction relationship is obvious. Often one really has just an accumulation or aggregation of documents relating to some matter because, apparently, the agency did not take the time to rationalize their arrangement. These accumulations can hardly be called "series" in the strict sense of the word, but arbitrarily we treat them as such—just as we are somewhat arbitrary about what constitutes a record group. They represent a block of material that has to be assigned a place in the arrangement. There is no succession of file units and therefore no obvious beginning or end, so that the special problem for this type of series is to determine its boundaries. One has to look for the common denominator in subject or provenance that separates this accumulation from other true or artificial series. Perhaps these papers or other materials were collected by some investigator because they were useful in a special matter he was handling. Perhaps they related to some special operation that came to a sudden end. Whatever their history and purpose, they must be identified by their boundaries and kept separate if they ever are to be understood and assigned their places in relation to the whole.

The different series, once they are identified, are the elements of the record group that at this level of arrangement are to be given a meaningful physical order that will later be reflected in the order of inventory entries on paper. Indeed, the entries of an inventory (which are the series) are probably at this stage on paper in the form of cards or slips that can be shuffled as the arrangement is being worked out.

Although the record groups and subgroups should have been established and their order decided upon at the second level of arrangement, the final allocation of series to subgroups (if not reallocation to other record groups) may have to await the detailed identification of series that comes at the third level of arrangement. Once all series are assigned to record groups and subgroups so that the boundaries of these are finally certain, the archivist looks within the group or subgroup and works out a logical arrangement sequence for the series so assigned.

It must be admitted that there is no one perfect arrangement sequence for series. Considerable variation is possible in any large record group, and no two archivists, no matter how experienced, would make the same decisions. But there are better arrangements and poorer arrangements, and the poorer one must be wrestled with until it is acceptable.

Arrangement of series is a relatively simple task if the records are the creation of a small, unified agency. Such a record group or subgroup, therefore, may be assigned to a younger archivist for training purposes. He will draw upon a few accepted principles such as the Dutch rule giving precedence to the correspondence series unless there happens to be a "backbone" series from which all else depends. Indexes and other agency-created finding aids usually precede the series they index. Facilitating and housekeeping records, if preserved, usually come last. In between, functions and the sequence of action within functions may govern the grouping of series. In larger record groups the series may be grouped according to chronological periods, by major breaks in the filing systems, or on a functional basis, and these groupings become also major divisions or breakdowns of the resulting inventory.

In most record groups of any age and size, however, there are almost certain to be many complicating factors. These may be caused by (1) changes in the organization; (2) changes in the functions; (3) changes in the filing schemes; (4) the existence of records from one or more predecessor agencies that have not been, or have been only partially, incorporated into records series created by the later agency; and (5) records that have been reclassified or otherwise reorganized for proper reasons, that have been incompletely reorganized (some ambitious scheme not carried through to completion), or that have been merely tampered with by would-be "methodizers" before being transferred to the archives depository.

The Dutch manual gives rules for dealing with these and many other complications that cannot be presented here. Although younger archivists with some experience can identify series in complicated record groups as well as they can in simpler ones, it is necessary usually for a more experienced archivist to take over and work out a rational arrangement. A person with experience can be expected not only to do a better job but to do it faster. It is a waste of time and money to employ a worker of too low a grade for arrangement work at this level. The arrangement finally decided upon should be approved by the division or branch chief having responsibility for the record group.

Arrangement of Filing Units Within Series

Although filing units within series may be single documents or single documents with enclosures and annexes, they are more likely to be assemblages of documents relating to some transaction, person, case, or subject, depending upon the filing policy or system used by the agency. The filing policy, in turn, is likely to be conditioned by the nature of the agency's operations. In the past these filing units were usually controlled in a system of registers and indexes that tied the whole body together in intricate but orderly fashion; and efficient servicing of the records now, as then, is dependent generally upon keeping the body in the same order so that all the contemporary finding aids remain valid as guides. These registry systems continue to be used, notably in the courts and regulatory agencies and in many other agencies that operate largely upon a case or project system. In still other agencies, however, they have been superseded by classified files without registry controls or with partial registry controls. In these modern instances the registry numbers do not control the filing order. Instead the filing units are the folders established for the classes of the classification scheme. All sorts of combinations may be encountered.

Arrangement work at this level, obviously, is not original arrangement; it is rather a simple but time-consuming checking operation to verify the original order and correct obvious displacements that have taken place over the years. It is necessary for efficient and certain reference service. No archivist has control over his records without it, and delay can soon cost more time, if the records are at all active, than is required to carry it out immediately after accessioning. Moreover, it is best done in connection with boxing and labeling. This is not to say that if a record group is without immediate importance from the point of view of service, or if it is never likely to be very active, such arrangement cannot be delayed or even dispensed with: when a decision such as this is made the records are boxed and labeled without close checking. Although nothing is so lost as a misplaced file, one can delay file unit checking until it can be seen that the records are active enough to justify the work. The highly active series in a record group should receive the more careful checking. These decisions, including the determination of priorities, should be made by branch chiefs on the basis of recommendations of their experienced professional assistants.

If the series is composed of numbered or lettered volumes, nothing is simpler than to arrange these in sequence on the shelves. It can be done by a laborer once the place for them is decided upon. Only when backstrip or other identification marks are missing, so that one must determine sequence from internal evidence, need an archivist or sub-professional employee, depending upon the complexity of the problem, be called upon. The alphabetical, numerical, or otherwise designated files (fastened together by various devices) or the folders containing loose papers are lined up and checked for order and completeness as they are placed in archives boxes, and a box list is prepared for labeling purposes. This becomes more than a routine job only if the agency's filing system is complicated or if an apparent arrangement has been disturbed intentionally or through accident or neglect. Inadvertent irregularities may call for considerable detective work in the records themselves and in outside sources to arrive at the explanation. Only when the facts are known can the archivists decide whether to allow space for what appears to be missing or whether to leave what appears to be an alien intrusion where he finds it. Some checking for irregularities can be done by the more intelligent and careful laborers and certainly by subprofessional personnel. It is more efficiently and reliably done by the latter if filing systems are complicated, for there are more elements to be watched. Perhaps three-fourths of the arrangement work on this level can be done by experienced subprofessionals; the degree of experience needed depends on the complexity of the filing system.

Frequently this level of arrangement calls for the integration of files drawn from different chronological blocks. The central files of an agency may have been accessioned in three chronological blocks—for example, 1905-10, 1911-15, and 1916-20—with so much overlapping that they cannot be serviced efficiently. Maintained originally in the agency as one series, they had been arbitrarily broken into period blocks, as the older files became less active, to facilitate interim storage in a records center. Now, permanent storage and frequent use for research call for restoring the records to their original order. As this is done certain categories that can be disposed of are dropped out; in other words, three or four tasks can be performed simultaneously. Ideally, so that the records can be shelved to stay, everything that has to be done to a series should be done in one multiple-purpose operation before it is boxed and labeled. Nothing is more wasteful than to have to go over and over the same records because all operations were not planned and carried through at once. Such multiple-purpose arrangement projects require at least subprofessional personnel of higher grades or professional workers in the beginning grades.

In many record groups there are rats' nests of bundles, irregularly sized papers, or other groupings that appear never to have been incorporated into systematically arranged and controlled series or that have been pulled out of such series for forgotten purposes and never put back, perhaps because a file clerk did not know where they belonged. The longer the records have remained in storage in attic or basement—so that over the years they have been serviced by many different persons, most of them unfamiliar with the old filing systems—the larger the rats' nests. Yet, they are often made up of fairly important records. Going through them calls for the skill of an archivist thoroughly familiar with not only the record group in question but also related record groups. Indeed, if the responsible person does not know the record group thoroughly, he had better keep away from the rat's nest. This is time-consuming arrangement work that must be done unless disorder is to be perpetuated, but is hardly ever done properly and efficiently by anyone but an experienced archivist of at least middle grade.

A final type of operation that may be encountered in the arrangement of file units is the deliberate reorganization of these units in cases where an arrangement different from the original one would seem to serve more efficiently to meet longterm reference demands. For example, an agency often lazily allows reports to pile up year after year, keeping those for each year together in some repetitive pattern, arranged perhaps alphabetically by jurisdiction. In reference service, however, the reports will almost always be called for by jurisdiction, which means that the archivist must draw them from as many places as there may be years involved. It is a relatively simple job to reorder the reports so that all for a jurisdiction are together in sequence. This is physical rearrangement, of course, but it is the simplest sort of rearrangement and does not really violate the integrity of the files. It can be entrusted to subprofessional personnel under proper supervision.

More complicated reorganizations may be decided upon if records have been so badly disarranged that the original organization cannot be fully restored with confidence unless excessive time is spent in research. One does not decide lightly to reorganize a series completely, for in the end the work can prove to be more difficult than expected. It is not easy to devise a new scheme; the records will not fit into any scheme of reorganization as well as they fitted into the original scheme; and they will not be the same body of records when so reordered even though all the documents have been worked into a new arrangement. In cases where an agency has allowed records to accumulate without organization, the archivist must decide whether to leave the records in this disorganized state (which he probably will do if they are not in much demand) or to devise an organization for them. Usually these are short series and the organization can be relatively simple; for example, chronological, alphabetical, or by personal name. Some organization is prerequisite if the records are to be microfilmed. The planning of such organization or reorganization must be by professional archivists of high grade and much experience. It may be carried out by middlegrade archivists working under supervision.

ARRANGEMENT

It is obvious that arrangement work on the level involving filing units is of various grades of difficulty and calls for the time of personnel of various grades from that of literate laborers through the subprofessional grades, and from the lower professional grades up to the middle grades. A professional archivist must supervise arrangement work performed by workers of any grade in the sense of spot checking, being present to answer questions, investigating gaps and irregularities, making decisions on whether to go ahead despite irregularities, bringing larger matters to the attention of his superiors, and the like. Planning and supervising arrangement on this level is work of considerable complexity and responsibility and should be done by middle-grade archivists and above. Finally, such projects before their inauguration should be approved by senior archivists and even division chiefs, depending on the amount of equipment and manpower involved or the lack of guiding precedent.

Arrangement of Documents Within File Units

A bound volume may contain many individual documents, but their arrangement was fixed at the time of recording; they cannot get out of order, nor can their order be altered. Loose papers are a different matter. Many ways have been tried over the years to keep related papers of a file unit together and in some kind of order, but none is entirely satisfactory. In the days before flat files, order was maintained by folding papers together. Modern ways to preserve the order involve the use of paper clips, wire staples, or rivets—the two last in connection with cover and backing sheets—or of folders and metal fasteners of various kinds within folders. In the days of folded records—roughly before World War I—enclosures were folded within the covering letters, and enclosures often had enclosures folded within them. A letter of transmittal might cover many enclosures, some of which had their own enclosures. This was true especially of legal records, vouchers, and reports. When records such as these are flattened, considerable ingenuity, careful checking, and use of folders or envelopes are all necessary to ensure that the proper documents are kept together and their relationships thus preserved. An archivist is likely to develop considerable admiration for the old system of folded records and the revealing endorsements on the middle fold, and he is not likely to want to unfold them permanently until the physical condition of the records requires that he do so. Increased handling to find and scrutinize flattened endorsements can result in more rapid deterioration than if the records had been left unflattened.

It is partly in connection with the flattening of records, then, that one is required to ensure that proper documents and individual sheets of paper are kept together and in a consistent order.

The other major process requiring arrangement within the file unit and down to the individual document is in connection with microfilming. There is an increasing amount of this these days as (1) scholars blithely order hundreds of dollars worth of film of records they have not seen, (2) we are trying to include more and more of our best and most valuable records in microfilm publications, and (3) we are filming vast quantities of records either with a view of destroying the originals or, contrariwise, to preserve them by encouraging the use of microfilm rather than of originals. One using film instead of originals suffers under many handicaps at best, and if the records are not in perfect order and filmed in a consistent manner—so that endorsements come first, for example, and enclosures are in their proper order and all sheets of a multipaged document are in order—the film becomes unusable and therefore useless. There are many instances of film made but never used in government agencies because the records were not carefully arranged beforehand.

One does not normally go within folders or cases to arrange original documents if they are going to be retained and used in their original form. If there is disorder, one can usually see by size or color of sheets which ones belong together and can, if he is interested in those particular records, puzzle out their arrangement more quickly and confidently than he could if they had been placed on microfilm in the same disorder.

Arrangement on this lowest level, then, is done chiefly in connection with flattening and microfilming (often both at once). It can be done by experienced subprofessional employees, or by lower grade—that is, less experienced—professional workers. It is usually a good task for a beginner because it familiarizes him with filing methods and the contents of files at the same time. Always a more experienced archivist should be on hand as supervisor, to answer questions and to iron out complications. Often arrangement of file units and individual documents is performed simultaneously, especially when records are being prepared for microfilming. This usually saves time and labor, but, insofar as the process becomes more complicated, a person of higher grade may be required. If the filing unit is the document, which happens in some files, arrangement on the file unit level and on the document level becomes one and the same job, usually a relatively simple one.

BOXING, SHELVING, AND LABELING

The five levels of arrangement described above have to do with the analysis and identification of records and with checking them to determine their proper arrangement. Presumably the decisions have been made and recorded on paper or are otherwise well understood. We have now to discuss the execution of the decisions. This can be done in relatively quick time by laborers, typists, and lower grade subprofessional personnel operating under higher grade subprofessional or professional supervision, depending on the complexity of the job. Usually the professional personnel responsible for decisions on arrangement should supervise their execution, lest time be wasted in identifying subgroups and series and determining their boundaries all over again. Checking arrangement on the file unit level and boxing the series can proceed with one crew while the supervisor works on the overall arrangement of the series. The shelving of the boxed series in the determined order is then the last operation except for typing and affixing the labels.

BOXING

Normally only loose papers are "boxed," that is, put into archival containers that afterwards are placed on shelves. In transferring a file to these containers, one tries to divide it at natural breaks (between file units if possible) and yet not to pack the box so tightly that records cannot be withdrawn or inserted without damage or so loosely that papers slump and bend and space is wasted. One checks the arrangement of the file units placed in the box and writes down the necessary data, usually the beginning and ending file numbers, for the label. Efforts are made to end a series in one box, without a waste of space, and to begin a new series in a new box. Unless the order of series has been worked out ahead of time with finality and the series are boxed in order, these boxed series will, of course, be given only temporary positions on the shelves. Only with smaller and simpler record groups or accessions is it likely that everything can be ready for shelving at once. Boxing can be the work of high-grade laborers or subprofessional employees. Professional personnel is rarely needed unless complicated arrangement work is being done at the same time and is really the controlling operation, of which the boxing is an inconsequential part.

SHELVING

Both boxes containing loose papers and bound volumes must be shelved. When the arrangement of their contents has been finished, the boxes can be shelved by laborers in locations and in the order, so far as series are concerned, that professional archivists have determined. This is largely a physical operation. The shelving of volumes, especially if they are of all sizes, is more complicated. Although it will be done with the aid of laborers, it will have to be closely supervised by professionals or experienced subprofessionals unless there are long runs of volumes, well labeled and of uniform size, to be set on the shelves. The supervisor should decide whether volumes are too large or too poorly bound to stand vertically on shelves. He must watch the order very closely if there are many series of a few volumes or of one volume each. He must approve any shelving of volumes out of order, deciding when enough space can be saved thereby to warrant it, or when the condition of the volumes demands it, or perhaps when the leaving of indexes and registers out of sequence so that they can be placed near desks or made available to searchers in a searchroom is desirable to save time or to permit a degree of self-service. These irregularities in the established order should be signaled by cross-references in the proper places.

Labeling is of two kinds: (1) of the containers and (2) of row ends in the stack areas after the shelving has been completed. The container labeling usually comes first. Lists of box contents should have been made up at the time of boxing. A container label must show the name and number of the record group, the name of any subgroup, the name of the series, and the particular contents of the box. It should also bear a number to show the place of the box in the record group or subgroup or at least in the series sequence. The first two or three elements, if they extend over a hundred containers or more, should be typed on stencils so that the labels can be processed in sheets; if this is done, only the contents of the individual boxes will need to be typed on individual labels. Sometimes there will be no subgroup. If a subgroup is well known, there need be shown only the number of the record group of which it is a part. Row-end labels must be typed in full, since each one varies so much in wording. Labels can be worked out by lower grade professional personnel or higher grade subprofessional personnel, but they should be reviewed by higher grade professionals before time is wasted in processing and typing. The affixing of the labels can be done by literate and careful laborers if work is reviewed by high-grade subprofessionals or low-grade professionals. The assignment of the lower or higher grade worker is determined by the complexity of the job.

There are of course reboxing, and reshelving, and relabeling jobs that follow after the internal disposal of accessioned material in order to consolidate the space gained by such disposal. They can be handled by the same grades of personnel that handled the original jobs of this nature. Occasionally there are major reshiftings of holdings as a record group or several of them are assigned to different areas. Such shiftings afford the opportunity to improve arrangement and correct any errors that may have been made originally. The planning of such a shift in order to get the most out of the available space in the new areas is usually work of professional level, but the execution can be by laborers and supervision by experienced subprofessional personnel.

REPORTING ARRANGEMENT RESULTS IN WRITING

For each level of arrangement except the lowest, there is likely to result some kind of archival instrument:

1. Depository level—an administrative issuance.

2. Record group level—a record group registration statement or summary for each established record group.

3. Series level—an inventory of the record group in which each series appears as a numbered entry.

4. Filing unit level—checklists of filing units for important series. These checklists are sometimes, for very long and important series, offered as separate documents, but more often they are presented as appendixes to inventories of the record groups. Very short series and series of lesser importance are deemed sufficiently accounted for in the inventory itself.

On the document level a written statement is not normally produced to reflect arrangement.

Most of these archival instruments serve a double purpose in that, although really produced as control documents to account for the holdings and show their arrangement, they serve also as finding aids. In one sense the depository-level document might be said to tell a searcher which way to turn when he enters the depository, the record group statement tells him which threshold to cross, the inventory tells him in which part of the room to look, and the filing-unit list tells him which unit to take off the shelf as likely to contain the document or documents he wishes to see. The searcher will not take these steps except in imagination as he consults the finding-aid documents, but some member of the archives staff must take them physically if the documents are to be made available to the searcher in a central searchroom.

It will be seen that with respect to finding-aid documents that reflect arrangement, which we may designate as primary finding aids, the real work involved is determining the arrangement. Presenting that arrangement in writing afterwards is a subsidiary activity. There are, of course, archival finding aids that do not follow the arrangement pattern of the records but cut across these patterns in index fashion. These may be designated as secondary finding aids. They must come later because established units of arrangement with fixed designations must first exist to which units of entry in secondary finding aids can refer. Thus, arrangement is the basic internal activity of an archival establishment. All other internal activities depend upon its proper accomplishment.

Organizing Photo Collections:
An Introspective Approach

Nancy E. Malan

Describing research for his book on early Texas oil, Walter Rundell recalls a visit to a museum with "splendid photographs, but they were completely unorganized, which is to say they were actually scattered all over the floor of a storage room."[1] An extreme example of the state of photograph collections? Perhaps. But perhaps not. Photography is a copy medium. The first step is to copy reality—a sports event, a ceremonious occasion, a construction site—from a dozen or more different angles. These original shots are then duplicated. Negatives are made into positives, or positives into copy negatives and back to positives, slides into duplicate slides, or wall or wallet-size enlargements, and so on until a single roll of film becomes an unwieldly collection of images. Consider the number of rolls of film passed over photography shop counters each year, and the fact that each one, like Topsy, may just grow. Eventually, if these images are deemed to have lasting value, they may find their way to a historical institution, where given the norm of ever-decreasing funds, limited staffs, and a paucity of storage space, they may be relegated to the storage room floor.

No matter the mitigating circumstances, a responsible curatorial institution must eventually get the photographs off the floor and into an order that will facilitate their retrieval and use. The task involves two basic processes: organizing or arranging the photographs and cataloging or describing them. Unlike book librarians, who abide by the *Anglo-American Cataloging Rules,* the picture professional will find no rule book of universally accepted standards. As Kenneth Duckett points out in *Modern Manuscripts:* "With the possible exception of manuscripts, no other body of historical documentation has had more diversity of arrangement and cataloging than photographs. There are few published guidelines that the curator can follow in establishing his collection, yet very early he will need to make decisions which materially affect its growth and use."[2]

Picture professionals lack, for example, a standard system for describing photograph collections, or individual photographs. There is no agreement on the information that should appear on a catalog card,

Reprinted with permission from *Picturescope* 29 (Spring 1981): 4-6.
[1]Walter Rundell, "Photographs as Historical Evidence: Early Texas Oil," *American Archivist* 41 (1978): 376.
[2]Kenneth Duckett, *Modern Manuscripts* (Nashville, 1975), p. 195.

its order or format, or the level of description. Some institutions describe thousands of photographs in a paragraph. Others risk rivaling the volume of photographs with the volume of catalog cards by cataloging and cross referencing each image onto individual index cards. Still others fail to do any descriptive work at all. They rely on the collective memory of experienced staff members to retrieve images that exactly suit the researcher's needs.

Given the lack of accepted standards, it seems appropriate to look to national institutions, with their reputed wealth of resources and expertise, for guidance. Both the National Archives and the Library of Congress, whose photographs number in the millions, have developed formats for group cataloging. Neither format is officially endorsed by the institutions using them nor by the archival or library professions they represent. At the Library of Congress work is only now underway on a manual for cataloging original, historical, and archival prints and photographs.* It is hoped that this manual, which will supplement the *Anglo-American Cataloging Rules*, will eventually be recognized as the national standard. In the meantime, the search for models must continue beyond national institutions.

Bibliographies like John Maounis's "Cataloging Historical Photographs" in the winter 1980 issue of *Picturescope* and Nancy E. Malan's "Selected Bibliography for Historical Photograph Collections" in the summer 1980 issue note a growing body of literature on the subject. But most of the entries take the case study approach, in which authors explain the peculiar needs of their institutions and describe the system developed to suit those needs. These articles may be useful to prompt the would-be cataloger's thoughts, but they do not necessarily describe procedures applicable or adaptable to other collections. In an age of sophisticated information retrieval systems, it seems reasonable to expect the existence of accepted rules for cataloging photographs, yet this expectation remains unfulfilled.

A similar hiatus exists in recommended procedures for organizing photograph collections. No sage as yet has written a manual describing the infinite variations on basic subject and numerical organization of photographs and the applicability or efficacy of these variations to specific types of photograph collections. The lack of standards, or even suggestions, is understandable when the range of materials defined as "historical photograph collections" is considered. Compare an institution that struggles to develop a suitable organization for two hundred images on a specific topic, like railroads, with one which has thousands of photo-

---

*The manual titled *Graphic Materials: Rules for Describing Original Items and Historical Collections*, compiled by Elizabeth W. Betz, has been published by the Library of Congress (Washington, D.C., 1982).

graphs documenting the broadest range of American life and culture. The problems and their solutions are quite dissimilar. In the latter case the use of general subject headings, like "railroads," might suffice. But in a collection of railroad photographs such a general heading would be useless.

An institution with one full-time staff member might do well to implement self-indexing files, so that researchers can work through them independently. Others with resources that allow for the microcopying of collections could consider organizing the copies in one way and the originals in another. Such a system would allow dual access, for example, by subject in the microcopy and by photographer in the original collection. The list of various types of photograph collections could go on for pages. The point is that the diversity of size, format, content, and quantity of photographs in historical collections makes the prospect of some uniform organizational scheme, to which all but maverick institutions would adhere, unlikely.

The conscientious picture professional, having searched for standards and surveyed existing literature, is likely to find himself or herself back where he or she started, wondering how to achieve bibliographic control of the collection on the now proverbial storage room floor. The answer lies not in universally accepted standards (which do not exist) or in procedures adopted by national institutions, but within each institution. Success depends on the institution's ability to assess its resources, the content and current state of its collections, and the needs of its users. The first step in achieving bibliographic control is for the staff to be institutionally introspective, to ask and answer the right questions. *Some of those questions are:*

Are we an archives bound by the principle of provenance?
The problem of organizing collections may be solved by invoking the principle of provenance. The provenance of a collection refers not only to its origins but to its internal order, which is maintained because it contributes to the overall significance of the materials. Photographs are simply boxed, labeled, and shelved in their original order. The staff is saved the task of reorganizing collections in the interest of preserving their integrity and may devote its energies to providing additional access, if necessary, through new finding aids.

How are our photographs and new accessions currently organized?
Whether an institution is formally bound by provenance or not, time spent on determining if and how collections are currently organized and on maintaining that order whenever possible is time well spent. The idiosyncracies of an existing arrangement may be minor and upon reflection wholly more acceptable than the burden of reorganizing hun-

dreds of unique images and their matching copies. It is tempting, particularly with new accessions, to disregard existing order in favor of having the new collection conform to existing institutional standards. Again, weigh the effort to plan and implement a new organizational scheme against efforts to facilitate the collection's use through an explanatory note, a new finding aid, or other written documentation. If there is no existing order, someone will have to create one.

Do groups of our photographs constitute collections, or are they unrelated items that can be part of a general photograph file?
For purposes of physical and intellectual control, it is useful to deal with photographs as collections rather than as individual items. To determine whether groups of photographs constitute collections, another series of questions needs to be addressed: Are the photographs the work of one photographer? Were they created by an individual or firm? Are they a common size or physical type? Do they depict the same subject, time period, or geographic area? Are they linked physically, as albums, 35-mm negatives, and contact sheets are? Are there caption lists, indexes, or other papers that would be difficult to match with the photographs if they were not kept as a unit? Does keeping them together aid identification? Has the donor requested that they remain together? Do they have an authenticity or special meaning that would be lost if they were separated (like a series showing progress on the construction of a building)? Do they have an internal order, an arrangement by subject, number, date or some other sequence? Are they a sizable addition to your holdings?
If your answer to most of these questions is "yes," the photographs are unified enough to be maintained as a collection, which can then be internally organized. Photographs that do not constitute collections may be placed into a general file, a catchall for unrelated items.

Is it necessary to refine our system to achieve item control or will group descriptions suffice?
Perhaps because of the influence of library card catalogs, which identify and help to retrieve individual books, it sometimes seems obligatory to provide similar control of individual photographs in a collection. For many collections, item control is an expensive luxury. If a collection includes one hundred views of Palo Alto and its environs, taken by the same photographer during a specified time period, it is perfectly legitimate to note the existence of these like-images on one group catalog card and to put the burden of locating a specific image on the researcher. Words that describe nuances of differences in photographs will never adequately substitute for the image itself. Researchers like and want to look at photographs rather than catalog cards. Allowing them that

opportunity by pointing them to collections rather than to word descriptions of individual images can prove more satisfactory for all parties involved.

It is also possible that most requests are for specific, individual items, and that item description is the most effective means of retrieval. Just be sure to thoroughly justify item cataloging before embarking on this time-consuming procedure.

Who are our users and how do they request photographs?
The purpose of organizing and cataloging photographs is a straightforward one: to make them accessible to researchers. In keeping with this goal, it is important to undertake some analysis of who comes to your institution and how photographs are requested. Are they professional researchers whose time is restricted by deadlines? Are they art history students concerned with the aesthetic value of original fine arts prints? Are they local residents whose afternoon reminiscences are prompted by images of local history? The needs of each of these groups are diverse and should be somewhat influential when planning access systems.

Pay attention too to the kinds of requests received. There is little point in organizing an Indian collection geographically if most photographs are asked for by name of tribe. If veterans of naval service ask for photographs by name of their ships, give some consideration to organizing the photographs, or an index to them, by name. Facilitating access encourages use, and increased use is in the interest of historical agencies and the field of history in general. A satisfied constituency is more likely to be a vocal and supportive one, a significant asset in fiscally conservative times that may threaten the existence of cultural institutions.

What are the most frequently requested topics?
Many institutions establish reputations for collections on particular subjects and therefore receive requests about specific limited topics. It may be that 80 percent of your requests can be answered by dealing with only 20 percent of the holdings. In such a situation, allocate an appropriately generous proportion of staff time and resources to these topics or collections. Make the system of replying to inquiries as efficient as possible through standardized replies to general inquiries, prepared lists citing frequently requested photographs, supplemental files made up of xeroxes or duplicate prints, image-bearing catalog cards, and other specialized finding aids. Although these finding aids may encourage the repetitious use of certain photographs, you will eventually spend less staff time replying to predictable inquiries. Additional work can then be done on other collections, with an eye toward publicizing their use as they are processed.

ARRANGEMENT

What can we practically achieve given limited funds and staff?
As noted earlier, it is a rare historical institution that has adequate funds and staff at its disposal. Priorities must therefore be established, talents and resources assessed, and a plan developed that suits both.

The experience of one national depository is instructive. Owing to its prestigious reputation and generous donors, it fulfilled its mandate to document world anthropology with collections covering virtually every geographic area in the world. The institution's director had a distinct interest in the anthropology of the North American Indian and for two decades devoted virtually all resources to the individual cataloging of photographs on this topic. The thousands of images on other topics remained inaccessible in the shipping cartons in which they were received. Researchers were denied access to them because they were unprocessed collections.

Under ordinary circumstances, it is not prudent to allocate 100 percent of the budget on 10 percent of the collection or to sacrifice over an extended period access to the bulk of your holdings for the sake of some small part. Since it is undoubtedly impossible to achieve bibliographic perfection, try to achieve at least some control over all the holdings before concentrating on a specialized area.

Resources, current status, collection content, users' needs—these are the primary factors to be considered before embarking on a system of bibliographic control. Data about them comes from observing and participating in the inner workings of your institution, from working with researchers, and from spending time (lots of time) with the photographs for which bibliographic control is needed. Only when you can comfortably expound on the questions posed above are you ready to do some serious planning for bibliographic control.

Aural and Graphic Archives and Manuscripts

Ralph E. Ehrenberg

W hile increasing awareness and sophistication of historians and other researchers in the use of nontraditional communication formats is encouraging the development of audiovisual programs at an unprecedented pace, procedures have yet to be fully defined for administering aural and graphic archives and collections.

Nonscript, nonprint materials share several common characteristics of form and content that set them apart from traditional textual materials. First, their physical attributes differ markedly. Paper, film, glass, celluloid, metal, plastic and cloth are all used as physical mediums. Moreover, their size may vary from a few inches to over many feet in length, as in the case of right-of-way maps or panorama drawings, while their composition—"the way in which they were brought together"[1]—may include albums, scrapbooks, volumes, atlases, sets, or single items. Consequently, aural and graphic materials pose special (and often related) problems of handling, storage and preservation.

Second, the medium of expression is graphic or aural rather than script or print. Archivists and curators, as well as researchers, are limited to languages—the projections, scales and symbols of maps, the pictorial designs of posters, the magnetic configurations of sound records—which establish definite parameters of expression and interpretation. Third, they have technical and aesthetic qualities not found in traditional archives. A knowledge of art, science and technology is often required to evaluate and service them adequately. Fourth, subject content is highly varied, yet concentrated or individualized. Aural-graphic languages are used to illustrate, evoke and promote ideas, events, things, places or persons, thus raising complex problems of subject control and retrieval. Finally, their creation (compilation, editing, printing and processing) is generally a group process involving two or more persons. The cost of creation therefore often tends to "weed out" useless records.

While these common characteristics illustrate a general similarity among aural and graphic records, they also reflect significant physical

Reprinted with permission from *Drexel Library Quarterly* 11 (January 1975): 55-71. The author is indebted to Nancy Malan and Leslie Waffen of the Audiovisual Archives Division, National Archives and Records Service, for their assistance in the preparation of the sections on photographic records and aural records, respectively.

[1]T. R. Schellenberg, *The Management of Archives* (New York: Columbia University Press, 1965), p. 322.

and substantive differences that affect basic archival and curatorial functions. This paper will discuss these differences under the general headings of graphic, photographic and aural records.

GRAPHIC RECORDS

Graphics are a form of communication which expresses ideas by lines and symbols rather than words. They can be divided into two classes: scaled and unscaled. Scaled graphics are exact representations of selected features of the earth's surface (maps, charts and cartograms) or of individual objects (engineering and architectural plans). Unscaled graphics are pictures created manually or mechanically by drawing or painting, and include engravings, illustrated broadsides, historical pictures and posters.

In the small or medium-size archives and manuscript collection, two kinds of graphics should be retained permanently: 1) manuscript and printed or processed graphics on which manuscript changes, additions or annotations have been made for record purposes, and 2) printed or processed graphics that are attached or interfiled with other documents of record character. Because of basic differences in form and content, the latter should be removed and stored as separate physical entities or photographically reproduced. The argument for retaining the integrity of a file unit is a compelling one that goes to the heart of archival principles and there are enough unfortunate examples of the careless removal of graphics to make custodians wary of perpetrating similar errors. On the other hand, the substantive content of many graphics will undoubtedly be lost if preventive measures such as physical removal or reproduction are not undertaken. If oversized graphics are removed, the custodian should indicate that such a transfer has taken place either by leaving a transfer card in the place of the original or by attaching a list of the separated items to the series or collection inventory. Conversely, separated items also should be marked in pencil to identify the series or collection from which they were removed.

ARRANGEMENT

Graphics should be arranged intact as a group by agency of origin or donor, in their original order if possible. By maintaining original order, intellectual integration of graphics and textual documents is facilitated and the identification of untitled, unsigned graphics is made easier. When provenance and *respect des fonds* are disregarded and graphics from various sources are interfiled into a general geographical or subject scheme, integration and identification become increasingly difficult and often impossible.

If the original order cannot be determined below the series or collection level, scaled graphics should be arranged by geographic area (maps and charts) or by model or structure (engineering and architectural plans).[2] Further subdivisions by topic and date can also be added. Elaborate published classification schemes have been prepared for scaled graphics and may assist the custodian in selecting area or subject terms.[3]

The National Archives of the United States and the Pennsylvania State Archives arrange scaled graphics on an organizational basis consisting of a hierarchy of administrative and geographic levels. The following levels of arrangement are normally included in descending order: 1) a record group or subgroup composed of records of an administrative unit at the bureau level of government, 2) a series or subseries composed of records reflecting the divisional level of government, 3) a file unit consisting of an assemblage of related documents, and finally 4) individual documents. I have described the application of this approach to map arrangement more fully elsewhere.[4] An example illustrating the organizational approach is taken from the Pennsylvania State Archives.[5]

Record Group 12 Records of the Department of Highways
   Subgroup Bureau of Construction
      Series State Roads and Turnpikes
         File Unit Eastern (Portion of Pennsylvania)
            Document Individual Maps

Another way of arranging scaled graphics while maintaining provenance is according to function. The objective of the functional approach is to arrange and classify records according to the purposes for which they were created or accumulated. No hierarchical system need be devised; therefore, it does not require an extensive knowledge of administrative or donor history to arrange the material or to research in it. Another advantage in the case of official government records is that natural series arranged according to function do not have to be divided

[2]Mary Larsgaard, "Map Classification," *Drexel Library Quarterly* 9 (October 1973): 38-39; Lyle F. Perusse, "Classifying and Cataloging Lantern Slides for the Architecture Library," *Journal of Cataloging and Classification* 10 (April 1954): 77-83.
[3]U.S. Library of Congress, Subject Cataloging Division, *Classification, Class G: Geography, Anthropology, Folklore, Manners and Customs, Recreation,* 3d ed. with supplementary pages (Washington, D.C.: Government Printing Office, 1954; reprinted 1966), pp. 177-181; Samuel W. Boggs and Dorothy Cornwell Lewis, *The Classification and Cataloging of Maps and Atlases* (New York: Special Libraries Association, 1945); Roman Drazniowsky, *Cataloging and Filing Rules for Maps and Atlases in the Society's Collection,* rev. ed. (New York: American Geographical Society, 1969).
[4]Ralph E. Ehrenberg, "Non-Geographic Methods of Map Arrangement and Classification," *Drexel Library Quarterly* 9 (October 1973): 49-54.
[5]Interview with Martha L. Simonetti, Archivist, Pennsylvania State Archives, June 21, 1973.

ARRANGEMENT

among several different record groups following each agency reorganization. The functional method seems particularly well suited for archives
of reasonably small political and geographical units and manuscript
collections.

Unscaled graphics differ markedly from scaled graphics. They do
not generally pertain to any particular place or area and may include a
variety of subjects, such as persons, things, phenomena and places. For
these reasons, unscaled graphics whose original order cannot be ascertained should be arranged and described in a manner similar to photographic records.

Following arrangement, each graphic is "titled" in pencil (normally
in the bottom right-hand corner of the verso) according to group or
collection number, series, file unit and document number or date. Titled
graphics should be stored unfolded in acid-free folders which are also
titled in pencil with the appropriate identifier in the lower right-hand
corner.

RETRIEVAL

Because researchers are more interested in the subject content of
graphics than in their organizational or functional relationships and
because the subject content is so varied, graphics should be described
individually or indexed graphically.

Descriptive elements vary according to type of graphic. For scaled
graphics the elements generally include series or collection name, area or
subject, title, author, date, scale (generally given verbally, "one inch to
two miles," or in representative fractions, 1:124,000), dimensions (height
by width) and medium. Descriptive elements are essentially the same for
unscaled graphics except that scale and area are not included.

A shelflist reflecting the arrangement scheme is useful as an internal
finding aid for quick reference and initial research. The shelflist may be
in page format and bound or in card format. Entries normally consist of
the entry or file number, title fragment and date, but can be expanded to
include substantially more detail, including content description and type
of material. The most detailed lists include an interpretation or analysis
and history of each graphic. Very few archives or manuscript collections
have the staff or the funds to prepare analytical descriptions. This is the
responsibility of the historian rather than the archivist or curator.

The conventional method for describing individual items is the catalog card. A properly designed card, cross-referenced by area, subject and
author or artist, provides multiple access points to any document. For
ease of reference, catalog cards can be color-coded: e.g., white for area,
blue for subject, yellow for author/artist. Subject cataloging is time-consuming, but a well-conceived preprinted form that includes selected sub-

ject blocks which can be checked off to indicate subject content will facilitate processing.

Graphic or map indexes provide another method of controlling maps individually. Published outline maps can be color-coded to show the coverage of selected sets or series of maps and charts that cover a particular geographic region. Indexes can be bound by region or stored separately in folders. Visual and graphic catalog cards that include maps or pictures of documents also speed up processing and reduce handling of originals.

Although collective description is more applicable to textual records, it can be adapted for graphics if they are thoroughly indexed by area and subject. Traditional inventories are particularly useful when graphics and textual records are closely related but stored separately. A copy of each inventory can be annotated by the archivist or curator to show where each entry is stored.

STORAGE AND HANDLING

Because of the nature of their origin (particularly scaled graphics), graphics have generally suffered some damage through use before the archivist or curator gets custody of them. The best and cheapest method of preservation is to place graphics in acid-free folders that are stored flat in standard map cases with sliding drawers no deeper than two inches, taking into account the heavy weight of full map cases. Floor weight load should be checked by a knowledgeable engineer to be sure that it will support the combined weight of oversized graphics and storage cases.[6]

Graphics must often be dissected to fit map cases although extremely large graphics should be rolled and stored in tubes. In no case should a graphic be folded. In time, acid deterioration along fold lines (which is easily observed by a brown, brittle appearance) will cause documents to literally fall apart.

Torn and deteriorated graphics should be reinforced and supported by acid-free rag paper, linen, nylon or muslin (attached by neutralized wheat flour paste or adhesive plasticized cellulose acetate foil laminated under heat and pressure) or enclosed in polyester (mylar) envelopes to strengthen them and prevent further tears and deterioration.

If extensive handling and use of certain individual graphics or series of graphics is anticipated, reference copies should be made. Since graphics are generally oversized, photostats or microfilm (70mm or 105mm) should be used in place of traditional forms of copying.

---

[6]Mary Galneder, "Equipment for Map Libraries," *Special Libraries* 61 (July-August 1970): 271-274.

PHOTOGRAPHIC RECORDS

Photographic records include all pictures that are produced on sensitized surfaces by the action of light and include still pictures, motion pictures and aerial photographs. Since motion pictures and aerial photographs are limited to a few specialized archives and manuscript collections, only still pictures will be discussed.

Because of the thousands of pictures produced daily, repositories must be selective in their retention policy. In general, pictures relating to the activities of an agency or donor, pictures having historical significance and pictures having value as works of art should be retained. Official pictures that can be disposed of are those that have had only a limited or one-time use, such as the thousands of photographs taken during a research project or identification photographs of large organizations.[7]

ARRANGEMENT

Photographic records consist of two forms: the original black-and-white negative or color transparency and the print. Normally, the negative or transparency is considered the record copy and the print a reference copy. In certain instances, such as purchased or donated photographs, the repository may only have a print. These unique prints along with annotated prints should also be considered record copies.

Since negative originals and unique prints are used for different purposes than reference prints, they should be stored and filed separately. The former should be used only for reproductive purposes. Continual use of originals and unique prints will result in damaging scratches, spots, and fingerprints. If they are valuable and frequently used, good quality copy negatives should be made. Ideally they should be housed in the photographic laboratory. At the very minimum they should be stored in closed stacks and restricted to staff use; in no instance should they be made available to casual researchers.

Negatives and unique prints should retain the original numbers assigned to them by the agency, firm or individual that produced them, and each series or collection should be maintained separately according to provenance and original order. Where order is lacking and it is not feasible to arrange by provenance, they may be arranged numerically simply by progressively registering each accession sequentially.[8]

A more sophisticated classification scheme has been devised by Paul Vanderbilt for the State Historical Society of Wisconsin. Each series or

---

[7]Joe D. Thomas, "Photographic Archives," *American Archivist* 21 (October 1958): 421.
[8]T.R. Schellenberg, op. cit., p. 328.

collection of negatives is assigned a Cutter code for the name of the series or collection originator or photographer.[9]

B 4   Bemis Collection
B 5   Billings Collection
•   •
•   •
•   •
B 58 Bittinger Collection

Individual film sheets are then assigned a unique control number by sequentially adding numbers to the series or collection number: B4-1, B4-2, B4-3 . . . B4-n.

Each sheet of film should be stored in separate acid-free, sulphur-free envelopes that are sealed along the edge rather than down the center. Center seam adhesives of old negative jackets retain moisture which will stain and eventually destroy film emulsion.[10]

Both jacket and sheet film should be notated with the same negative number so that negatives will not become lost. The negative number can be hand-scribed on the film emulsion or photographed on a strip of high contrast sheet film which is attached to the sheet negative.[11]

RETRIEVAL

Excessive handling eventually destroys negative originals and unique prints. To minimize handling, a good control system is imperative. A self-indexing reference print file that is keyed to the negative file should provide adequate intellectual control of the negative file.[12] Multiple point access to the print and negative file can be obtained by additional indexes and catalog cards arranged by subject.

To establish a self-indexing file, inexpensive photographic reference prints are made of significant original negatives and unique prints. These prints should be either placed in standardized (generally legal-size) acid-free, low-sulfur envelopes or dry mounted on 100 percent rag paper for support. Mounting is time and space consuming but provides good protection against curling and damage.[13] For convenience, copy negatives can be filed with prints, provided that they are stored in separate negative jackets.

[9]Paul Vanderbilt, "Filing Your Photographs: Some Basic Procedures," *History News* 21 (no. 6, June 1966): 5-6. Technical Leaflet 36.
[10]George T. Eaton, "Preservation, Deterioration, Restoration of Photographic Images," *Library Quarterly* 40 (January 1970): 93.
[11]Paul Vanderbilt, op. cit., p. 6.
[12]Renata V. Shaw, "Picture Organization Practices and Procedures," *Special Libraries* 63 (October 1972): 448-456; (November 1972): 502-506.
[13]Paul Vanderbilt, op. cit., p. 3.

ARRANGEMENT

The reference file can be organized according to four main categories: portraits, places, subjects, and events. While portraits are filed alphabetically by name of individual and generally pose few problems, the remaining three categories require the establishment of authority files to standardize retrieval terms. Special emphasis should be given to local subjects. For the geographical file, the custodian will find the references cited above for scaled graphics useful; for the subject file, the subject headings for the picture collection in the Newark Public Library are helpful.[14]

Each reference print or mount and corresponding envelope must be captioned for identification. The amount of information depends upon the category and level of retrieval desired, but all captions should include the file designation (Portrait File, Geographic File, etc.) title (subject/name/place/event), date of image, photographer, restrictions, provenance and negative number.

Determining the title and related caption information is sometimes difficult. Internal evidence that helps to identify textual and graphic records is often lacking. That is why it is important to arrange negative originals and unique prints according to provenance. Their organizational origins may help "to identify the time and place at which they were produced and the subjects to which they relate."[15] Another problem is that the historical significance of the subject content may differ from the photograph's original purpose. A classic example concerns a photograph made by the Office of Public Buildings and Grounds, a federal agency established to erect buildings and monuments in Washington, D.C. It is an image of two small children and their nanny, all three in high button shoes and prominent hats, the maid with her starched, ankle-length white apron. The photograph is filed by the agency of origin under Meridian Hill Park and captioned, "View showing texture of concrete in lower wall. Maid with small children in view."[16]

Captions can be typed on acid-free paper and dry mounted or hand written on the back of pictures or mounting boards. Pressure sensitive labels should not be used because the adhesives dry up and the labels fall off. To write on the back of a photograph, place the photograph face down on a sheet of glass and use a soft pencil.

Collective descriptions, such as inventories or guides, are useful for publicizing significant groups or collections. Standard descriptive procedures are recommended: a brief history of the photographic activity that

---

[14]William J. Dane, *The Picture Collection; Subject Headings,* 6th ed. (Hamden, Conn.: Shoe String Press, 1968).

[15]T. R. Schellenberg, op. cit., p. 325.

[16]Example suggested by Nancy Malan, Archivist, National Archives, September 12, 1974.

produced the group or collection should be followed by the identification and description of the individual series.[17] Each entry should describe one series and these should be grouped either by administrative subdivision, by subject or by type.

Series entry descriptions should include a title line and descriptive paragraph. The title line consists of the subject to which the material relates, inclusive dates (as well as significant gaps), type of photographs and quantity. The descriptive paragraph should include information concerning the origin, subject and composition of the photographic series.

STORAGE AND HANDLING

General storage and handling procedures have been mentioned above but special reference must be made to the problem of humidity and the storage of certain types of photographic negatives. Relative humidity should be maintained between 40 to 50 percent. Fungus growth is encouraged above 60 percent while film brittleness, curl and static charge result from very low humidity.[18] Temperature should be maintained at the same level that is recommended for other permanent records.

The three types of photographic negatives that require special attention are cellulose nitrate base film, glass plates and color transparencies. All three must be stored separately from "safety" or cellulose acetate base film which comprises the bulk of current film production.

Nitrate film in a deteriorated state is combustible and highly inflammable when tightly packed in envelopes or film cans and stored in a warm place. Cool temperatures and individual storage reduce the threat of deterioration and combustion, but it is still advisable to replace nitrate film with acetate copy negatives.

Nitrate base film can be identified by year of production and by testing. Most film produced during the period 1890-1930 (and aerial film from the late 1930s and early 1940s) was on nitrate base. Paul Vanderbilt describes the procedure for testing nitrate base film:

> To identify nitrate film, cut a long thin sliver from a sample margin and touch a match to it. If it burns briskly with a yellow sparkling flame and leaves a crisp, black ash, it is nitrate; if it burns only slowly or goes out and leaves a whitish melted mass between the unburned part of the ash, it is acetate or safety film. Then examine the notching code and treat all films similarly notched accordingly. Safety film generally carries the imprinted word "safety" in the margin. Some films are not notched and hard to identify

---

[17]T. R. Schellenberg, op. cit., p. 339.
[18]George T. Eaton, op. cit., p. 95.

and there is such a thing as a laminate of safety and nitrate bases. With experience, one learns to tell the differences, in most cases, by appearance.[19]

Glass plates that have permanent value should be stored vertically either in archives boxes or envelopes separated by cardboard padding or in slotted plywood boxes. The weight of glass plate negatives poses a similar problem to the weight of map cases. Depending on the number of plates involved, it may be necessary to provide storage areas with reinforced flooring. When stored on shelving, glass plates should always be placed on the lower shelves to prevent toppling and to make handling less dangerous.

Color transparencies also require special attention. The organic dyes in color film are not permanent but will change less rapidly under cool storage conditions. Color film, therefore, should be stored at 40 F and 30 to 40 percent relative humidity for maximum protection. For security and references purposes, black-and-white copy negatives should be made.

AURAL RECORDS

Aural records are "sound-storing artifacts" that include a variety of sound recording and reproduction devices in the form of cylinders, discs and magnetic tapes.[20] Like other nonprint, nonscript material, sound recordings may complement the written or printed word (through rhetorical style, nuances and intonations) but they also have the quality to convey a "literal message," an attribute not found in any graphic medium.[21]

Most "sound archives" are primarily interested in mass-produced vocal recordings. The type of recording one is likely to find in an archives or manuscript collection, however, is likely to be unique spoken word or musical recordings. These should be retained particularly if they concern an activity or function of the agency of origin or donor. Examples of official sound recordings from the Oregon State Archives that have permanent value include proceedings of board and executive committee meetings, investigative reports, field notes, trip reports and oral presentations before courts and boards.[22]

Because of their rarity, Edward A. Colby also recommends that the following mass-produced vocal recordings be saved: early recordings (to 1909), "representative collections of early recordings as tangible or at

---

[19]Paul Vanderbilt, op. cit., p. 6.

[20]Gordon Stevenson, "Discography: Scientific, Analytical, Historical and Systematic," *Library Trends* 21 (July 1972): 106-107.

[21]Walter L. Welch, "Preservation and Restoration of Authenticity in Sound Recordings," *Library Trends* 21 (July 1972): 83.

[22]James D. Porter, "Sound in the Archives," *American Archivist* 27 (April 1964): 328.

least visible artifacts in the history of recorded sound," and out-of-print recordings.[23] Finally, all oral history sound recordings should be permanently retained even when a transcript is made, because most transcripts are not verbatim renderings of a tape.[24] They have often been edited both by the transcriber and the interviewer. Moreover, a typed transcript cannot reflect the tonal qualities of the voice.

<h2 style="text-align:center">ARRANGEMENT</h2>

Arrangement and classification schemes have not been standardized for aural records. Christopher Barnes briefly describes eight different methods of arrangement which can be grouped under three broad categories: numerical, provenance and thematic.[25] In numerical arrangement, each sound recording or accession is organized sequentially by number while thematic arrangement is alphabetically by subject, theme or event.

Arrangement by provenance poses special problems for sound recordings. Like photographs and unscaled graphics, aural records are generally created sporadically and do not necessarily reflect any special activity or function. Because of this, aural records in the custody of the Audiovisual Division of the National Archives of the United States are arranged by agency of origin and thereunder serially by number.

<h2 style="text-align:center">RETRIEVAL</h2>

No commonly accepted format of description has been formalized. Basic elements of a sound recording consist of the physical artifact and the data recorded. Level of control depends upon the emphasis placed on each of these elements. Description of the physical artifact should include group or collection number, item number, title, date, type of sound recording, number of recordings (two-track, one side, etc.), time/footage and speed (7.5 inches per second, 33 rpm, etc.).

The descriptive element of an entry or catalog card should include information concerning the sound data's origin and general references to major subjects, themes and events. The latter is complicated by the necessity of using visual senses to interpret aural senses. In describing textual and graphic records, the archivist or curator can use written words and visual symbols to describe written words and visual symbols. But when verbal communication of sound recordings is "extracted for

---

[23]Edward A. Colby, "Sound Scholarship: Scope, Purpose, Function and Potential of Phonorecord Archives," *Library Trends* 21 (July 1972): 11.

[24]Norman Hoyle, "Oral History," *Library Trends* 21 (July 1972): 73.

[25]Christopher Barnes, "Classification and Cataloging of Spoken Records in Academic Libraries," *College & Research Libraries* 28 (January 1967): 49-52.

197

the purposes of description and identification, it must be transferred from one frame of sensory perception to another. This cannot be done without some loss of information."[26]

Description of individual sound recordings in the form of catalog cards or special lists is generally more useful than collective description. The latter, however, is helpful as a reference tool if organized around a series or collection, a subject or a theme, and is carefully indexed.

The retrieval of sound data is made more complex by the need to electronically reconvert the physical and magnetic configurations stored on various physical mediums into auditory symbols before they can be used.[27] Reconversion raises various technological and ethical problems.

Like photographic original negatives and prints, original sound recording cylinders, discs and magnetic tapes are fragile and will deteriorate with use. The data stored on the recordings, therefore, must be transferred from originals to duplicate copies that are used for reference and cataloging.

Available equipment for rerecording originals varies. Most authorities recommend professional recording equipment but portable home-use magnetic tape recorders/reproducers capable of rerecording high-fidelity sound on quarter-inch tape are satisfactory for the small or medium-size archives or collection. The type of tape most often recommended is polyester (mylar) magnetic tape because of its exceptional resistance to wear. Furthermore, polyester contains no plasticizing agents that can evaporate under certain conditions of humidity and temperature, leaving tapes brittle and weak.

Choices of tape speed, size and tracks still remain open to question. The Oregon State Archives rerecords on a reel-to-reel format at 3.75 ips while the National Archives uses 7.5 ips.[28] Reel size is also a problem. The larger the reel, the more economical. But a 10½ inch reel requires proportionally more access time than a smaller reel. The same is true of multiple-track recordings. While it is less expensive to use multiple-track recordings, access becomes more arduous.

Each duplicate tape should include a blank leader and trailer to reduce wear, facilitate threading and aid identification. It can be color-coded to identify master copies from reference copies or leaders from trailers. Identification should include the reel's identification number, recording speed and number of tracks. Finally, leaders and trailers should include a control signal, "recorded at a standard volume level, [to serve] as a basis for comparing and determining the condition of the tape

[26]Gordon Stevenson, op. cit., p. 107.
[27]Edward A. Colby, op. cit., p. 14.
[28]James D. Porter, op. cit., p. 330.

in the future."[29] The control signal serves the same function as a microfilm grey or color scale.

Rerecording also enters the ethical realm. For instance, no effort beyond the correction of technical problems should be made to manipulate or distort the original sound, such as amplifying a weak voice. The value of sound rerecordings is in their ability to recreate the exact quality of the spoken or vocal voice. Of course, it is also unethical to edit by addition or deletion. Inadvertent breaks or tears in original recording tape should be flagged or noted by colored tape to warn the reader that an omission may exist.

Special equipment is also needed for reproducing or playback. A separate playback unit is recommended to eliminate the possibility of accidental or deliberate erasure. If this is not feasible, a combination recorder/reproducer should be modified by disconnecting the recording/erasing head. Earphones are also recommended so that other users will not be disturbed during playback.

STORAGE AND HANDLING

Proper storage and handling are basic to the preservation of aural records; once they have been damaged, their content may be irretrievably lost. Because of the variety of materials, storage and handling techniques differ for each sound recording form.

Cylinder sound recordings were developed by Thomas Edison in the 1880s and produced until his death in 1931. There are two types: wax and celluloid. The wax type are particularly fragile and must be stored in a dry environment. Deterioration of wax cylinders, which results not from fungus but from moisture penetrating the wood flour, phenol gum cores, can be retarded by *avoiding* air-conditioned, humidified storage.[30]

Wax-type cylinders should be stored upright in fleece-lined boxes on cardboard tubes that permit the free flow of air around the cylinders and keep them from touching one another. Because of their fragile nature, they must not be stored in sliding drawers or handled by ungloved hands. The shock from sliding drawers and the heat of fingers can actually break the cylinders.[31]

Celluloid cylinders are hardier but should also be stored in an upright position on end and should not be allowed to touch one another. Celluloid cylinders are often distorted from cardboard inserts or plaster of paris linings that have swollen and disintegrated from dampness.

---

[29]Ibid., p. 334.
[30]Walter L. Welch, op. cit., p. 91.
[31]Ibid., pp. 92-94.

These have to be cleaned and the distortion corrected before they can be rerecorded.[32]

There are four types of disc sound recordings: shellac, acetate, lacquer and vinyl. The acetate and lacquer discs are less durable than vinyl and shellac and should be handled and used accordingly. Glass was used as an acetate base during World War II and poses special problems because of its fragile nature. All large discs should be stored on end, on heavy utility shelves (although vinyl discs are lighter and can be stored on standard library shelving), supported by dividers and grouped by type to prevent warpage.[33] Vinyl 45 rpm disc recordings may be stored in file drawers because of their light weight and for space economy.[34]

Magnetic tapes should be stored vertically on edge in their original containers on metal shelves. The accumulated weight of flat stacking may distort reels or damage tape edges. Exposure to magnetic fields, which can cause erasure, and ultraviolet light should be avoided. Temperature control and relative humidity should be the same as for discs and other archival documents. Magnetic tape should be loosely wound on reels to prevent physical tape distortion and print-through. Periodic playback (at least once every two years) will relieve strains on the tape.

[32]David Hall, "Phonorecord Preservation," *Special Libraries* 62 (September 1971): 357-358.

[33]Walter L. Welch, op. cit., p. 95.

[34]James D. Porter, op. cit., p. 334.

Chapter 6
Description

A rchival description is the process of establishing intellectual control over records and personal papers through the preparation of finding aids. Finding aids—whether published, unpublished, or in automated form—provide information on the content and nature of records and personal papers that is necessary to permit staff to identify and control the materials and to assist researchers to use them. Finding aids produced by an effective description program therefore are essential for sound archival management.

In her essay "Efficient Finding Aids: Developing a System for Control of Archives and Manuscripts" (1981), Lydia Lucas reviews the goals of an institutional description program and the interrelationships between different finding aids. Based on experience of the Minnesota Historical Society, Lucas proposes an integrated description program which, although originally developed as a manual process, offers the possibility of efficient automation.

Inventories and registers traditionally have been considered the basic finding aids for descriptions of bodies of institutional records and personal papers, respectively. In "The Preparation of Inventories" (1982), Edward E. Hill provides detailed instructions for writing inventories of records in the National Archives. His paper provides practical information concerning the purpose, scope, organization, content, style, and format of inventories in the National Archives. Katharine E. Brand reviews the development of the register for personal papers as it evolved in the Library of Congress Manuscript Division in her article "The Place of the Register in the Manuscripts Division of the Library of Congress" (1955). Brand emphasizes the ability of the register to provide a standardized format for description while at the same time encouraging necessary flexibility and judgment. Even though these articles discuss descriptive practices at specific institutions, the practical information they provide can be of value to archivists in many different repositories.

Virginia Purdy discusses another form of finding aid in her article "Subject Guides" (1984). The goal of an effective subject guide is to direct archivists and researchers to many different documentary sources relevant to a particular subject of inquiry. Such guides are an important tool that can lead archivists and researchers to material in unexpected places that might otherwise be overlooked. They too can be important elements of institutional description programs.

Efficient Finding Aids:
Developing a System for Control
of Archives and Manuscripts

Lydia Lucas

Those of us from repositories that don't have automated finding aid systems tend to feel a bit defensive, probably a bit jealous, around those from repositories that do. Disparities in size, in fiscal and personnel resources, and in access to technical expertise have constituted barriers that fostered a perception of automation as beyond the means of most of us, and therefore beyond our immediate aspirations as well. The interests, concerns, and priorities of institutions so far advanced may seem irrelevant to the creation and use of the manual finding aid systems employed by the rest of us.

The last few years, however, have seen the development of cooperative projects offering an opportunity for participation by institutions of all sizes, all types, and all stages of development. The national repository guide and data base being developed by the National Historical Publications and Records Commission; the Washington Records Project that is preparing guide entries to records and manuscripts throughout that state; and the four state, Midwest State Archives Guide Project are examples, currently in progress, of projects designed around contributions from a number of repositories, relying upon information derived from the finding aids of those repositories.[1] Future years will see more such cooperative ventures, and with them will come the expectation that other repositories will eventually be able to structure and submit appropriate input data. Even those repositories whose internal procedures remain entirely manual may find it desirable and possible to prepare finding aids that can serve the needs of automated systems as well.

Besides being eyed as potential nourishment for automated systems, finding aids in today's repositories are beset from other directions. They

Reprinted with permission from *The American Archivist* 44 (Winter 1981): 21-26.

[1]Larry J. Hackman, Nancy Sahli, and Dennis A. Burton, "The NHPRC and a Guide to Manuscript and Archival Materials in the United States," *American Archivist* 40 (April 1977): 201-5; *Report of the Conference on Automated Guide Projects*, NASARA, St. Louis, Missouri, 19-20 July 1977; "The NHPRC Guide/Data Base: An Introduction," April 1979, information packet distributed by NHPRC; Lawrence R. Stark, "The Transition of Automation in Multi-Repository Guides," unpublished paper delivered at the annual meeting, SAA, October 1979; Max J. Evans, "The Midwest State Archives Guide Project: A Status Report," unpublished paper delivered at the Midwest Archives Conference, Spring meeting, May 1979.

must be adaptable to collections of increasing variance in size, complexity, types of materials, and content value. They must serve more users with a wider range of individual needs than ever before. In many reference situations, they must be sufficiently self-explanatory to permit a substantial degree of independent use by the research public.

With needs and demands nearly always far outstripping staff resources, practicality suggests that a single finding aid system should address simultaneously as many of these imperatives as possible. The ideal inventory or register must be efficient, in a format permitting the processor to record a maximum of usable information in a minimum of time and space. It must be easy to maintain, encouraging updates, changes, and addenda. It must enable a potential user to grasp the essence of a collection at a glance, to judge whether the collection includes items relevant to that user's research topic, to locate references to those items in the finding aid, and then to identify precisely that portion of the collection that contains them. The user would have been specifically directed to that inventory through some sort of repository-level index or similar access medium.

Consistent attainment of such an ideal may be beyond the scope of mortal man. There are, however, some general principles and practices that contribute to the ease and efficiency with which finding aids can be produced, maintained, and used. Contemplating potential future automation might be one way to help bring these practices into focus and develop a rationale for their systematic application.

The Minnesota Historical Society's finding aids system is far from new; its core structure of individual collection inventories with access provided through a dictionary card-catalog has been in use since the 1920s. It is similar to the systems found in other repositories of comparable size, and no aspect of it is yet automated. But its most recent form was shaped quite consciously out of, among other things, a particular experience with automation. It illustrates the evolution of one repository's approach to finding aids, and the adaptations it made in both theory and practice to anticipate future automation. At the same time, we have found it to be an efficient and effective manual system.

A dozen years ago, we were preparing what might be called "scholarly" inventories. The core of each inventory was a narrative description of the collection. Often, the description was a sort of research essay in which the processor advanced through the papers, discoursing at greater or lesser length about their content, until he reached the last box and there was nothing more to be said. As a substitute for the calendaring approach, this type of inventory was informative, with extensive detail and considerable analysis and interpretation; but it had some increasingly bothersome deficiencies. The essay approach did not incorporate the concept of a separate scope note, box list, or other concise overview of the collection's character. Lacking this, it was difficult to obtain a clear sense of what the topical foci of the papers were, what materials bulked largest in quantity or importance, whether cited specifics highlighted aspects of a significant topic or represented the processor's whim, and often where they were physically located within the collection.

The card catalog, then as now based on a unit card system with fairly extensive author and subject tracings, and occasionally an analytic card for a specific item or series, was not designed to do more than direct its user to the inventory. The researcher then had to read the entire inventory, having no way to judge whether he needed to or not.

This system itself had arisen in part as reaction to a still earlier approach in which the card catalog had been used as the primary information medium. Many collections had been cataloged in more detail than they were described; names, in particular, often appeared in the card catalog without being mentioned in the corresponding collection inventory.

The finding aid system as a whole recognized only unprocessed collections, not yet entered into the system, and collections that had been described and/or cataloged in detail. For many years there was no pressing need for an intermediate status.

These problems became obvious in the late 1960s, when we became involved in the testing phase of the SPINDEX II program for automated description of archival materials. Our experimentation centered on producing a file-list printout and keyword index for forty boxes of Northern Pacific Railway, General Manager, subject files. We also formatted (but never had keypunched) some lists and indexes for selected manuscripts materials.

We bowed out of the SPINDEX project rather early. The immediate reasons were lack of funds, departure of a key staff person, and the frustrations of trying to apply and de-bug a program that was insufficiently developed for our needs. But the underlying reason was that we didn't really know what those needs were. Not only did we lack a clear conception of what we realistically could and could not expect the program to provide, we also had not clearly defined why we wanted computerization. It was surely progressive, and a Good Thing; but no gaping deficiency in our finding aid system had been defined as being both vital to our program and insoluble without automation.

In fact, we were operating under the delightful assumption that if one fed in file titles and permuted their keywords, the computer would structure the files—an attractive substitute for the lengthy tasks of arrangement, analysis, and description. Unprocessed collections could easily be brought under control, and processed collections could be indexed and correlated at will. What was missing was *context*—summaries of collections and series and types of files giving meaning to the lists and indexes that might be produced by characterizing the collection as a whole, and reflecting their relationship to it. We knew what all the file titles were, but the format offered no way to express what was in them. Nor did it provide a means of dealing effectively with lengthy series of uniform folder titles, such as "Correspondence." It was impossible to judge what a series might require in more precise file identification, indexing, and correlating, or how to devise logical control numbers. Lacking, too, was a realization that data formatting and keypunching were noticeably more time-consuming and expensive than just typing file lists, and should be expected to yield proportionate benefits. In sum, manipulating isolated file or folder-level data did not offer us a viable way to deal constructively with anything but random subject files, and, in fact, the sole survivor of our first foray into automation is the General Manager printout, which is of just such a file.

So we abandoned SPINDEX II, not without a guilty sense of being Neanderthals at heart, and began to cope with what was becoming an intimidating backlog of unprocessed collections. But in doing so, we very consciously drew on our SPINDEX experience to develop processing priorities and inventory formats that we hoped would both improve our existing manual system and accommodate whatever we might want to do in the future (including another attempt at automation, should an appropriate occasion arise).

When the occasion did arise, nearly ten years later, we were delighted by the ease with which we could prepare automated input from manual finding aids, and in turn could modify details of these finding aids to match the input format. We are currently participating in the Midwest State Archives Guide Project, an NHPRC-funded cooperative project by the state archives of Illinois, Indiana, Minnesota, and Wisconsin to produce guides to public records using the SPINDEX III program. One of the project's specific goals is to explore the practicality of developing such guides from existing finding aids of varying formats and levels of detail.

Data entry for this project is at the series rather than the file-title level. The series are placed within an overall organization scheme before being assigned the control numbers that will fix their location in the registers, guides, and checklists generated from the project's data base. The index will be cataloger-produced rather than created from keywords in existing series titles and descriptions, since another project goal is to explore the use of common terminology for certain topics and record types common to the public records of many states. The cooperating institutions record, in a standardized format, as much or as little data as their finding aids offer, and send the data to the State Historical Society of Wisconsin for computer input and manipulation. A prototype guide from the pilot stage of this project has been produced. The implementation stage, now in progess, will enter data on as many series as possible, permitting the creation of more comprehensive guides and checklists.

I think the most important thing we have learned from these two ventures is that an automated finding aid system and a manual system are not two independent entities. They are inextricably linked. The SPINDEX III training sessions stress, and our own experience has confirmed, that a poor manual system cannot be transformed into a good automated system. In fact, an automated system should be planned as though it were going to be a manual one, exploring where and why automation will be beneficial, and how the system should be structured to facilitate it. An automated system should enhance or perhaps replace a viable manual system, not attempt to compensate for the deficiencies of an inadequate one. If anything, it must be even more simple, more straightforward, more obvious. Automation, though it tolerates wide variance in data, does not tolerate idiosyncrasy.

Our current finding aid system evolved in part out of this understanding, and in part out of the realization that the one-place narrative inventory suffered in its own way from the same deficiency as did the piecemeal file approach: lack of summary, absence of context. The system is now grounded in two interrelated principles: basic bibliographic control over all collections, and a "building-block" approach to inventories. Both principles start at the accessioning process and carry through to the final inventory for a fully processed collection.

As a collection is accessioned, a main entry including title, date span, and quantity is established; a preliminary scope and content statement is drafted; and a summary list or description of box contents is prepared. If necessary, enough time is invested in organizing the papers to ensure that the contents of each box can be defined and recorded somehow. Accuracy will be compromised at this stage, if necessary to maintain the accessioning momentum. The emphasis on basic controls reflects a paramount institutional priority: never should there be anything in our possession for which we cannot produce the information needed to identify it and its components, and to service it for the donors and the public. Also, incidentally, it helps remove a psychological burden when the backlog is no longer the unprocessed unknown but represents the first stage in a processing continuum.

Processing refines the principle embodied in the accessioning process: maximum accessibility gained as straightforwardly as possible. Inventories, especially for larger collections, are structured in progressive levels of detail, one leading into the other. Biographical or historical data and an improved scope and content note, followed by a summary box list and perhaps brief series summaries, introduce the collection and provide an overview that a user can scan quickly to judge whether it may be pertinent to the user's research. These can then be supplemented, as needed, by more detailed series descriptions, folder or file lists (selectively annotated with content notes), special lists, or citations to specific items. Description of a long run of chronologically arranged papers can be subdivided by date spans or other appropriate segments, or a general description can be followed by references to more diverse materials. Data sheets, originally intended for SPINDEX II input, now supplement some inventories as a way of recording a great deal of detail about individual folder contents, without cluttering up the main inventory.

Presenting the collection in identifiable units, and visually distinguishing the summary portions of the inventory, offer the researcher ready access to information about particular parts of the collection without burdening that researcher with irrelevant detail. Preparation of the inventory can stop, if necessary, at any level and still yield a cohesive finding aid. The archivist has considerable flexibility in selecting descriptive alternatives and depths of analysis appropriate to each collection. The format also tolerates personal predilections and differing degrees of skill and experience among processors.

We found that conscious adoption of these two principles offered a perspective on finding aids in general. Do calendars, for instance, or lengthy folder-by-folder descriptions, provide a refuge from the need to summarize and thereby omit precious specifics? Have we been writing narratives more for their literary qualities than for functional use? Will users think us any more sophisticated because we produce either literary or endlessly detailed inventories? Scope notes, box lists, and annotations, especially for larger or more homogeneous collections, can be just as informative, simpler to prepare, and easier to scan. Use of these devices does not lessen the amount of analysis time or intellectual effort on the part of the archivist, but does offer a format whereby all of this input can be channeled toward recording information instead of being devoted to the construction of narratives or the repetition of bibliographic details.

A format that uses scope notes and series summaries to reflect the essence of a collection encourages the archivist to view the papers as a whole and to develop a concise statement of vital information that can stand independent of subsequent details. Compartmentalizing the inventories makes it possible to view them as being readily updatable, as dynamic rather than static. Revisions or additions can be made at any point and only affect a page or two. Detailed lists and appendixes, should they prove useful, can be inserted at any time without requiring that the rest of the inventory be redone. If inventories are prepared in a looseleaf format, such modification becomes a routine part of an ongoing program of finding aid maintenance and improvement. In fact, once we had become comfortable with the concepts of basic controls and levels of detail, we realized that a single finding aid system could accommodate wide disparities in information for both processed and unprocessed collections, since the system is readily updated by replacing preliminary inventories and card sets with more detailed ones.

Other considerations of inventory construction follow naturally. Inventories should be predictable, with the same basic elements having roughly the same relationships from inventory to inventory. Inventories should be easy to scan visually and refer to, with generous use of subheads, section breaks, indentations, and lists. The physical layout of inventories should help ensure that basic data are consistently recorded, by providing definite places where such data belong and where their absence will be conspicuous. Standard formats (of headings, for example), where the required elements can be formalized, help encourage precision and accuracy at crucial points. Dates and quantities should be a part of all entries, so that the reader does not have to guess.

An inventory that is seen as the core of a control system becomes the single place where a researcher can find all of the recorded information about a collection. Other types of finding aids—compiled guides and subject lists on the one hand, card catalogs or analogous repository indexes on the other—find their places in the system by linking with this core. A subject guide, for instance, should not contain information that cannot also be found in the inventory. Catalog entries should not be used in lieu of inventory references to authors and subjects.

Seeing the inventory as the system's core helps also to define the role of a repository index (in our case a card catalog), which becomes more clearly an index to all of the inventories rather than an independent descriptive medium or a means of direct access into the papers. Catalog entries are derived from information in the completed inventory, and nothing appears in the catalog that is not mentioned and placed in context in the inventory to which it refers. We have found that the ease and flexibility of preparing and maintaining a card catalog are enhanced if its use is limited to this primary function and it is not expected to offer more extensive or varied information than its format can accommodate.

A card catalog shares a particular advantage with the compartmentalized inventory: because it comes in small segments, one reference on a card, it can readily be updated or expanded by replacing or adding cards. The cards of one collection need not look exactly like those of another, and outmoded cards need not be replaced every time a change in format is made.

Also, use of a repository index as an access medium reinforces the need to characterize each collection in a way that will clearly distinguish it from all others. For manuscripts, this is done through a distinctive title, usually combined with a catalog number. For archival records, we have established a hierarchical record group/subgroup/series/file identification that can, if necessary, be expressed alpha-numerically. Although a card catalog can accommodate lengthy collection or series titles, other types of indexes become unwieldy unless titles can be converted to symbols of some sort. This is of crucial importance when we contemplate an automation project that will require reliance on unique collection or series control numbers for manipulation of data elements.

The aim of our finding aid system is to enable us to peel off information at any point and have self-contained input for a variety of potential information systems, manual or automated, in-house or otherwise: catalogs, guides, indexes, shelflists, bibliographies, checklists, central reference services. Contemplating the requirements of automation helps reinforce this approach, for a viable automated system is structured; deals with identifiable units; requires that certain pieces of data be found in certain places, recorded in a standardized manner; does not readily accommodate long narratives; is oriented toward the discrete and specific; and takes no account of literary style or nuances.

Having developed our finding aid system this far, we now know what we need that a manual system cannot give us. These needs all go beyond what can be accommodated by more traditional finding aid formats and procedures: (1) updatability of *compiled* finding aids (as opposed to individual inventories), particularly of checklists to public records, special subject lists, microfilm sale lists, and similar consolidated reference tools that should be updated regularly; (2) effective subject access to bodies of records (railroad and public records, for example) that are hierarchically arranged and often interrelated in such a way that individual series cannot be assigned discrete names and catalog numbers; in other words, they cannot be handled readily or comprehensibly by a standard dictionary catalog; (3) subject access to random files, such as numbered subject files or related files from several series or collections; and (4) linkage with data in other institutions.

In coming full circle to a second computerization project, we have what we hope is a better grasp of our priorities, our capabilities, our needs, and the way we would like to see those needs addressed. Without a manual system that helped us pinpoint them and judge their importance, we would probably never have come to this understanding.

The Preparation of Inventories at the National Archives

Edward E. Hill

his staff information paper contains instructions on the preparation of inventories, indi-
cating their purposes and scope, their organization and content, and
their style and format.

PURPOSE AND SCOPE

A records inventory is, as its name implies, a description, or listing,
of records that is designed to provide information on their character and
quantity. In it the character of records is defined in terms of their
arrangement, their administrative and functional origins, their types,
their inclusive dates, their content, and their relationships to other
records.

There are two series of published inventories—preliminary inventories and inventories. A preliminary inventory is considered to be provi-
sional in character. It is intended primarily for internal use, not only as
an initial finding aid but also as a means of establishing inventory control
for various administrative purposes over records that are part of the
National Archives of the United States. An inventory, as opposed to a
preliminary inventory, is prepared after the records have been analyzed
to determine their completeness, to eliminate disposable materials, and
to arrange and to describe in greater detail the remaining records. It is
particularly suitable for records of terminated agencies for which further
additions or disposals are not anticipated.

In content and form, preliminary inventories and inventories are
essentially the same. Except when noted, the discussion in this paper
applies to both.

Eventually an inventory should cover all the records in a record
group. Descriptions for major subgroups in a record group, such as the
records of one U.S. district court, should be entered into the system as
they are completed; sometimes it may be desirable to publish that part of
the inventory for a self-contained major subgroup as a preliminary
inventory. The parts must be carefully planned to permit coverage of all
the records in the record group without overlapping.

Reprinted from National Archives and Records Service Staff Information Paper 14, "The
Preparation of Inventories," (Washington: National Archives and Records Service, 1982),
with slight revisions by the author.

DESCRIPTION

Inventories of records that are part of the National Archives of the United States are now produced by computer, using the system known as NARS A-1. Older inventories prepared before the introduction of the computer system that are considered satisfactory are being entered into the system. Some of the computer-produced inventories will be edited and published as in the past; others will be available only as computer printouts, either on microfiche or on paper.

A major advantage of a computer-produced inventory over a published or processed one is that it can be kept current. Whenever new records are added to a record group, they are described for the NARS A-1 system. If there is an inventory, it is revised. If there is no inventory or there is an incomplete one, progress is made in compiling one. Other changes, such as disposals, transfers, remeasurements, and changes of record group may be recorded also.

The same kinds of information that appear in published inventories are also in NARS A-1 inventories. When no published inventory exists or an inventory is not current, this information can be retrieved on a printout and made available to the public. Also there is additional information that can be put on the right side of the printout for staff use. Every element in an inventory is assigned a control number that identifies its location in the inventory. Also the unit of physical custody and the location of the records on the shelves is recorded so that a location register can be provided. There are line numbers for ease in updating descriptions, and there is space for comments of various kinds.

CONTENT AND ORGANIZATION

An inventory should contain the essential facts that serve to identify and describe the records. These facts should be provided in an introduction in which the origin, or provenance, of the record group as a whole is analyzed; subgroup sections, with introductions when appropriate, for administrative units of the creating agency or for records relating to some function, activity, or subject; and entries in which identifiable units of records (series) are described. Appendixes containing readily available information on the content, arrangement, or history of the records may be appropriate; for longer, more complex inventories, an index is useful. Published inventories have a table of contents, which presents in outline form all the main and subordinate headings. They also have a title page, a page for Library of Congress cataloging data, a foreword, and a preface, all of which are discussed in the section on format and style.

GENERAL INTRODUCTION

The purpose of the general introduction is to describe and identify the record group as a whole. It should contain general information on the administrative origins of the record group, the functions reflected, and, if helpful, the types of records in the record group, their organization, and their relationships to other records.

Most record groups are for the records of a single agency or other unit and, if the records are present, its predecessors. The introduction should provide information on the history of the organizational unit that created or assembled the records, showing the unit's predecessors and its authorization and establishment by law, Executive order, or other means; its major functions; and its major subdivisions under which the series within the record group are described. A breakdown of the organizational structure beyond the major subdivisions usually is unnecessary in the general introduction. Detailed information on administrative origins and functions should be included, when needed, in the main body of the inventory, either in subgroup level introductory statements for the particular units or in entries for series of records to which such information relates. Do not include in the general introduction minor details of organizational development not essential to an understanding of the historical origins of the record group or any of its series.

If the record group includes records of predecessor units, the amount of information about them in the introduction depends on how their records were handled. If there are still identifiable series of records of a predecessor unit, detailed information should be in a subgroup introduction for the descriptions of those records. If, however, the records of the predecessor unit were merged with those of the successor agency, information about the predecessor unit should be in the general introduction. Sometimes a record group includes records of units related to but not subordinate to a major unit, such as the records of the Committee of Special Advisors on Reclamation, which are among the records of the Bureau of Reclamation. Mention these related units only briefly in the general introduction, explaining why their records are included in the record group, and provide most of the information in the subgroup-level introductory or appropriate series description.

For collective record groups, which include the records of a number of separate units that are related only by some similarity of function (for example, claims commissions) or common origin (for example, Presidential commissions), the general introduction may be only a brief description of the general nature of the record group and its organization. This type of record group particularly lends itself to published preliminary inventories for subgroups.

A standard paragraph in introductions gives the broad subject and specific cutoff date of the inventory, the volume of records, the title of the record group, and, if desired, the overall dates of the records. For example:

DESCRIPTION

The records described in this inventory are those of the government of the District of Columbia that were in the National Archives of the United States as of April 1, 1974. They amount to 35.70 cubic meters and are designated as Records of the Government of the District of Columbia, Record Group 351.

Other information on the content and organization of the records and the recordkeeping practices of the agency also may be included. Avoid, however, merely summarizing the table of contents.

Give references to related records in other record groups or outside the National Archives. Some brief indication of the nature of the relationship should be given:

More recent records of estimates of Government receipts and expenditures are in Records of the Office of Management and Budget, Record Group 51.

Bibliographical citations also may be given.

Information about general or specific restrictions may be included in the general introduction, introductions to subgroups, or series descriptions, depending on how broadly they apply.

In the last paragraph, if applicable, explain collective authorship and acknowledge other persons who contributed. For published inventories give the name of the editor. For example:

This inventory was compiled by John Adams and revised by Thomas Jefferson. Gilbert Stuart prepared the entries for the audio-visual records. The editor was Benjamin Franklin.

A list of names of the heads of the agency (with dates of appointment) is often placed at the end of the introduction, or it can be an appendix. Organization charts can be used to illustrate the introduction or can be placed in an appendix.

Introductory statements should be strictly objective and factual in content and should be organized in some coherent system, which will vary according to the nature of the particular record group. The following outline is intended as a suggestion only:

I. History and functions of the administrative unit
    1. Predecessors
    2. Authorization and establishment by law, Executive order, or other means
    3. Functions
    4. Organization by major groups or functions

II. Records
    1. Analysis by types and major groups (units or functions)
    2. Arrangement

3. Relationships to other records
   a. Within the National Archives of the United States
   b. Outside the National Archives
4. Bibliographical citations
5. Restrictions

III. Acknowledgments

IV. List of agency heads

SUBGROUP INTRODUCTIONS

Introductions for subgroups should be used whenever appropriate. There are no fixed requirements for contents; include only what is needed to understand and use the records. The information should not be duplicated in the general introduction or in series descriptions. Information that may be appropriate includes the administrative history of the subordinate unit or function, explanation of the process of the creation of the records, applicable restrictions, citations of microfilm publications, and cross-references to related records.

SERIES ENTRIES

The normal unit of entry for all National Archives inventories is the series. A series usually is established at the time documents are filed in it by the originating office and, unless afterward rearranged or disarranged, is usually maintained in its original order. In most cases the series consists of documents, volumes, folders, or dossiers arranged in some serial order, such as alphabetical, numerical, or chronological. In other cases a body of records is designated as a series because of some unifying characteristic other than serial order; usually such records were kept together because they are about a particular subject or activity, were kept by a particular office or unit, or are of a particular type or form. Even these series, however, usually have some sort of arrangement pattern. If there are a number of disparate items, they may be described under such a title as MISCELLANEOUS RECORDS; however, this should be avoided as much as possible. Sometimes such items have merely become separated from other series and should be returned to their proper places. It is usually better to have one series contain a folder or two that do not fit the pattern of the series and call attention to this fact in the description rather than to have numerous small series of such items.

There are a variety of ways to determine the originating office of a series. Often there are endorsements or stamps to indicate the receipt of documents. Names of persons to whom they were routed may be written on them, or carbon copies may be marked to show the recipient. File

DESCRIPTION

markings and backstrips of volumes may give clues. Even such minor things as the color of labels for folder headings or the style of typing or writing may help. Indexes, registers, dockets, and other finding aids may indicate the office. Sometimes clerks or typists put their initials on documents. The subject or nature of the records may be of some use.

Title Entries

The title entry for each series must have an entry number, a title, the inclusive dates of the records, and a quantity statement. An example of a complete title entry as it appears on a printout is:

221. RECORDS RELATING TO DEFENSE TRAINING COURSES.
    1941-1942   30 cm, 1 ft.

In a published inventory it would be slightly different:

221. RECORDS RELATING TO DEFENSE TRAINING COURSES.
    1941-42. 30 cm, 1 ft.

Ideally entry numbers should be in a straight numerical sequence. If there are 36 entries, they should be numbered from 1 to 36. In practice, however, this cannot always be done. If a new entry is inserted between two previously existing entries, a letter of the alphabet should be appended to the number for the first entry, for example, 22a. If additional entries are inserted at this point, continue through the alphabet to 22z and then start a new alphabetical sequence, 22aa, 22ab, etc. If series are disposed, there may be gaps in the numbers. Before an inventory is published, however, the entries should be renumbered in a straight numerical sequence.

Titles should be as specific, distinctive, and descriptive as possible. The title used by the agency may be used as a series title if it is appropriate or if it has special significance. The Bureau of Indian Affairs, for example, used the term "special files" for a distinct series consisting principally of letters relating to some subject drawn from the general series of letters received by the Bureau. The term was used consistently on endorsements, in registers, and on cross-reference sheets; it is well known by persons doing research in the records; and the term itself connotes a gathering of related records. Agency titles that are incorrect (such as calling a register an index), jargon ("flat files," "E" wires, RAC licenses), or vague ("subject files") should be avoided if possible. When not using the agency title will cause confusion (if, for example, it appears on the backstrips of volumes), it may be added to the devised title as an alternate title in parentheses and with quotation marks or it can be explained in the series description.

All titles should have an indication of the type or types of records. If there are more than a few types it may be necessary to use such general terms as "central files" or simply "records." "Type" denotes form and use; below is a list of many of the more common types identified in existing inventories.

abstracts	drawings	photographs
aerial photographs	endorsements	plans
affidavits	estimates	plats
agreements	exhibits	posters
announcements	filmstrips	powers of attorney
applications	graphs	proceedings
architectural drawings	histories	publications
authorizations	indentures	questionnaires
awards	indexes	receipts
bids	instructions	registers
bills	inventories	regulations
bonds	issuances	releases
books	journals	reports
briefs	judgments	resolutions
bulletins	ledgers	returns
certificates	letters	rolls
charts	lists	rosters
circulars	logs	schedules
clippings	manifests	slides
commissions	maps	sound recordings
computer tapes	memorandums	specifications
contracts	memorials	speeches
correspondence	messages	statements
cross-reference	minutes	subpoenas
daybooks	motion pictures	summaries
decisions	newsletters	tables
deeds	notes	telegrams
depositions	notices	tickets
despatches	notifications	transcripts
diaries	opinions	video recordings
digests	orders	vouchers
directives	patents	warrants
discharges	payrolls	writs
dockets	petitions	

There are many other types of records, often of a technical nature, such as the various types of legal documents found in files for court cases. As much as possible, use nontechnical language. If it is necessary to use terms that a person untrained in the particular technology is unlikely to know, explain these terms in introductions, series descriptions, or a glossary.

DESCRIPTION

Be careful to distinguish between types of records and processes, activities, etc. The impeachment of Andrew Johnson was a process, not a type of document. The series title might be:

RECORDS CONCERNING THE IMPEACHMENT OF ANDREW JOHNSON.

Statistics are not documents but information found in documents—tables, reports, etc. The title of a report, motion picture, or other record is not necessarily an adequate series title. BRUSSELS WORLD'S FAIR or BROADCASTING STATIONS OF THE WORLD, for example, are incomplete titles because they do not indicate any type of record. Instead use:

MOTION PICTURES OF THE BRUSSELS WORLD'S FAIR.
REPORTS CONCERNING BROADCASTING STATIONS OF THE WORLD.

There are cases in which the distinction between types of records and activities is not too clear. A person filing a claim, for instance, might conceivably submit a document called a claim. More likely, however, the person will submit a number of documents supporting the claim, thereby making the claim a process rather than a type of record. Similarly, it is best to consider an appointment as an action and the document created by it as a certification (or notification) of appointment.

Be as specific as possible in identifying types of records. Do not use "records" if they are all or predominantly of one or two types. If a series consists mostly of one or a few types of records but there are also some other types, use the principal types in the title and explain in the description:

Included are some tables and charts.

Do not use redundant or superfluous words. The title GENERAL CORRESPONDENCE is enough; GENERAL CORRESPONDENCE FILES is unnecessary and even GENERAL is not needed if there are no specific correspondence series. "Files" should not be used alone, even when there is no other indication of type of record in the title; use CASE FILES or CENTRAL FILES. Avoid the term "materials" as a synonym for records and use MISCELLANEOUS as little as possible.

After determining the type or types of records, consider other characteristics that will help distinguish a particular series from other series. Some of these characteristics are administrative origins of the series, functions of the originating unit, subject matter, and frequency of serial documents. Any one of these or a combination may be used as part of the series title, but, as much as possible, avoid repeating information. If a subgroup heading is RECORDS OF THE ALASKA DIVISION, for a series title use LETTERS SENT, not LETTERS SENT BY THE

ALASKA DIVISION. The title, however, may include nonrepetitive information that helps identify the office or official that performed the action reflected in the series:

ANNUAL REPORTS OF THE DIRECTOR.
CORRESPONDENCE OF OTIS A. SINGLETARY.
RECORDS OF THE OFFICE OF THE CHIEF CLERK.

Samples of titles that provide information on functions are:

PRICE DETERMINATION CASE FILES.
CORRESPONDENCE RELATING TO INVESTIGATIONS.

Reports might relate to inspections, surveys, or the progress of particular activities:

ROAD SURVEY REPORTS.
FINAL CONSTRUCTION REPORTS.
PROGRESS REPORTS ON WPA PROJECTS IN STATE AND LOCAL PARKS.

If the type of records is applications, the title might indicate that they are of a specific kind or that action was taken on them:

APPLICATIONS FOR PRICE ADJUSTMENTS.
DISAPPROVED APPLICATIONS.

Examples of titles that give information on subject matter content are:

REPORTS CONCERNING THE EUROPEAN CORN BORER.
FOREST FIRE REPORTS.
RECORDS CONCERNING FORMER STUDENTS.

The addressees or writers of documents may be specified in the title by office, occupation, position, name, or other identification:

RESOLUTIONS RECEIVED FROM THE SENATE.
LETTERS SENT TO BANKERS.
LETTERS RECEIVED FROM CUSTOMS COLLECTORS.
AFFIDAVITS OF PREEMPTION CLAIMANTS.
DIARY OF JOSEPH C. GREW.

Reports may be identified by indicating that they are narrative or statistical in character or that they were produced at annual, monthly, weekly, or other intervals:

NARRATIVE REPORTS.
ANNUAL STATISTICAL REPORTS.

DESCRIPTION

To titles such as these, information on administrative origins, functions, or subjects can be added for even fuller series identification:

SUPERINTENDENTS' ANNUAL NARRATIVE REPORTS.
ANNUAL NARRATIVE INSPECTION REPORTS.
MONTHLY STATISTICAL REPORTS ON TRACHOMA.

There has been some confusion about the term "correspondence." Properly, correspondence is letters exchanged. Inventories describing records to approximately 1900 use this term when there is both incoming and outgoing correspondence. If there is just one or the other, "letters sent" or "letters received" is used. In modern records systems adopted since 1900, correspondence is usually in the central files of the agency along with other types of records. It is usually best to identify these records by a title such as CENTRAL FILES or GENERAL RECORDS rather than CORRESPONDENCE.

Include information on the arrangement of a series in the title only if it helps indicate the substantive character of the records or helps distinguish the series from other series. Thus the title CHRONOLOGICAL CORRESPONDENCE, which distinguishes letters accumulated on a day-to-day basis for office reference from those filed as official, is a suitable series title. Ordinarily such terms as "decimal files," "alphabetical files," or "subject files," although used in the file unit of the agency that created the records, are not descriptive enough for a series title, and therefore a title must be devised. There have been agencies, however, that arranged similar records according to more than one filing system at the same time, and sometimes the use of these terms is needed to distinguish one such series from another.

The dates of creation or accumulation of records in a series are handled separately (see second paragraph following), but other dates may be made part of the title. They may be the dates of the subject matter of the records or they may be the dates of records used to produce finding aids or other material:

CORRESPONDENCE OF THE BOARD PERTAINING TO THE 8-HOUR-DAY CONTROVERSY OF 1916.

COMPUTER TAPES CONTAINING COUNTY AND STATE POVERTY STATISTICS EXTRACTED FROM THE 1970 CENSUS.

Use entry numbers as part of a title only when they are necessary to avoid long and complicated titles. Say INDEX TO LETTERS RECEIVED, for instance, not INDEX TO ENTRY 5, and include a cross-reference to the entry number(s) in the description.

Inclusive dates during which the accessioned records were produced or accumulated should be given as part of the title entry. On a computer printout the dates appear on the line below the title. In a published inventory they are immediately after the title. These dates are not necessarily the same as those of individual documents in the series. Documents in court case files, for instance, are dated by when they were created by or presented to the court, even though individual exhibits presented to the court may be of a much earlier date.

Put explanations of any gaps within the date span in the first paragraph of the description. Dates should be as specific as possible, to the month and day if this can be determined. If no dates can be determined, use "N.d."; if only one is missing, use a question mark for it. If only approximate dates can be determined, use "Ca." and years, no months or days.

The dates for a finding aid being described as a series should be those when it was prepared rather than those of the records it accompanies. The dates of the records may be made part of the title:

LISTS OF CONTENTS OF 1800-70 POPULATION SCHEDULES. 1901-3.

However, finding aids, such as registers, indexes, and dockets, that were part of a continuing records control system may be assumed to have the same dates as the records they control, even though work on them may have fallen behind sometimes.

Generally, it is best to use as broad a date span as possible without being seriously misleading. For series in which a few documents are dated earlier or later than the main body, use the narrower dates and explain in the first paragraph of the description that there are some earlier and later documents. This will avoid being misleading and also avoid the difficulty of determining the dates of the earliest and latest documents, especially when records are arranged according to a subject classification system. It is likely that earlier documents were incorporated into the series during the main period of creation of the series and that later documents were inquiries about business long since completed.

The quantity of records in the series should be indicated in linear terms, either in metric measurements or in feet and inches. Metric measurements are preferred except possibly when completing or revising an older inventory with measurements in feet and inches.

Arrangement and Narrative Description

The arrangement and narrative description is used to explain the character of the records in detail. Any information not given elsewhere in the inventory may be included. Usually two paragraphs will suffice, one for the arrangement statement and related information and the other for the description of content and related information. There is no objection, however, to dividing the content statement into several

221

DESCRIPTION

paragraphs. This may be particularly appropriate for bibliographic citations, citations to microfilm publications, and cross-references.

In the first paragraph any needed information may be given on the arrangement of the records, gaps in the records and other discrepancies, and finding aids prepared by the agency that are part of the series.

An arrangement statement is necessary except possibly when there is only one item or there are a few items that are individually named as part of the description. If no arrangement pattern can be discerned, say "Unarranged," but this should be avoided as much as possible. There is usually at least some sort of rudimentary arrangement; if not, perhaps one can be imposed.

The arrangement statement should be precise. "Arranged alphabetically" is not enough. Specify whether it is by correspondent, subject, place, agency, something other than these, or some combination. If the arrangement is not strictly alphabetical but, for instance, just by initial letter of surname, this should be explained.

"Arranged chronologically" by itself implies that the records are arranged chronologically by date of document or, for entries in a document, such as a journal or register, in order of entry. If there is some other chronological order, such as by date of receipt, this should be indicated. If the chronological order is not exact but only, for example, by year, month, or week, state this.

For a geographical arrangement indicate the kinds of places for which there are records and the geographical pattern that is used. Comparatively few series are arranged strictly geographically; plats, arranged by township and range, are one example. If records are arranged by region or district, there is likely to be some sort of geographical order. More frequently, however, records are arranged alphabetically by name of geographic unit or place.

Saying that records are arranged numerically means little. Presumably there was some system for the numbering, and the numbers were used primarily for identification. Often it is a chronological or alphabetical system:

Arranged by certificate number assigned in chronological order by date of issue.

Arranged by date of issue and numbered consecutively, from 1 to 658.

Arranged by claim number, which was assigned in alphabetical order by name of claimant.

If there is a numerical subject classification system, the records are arranged by subject and numbers represent specific kinds of subjects, such as geographic areas, industries, or occupations. There may be a coding system: arranged in numerical sequence by state code, thereun-

222

der by race code, and thereunder by county code. If the logic of the numbering cannot be determined, at least try to name whatever is represented by the numbers:

Arranged by project number.

If the records are arranged by a classification system, at a minimum say what kind of a system it is and, if possible, indicate where a copy of the classification system may be found. Some of the major headings may be indicated, although often this fits better later in the description. For more important series consider using a list of headings (either complete or select) as an appendix. Most classification systems are by subject and perhaps partly by type of record, and there usually is a predetermined pattern with classifications identified by number or letter of the alphabet or some combination. Decimal systems are one of the most popular numbering techniques. Sometimes, however, there is no real pattern; the next number or other identification was assigned to each new subject heading established.

There is little point in giving just the first and last classifications with no indication of what comes between (arranged by an alphabetical-numerical subject classification scheme beginning with A-1, Animals, and ending with Z-8, Minerals). If a system is widely used, such as the War Department decimal classification system, or at least is used for a number of series, show how it was used for the particular series. Are certain headings used more than usual or were adaptations made for the particular records?

Some series are arranged by subject or by type of record or a combination but in no apparent order; this is often the case with office files of officials.

Records often have more than one level of arrangement, especially records arranged according to a classification system. At a minimum the records under any one classification should be arranged in some order, often but not always chronological. Records under different headings may be arranged in different ways. The classification system may not even be the primary arrangement:

Arranged alphabetically by park and thereunder according to a decimal classification system. Within each decimal classification the records are often subdivided by more specific subjects or names of individuals, States, government agencies, or other appropriate headings, most frequently, in alphabetical order. Within individual headings and subheadings, documents are usually in chronological order.

Indicate all levels of arrangement. The amount of detail that should be included will depend in large part on the importance and size of the series. Another factor is how widely the system is used. It usually is not necessary to go into detail on a commonly used system, such as the War Department decimal classification system. A system unique to one agency and perhaps used for only one series may require an elaborate explanation.

Note exceptions to and variations in the arrangement:

The letters are arranged for the most part chronologically but sometimes those received from one person during a calendar year are grouped together with the first one received.

Arranged alphabetically by initial letter of surname for the period 1877-81, with the entries for 1882 and 1883 appended at the end of the schedule.

Sometimes it may be appropriate to refer to the physical form in the arrangement statement:

Arranged chronologically in three binders.

Explain any gaps and apparent discrepancies in the dates, such as when there are documents dated before or after most of the records or when records accumulated by a unit during certain years were created by someone else earlier—items in a reference collection, for example. Explain any other gaps in the records:

There are no records for the letters A-D.

No records were preserved for the following decimal classifications . . .

Some of the maps and fieldbooks were destroyed by fire in April 1948.

The volume is labeled "Journal B," but no other journals have been found.

Cite finding aids that are part of the series, such as indexes in the fronts of volumes or a list of file headings at the beginning of the series:

Each volume is indexed by name of school.

The first map serves as an index to the other maps.

Finding aids that are a separate series or are nonrecord should be mentioned later.

Usually information on the types of records is given at the beginning of the second paragraph, although this position may need to be used to provide information on the administrative origins of the records if it is important and has not appeared in the appropriate introductory:

This commission was created by an act of Congress dated July 15, 1870 (16 Stat. 309), and was composed of the Mayor of the city of Washington, the Secretary of the Interior, the Commission of Public Buildings and Grounds, the Architect of the Capitol Extension, and two men appointed by the Mayor with the advice and consent of the Board of Aldermen. The commission was to undertake the dredging of the canal, or, if it deemed best, the arching of the canal to convert it into a sewer.

If the title line uses RECORDS or some other general term, list the main types of records in the series:

Correspondence, memorandums, narrative and statistical reports, tables, schedules, procedural issuances, photographs, and other records.

Indentures (chiefly deeds for assignments of shares of stock), contracts, resolutions, legal opinions, court judgments, notes for loans, lottery tickets, copies of legislative bills, and other records.

Chiefly reports, but include minutes of staff meetings, issuances, directives, newspaper clippings, copies of speeches, transcripts of telephone calls, and correspondence.

A typical case file contains copies of the loan application, the report of an engineering survey, the loan brief, a letter of January 25, 1946, pertaining to the cancellation of the loan or cancellation of the authority to execute the participation agreement in the loan, and related correspondence.

List the types of records in some logical order. Common ways are to put them in the order of quantity or importance or a combination of the two. It may also be chronological in the order in which a sequence of documents was usually created or accumulated:

Subpoenas, transcripts of testimony, opinions of the boards, and decisions of the Secretary.

Try to put similar or related types of records together and avoid listing a general type of record in one place and more specific examples of the same type somewhere else. Instead say:

Progress and other reports.

Annual, monthly, and weekly narrative reports.

If a specific type of record is named in the title, try to avoid the same terminology in the description. If the title uses CORRESPONDENCE, the description might say:

Letters received and letters sent.

For ROSTER OF EMPLOYEES:

A list of employees in local offices.

The description of types can be an appropriate place for information on the physical form and related peculiarities of the records if it is not repetitive:

225

DESCRIPTION

Index on 3- by 5-inch cards.

Printed copies of congressional hearings . . .

Minutes of meetings of the stockholders in a volume labeled "Letter Book A."

The description of types may also be an appropriate place for information on the administrative origins of the series not given in the title:

Reports of school social workers.

Carbon copies of letters signed by the Secretary of the Treasury or an Assistant Secretary in reply to inquiries regarding . . .

A narrative report, with . . . . The survey was made under the direction of the U.S. Public Health Service.

This is the report of Special Agent John Hutchins, who had been assigned to investigate the charges made against Deputy Collector of Customs William C. Gray.

Frequently there is information on the functions, activities, and other subjects reflected in the records. It is not necessary to separate such information from types of records. Sometimes subjects may be identified with a particular type:

The records consist of affidavits of witnesses concerning the disputed ownership of cotton, opinions of Treasury officials on the validity of claims, and claimants' petitions for the proceeds of cotton sold.

The content information can be an elaboration of the title:

REPORT ON EMIGRATION.

. . . .

The report was concerned with 2,000 families expected to emigrate to northeastern North America and contains information on the area.

SURVEY JOURNALS.

. . . .

The journals consist of narrative accounts of the boundary surveys conducted and of the organization and progress of the survey teams.

This kind of information can be a listing, either in the same sentence with the types of records or in a separate sentence:

Correspondence, memorandums, legal opinions, maps, agreements, and related records pertaining to activities and problems of borrower cooperatives.

Affidavits, petitions, powers of attorney, and other records concerning individual claims presented to the commissioners.

Annual, semiannual, and monthly statistical reports on standard forms. They concern medical work done outside agency or school hospital buildings or attached dispensaries, and they give information concerning calls, treatments, births, deaths, diseases treated, examinations, and laboratory tests.

Even if the series is limited to one function activity, or subject, it is often advisable to provide more specific information than is given in the title:

RECORDS RECEIVED RELATING TO THE CONSTRUCTION OF CANALS.

. . . .

relating to the construction of the Alexandria, Chesapeake and Ohio, Dismal Swamp, Louisville-Portland, and Norfolk canals.

LETTERS RECEIVED CONCERNING MUSKOGEE TOWNSITE.

. . . .

The letters relate to the appraisal of lots, disposal of Indian homesteads to be added to the townsite, individual claims, investigations of fraud, and other pertinent subjects.

The subjects may be geographical place names:

There are reports for the following States: Alabama, California, Indiana . . .

If the title sufficiently identifies the type of record, the description may begin with information on content. This is especially true for such records as registers, indexes, and lists:

REGISTER OF U.S. DEPOSITORIES.

. . . .

The entries give name of the bank, the amount of its capital and securities, and the names of its principal depositors.

Often, particularly with correspondence, it is desirable to name writers and addressees, either individually or in groups:

Letters to Members of Congress, Chairmen of the Senate and House Committees on the District of Columbia, heads of Federal agencies, heads of local departments of government, attorneys, businessmen, and others.

Copies of notes exchanged between the Department of State and the British Embassy at Washington and copies of instructions to and despatches from the U.S. ambassador at London relating to . . .

If there are numerous subjects, just as with types of records, they should be grouped in some logical order. Most often this means going from the most important to the least important in terms of significance or quantity or both. There should be an attempt to keep related subject areas together. Do not, for example, say:

227

DESCRIPTION

> ... issuing of checks, bids for furnishing coin bags, outstanding checks, remittances of penalties, security bonds, and other matters concerning checks.

Put everything about checks together:

> ... issuing of checks, outstanding checks, and other matters concerning checks; bids for furnishing coin bags; ...

Subjects can also be listed in the order of a files system or a listing of subject headings (these can instead be put in a separate appendix). They may follow the order in which the information is given in the entries of a register. At other times, particularly for activities, there may be a chronological order:

> ... relating to applications for enrollment, investigations, consideration by the committee, its decisions, and notification of the applicant.

If there are a number of similar series of well-known types of records—payrolls, for instance—or if there are similar series within the same record group for different administrative units which usually kept the same types of records relating to the same subject, sometimes only the arrangement statement may be necessary.

Series descriptions should emphasize the essence or typical character of the records rather than unusual items. Occasionally, however, it is advisable to note a document or information that has particular significance or that one might not expect to find:

> Some of the principals involved were Samuel Colt, Rudyard Kipling, Oscar Hammerstein, and the Sultan of Turkey.

> The documents of conveyance, assignment, and surrender of the charter to the Chesapeake and Ohio Canal Co. are among the records.

> Included with the letters are drafts of a convention relating to the Alaskan boundary line.

Cite microfilm publications when applicable:

> This volume has been reproduced by the National Archives and Records Service as part of Microfilm Publication M605, *Records of the City of Georgetown (D.C.), 1800-79.*

> This volume has been reproduced as NARS Microfilm Publication M142, *Letter Book of the Arkansas Trading House, 1805-1810.*

The title of the microfilm publication may be omitted if it is identical to the series title under which it is cited or so nearly the same as to be redundant. If a microfilm publication includes an entire subgroup or numerous series of a subgroup, the title of the publication need be given only in a subgroup introduction. If there are many microfilm publications, consider listing them in an appendix. City any other publications:

> Most of these papers have been printed in volume 5 of *Papers Relating to the Treaty of Washington* (Washington, Government Printing Office, 1872).

Cite any finding aid that is not part of the series. If it is another series, give a cross-reference; if it is nonrecord, give some indication of its form and availability. Also give cross-references, if readily available, to any other closely related records in another series or another record group or outside the National Archives, indicating the nature of the relationship. In cross-references do not confuse entries (i.e., descriptions of the records) with the records. Do not say:

> The letters registered in the volume are also registered in entry (or series) 198.

Instead say:

> The letters registered in this volume are also registered in the main series of registers of letters received (entry 198).

> There are other accounting records among the letters received described in entry 3.

> There does not appear to be any duplication of the resolutions described in entries 131 and 132.

For the sake of brevity, however, it is acceptable to give only an identification of the records and the entry number when the intention is to refer to the series description:

> For a register of the letters, see entry 28.

Even though strictly speaking the reference should be:

> For a description of a register of the letters, see entry 28.

An example of a cross-reference to related records other than finding aids in the same record group is:

> There are allotment schedules for the Indians of Michigan among the records described in entry 343.

Examples of references to records not in the same record group are:

> Additional records of the New York customhouse are in the records of the U.S. Customs Service, Record Group 36.

DESCRIPTION

The George A. Trenholm papers and the Confederate States of America collection in the Library of Congress also contain letters received by the Secretaries of the Treasury.

Descriptions at the subseries level are unusual in inventories, but if any are prepared, they should follow the pattern for series descriptions.

Grouping Series

A logical scheme for grouping the series within the record group should be devised for most inventories. The scheme should be chosen that is best suited to show the character and significance of series while minimizing the necessity for changes in the scheme to accommodate later accessions. It is possible to use one or a combination of the following schemes: organizational, functional, chronological, or geographical, or according to type of records. In practice most of the more complicated inventories that have been done use a combination of methods, and there are small inventories in which there is no grouping of series.

The organizational method of grouping series is preferred when it is practicable; it has been used in most past inventories at least in part. When there are frequent reorganizations, it may be feasible only in combination with a chronological or some other scheme. Series normally should be described with reference to the administrative units that created them. Under an organizational method the series are grouped to reflect the hierarchical levels within the agency, such as the bureaus, divisions, branches, and sections. If there are general records of the agency, in most cases they should be described first. Such records were usually kept in a mail and files unit, but they should not be considered as records of that unit if they relate to the business of the agency as a whole. Records of high officials, such as Cabinet secretaries, bureau chiefs, and their principal assistants, usually come next; however, there are cases when they might be considered more significant than the general records. The records of the commissioners of a regulatory commission documenting their decisions, for example, might be regarded as more important than the general records of the agency that assists the commissioners in arriving at their decisions. Next come the records of the subdivisions of the agency. The major subdivisions may have subordinate units at several lower levels. Divisions may be divided into branches, which in turn are divided into sections. Headquarters records precede field office records, and records of antecedent units precede those of their successors if they have been maintained as a separate entity. If records of units that are related to but not part of the principal agency are in the record group, they are usually described last.

It is best to start with the records of the units concerned with major program policy and functions and proceed to those with more strictly administrative duties, such as supplies and personnel. There are problems, however, with such units as offices of executive directors and administrative divisions that were concerned with both policymaking and low-level administrative matters; there has been some tendency to place them toward the top of the hierarchy. Many patterns can be used because it rarely is possible to rank the units in a precise order of importance.

Frequently there are complications resulting from reorganizations. One way of overcoming them is to base the hierarchy on that of the organization at a given date. An example of an inventory arranged according to the organization on a particular date is that for the records of the Smaller War Plants Corporation (PI 160).

The single date method works best with an agency with a short period of existence and limited functions. If a single date method is used for a terminated agency, the date is usually either that of the last organization or, if the agency was gradually dismantled, that of the last organization when it was at full strength. The organization of a unit in charge of terminating the affairs of an agency should not be used. For an agency still in operation, the hierarchy may be based on the current organization or the one in effect for the most recently accessioned records. The latter makes it more difficult to update the inventory when more records are accessioned.

Agencies of long duration and several reorganizations may sometimes be handled by establishing different hierarchies for different periods of time. This method is routinely used when there is a succession of agencies, with separate hierarchies established for each predecessor. See, for example, the inventory of the records of the Bureau of Agricultural and Industrial Chemistry (PI 149). It may also be used when adding to older inventories based on hierarchies that were appropriate at the time of compilation but that are obsolete for new accessions; it may be possible to establish a new hierarchy for the more recent records and keep the older hierarchy essentially unchanged for the older records.

A second way of solving the problems posed by reorganizations is to use a chronological pattern for the order of the organizational units within a hierarchy. The units may be arranged by date of establishment as is done in part in the preliminary inventory of the Washington headquarters records of the Bureau of Refugees, Freedmen, and Abandoned Lands (PI 174). Alternatively, they can be grouped to place related units together. This can be done in combination with a chronological order, as in the inventory of the records of the Bureau of Indian Affairs (PI 163), in which records of divisions that succeeded or were broken off from one of the original divisions are described following the records of that division.

DESCRIPTION

A second scheme for grouping series is a functional one. The series are described under the functions that brought about their creation. Frequently this is less difficult to establish than the organizations that created them. This is particularly true if functions remained relatively unchanged but there were many administrative reorganizations. The use of functional headings is illustrated in the inventory of the records of the Public Buildings Service (PI 110). Functional headings are more commonly used as lower level headings in an inventory hierarchy using units as major subheadings, although some of these lower level headings may be regarded more as activity or subject headings than as functional ones.

If the series cannot be analyzed under organizational or functional headings, other methods of grouping them may be followed. In the inventory of the records of the House of Representatives (PI 113), the order is chronological; the series are arranged by Congress. The series may be in a geographical order as in the inventory of the records relating to international claims (PI 177). In the inventory of the records of the Solicitor of the Treasury (PI 171) they are by type of record. In the inventory of the records of the Office of the Chief Signal Officer (PI 155) there is a combination of chronological periods with types of records.

These methods may be combined at any hierarchical level in the inventory or within any subgroup. In the inventory of the records of the Bureau of Indian Affairs (PI 163), for instance, all the methods named above are used somewhere.

The practice of having separate sections for description of nontextual records when the rest of the inventory follows another pattern should be avoided. If possible, fit these records into the hierarchy used.

Order of Series

The order in which series should be identified and described under a given subgroup heading should follow a reasonably logical pattern, reflecting when appropriate the interrelationship of different series.

Entries for finding aids should precede the series for the records they serve. Indexes should come before registers or dockets. The discussion below includes any finding aids that accompany records even though they are not specifically mentioned.

Usually it is best to go from the general to the specific. First come series relating to the full range of functions and activities of an organizational or equivalent functional (or other) subgroup, followed by those relating to more specific activities or subjects. Typically, general correspondence series precede other series of a general nature. See the inventory of the records of the Bureau of Agricultural and Industrial Chemistry (PI 149) for examples of this kind of order. There are times, however, when other records are considered more basic than the general correspondence, either because of the particular importance of some other type of records, for example minutes or decisions, or because the general correspondence is comparatively inconsequential or incomplete. See pages 11 and 12 of the inventory of the records of the National Mediation Board (PI 179) for a subgroup in which case files are ranked above a small series of general correspondence.

When there are successive series of essentially the same records, such as general correspondence arranged according to different file systems for different periods of time, they should be put in chronological order.

Some form of chronological order is often used for the more specific entries in a subgroup. When the series are not particularly related to one another, they may be in order by the date of the earliest document in the series. This is done in PI 149, mentioned above. When the series are related, they may be put in the order in which a function was performed, going, for example, from applications to discharges. In the inventory of the records relating to international boundaries (PI 170), the order is generally that in which the boundary commissions did their work.

There may be an attempt to put specific series in order of importance. There is likely to be considerable difference of opinion on the ranking; however, it is generally agreed that series reflecting functions or activities should be placed before reference materials.

It also may be possible to arrange series by administrative hierarchy. This is most common when there are only one or two series of records each of comparatively low-level units that do not seem to warrant a subgroup heading.

APPENDIXES

Appendixes provide supplementary information about the administrative origins and history of the agency and records and about the contents of series. They can include lists (select or complete) of file classifications, subject headings, individual documents, projects or administrative units for which there are records on microfilm, and officials or other persons as well as organization charts, bibliographies, and glossaries. If an appendix relates to a subgroup or specific series, provide reciprocal cross-references. In general, appendixes should be provided for only the most important series, such as central files, and series with a high proportion of disparate items of particular interest, such as reports or publications.

INDEX

Indexes should be prepared only for larger, more complicated inventories. The general introductions, introductory statements for sub-

233

groups, and series descriptions should be indexed, but appendixes should not. Series descriptions should be indexed by entry number and introductory material by page number, which can be distinguished from an entry number by the use of the abbreviation "p." or by boldface type.

Index names, places, and subjects (including functions and activities), but not types of records. Try to avoid indexing under multiple headings. Instead of indexing expositions under both their individual names and the general term "expositions," index under the individual names of expositions and under "expositions" say:

Expositions, 22, 48, 79, p.129.

See also names of individual expositions.

For detailed instructions on indexing, consult *Indexing; Principles, Rules and Examples*, by Martha Thorne Wheeler, as revised by Janet M. Strube, Bulletin No. 1445, 5th ed. (Albany: New York State Library, 1957).

FORMAT AND STYLE

If an inventory is properly prepared for entry in the NARS A-1 system, the computer will take care of the format. A typical entry produced by the computer is as follows:

19. RECORDS RELATING TO THE INLAND WATERWAY SURVEY.
1942-1944   30 cm, 1 ft.

Arranged by subject and thereunder chronologically.

Mostly correspondence and memorandums, but there are also reports, maps, and newsclippings. They concern the 1943 survey of the Orinoco-Casinquiare Canal-Rio Negro waterway and were accumulated in the office of J. Stanton Robbins, Director of the Commercial and Financial Division. Other records relating to the survey are described in entry 32.

A somewhat different format for the title entry in published inventories has already been noted.

The National Archives follows the *U.S. Government Printing Office Style Manual* in all questions of capitalization, spelling, compound words, abbreviations, numerals, punctuation, and italics (underlining). Do not strive for variation in terminology; it is easier to understand descriptions if the same terms are used consistently. Avoid excessive use of abbreviations, particularly for names of lesser known administrative units. Within the general introduction and any subgroup, use the full name of well-known persons at least once and more often for lesser known persons.

Use complete sentences except for the first sentences of the arrangement and content paragraphs in a series entry:

Arranged chronologically.

Periodic lists showing the designations and locations of all Civilian Conservation Corps camps: . . .

Reports, correspondence, memorandums, maps, photographs, clippings, and other records. The records relate to the investigation of . . .

The Place of the Register in the Manuscripts Division of the Library of Congress

Katharine E. Brand

On page 7 of the preliminary "Rules for Descriptive Cataloging in the Library of Congress . . . for Collections of Manuscripts," which has recently been issued, there appears the following direction: "If the repository has on file an unpublished guide to the organization and content of the collection, this should be noted."

Well to the fore among such "unpublished guides" in the Library's Manuscripts Division is the register. This has become the very backbone of the Division's work in organizing collections of manuscripts for use. Its development, as was suggested in an article in the *American Archivist* for April 1953 has been gradual.[1] Registers were prepared, in the first instance, in order to maintain control over the Division's holdings and to aid the researcher in his use of material and the staff in replying to reference inquiries. Their use by readers and staff members has shown where improvements could be made. The labors of the Library's Committee on Manuscripts Cataloging over a 2-year period, and the rules which have emerged therefrom, have suggested other changes. The Division's experience both with the preparation and with the administrative use of registers has also resulted in valuable suggestions for revision. In consequence there have emerged, in fact, not only improvements in the register itself but also a new kind of instrument—the short-register, familiarly known in the Division as the "short form"—which is designed to control and describe material not sufficiently extensive or complex to warrant the preparation of a full-length register.

For each accession received in the Manuscripts Division, whether it be a single manuscript or a group of manuscripts, there is now prepared either a full-length register or a short-register. A collection of personal papers, being as a rule both extensive and complicated, is likely to be described in a full-length register. This is true also of a substantial collection of records of a nongovernmental organization. But a single manuscript, or a small group of manuscripts, or even a considerable group in one simple series is, in most cases, described by a short-register. The sample "John Doe" registers (appendixes I and II, below) will suggest

Reprinted with permission from *The American Archivist* 18 (January 1955): 59-67.

[1]Katharine E. Brand, "Developments in the Handling of Recent Manuscripts in the Library of Congress."

why this is so. The short-register consists of a mimeographed sheet, to be filled in by the processor; while the full-length register, which varies widely according to variations in the papers or records described, is prepared on plain sheets, according to a generally prescribed form and sequence to be sure, but without benefit of mimeographed headings. The same essential information, however, appears in both cases: title, accession number, date received, source, status, and so on. The information is assembled from various sources, one of the most important of which is the Division's case file, which consists, as its name implies, of case histories of manuscript holdings—that is, all the documents which have been created in the acquisition, custody, and reference use of each collection. When the register is completed, two copies go at once into the case file, one to bring the record up to date, the other to be available for interlibrary loan when donor restrictions permit.

In addition to their other uses, registers and short-registers are designed also to make necessary information quickly and easily available to the cataloger when the group cataloging of the vast holdings of the Manuscripts Division, according to the new rules, is begun.[2] In the full-length register, part I should furnish the cataloger with information necessary for establishing a main entry and title; physical description; location; reference to published descriptions and to indexes or other unpublished guides in the repository (of which the register itself is, of course, one); restrictions on access, if any; proprietorship of literary rights, when not dedicated to the public; and provenance. Parts III, IV, and V, or some combination of these, should furnish the information necessary for preparing added entries, references, and analyticals, for establishing the form of the document (if it is not original), and for writing scope and content notes. The short register should furnish the same information in capsule form.

The two deviate most widely in the description of the material itself. The register includes a carefully drawn description of series, a container list, and in many cases a partial list of correspondents, but in the short-register a very brief description usually suffices. This may take the form of a list of letters or other papers, with dates and in some cases content notes, or it may be a paragraph description if the material does not lend itself usefully to list treatment. In either case, significant names ad subjects are brought out in this section.

The form of registers and short-registers is, we think, extremely important, not at all because it purports to be the only correct method of procedure but because *some* established and standardized form is essential where so many different workers and so many different users are

[2]See Robert H. Land, "The National Union Catalog of Manuscript Collections," in *American Archivist*, 17:199 (July 1954).

involved. The form that has been developed is proving to be adaptable, reasonably easy to prepare if the necessary information has been assembled, and usable from the point of view of the reader who comes to it in search of information.

We who have worked with manuscripts and have prepared these registers find that they serve as a useful discipline in the task of processing the material. The worker engaged in organizing a difficult and complex collection of papers is often much helped by keeping well marshaled in his mind the various kinds of information he will need for the completion of a register. The biographical note, which is ordinarily prepared in rough at the outset of an extensive processing task, will, if a chaotic group of papers is concerned, help the processor to find his way through the labyrinth by suggesting what he ought to look for and identifying material about which he would otherwise be uncertain. When he comes upon what appear to be series or parts of series he must watch for their structure, remembering that he will need to know this in drafting his description of series. As he records, on rough working cards, the dossier headings in a developing subject file, he will be inclined to execute even these working cards in the prescribed form so that a container list can be typed, in part, directly from the cards. And when, after the organization of the papers is nearly completed, the processor begins the drafting of the register, it happens more often than not that he must return to his volumes and boxes, must recheck his folder headings and his shelf reading here and there, in order to supply all the information upon which the "John Doe" sample insists. Short registers deal, of course, with far less complicated groups of materials, but they, too, often serve as a kind of check that the processor himself applies to his own work.

We are well aware in the Library's Manuscripts Division—as what overburdened repository is not?—that processing depends on staff, and staff depends on funds. Occasionally, therefore, when interest in a large group of newly received material is unusually keen or when for some reason the papers must be used by readers before the staff has been able to complete their organization, it is necessary to do a partial processing job. In such cases we have experimented with the preparation of a partial register, that is to say, one which presents as much information as possible about the whole collection, in parts I and II, but which, in matters covered by the other parts, concerns only such of the papers as have actually been processed for service. This is a useful detour around a difficult situation, but we employ it only when we must, because it is dangerous. Such a partial register may, in spite of the fact that its incomplete character is carefully spelled out at the beginning, give the user a false sense of having sufficiently "covered" a group of papers; and it may tend also to give the Division itself an equally false sense of having completed a job! But if care is taken at both these danger spots, the partial register can at times serve a very useful purpose.

At all points it is necessary to emphasize, and emphasize again, the need for judgment. There are no hard-and-fast rules to cover every situation, much as one may wish there were. The "John Doe" whose papers are described in the sample registers obviously led an oversimplified life. The handling of his diaries, his general correspondence, his speech file, and the packet of papers assembled by his biographer is intended to *suggest* methods of handling similar and also other types of actual material in the papers of his flesh-and-blood counterparts. But this is a suggestion only. Every manuscript collection differs somewhat from every other manuscript collection. Although general principles and precedents that have been proved workable are of real help, nothing can relieve the manuscript worker from the necessity of using his own judgment. And nowhere is that more true than in the last and in some ways the most important step of all—the careful and intelligent recording, in properly prepared registers, of what has been done.

Two sample forms follow, both of which are now in use in the Manuscripts Division: a register; and a short-register. Both record the handling of the literary remains of that well-known and extremely useful figure, John Doe.

SAMPLE REGISTER

LIBRARY OF CONGRESS
MANUSCRIPTS DIVISION

[Form number]   *Processed by:* AJC
Revised 10/27/54   *Date:* 5-11-54

JOHN DOE PAPERS

Acs. _____; _____, _____
II-41-F, 4 to L, 3

The papers of John Doe, banker, cabinet member, and author, were deposited in the Library of Congress in 1930 and 1941 by Mrs. John Doe. In 1952 Mrs. Doe converted the deposit to a gift.

Linear feet of shelf space occupied: 110.5
Approximate number of items: 71,450*

For ten years, or during the lifetime of Mrs. John Doe, whichever period is shorter, the papers may be used only by permission of Mrs. Doe.

Literary rights in the unpublished writings of John Doe in these papers, and in other collections of papers in the custody of the Library of Congress, have been dedicated to the public, except that these literary rights are reserved to Mrs. John Doe during her lifetime.

A press release on the John Doe papers was issued by the Library of Congress on _____; a note appeared in the Library's *Information Bulletin*, _____; and the material was described on p. _____ of the Library of Congress *Quarterly Journal of Current Acquisitions,* _____ (Vol. __, No. __).

II. *Biographical Note*

1870   Born, Boston, Massachusetts
1891   B.A., Amherst College
1892-4   Harvard Law School
1895   Admitted to bar and began law practice, in Massachusetts
1900-12   President, Hamilton Bank, Boston, Massachusetts
1913-17   Secretary of the Treasury
1918-24   Chairman, Federal Reserve Board
1925   Died, Washington, D. C.

Author of: _____ . 1914
_____ . 1920

*A large group of pictures, mounted and unmounted, was transferred to the Library's Prints and Photographs Division; 16 maps to the Map Division; and 40 records of speeches to the Music Division. All of these are available for use without special permission.

*Contain-
ers*   *Series*

1-15   Diaries. 1891-Aug. 1925. 15 containers.
          In 32 bound volumes, chronologically arranged. The fol-
          lowing volumes are missing: 1899; 1920; 1921.

16-176   General Correspondence. 1896-1925. 161 containers.
          Letters sent and received. Chronologically arranged by
          months.

177-189   "Personal Correspondence." 1898-1925. 13 containers.
          Letters sent and received. Alphabetically arranged by
          names of correspondents.

190   "Personal Correspondence" of Mrs. John Doe. 1905-25. 1
          container.
          Mainly letters received. A few handwritten copies of letters
          sent are included. Chronologically arranged by days.

191-195   Material Relating to the Death of John Doe. 1925. 5 containers.
          Mainly letters received. Some newspaper clippings and sev-
          eral biographical articles are included. The clippings and arti-
          cles have been segregated, but otherwise there is no
          arrangement.

196-225   Subject File. ca. 1880-1925 [mainly 1891-1924]. 30 containers.
          Memoranda, reports, financial papers, maps, photographs,
          memorabilia, clippings, etc. All correspondence has been with-
          drawn and filed in the General Correspondence Series. The
          folders are alphabetically arranged by subject. There is little
          arrangement within folders.

226-250   Speech, Article and Book File. 1906-24. 25 containers.
          Handwritten, typewritten, near-print, and printed copies
          or drafts of speeches and articles; also manuscripts and galley
          proofs of John Doe's two books. Chronologically arranged.

251-253   Biographer's Papers. ca. 1925-30. 3 containers.
          Correspondence, notes, manuscripts, etc., relating to John
          Doe, assembled by Joe Doaks (who died in 1930 without having
          completed the biography of Doe). The correspondence has
          been separated, but otherwise there is no arrangement.

254-274   Scrapbooks. 1906-25. 21 containers.
          Clippings from newspapers and magazines, mounted in 26
          scrapbooks. The material relates to John Doe and his activities.
          The volumes are chronologically arranged, and there is general
          chronological arrangement within each volume.

IV. *Container List*

Nos.	_Contents_

226   Speech, Article and Book File. 1906-08
227   "   "   "   "   "   1909
228   "   "   "   "   "   1910-12
229   "   "   "   "   "   Jan.-June 1913
230   "   "   "   "   "   July-Dec. 1913
.
.
.
251-2   Biographer's Papers. Correspondence
253   "   "   Notes, Manuscript, etc.
254   Scrapbooks. 1906-07
255   "   1908
256   "   1909
.
.
.
274   "   1925

V. [Optional Section]*

Among the correspondents of John Doe are the following persons:

Calvin Coolidge	1923-24
Charles S. Hamlin	ca. 1906-20
Henry Cabot Lodge	ca. 1910-15
William G. McAdoo	ca. 1913-24
Elihu Root	1910-11
Woodrow Wilson	ca. 1913-23

Bases for Estimates
(for Staff use only)

Average number of items in letter-size metaledge container: 300
   "   "   "   "   " legal-size   "   "   300
   "   "   "   "   " 3-inch box-portfolio   150
Number of letter-size metaledge containers in 1 full press: 36
   "   " legal-size   "   "   " " "   "   30
   "   " 3-inch box-portfolios   " " "   "   32 [or, if
                                                              crowded,
                                                              36]

Number of linear feet per shelf: 2.42

*If more detailed information can be easily assembled by the processor (such as the approximate number of letters found in each case, or the specific dates of certain significant letters), such information may be added to this optional section of the register.

SAMPLE SHORT-REGISTER

MANUSCRIPTS DIVISION

0127-4   *Processed by:* AJC

Revised 10/27/54   *Date:* 10-30-54

Title: John Doe Diary   *Ac. no.:* _____

   Addition to: John Doe Papers   Material rec'd. on: _____

Source: Mrs. John Doe   *Location:* II-41-L, 4

Status: Gift

Linear feet: 1.25   *Approx. no. of items:* 4   *No. of containers:* 4 (vols.)

Restrictions: For ten years, or during the lifetime of Mrs. John Doe, whichever period is shorter, the diary may be used only by permission of
Mrs. Doe.

Literary rights: The literary rights in these diaries have been dedicated to the
public, except that such literary rights are reserved to Mrs. John Doe
during her lifetime.

Description: The diaries of John Doe (Secretary of the Treasury, 1913-17;
Chairman, Federal Reserve Board, 1918-24), cover the years 1913-24
and are contained in 3 original autograph volumes and a photostat
volume, reproducing a 4th autograph volume, the original of which is
in the possession of Mrs. John Doe. The diaries include a number of
detailed descriptions of Cabinet meetings; comments on the activities
of the Federal Reserve Board during World War I and in the years
immediately following; descriptions of social events; and a number of
entries of purely personal and family significance.

   A note on the John Doe diaries appeared in the *Information Bulletin,*
— .

*[Note to staff: In rare cases it may be advisable to attach a separate biographical
note, or a container list.]*

Subject Guides

Virginia C. Purdy

W ho would think to look for information about the management of small grocery stores in the series of federal records labeled "Closed Cases of the Stamp Program, 1939-43," in the Records of the Surplus Marketing Administration, Record Group 124 in the National Archives? Probably no one would, except the archivist with long experience working with the records of the various component agencies of the U. S. Department of Agriculture. Yet in these records, in case after case, the deposition of the owner of the "mom-and-pop" corner grocery explains that it was his wife or his daughter who was minding the store when the food stamps were misused, and a picture gradually emerges of a kind of economic enterprise and a way of life that has all but disappeared.

Unfortunately, archivists do not live forever, and some of them even retire. Each one leaves the archives with a head full of knowledge about the subject content of holdings and about relationships among collections and record groups that will take years for successor archivists to develop. Until the day when every repository has complete computer-assisted subject access to its holdings, the best solution to this problem may be the subject guide or other subject-oriented description.

Although the desirability of including subject guides in archives description programs has long been accepted, archives administrators have not given them high priority. In 1940 when the National Archives Committee to Study Finding Aids was deliberating, Solon Buck proposed surveys of materials "on a general subject . . . as a starting point for the scholar." Ernst Posner replied that this would be useful, but he added, "On the whole, archivists have refrained from taking the first step in giving [such] information because they were afraid of the responsibility for the outcome of the studies." In another connection, Posner observed that content description is "one of the most difficult tasks with which an archivist could be faced," and it "will always have a very subjective character because it will depend on an evaluation by the archivist. . . ."[1]

T. R. Schellenberg also noted the problems associated with "description according to pertinence." "The subject approach," he wrote,

---

Essay prepared by the author for *A Modern Archives Reader*.

[1] Minutes, April 5, 1940, Committee on Finding Mediums; Records of Accessioning, Preservation, and Classification: Finding Aids, 1935-44; Records of the National Archives, Record Group 64, National Archives (hereafter cited as RG 64, NA).

is a difficult one and the archivist is justified in taking it only where it serves to make information available to a considerable class of users. . . . The general public, as a rule, is unfamiliar with the hierarchical structure of a government and considers subjects without regard to the government agencies that dealt with them. To promote the fullest exploitation of its holdings, therefore, an archival institution is justified in developing a program of analyzing records in relation to subject matter rather than their provenance.[2]

For all the reluctance on the part of archivists to undertake subject guides, they are the most "user-friendly" of the finding aids in the archivist's arsenal. A well researched and well written guide can also be of immense use to a reference archivist both because it guides the archivist to pertinent records and because it provides researchers with enough information to enable them to frame their reference requests in more specific and generally better informed terms. In addition, though the subject of a particular guide may be of great interest only to one generation of scholars or to a particular group, the guide can often be used to access other related subjects difficult to get at through the traditional inventory. Therefore, guides have been prepared for records on one subject in a single repository and in a number of repositories, often in a given geographical area. Most of what follows deals with subject guides to materials in one repository, although multi-repository guides also will be considered. Many of the examples are drawn from such guides.

There appears to be a consensus that a repository should first set its house in order, at least to the point of issuing a general repository guide and inventorying its most important record groups or collections, before launching any subject guides.[3] An archives should have a grasp of the total universe of its holdings that may be useful to researchers working in many different areas before it concentrates its resources on the needs of researchers in one particular field. It is also much easier to select records relating to a single subject from record groups and collections that have been inventoried. The compiler of a subject guide may refer to uninventoried records in ways that may not be clear to the reference archivist using the guide in the future. This will not be the case if series have been established and titled before the subject compiler begins surveying.

Several considerations govern an archives' decision to produce a subject guide and the choice of a subject. Frequently a guide will be part of the celebration of a particular anniversary, as was the case with the

---

[2]T. R. Schellenberg, *Modern Archives* (Chicago: University of Chicago Press, 1956), p. 219.

[3]David B. Gracy II, *Archives and Manuscripts: Arrangement and Description* (Chicago: Society of American Archivists, 1977), p. 19.

Civil War guides published in the 1960s[4] and those dealing with the Revolutionary War that appeared in the 1970s.[5] Other guides have been launched because of user pressure, in the form of either repeated questions about the same subject or frequent suggestion that a guide is needed. One suspects that the repeated questions prompted the Shakespeare guide that contains a brief essay on the authenticity of every document in the British Public Record Office relating to William Shakespeare.[6] Researchers in large repositories have greater need for records description by pertinence than those in smaller institutions, which are more likely to provide subject access by means of a card catalog.

Certainly there are fashions in research, most recently the interest in black history and women's history. But a better reason for producing guides in these two areas is the elusiveness of the records. The North Carolina State Archives published a *Guide to Women's Records* in 1978.[7] Most of the records described were part of collections of personal papers of famous men. Andrea Hinding has noted that the initial survey of archives for *Women's History Sources*[8] often elicited the response, "We have no records about women," until survey staff members gently urged the archivists to look in family, organization, and men's papers.[9] The researcher of women's history can often find pertinent records by searching for feminine names. The historian of American blacks does not even have this faint clue; hence the number of guides and documentary publications in the field.[10] The intricacy of the subject is the reason

---

[4]Kenneth W. Munden and Henry Putnam Beers, comps., *Guide to Federal Archives Relating to the Civil War* (Washington: National Archives and Records Service, 1962); *Guide to Civil War Records in the North Carolina State Archives* (Raleigh: State Department of Archives and History, 1966); *Michigan Women in the Civil War* (Lansing: Civil War Centennial Observance Commission, 1963).

[5]Stephan Bielinski, comp., *Guide to the Revolutionary War Manuscripts in the New York State Library* (Albany: N.Y. State American Revolution Bicentennial Commission, 1976).

[6]N. A. Evans, comp., *Shakespeare in the Public Records*, Public Record Office Handbook No. 6 (London: Her Majesty's Stationery Office, 1964).

[7]Catherine E. Thompson, comp., *A Selective Guide to Women-related Records in the North Carolina State Archives* (Raleigh: State Department of Archives and History, 1977). See also David J. Olson, comp., *Bibliography of Sources Relating to Women* (Lansing: Michigan Department of State, Michigan History Division, 1975); and James P. Dankey and Eleanor McKay, comps., *Women's History Resources in the State Historical Society of Wisconsin*, 3d ed. (Madison: The Society, 1976).

[8]Andrea Hinding, ed., *Women's History Sources: A Guide to Manuscript Collections in the United States*, 2 vols. (New York and London: R. R. Bowker, 1979).

[9]Hinding, "An Abundance of Riches: The Women's History Sources Survey," in *Clio Was A Woman: Studies in the History of American Women*, ed. by Mabel E. Deutrich and Virginia C. Purdy (Washington, D.C.: Howard University Press, 1980), pp. 23-30.

[10]Amistad Research Center, Fisk University, "Some Archival Sources on Negro History in Tennessee," (Processed, 1969); Paul Lewinson, *Guide to Documents in the National Archives for Negro Studies* (Washington: American Council of Learned Societies, 1947).

given by the compiler of *The Fur Trade in Minnesota* for preparing a guide to records on this subject. He hoped that the guide would "clarify inter-relationships among collections of pertinent records and . . . point out some of the complex relationships . . . within the trade."[11]

Archivists may wish to "encourage research in unworked areas." Waldo Leland declared that this was the purpose of the many guides to materials for American history in countries abroad that were produced by the Carnegie Institute of Washington during and after J. Franklin Jameson's tenure as Director of the Department of History and Research.[12] They may also wish to emphasize holdings in an area not always associated with a particular institution. While the West Point archives would hardly do a guide on the subject of military education, it might well consider writing one on records useful for the study of engineering history.

A final consideration may be the expertise of the staff. Often a subject may be chosen because an archivist with special interest in it is available to prepare a guide.

There is no prescribed method for preparing a subject guide. In a large institution all staff members might be requested to prepare descriptions of records relating to the subject in the holdings in their custody. This system has the advantage of drawing upon the knowledge of the archivists who deal with the same records day after day, but it may produce a composite work of uneven quality. One person or two at most, should be responsible for compiling the submissions into a final manuscript to ensure uniformity in style and format. *A Guide to Documents in the National Archives for Negro Studies* was prepared by Paul Lewinson for the American Council of Learned Societies Committee on Negro Studies. The preface states that Lewinson "directed the collection of information used and prepared the survey in its final form."[13]

Usually one staff member undertakes a guide to records about a subject in all the holdings of a repository. Ideally this person should know the literature about the subject and the trends of current research in the field. A familiarity with names and related places and subjects will lead such a searcher into records that a less well-versed person might overlook. Even with a single compiler, however, a guide should be considered an institutional project to which all staff members will contribute as they can.

For the most part, research and description should be at the series, not the item level. It is not the purpose of a guide to do a researcher's

[11]Bruce M. White, comp., *The Fur Trade in Minnesota: An Introductory Guide to Manuscript Sources* (St. Paul: Minnesota Historical Society Press, 1977).

[12]*Dictionary of American Biography*, s.v. "Jameson, J. Franklin."

[13]Lewinson, *Guide to Documents*, p. v.

work, but to *guide* him or her to records that may be useful, from which he or she may discover significant items for his or her study by a careful page-by-page examination. If archivists undertake a detailed description below the series level for one subject, they may never find time to cover other, perhaps equally important, subjects. Philip Hamer's analysis of the "Project for the Preparation of Guides to the Documentation of the Experiences of the United States Government in World War II" included a statement of purpose that influenced the format: "The whole purpose . . . should be to give the reader an overview of the whole range of sources within the field of his particular interest, [and] indicate the bodies of materials he should investigate. . . ."[14] Probably the most difficult aspect of the compiler's work is knowing when to stop searching.

A compiler goes about data gathering using much the same methods as those employed by any searcher in original sources. Collections or record groups are selected for surveying according to the apparent relevance to the subject of the activities of the creator of personal papers or the function of the agency or institution that created the records. The compiler cannot expect to find and describe every record relating to the subject; in fact, whole record groups may be overlooked by a competent archivist without causing embarrassment. A researcher investigating the records that are described in the guide will probably find his or her way to other records by pursuing leads and internal evidence provided in the records examined.

For consistency and efficiency in surveying records, the compiler will probably wish to devise a form containing space for each kind of information that may be available or useful for a given series. Although all of the following fields may not be required for every series, having them on a form provides a checklist for the compiler so that all are at least considered, eliminating many return visits to the records. Suggested fields are: date of survey; record group or collection name and number; series name, dates, volume, and arrangement; description; finding aid; stack location; and the name of an archivist who may be able to help a researcher use the series. An arbitrary number assigned to each form facilitates reference to notes taken during the survey if the number is inserted in the margin of the manuscript of the guide at the point where the series is mentioned.

There are almost as many ways to organize a guide as there are guides. The plan should make it easy for a user to locate the records needed, but should also take into account the ease of compilation, lest the work go on for years without producing a final product. Researchers applaud guides that are arranged entirely by subject or function so that

---

[14]Functional Classified Files 36.5—World War II Guide Project, Records of the Archivist of the United States, National Archives and Records Service, RG 64, NA.

all records about a particular event, person, or topic are described together, but the difficulty of preparing entries for this type of description is considerable, involving much repetition when a series clearly relates to more than one topic. A greater degree of subjectivity also creeps in, because more rests on the compiler's judgment of the relevance of materials to subtopics than is the case with other types of arrangement of entries.

The archivist finds his or her work facilitated by noting all records related to the general subject of the guide in one record group or collection before proceeding to another. This is certainly the most common approach, but it is less enlightening to the researcher.

F. Gerald Ham, in his *Labor Manuscripts in the State Historical Society of Wisconsin* strikes a compromise by arranging entries by type of creator: "[National] Labor Unions; Educational, Social, and Political Action Organizations; Miscellaneous Papers; Personal Papers; Wisconsin Labor Organizations; and Labor Materials in the State Archives."[15] Probably George S. Ulibarri discovered the happiest medium in the organization of his guide to records in the National Archives relating to Alaska. Chapter headings deal with broad subjects like "Natural Resources" with subheadings like "Mining and Mineral Resources," but under each subtopic entries are by record group in strict numerical order.[16]

Although it is not a subject guide, Philip M. Hamer's *Guide to Archives and Manuscripts in the United States*[17] seems to have set the pattern for guides to records in a geographical area. Like Hamer's, most guides of this type are organized alphabetically by place name and thereunder alphabetically by name of repository. *Resources on the Ethnic and Immigrant in the Pittsburgh Area*[18] provides a historical note about each repository followed by a summary description of relevant collections. A variation is in *Guide to Dutch-American Historical Collections of Western Michigan*;[19] it is arranged alphabetically by name of collection with the repository noted in the narrative description.

The entries in a guide should describe each body of records in enough detail to help a user at a distance from the repository to decide whether or not a letter of inquiry or a visit would be worthwhile and to

---

[15]F. Gerald Ham, *Labor Manuscripts in the State Historical Society of Wisconsin* (Madison: The Society, 1967).

[16]George S. Ulibarri, *Documenting Alaskan History: Guide to Federal Archives Relating to Alaska*, Alaska Historical Commission Studies in History No. 23 (Fairbanks: University of Alaska Press, 1983).

[17]New Haven: Yale University Press, 1961.

[18]Robert E. Wilson and Frank Zabrosky, comps., (Pittsburgh: Pittsburgh Council on Higher Education, 1976).

[19]Herbert Brinks, comp., (Grand Rapids and Holland, Mich.: Dutch American Historical Commission, 1967).

ensure that an archivist in the repository can locate the records described. Extant guides range in detail from the *Guide to Ohio County and Municipal Records for Urban Research*,[20] which supplies series title entries only, to the lengthy narratives of the *Guide to Federal Archives Relating to the Civil War*,[21] which provides a good deal of administrative history of each agency cited. To reach a judicious decision on this matter, a compiler might ask: "How much information do researchers actually need to have about records to determine their pertinence to a research topic?" The name and dates of each relevant series in a record group or collection, the volume of records, and the percentage or portion of those that are pertinent to the guide are basic elements of guide description. Also important is an indication of the configuration of the records: whether those about the subject are all together under a convenient subject heading in a correspondence series, for example, or "scattered through." Sometimes it is only possible to state that "a few" or "many" of the items relate to the subject. If the researcher sees "scattered through" or "a few" in the description of a series of many linear feet, it should alert him or her to the fact that it will either take a long search to find what is there or it may not be worth the time to go through the material. Occasionally it is useful to explain why the records were created by this particular agency or person, especially if they appear in a totally unexpected place, but it is seldom necessary to prepare complete administrative histories or biographies in a subject guide. If researchers are interested and do not already know the background information, they can turn to inventories and other sources.

Hamer summed up his instructions on the compilation of a guide to World War II subjects:

> Each chapter should be in the nature of a description and critical essay on the sources rather than a formal listing, . . . should be suggestive of informational uses of the materials under discussion, and should be as readable as may be.[22]

Since 1946 subject guides have become somewhat more specific than these directions suggest, but being "as readable as may be" is still good advice.

However a guide is organized, additional subject access can be provided by a good index or indexes. While description is being written, the compiler would be wise to bear the index in mind, making certain that indexable subject terms are put into the text. Archivists frequently

---

[20]Paul D. Yon, comp., *Guide to Ohio County and Municipal Records for Urban Research* (Columbus: Ohio Historical Society, 1973).

[21]See note 4.

[22]See note 14.

remind researchers that indexes to finding aids are indexes to the descriptions only, and not to the records themselves. Guide compilers need to remind themselves of the same thing. A good old-fashioned practice is to compile a thesaurus of index terms as the descriptive entries are written, thus ensuring that a name or a subject term is in the same form every time it appears. A common practice nowadays is to underline key words and write implied terms and qualifiers in margins and let the nearest handy computer or word processor sort them alphabetically for further editing. In either case, some kind of numbering system for entries in the text will permit indexing of the manuscript instead of postponing this time-consuming activity until the page proof stage. Of course, no index is possible for a guide consisting only of unrevealing series titles[23] or location symbols.[24]

The forematter of any work is usually written last. Compilers often complain that no one ever reads an introduction, but a good guide must have one. Users can ignore it at their own risk. It should include a statement about the scope of the guide. Are the records described those of one institution or of a group of institutions? Perhaps only a portion of the holdings have been surveyed. Why? Are there other closely related materials that the searcher might find useful? If the guide is to records about a group of people, is it about all of them or just those in a certain area? Noting what is not covered is almost as important as pointing out what is covered.

Waldo Leland's introduction for the *Archives of the Ministry of Foreign Affairs* (Volume II of *Guide to Materials for American History in the Libraries and Archives of Paris*) is admirable. Leland states the purpose of the compilation, where the volume fits into the series of finding aids sponsored by the Carnegie Institute of Washington, gaps in its coverage and the reason therefor (World War II), the organization of the archives, available finding aids and reproductions of documents, and even the location of his notes: "All the notes taken in Paris on which this volume is based have been deposited in the Library of Congress. . . ."

A good example of mentioning what is not covered is found in Aloha South's introduction to the *Guide to Federal Archives Relating to Africa*.[25] She tells the reader that while many of the series described in the guide are available as microfilm publications, she has not included that information in the guide. Searchers must consult a microfilm catalog to ascertain which titles are available.

---

[23]See note 20.

[24]John Albert Robbins, comp., *American Literary Manuscripts*, 2d. ed., (Athens: University of Georgia Press, 1977).

[25]Waltham, Mass.: Crossroads Press, 1977.

A repository subject guide need not be prepared by repository staff. The Carnegie guides are cases in point. So are two subject guides to records in the Public Record Office of Great Britain. Although both were published by the British government, the compilations were made by two social scientists working under a grant from the Social Science Research Council to the University of Kent. The first guide, *Records of Interest to Social Scientists, 1919 to 1939: Introduction,* is described as a prolegomenon of an extensive series to be prepared in this manner, and in the preface of the second, the compiler expresses delight with "topic guides" as a "new way of approaching the vast amount of material on contemporary history that is now open for public inspection at the Public Record Office."[26]

While we know of no guides that have been prepared by potential users under foundation grants in the United States, the *Guide to Federal Archives Relating to Africa* was proposed by the African Studies Association and published with a National Endowment for the Humanities grant to the Association. *Documenting Alaskan History: Guide to Federal Archives Relating to Alaska* was published by the University of Alaska Press with the support of the Alaska Historical Commission. Perhaps someday graduate programs for archivists will consider the preparation of a subject guide to certain records one way of fulfilling the requirement for thesis or major project.

Thus far we have largely been considering full-scale book-length subject guides, but there are several other forms of the genre. The heart of almost any archivist leaps at the opportunity to publish a subject essay in a journal of history, but such opportunities are rare.[27] And many archivists have been asked to present a paper on resources for a particular subject at a historical society annual meeting only to discover that the audience attending the session is composed entirely of other archivists. Some repositories make short essays about records dealing with a single subject a part of their publication program. *Reference Information Papers* at the National Archives and *Archives Information Circulars* at the North Carolina State Department of Archives and History are examples. As a part of its subject oriented conferences, the National Archives has scheduled

---

[26]Brenda Swann and Maureen Trumbull, comps., (London: Her Majesty's Stationery Office, 1971); idem., *Records of Interest to Social Scientists: Unemployment Insurance, 1911-1939* (London: Her Majesty's Stationery Office, 1975).

[27]But see: W. Neil Franklin, "Materials in the National Archives Relating to Vermont," *Vermont History* 27 (July 1959): 240-55; Richard S. Maxwell, "Louisiana and Its History: A Discussion of Sources in the National Archives," *Louisiana History* 13 (Spring 1972): 169-180; Nathan Reingold, "Resources on American Jewish History in the National Archives," *Publication of the American Jewish Historical Society* 47 (June 1958): 186-195; and Meyer Fishbein, "Business History Resources in the National Archives," *Business History Review* 38 (Summer 1964): 232-257.

one or more resource papers by members of its staff; these are then published in the conference proceedings. *Archivaria* devoted much of its fourth issue (Summer 1977) to sources for labor history.

Finally, who can be expected to use these "user-friendly" finding aids? In many cases, archivists and librarians may be the principal users of subject guides and derive the greatest benefit from them. They provide greater intellectual control over a repository's holdings and enable the good reference archivist to steer researchers confidently toward useful records in the home repository and in other repositories that have produced subject guides.

Most guides are undertaken, however, with high hopes that they will attract high-level scholarly researchers to the holdings described. Experience seems to indicate that this does not always happen.[28] Nor do guides appear to influence the habitual patterns of researchers, who use footnotes in monographs and journal articles and personal contacts more extensively than bibliographies and subject guides. Even the existence of descriptions of holdings on a national scale does not prevent a writer from basing a paper on resources in his or her own area.[29]

On the other hand, any archivist who has enjoyed a researcher's delighted excitement on being shown a subject guide in his or her own field must conclude that the long, hard job of preparation was all worthwhile. All scholars may not approach a research project as archivists do, through the bibliographic route, but most are happy to find that there are road maps into the archival thicket. To fracture another metaphor, it is good to have water to which horses may be led; they usually drink.

---

[28]Roy Turnbaugh, "Published Guide: The Morning After," paper delivered at Society of American Archivists annual meeting, Boston, 21 October 1982.

[29]Nancy Sahli, "National Information Systems and Strategies for Research Use," paper delivered at Spring 1983 meeting of the Mid-Atlantic Regional Archives Conference, New Brunswick, N.J., 21 May 1983.

Chapter 7
Reference

R eference is the process of making information in the holdings of an archival repository available to users. It can be seen both as the general process of providing records or information about them to the researcher and as the special effort required to identify particular materials in response to an individual reference request. Both elements of reference are fundamental to every archival program.

In "Reference" (1982), George Chalou gives a conceptual outline of the techniques used in providing records or information about them to users. He observes that reference service is the convergence of three elements: the researcher who seeks information, the records that are the source of the information, and the staff archivist who brings together the researcher and the records. The many facets of reference service and appropriate attitudes and goals of the repository and its staff are outlined in this common-sense approach to a basic function.

Mary Jo Pugh views reference from a different perspective in her essay "The Illusion of Omniscience: Subject Access and the Reference Archivist" (1982). She notes that the principles and methodology of archival arrangement and description have a direct effect on a researcher's success in identifying records relating to a particular inquiry. Based on this observation, Pugh reviews the theory and techniques of archival arrangement and description and relates these functions to the needs of users. She also questions some of the traditional assumptions concerning reference activities and proposes methods to improve the effectiveness of description programs for better reference service.

Reference

George Chalou

Archivists, manuscript curators, and librarians share something very important. In truth, what they share reaches to the very heart of why historical societies through the years have collected and organized records. Through record keeping, persons, institutions and governments have the means of retrieving the essence of their past activities. Those who provide reference service are engaged in making records, historical manuscripts and books available. This means constant interaction with the user of the documentary resources in our custody. Because reference service is an action function and because reference work is never quite done, seldom is there an opportunity for a reference staff to reflect on the nature of reference service.

If one could peer through the roof and ceiling of an institution, this typical and dynamic scene might be viewed. He might see large financial account books being loaded on a record cart to be delivered shortly to a user in the reference room. There one might see a researcher and a staff person in animated conversation. Facial expressions and body language indicate that this is where the action is taking place. The records, the staff member, and the researcher have come together. The viewer might just have witnessed what could be termed the point of convergence.

All three of these necessary elements of reference service—records, staff and users—must be properly prepared and combined for maximum benefit. Because reference service takes so much of a staff's time, little thought is given to the analysis of this service. Yet careful study and attention must be given if institutions desire to continue providing high-quality reference service. The first element, the records, is inanimate and, of course, reflects what the creators, transmitters and recipients of the records have done with them. Records that are created on a stable physical base and are properly maintained will be in better condition for users. Proper preservation of records and historical manuscripts must take precedence over the needs of researchers. Making a fragile document available to one person could destroy the document forever, or more probably, could mean an expensive repair for an organization. Records also must be boxed, labeled and arranged in order to help your users and your staff. In addition, the more finding aids, such as invento-

Reprinted with permission from *A Manual of Archival Techniques,* edited by Roland M. Baumann (Harrisburg: Pennsylvania Historical and Museum Commission, 1982), pp. 47-53.

ries, calendars, indexes and guides, an organization prepares the more efficient the reference operation.

The reference staff should hold positive attitudes toward people and provide a service to researchers. This underlying attitude is very important and should be demonstrated throughout the organization. However, wanting to help a researcher is sometimes not enough if the organization does not have adequate reference staff. Administrators should study the past reference load in order to prepare for heavy-use periods. College vacations or holiday breaks usually bring more users into a library or historical society facility. Most organizations have back-up personnel who can be called upon for temporary duty during unexpectedly heavy researcher use.

The users of a particular institution's holdings may represent a cross section of the research community or a specialized clientele. Many factors affect this composition, but the subject matter of the records is the most significant. The particular location of the library or archives and the quality of service researchers can expect are also important. An institution has control over the quality of records and staff, but possesses little control over the quality of researchers. Those persons, however, who read the secondary literature on their topic and carefully design their research before using records will be easier to work with and will profit more from a visit to a research facility.

Well-prepared users, a motivated and trained reference staff, and properly maintained records come together in such a way that all three benefit. If one element is weak, then less than full utilization of the records will occur. If the staff is inadequate and the user unprepared, the most carefully maintained and fully described records will be underused. It is important that every repository do all that it can to develop all three elements—records, staff and users.

In addition to understanding the nature of reference, it is important to distinguish the various forms of reference service. Some researchers visit facilities but many more write or telephone and ask assistance. Your institution should know what percent of reference-staff time is devoted to written or telephonic service. If the same questions are raised—such as the hours and days open for business—a set of instructions or form letters should be printed for distribution. There should be no need to play twenty questions with researchers if the same questions and answers are involved time after time. Staff time is limited and valuable. Written procedures or guidelines for researchers are also valuable in providing guidance and on-the-job training for your staff. Managers and supervisors should be especially sensitive to the opportunities for printed information that can be sent by mail. A reference person would not force a researcher to wait two hours in order to search and answer a reference inquiry received the previous day.

It is essential that reference personnel understand the importance of the personal interview of the researcher. This step in the reference process is a crucial and demanding responsibility; however, an archivist or curator should have a positive attitude toward the person being interviewed. Care and attention should be given equally to both the well-known scholar and a person who wants information from the records of a local nineteenth-century business. Encourage the staff to view the personal interview of the researcher as an opportunity rather than an onerous task.

In the beginning of the interview the archivist should ask a series of questions which permits the researcher to define his or her subject. The archivist must be a good listener and ask questions which cause the visitor to define whether the topic is more extensive (scope) or more intensive (depth). If the researcher expects to do both, the interviewer must ask how much time the researcher expects to take using the records. The researcher may be unrealistic because of the volume of the records or manuscripts or the lack of finding aids. Share your view with the researcher, and tactfully suggest that it may not be possible to research everything he or she desires. In general, do not be afraid to make suggestions and offer advice. Final decisions, however, rest with the researcher. Because most searchers have limited research time at any one institution, it is wise, as a general rule, to provide him or her the series or records or manuscript collections which are most likely to yield pertinent information. If a researcher has almost unlimited time, direct him or her from the most probable to the least probable sources. An exceptional searcher may be willing to search your entire holdings. Remember that important historical documentation can be found in the most unlikely places. If the researcher insists on discounting reference-staff advice and desires to work in other collections, do not resist this. Few researchers will complain at the end if the reference person has outlined all the options during the interview.

The institution's reproduction procedures, fees and research rules should be explained at the outset. A sheet or brochure explaining these procedures is very useful and should include information pertaining to copyrighted material in the custody of the institution. Under certain conditions, the copyright law which took effect in 1978 grants the archivist more discretion in furnishing users reproductions of copyrighted material.

There are several functions comprising general reference service, but the two most important categories are information service and document service. Within information service, it is helpful to understand the difference between information from records or papers and information about records or papers.

If a staff person extracts the date of death of an individual from a personal-papers collection and supplies this information to the searcher, information from the record is furnished. It is simple to extract brief, factual data from documents. Names, dates, occupations or place names extracted from records can sometimes be placed within form letters especially designed to efficiently process high-volume, repetitive requests. A properly designed and correctly used form letter can save reference and clerical staff considerable amounts of time.

If, however, a historian asks an archivist to find what prompted a politician to make a particular speech or critical policy decision, the answer would be more difficult and the archivist would begin making judgments that only the researcher should make. Some reference persons forget that they are assisting the researcher and are not themselves acting as researcher. The public does not expect the reference librarian to know all the information contained in all the books in his library. Likewise, the researcher should not expect the archivist to know all the factual data in the records in his custody. The research public has a right to believe that the archivist knows as much about the records as possible. It is important to know about the finding aids to manuscript collections or archives. The most valuable finding aid, however, is the reference person—not a prepared guide, index or inventory. In many cases this most valuable finding aid evaluates and furnishes the prepared finding aids to the researcher. Knowing what major topics are included among records is very important because many researchers orient their research around major subjects, such as the American Revolution, Civil War, religion and transportation. A reference staff should constantly strive to gain additional knowledge about holdings. If donors impose restrictions on their personal papers, the reference person should be aware of this. Knowing how to obtain information about records or papers is very important.

The other major function involves making the records available. This includes bringing the records to the research room, making reproductions of records, and loaning of documents. It is wise not to make two series of records available to researchers at the same time. This will avoid the possibility of researchers mixing records from different agencies or offices. In addition, every request for records or papers should be indicated on a request form which best meets the institution's needs. The making of reproductions is a major responsibility of an institution's reference staff and cannot be taken lightly. Academic researchers are more likely to place large reproduction orders, and constant monitoring of such orders is needed to ensure accurate and prompt service.

Reference service is a dynamic, constantly changing relationship between researcher and archivist. There is one policy or principle, however, that should influence all reference activity. This has come to be called the policy of equal access. In 1973, and again in 1978, the Society of American Archivists supported this position. Briefly stated, it proposes that all repositories of research materials make available their holdings on equal terms of access. This policy is well worth striving for in all repositories of historical documentation, but achieving it is quite difficult. The nature and mission of an institution will greatly affect the ability to attain this ideal. Private research institutions, financed by private funds, will more likely place priorities on certain types of requests. No institution—public or private—can avoid exceptions to the policy of equal access. Nevertheless, disregard of this practice will open your institution to charges of favoritism. The arbitrary or widespread disregard of equal access of documentation is also an intrusion on the tradition of scholarship.

The policy of equal access does not mean that any question asked should be answered. Most institutions must impose some limitations on what it considers legitimate reference service. These limitations must be applied consistently to all researchers. The first in importance is the ability of your archives to stop or limit reference services to someone who has violated user procedures made known when the person applied for research permission. The careless use of original materials or theft of documents is sufficient cause for withdrawal of the researcher-use privilege. Care should be used when this is done in order to avoid legal complications. Keep in mind, however, that the preservation of records must remain the first priority.

In the National Archives and Records Service, persons seeking general information relating to widely known events, persons or historical trends are referred to published works that are in a public or university library. The second limitation is that a reference staff should avoid doing substantive research for a requester. Admittedly, there is the question as to what constitutes substantive research, and every institution must define this area for its staff. In order to provide equal access it is sometimes necessary to limit the quantity of items per written or telephonic request. Obviously, a request that listed six hundred documents to be located and reproduced could be such a staff burden that other requests would be delayed or not answered. In order to process other requests and provide equal access, it might be necessary to inform the researcher that only thirty items were searched for and that subsequent requests be limited to thirty items. The standards set for quantity requests are arbitrary but they should apply equally.

Equal access must be set aside in special cases because of statutory requirements, court order, agency or corporate needs, overriding public interest, or the establishment of individual benefits. In this connection custodians of public records have special obligations. Both careful judgment and common sense must be considered if certain requests are moved ahead of requests received earlier.

In addition there are various restrictions of access, which can be placed into four general classes: statutory restrictions, governmental agency restrictions (federal, state, local), institutional restrictions, and donor-imposed restrictions. Any acquisition or accessioning program is predicated on the assumption that the documentation acquired will be used sooner or later. Archivists or manuscripts curators must honor such restrictions, but likewise they should work toward maximum release of materials as soon as possible.

The Freedom of Information Act of 1966 (amended in 1974) exempts from disclosure certain types of information found in records of the Executive Branch of the U.S. government. Other federal, state and local laws or regulations prohibit the release of other information or types of records.

Many private repositories have records or personal papers in their custody which document a private or confidential relationship. The personal papers of a lawyer might have information relating to the plea of a client in a felony case. Information given in confidence is a very sensitive issue and must be handled carefully. Any repository holding this type of documentation should have the capacity to develop and use restrictions. Few persons (corporations included) simply donate their materials to a repository without imposing some restrictions to access. These limitations should be a part of the deed of gift. Institutions acquiring personal-papers collections must weigh both the number and the time period of restrictions offered by donors. No hard-and-fast rule on how to make acquisitions can be designed.

It is important to know how to judge when reference service meets the high standards that it should. There are indicators that can be weighed. The protection and care an archives staff provides its holdings are very important. Careless and rough handling of records should not be permitted. Thoroughness in the reference service in your institution is another indicator which must be examined. If reproduction orders are carelessly processed, and follow-up letters are never written, reference supervisors must take action. Courtesy to the researcher is a consistent hallmark of high-quality reference service. Archivists and manuscript curators make documentation available in a prompt and professional manner. This does not mean, however, that the reference person is a servant of the researcher and that he or she must do what the researcher desires. Firmness is sometimes a very important quality in relating to difficult researchers.

Another indicator of professional-quality reference service is the cooperation that takes place among the institution's reference staff. Staff members should help each other voluntarily and share their particular strengths when performing reference service. Widespread rivalry or professional jealousy does little to build staff *esprit* and usually breaks down communication among the staff. Usually the research clientele suffers.

The last indicator is the recognition by researchers of reference services performed. This may take many forms—a sincere but short statement of appreciation when a researcher finishes, or a thank-you note or letter to the archivist or to the director of your institution. By word of mouth, researchers will urge others to visit your facility or warn them to stay away if their experiences were unpleasant. In some cases researchers will acknowledge their debt to archivists in their publications. Some authors will send a complimentary copy of their book or article to the reference person along with a personalized inscription. The composite recognition of an institution's reference services is very important and must be evaluated constantly.

In conclusion, an institution must be committed to the goal of making its documentary resources available to its clientele in a professional and expeditious manner. This commitment to research and a better grasp of the human past must motivate those who make our documentary heritage available. Striving toward this goal is a constant duty.

The Illusion of Omniscience:
Subject Access and the Reference Archivist

Mary Jo Pugh

Current theories of subject and information retrieval are predicated on the experience and needs of libraries and information centers and do not effectively address the needs of archives. Both libraries and archives seek to aid users in locating information. The problems faced by the two institutions, however, are as different as their materials, organizing principles, and descriptive techniques. A comparison of the two institutions illustrates some of the difficulties facing the reference archivist seeking subject retrieval of archival and manuscript materials arranged according to the principles of provenance and original order.

Archives and libraries differ most obviously in the materials they collect. For the most part, libraries collect books and other published materials which are produced in multiple copies in relatively uniform sizes and formats. Generally, a book is created quite deliberately by an author, as a literary product treating a particular topic. On the other hand, archives accession unique documents which vary widely in size and format. The documents are usually created by many authors as the byproduct of personal and organizational activity. Rarely are they self-conscious literary productions.Unlike a book, which can stand alone as an author's thoughts on a single topic, archival documents generally make sense only as part of a group of records. Record groups reflect the many activities which created them and may be useful for many subjects.

Retrieval of individual books relating to a specific subject is a primary goal for the library, and librarians have devised both classification and cataloging techniques to accomplish subject retrieval. On the other hand, subject retrieval of individual documents has not been a primary goal for most archivists. Library classification brings books treating the same subject together on the shelf, thereby creating one important and powerful mode of subject access. The classification notation gives each book a unique number which identifies its primary subject. Any classification scheme assumes a community of users, and the development of the scheme and the location of any given book within it will in part be determined by the perceived needs of the users. For example, a book on the history of religion among American blacks can be located with books on religion, or with books about blacks, or with books about U.S. history,

Reprinted with permission from *The American Archivist* 45 (Winter 1982): 33-44.

but because the book can be physically located in only one place, only one aspect of the subject treated by the book can be retrieved through the classification scheme alone.

Archivists reject the idea of rearranging documents to fit a predetermined classification scheme. Archivists respond instead to the unique, organic, and activity-based quality of records. Basic to archival arrangement is the canon that records cannot be arranged according to an enumerative scheme but must be arranged according to the principles of provenance and original order, reflecting the processes that created them. The subject matter of individual documents can only be understood in the context of related documents created by the same activity. Records are valuable not only for the information found in them but also for the evidence they provide about the processes that generated them. Consequently, the relationships among activities reflected in the records must be preserved. The archivist is as responsive to the needs of the creator of the record as to later users.

T.R. Schellenberg recognizes that all later users may not find archival order useful but defends archival arrangement according to the principles of provenance and original order:

> While this arrangement will not bring together records by subjects that will meet all the research needs of scholars, it is the only workable way of placing records in order while preserving their evidential values on government functioning. . . . The archivist, therefore, should resist any efforts on the part of scholars to induce him to arrange records according to any abstract system of universal subject classification.[1]

Archivists further maintain that a usable original order remains usable. Because human activity created the records and because later users are interested in that activity, retaining records in the order generated by the original activity allows access through analysis of function, a powerful mode of access. Archivists also recognize that many records are self-indexing when original order is maintained. Physical arrangement, however, whether in the archives or the library, can offer only one mode of access. In the office of origin, physical location is usually sufficient to retrieve documents, but it is not enough in the archives. Since no library classification scheme or arrangement of records meets the needs of all users, cataloging of books and description of records are employed to provide intellectual control of the holdings.

In the library, cataloging, like classification, serves two purposes. Library cataloging describes each item according to standardized prescriptive rules and also offers multiple access points—typically author,

---

[1]T.R. Schellenberg, *Modern Archives: Principles and Techniques* (Chicago: University of Chicago Press, 1956), p. 188.

title, and subject—for the user. Standardized lists of subject headings relate subjects represented in the library to each other by means of cross references. Standard practice allows for cooperative cataloging and shared information. Archival methods of group description, on the other hand, analyze the function and structure of the records rather than providing item description and multiple access points. Each record group tends to be described as an isolated entity, and there is little standardization among institutions.

American archival institutions and manuscript repositories have used a wide variety of descriptive media; the forms most prevalent today are the inventory or register, the card catalog, and the guide. In purely archival agencies, the inventory quickly became the basic finding aid; the card catalog is rarely found in such institutions. The card catalog is more likely to be found in manuscript repositories, but even there the register is widely accepted as the basic finding aid.

In favoring the descriptive inventory or register, archival agencies which do not use a supplementary card catalog or its equivalent may find it difficult to provide for multiple access points, especially subject access. Manuscript repositories are more likely to use a card catalog or its equivalent to provide multiple access points and subject access. The *National Union Catalog of Manuscript Collections* (NUCMC) serves this function for many manuscript repositories, but not for archival agencies strictly defined.[2]

The repository guide is one solution to the need for multiple access points. Publishing a guide is universally described as a mandatory obligation. The SAA's glossary defines the guide as "a finding aid at the repository level that briefly describes and indicates the relationships between holdings, with record groups, papers, collections, or comparable bodies of material as the units of entry."[3] A guide, however, is as significant for its index as for its descriptive matter. For many purely archival institutions, the guide index is the only comprehensive, multiple access tool offering a subject approach. The importance of the guide for most archival agencies cannot be overstated, but it is usually recommended for only one of its two vital functions. Too often the index to the guide is a hastily contrived addition to the descriptive matter.

Subject access is achieved in some institutions through the preparation and publication of special subject guides on topics of interest, such

[2]The influence of the *National Union Catalog of Manuscript Collections* should be studied and evaluated in this context. See, for example, Richard Berner, "Observations on Archivists, Librarians, and the National Union Catalog of Manuscript Collections," *College and Research Libraries* 28 (July 1968): 276-80.

[3]Frank B. Evans, Donald F. Harrison, and Edwin A. Thompson, comps., and William L. Rofes, ed., "A Basic Glossary for Archivists, Manuscript Curators, and Records Managers," *American Archivist* 37 (July 1974).

as the *Guide to Materials on Latin America in the National Archives* (Washington, D.C.: Government Printing Office, 1974) or various "reference
information papers" on special topics. Other kinds of special aids may
outline search strategies for common problems presented to the
archives. On the national level, subject surveys such as the *Women's History Sources: A Guide to Archives and Manuscript Collections in the United
States* (New York: Bowker, 1979), provide access for some users.

Archival methodology has significant consequences for subsequent
reference practice. In the library the user is expected to understand the
basic principles of classification and cataloging, to use subject entries
from the card catalogs, and to retrieve books from the shelves. There is
no analogous procedure in most archival agencies.

Archival theory includes a number of assumptions about the user
and subject access. The archival system is predicated on interaction
between the user and the archivist. Indeed, the archivist is necessary,
even indispensable, for subject retrieval. The archivist is assumed to be a
subject specialist who introduces the user to the relevant records through
the finding aids and continues to mediate between the user and the
archival system throughout the user's research.

Schellenberg, for example, believes that subject access flows naturally from the archivist's firsthand knowledge of the records. He argues
that reference activities should not be segregated functionally because an
archivist servicing records must have the firsthand knowledge of the
records that comes from processing them. Reference assistance to users
should be a logical outgrowth of other archival activities:

> An archival institution should be organized, in the main, on a subject-mat-
> ter, not a functional basis. By this I mean that it should be so organized that
> its staff will be assigned archival work on the basis of its relation to subject
> areas or fields of inquiry, not on the basis of its specialized professional
> nature. A knowledge of the principles and techniques of arranging, describ-
> ing, publishing, and servicing archives should be developed with respect to
> particular bodies of archives. . . . By applying the knowledge in this manner,
> moreover, a special knowledge is gained of the archives—of their content,
> their arrangement, their significance for research uses and the like. . . . An
> archival institution, therefore, should be organized in a manner that will
> most effectively develop subject-matter knowledge in its staff.[4]

In Schellenberg's view the archivist serves as an indispensible intermediary between the user and the records because, in his words, "No matter
how well finding aids are prepared, they cannot impart all the knowledge that is in the head of a well-informed archivist."[5] Richard Lytle

---

[4]Schellenberg, *Modern Archives*, pp. 126-27.

[5]T.R. Schellenberg, *The Management of Archives* (New York: Columbia University Press,
1965), p. 109. See also Richard H. Lytle, "Intellectual Access to Archives: Provenance and

REFERENCE

confirms this observation. In his analysis of retrieval methods in archives, he found that "retrieval performance scores appeared to be primarily a function of the experience of the searcher with the method used."[6]

In his description of the interaction between user and archivist, Frank Burke emphasizes the personalized nature of research in provenance-based archival agencies. He notes that the records are arranged and described in terms of organization, function, and hierarchy. The researcher, however, usually presents a subject request. Only the archivist with his[7] knowledge of the subject matter of the records and knowledge of the functional and administrative structure of the agencies producing the records is able to match researcher requests with archival material.[8] Richard Lytle sums up the traditional method succinctly:

> Subject retrieval in the P (Provenance) Method proceeds by linking subject queries with provenance information contained in administrative histories or biographies, thereby producing leads to files which are searched by using their internal structures.[9]

An example of this interaction between user and archivist is found in the Spring 1980 issue of *Prologue*. Donald M. Sweig based his article, "Reassessing the Human Dimension of the Interstate Slave Trade," on manifests of ships transporting slaves from Alexandria, Virginia, to New Orleans in the 1820s and 1830s. The article won the Charles Thompson Prize, and the author expresses his appreciation to James Harwood of the National Archives, "whose cooperation and knowledge of the records of the U.S. Customs Service brought the manifests to hand."[10]

A second assumption about subject access in the traditional provenance-based system is that the system will work only if the user supplies information extrinsic to the finding aids. Any access system depends upon some degree of independent knowledge on the user's part, but archival access systems rely most heavily on it. Philip Brooks, Richard Berner, and Howard Peckham are among the many archivists who expect the researcher to associate names of people and organizations with the activities and events related to his topic. These associations link

Content Indexing Methods of Subject Retrieval," *American Archivist* 43 (Winter 1980): 71-72.

[6]Lytle, "Intellectual Access to Archives: Report on an Experiment," *American Archivist* 43 (Spring 1980): 194.

[7]Masculine pronouns are used generically throughout this article.

[8]Frank Burke, "The Impact of the Specialist on Archives," *College and Research Libraries* 33 (1972): 312-17.

[9]Lytle, "Intellectual Access to Archives: Provenance and Content Indexing Methods of Subject Retrieval," p. 64.

[10]Donald M. Sweig, "Reassessing the Human Dimensions of the Interstate Slave Trade," *Prologue* 12 (Spring 1980): 5.

the topic with the personal and organizational records held by the archival agency.[11]Berner states:

> In the course of this preliminary research the user will have associated names of persons and organizations with his particular subject. He will, in fact, have done this so precisely and in so personal a manner that no describer of the manuscript group would be able to anticipate his needs. Whatever painstaking subject analysis of items and series that the describer might make would be largely a superfluous substitute for the minute name/subject association developed inherently by the researcher in his preliminary study.[12]

He hypothesizes that as many as 90 percent of users link their subject to proper names.[13] Many archivists imply that the "serious" researcher who does his homework and prepares carefully identifies the collections and record groups he needs before he even gets to the archives. The archivist then has only to give the user the proper inventory or register.

Berner discusses an example. In describing the records of the Council of Churches, the archivist may use a subject heading for "Japanese-American Evacuation and Relocation" to account for a subseries of records dealing with that subject. However, Berner adds the following:

> . . . it should be noted that normally any reasonably knowledgeable user would have known already that the Council of Churches had been active on behalf of Japanese-American evacuees and this name association with this special subject would really be sufficient. . . .[14]

Two other assumptions about subject access in provenance-based archival agencies center on the nature of historical research. Archivists assume that the user wants high recall and does not care if he gets low precision. In other words the user is expected to wade through many irrelevant documents to be certain he has seen everything of interest.

Archivists also expect the research process to be heuristic or iterative. As the researcher works his way through materials, he accumulates more names and events which he then tries to link with other record groups and collections. A continuing interaction with the reference archivist is required.

---

[11]See for example, Philip C. Brooks, *Research in Archives: The Use of Unpublished Primary Sources* (Chicago: University of Chicago Press, 1969); Richard Berner and M. Gary Bettis, "Description of Manuscript Collections: A Single Network System," *College and Research Libraries* 30 (September 1969): 405-16; and Howard Peckham, "Aiding the Scholar in Using Manuscript Collections," *American Archivist* 19 (July 1956): 221-28.
[12]Berner and Bettis, "Description of Manuscript Collections," p. 411.
[13]Richard Berner, "Arrangement and Description of Manuscripts," *Drexel Library Quarterly* 11 (January 1975): 51.
[14]Ibid.

The standard procedure is not without its critics. Many archivists are concerned about the adequacy of the intellectual control of archival materials and feel that traditional methods based on the assumptions described above do not deal effectively with the problems presented by users. A closer examination of the assumptions underlying current practice may illuminate the special concerns of the reference archivist.

The current practice of arrangement and description in archival agencies does not focus primarily on user needs. Processors tend instead to focus on the records, partly because the records are unique and partly because the archival agency is part of a larger parent organization. While few archivists question the principle of provenance, most will admit that its corollary—original order—is not always revealing to users outside the originating department. Archivists often inherit office filing systems which were poorly conceived, badly maintained, and dependent on the decisions of file clerks for the location of particular files or items in a file. Inherited file headings are often not meaningful and repeating them in our inventories is not always helpful to the user. Listing "Director's correspondence, A-Z" tells the user very little, but inventories are too often such lists. Many descriptions tend to capture only the order, not the substance, of the records. Simply recapitulating the order of the records in the inventory offers only unidimensional access through arrangement; it makes serial scanning of the records more effective.

Guides, so crucial for subject access, are out of date before they are published. Traditional published guides are not easily updated and appear infrequently. For example, 13 years passed between guides at the Michigan Historical Collections, and at the National Archives 26 years passed between guides. Entries in the guide cannot be manipulated or changed. To supplement the static guide, we need an ongoing system of elements which can be manipulated.

The myth of the immortal, omniscient, indispensable reference archivist must also be examined. Current practice relies too heavily on the subject knowledge and memory of the individual archivist, and is too dependent on the personalities of the researcher and the archivist. In order to help the user, the archivist must associate subject matter with record groups and collections. Some users can discuss topics so as to stimulate these associations in the archivist's mind. Other researchers feel the initial interview is an invasion of their privacy or fail to use terms which bring forth a meaningful exchange. Unfortunately, either party may be rushed or distracted.[15]

---

[15]The Loewenheim case implied that archivists may be held to higher standards than our systems are capable of producing. See Herman Kahn, "The Long Range Implications for Historians and Archivists of the Charges Against the Franklin D. Roosevelt Library,"

Archivists have not analyzed the elements which comprise a successful reference interview and have not studied the process of question negotiation in the archival setting. The archivist seeks to understand the full ramifications of the inquiry and tries to understand what the user really wants to know, which often differs dramatically from the initial question. The archivist also helps to refine the question in view of the sources and to conceptualize a search strategy.

To depend on the subject knowledge of a particular archivist leaves too much to chance, since the quality of reference service may vary from day to day as individuals take leaves for illness, meetings, or vacations. Reference service may vary from year to year as archivists transfer or retire. In large organizations, seasonal variation or turnover may not be a major problem. In small organizations it can be devastating.

Furthermore, many archivists do not have the opportunity to develop the subject specialization recommended by Schellenberg, because archival institutions are not always organized along subject lines. Processing and reference activities are often divided functionally between two people or two departments. Records are often processed by student interns or by temporary personnel paid by grant funds. In many institutions, reference activities are rotated among all members of the staff, sometimes for periods as brief as two hours, and continuity with the researcher is lost. Unfortunately, in too many institutions, the reference responsibility is seen as a series of interruptions better delegated to a paraprofessional while the researcher is left to shift as best he can.

Like these assumptions about reference service, our assumptions about users are also untested. We have not explored the needs of the users as they approach the record. Archivists often assume the user is a subject specialist, a post-doctoral scholar, or, at the very least, a doctoral candidate at the dissertation stage. Yet registration forms reveal many other users, and use statistics indicate that research use is growing most rapidly in nontraditional areas. Administrators and staff of the parent institution, students at all stages of training, ecologists, archaeologists, preservation planners, urban planners, journalists, lawyers, amateur historians, local historians, and genealogists are among users of archival sources.

We do not know how users, whether scholarly or nonscholarly, approach the record. Is it true that 90 percent of users use proper names as their primary mode of access? It is difficult to know how many requests enumerated in terms of persons and organizations actually conceal a subject request and are presented in terms congruent with the

---

American Archivist 34 (July 1971): 265-75; and Richard Pollenberg, "The Roosevelt Library Case: A Review Article," in the same issue, pp. 277-84.

archival system simply because users have learned that is the only way they will get a response from the system.

In 1977 the Committee on Finding Aids of the SAA circulated a questionnaire to reference staff to test the hypothesis that well-prepared scholars would primarily use the name approach. The questionnaire analyzed researcher use of proper names, topical subjects, geographical place names, and chronology when approaching the finding aids. Use of these four modes was compared with the amount of preparation the researcher had done before arriving at the research institution.

In response to the questionnaire, researcher registration forms at the Michigan Historical Collections were examined for the six-month period for July through December 1976. Nearly 40 percent of the users (61/156) were judged to have read extensively on their subject. Another 40 percent were unprepared (62/156). The remaining 20 percent had done some preparation. In this sample, preparation of user was not a good predictor for mode of access. Roughly half of all users, regardless of preparation, began with a subject approach or used the subject approach offered by the card catalog.

Another study by Michael Stevens in 1977 sought to discover how historians use finding aids in their research. Stevens sent questionnaires to 123 American historians with doctorates teaching in history departments in Wisconsin. He found from their responses that the formal system, including such tools as NUCMC, was relatively ineffective in providing information to historians. Most historians relied on other historians, either through previously published works or by word of mouth. His findings indicate that historians use both names and subjects as access points. Although names predominated, subject terms were used by a considerable minority of the historians.[16]

We also need to know more about the operation and efficacy of the name approach. Without a subject approach provided by a card catalog or guide, the researcher must check all names of possible interest against all inventories and registers to see if the archival agency has the records of the particular individuals or organizations. Even a rudimentary subject approach will lead directly to at least some of the relevant collections and record groups. The researcher can still check other names against the finding aids if he suspects the adequacy of the subject approach. A good subject approach may lead to sources that the researcher has not considered.

The relationship between the type of research project and the modes of access also needs to be studied. Not all research topics are accessible through the traditional modes. The new fields of historical

---

[16]Michael E. Stevens, "The Historian and Archival Finding Aids," *Georgia Archive* 5 (Winter 1977): 64-74.

inquiry and current interest in cross-disciplinary research have created a revolution in readers' expectations and needs. Researchers interested in social, demographic, cultural, ethnic, or economic history, for example, have new needs. A researcher investigating farm labor in the 19th century is interested in the most anonymous of Americans and will not have associated proper names with his topic no matter how extensive his research or his previous reading. It is obvious that the researcher must ultimately reach the names of the persons and organizations which created the papers and records documenting the activity of interest, but the problem lies in linking the known activity with the unknown actors. A cultural geographer interested in the uses of the Huron River in Washtenaw County, Michigan, must find his way to the industrial schedules of the U.S. and Michigan censuses to find mills and their output. Frank Burke uses another example to illustrate the impact of recent research:

> It is one thing to do archival research on the role of the Committee on Fair Employment Practice in World War II, it is quite another to enter the National Archives with a topic such as the social and economic condition of the Afro-American in the New Deal era.[17]

In the first case the archivist would give the researcher the Preliminary Inventory Number 147 for Record Group 228, the records of the Committee on Fair Employment Practice, and offer help in using the files. In contrast, the second search would require, first, an effort to translate "Afro-American" and "New Deal" into historically contemporary terms, and, second, a joint analysis by the researcher and the archivist of federal activity in the 1930s to locate federal agencies, both civilian and military, that influenced or recorded the economic and social conditions of blacks during the period.

It is folly to expect the reference archivist to remember all administrative histories, biographical sketches, series descriptions, and container lists required to translate subject requests into names of record groups or collections. Archivists need to be able to build on the work of predecessors and colleagues. Reference archivists need an alphabetical, updatable, multiple-subject approach even if the readers never use it. It is true that no system of finding aids will be able to make all the associations and intuitive leaps of the imagination that result from a fruitful interchange between archivist and researcher. No finding aid will replace reference assistance or relieve the researcher from the need to associate a subject with names, dates, and other specific access points, but we must codify what we can.

Archivists have the methodology to provide better subject access. Richard Lytle usefully differentiates between provenance-based descrip-

[17]Burke, p. 315.

tive systems and content-indexing systems. In the provenance-based system, descriptive information "derives only from what is known *about* the file—the activities of the creating person or organization and the structure or organizing principles of the file itself." In the content-indexing system, deriving from librarianship, "information is gleaned by an indexer who examines the records."[18] Lytle provides a useful theoretical distinction and he has greatly influenced this paper, but he presses the distinction too far. As he admits, the two systems often "occur as complementary approaches within a given repository," and he further states, "The two methods may be summarized as two dimensions of subject access to archives."[19]

We need both modes to satisfy the needs of reference staff and users. Determining information about provenance and determining information about content are not contradictory or mutually exclusive activities. The analysis of records is central to archival activity. Schellenberg's views are instructive:

> While preparing an inventory, an archivist gains a knowledge of the origins, structure, and content of an archival group that is very useful to him in reference service and later descriptive work. Its preparation is a kind of discipline for him, for while preparing it he is required to do those things that are always necessary to acquire a knowledge of records. These relate to a study of the organization and function of an agency, which he must know if he is to understand the records it produced; a dissection of the archival group into its constituent parts . . . and an identification of the record type and a description of the content of each of the series.[20]

Analysis of both provenance and content can and should be part of our daily work. Archivists tend to be too passive and bureaucratic when writing inventories and registers. Inventories, which should be the major intellectual accomplishment of our profession, are too often merely lists of container and file headings. In the agency history or the biographical sketch, in the scope and content note, in the subgroup or series description, the archivist has the opportunity and the obligation to analyze in some detail the content and potential use of the records as well as the function and composition of records. Frequently only the processing archivist will see the collection or record group as a whole. Preparing a sensitive, perceptive, provocative essay on the strengths and weaknesses of records for research use is difficult. It requires historical knowledge, imagination, and the ability to write clear prose. It is also difficult to assess records for current research interests and to anticipate other uses

---

[18]Lytle, "Intellectual Access to Archives: Provenance and Content Indexing Methods of Subject Retrieval," p. 64.

[19]Ibid., pp. 65, 74.

[20]Schellenberg, *The Management of Archives*, p. 220.

of the records. But if we are unable to assess and analyze the records, why are we saving them? Human activity generates records, and although current users may not be interested in particular activites, they are part of the human experience. Archivists knew of the activities of blacks and women from our records before historians discovered them. Archivists knew the universals of human experience—birth, family, education, work, aging, and death—long before they became elements of historical analysis. Archivists, however, did not always identify these historical elements in descriptive programs. Manfred Kochen suggests that a good information retrieval system is one that helps people to ask better questions.[21] Archivists in their inventories and registers have unlimited opportunities to suggest areas of study.

Archivists have long sought to differentiate archival arrangement and description from library classification and cataloging. In the process, archivists may have unnecessarily neglected the idea of subject access. The double step of indexing inventories and registers and cumulating the index entries offers one way to gain subject control in a manual system and provides the data for eventual transfer to automated systems. SAA's Committee on Finding Aids noted that indexes are rarely used in inventories or registers. The Committee, however, errs in defining indexing too narrowly as "rearranging entries from container or item listings into an alphabetical, subject, chronological or other sequence."[22] It is not necessary to restrict the index to the container or item level. Indexing can be keyed to any of the other levels of description as well, as it is in the guide. Such indexes can be cumulated into a master index for the repository.

These ideas are not new. Variants of this proposal are described by Ruth Bordin and Robert Warner, Kenneth Duckett, David B. Gracy II, and Schellenberg.[23] Richard Berner offers a comprehensive and well-developed model. He suggests that archivists use a card catalog or index-posting sheets to index the inventories or registers rather than the

[21]Manfred Kochen, *Principles of Information Retrieval* (Los Angeles: Melville Publishing Co., 1974), pp. 54-55.

[22]Society of American Archivists' Committee on Finding Aids, *Inventories and Registers: A Handbook of Techniques and Examples* (Chicago: Society of American Archivists, 1976), p. 32.

[23]Ruth B. Bordin and Robert M. Warner. *The Modern Manuscript Library* (New York: Scarecrow Press, 1966); Kenneth Duckett, *Modern Manuscripts: A Practical Manual for Their Management, Care and Use* (Nashville: American Association for State and Local History, 1975); David B. Gracy II, *Archives & Manuscripts: Arrangement and Description* (Chicago: Society of American Archivists, 1977); and T.R. Schellenberg, *The Management of Archives*, pp. 253-89. Richard Berner has written widely on this subject. Two important articles are Richard M. Berner and M. Gary Bettis, "Description of Manuscript Collections" and Berner's "Arrangement and Description of Manuscripts" cited above.

records. The card catalog or index-posting sheets thus lead the reference archivist or the user to the proper inventory or register, which then leads into the internal arrangement of the record group or collection.

Subject analysis and indexing are time-consuming, but increased effort at the input stage may reduce the amount of searching time at the output stage. Archivists have only begun to measure input costs for processing and have rarely measured output costs. Reference department salaries may be charged to output costs but it is difficult to quantify other output costs—the costs of unanswered questions, the cost of researcher time spent searching through irrelevant documents, or the cost to an agency administrator of failing to locate a needed policy statement.

In setting up an indexing system, we must consider the concept of literary warrant, that is, the vocabulary of the system must be based on the material we put into it, not forced to conform to any purely theoretical scheme.[24] Archivists will probably reject an enumerative list of subject headings that gives little freedom to the indexer and that is unresponsive to the variety of information in and about our records. A more synthetic system that gives the indexer the principles to specify subjects as they arise will be more suitable. Without adequate control of vocabulary, recall will drop. A rich entry vocabulary, a large list of the non-preferred synonyms, enables the system to move easily from the natural language of users and the records to the more controlled indexing language. An indexing system must provide syntax as well as vocabulary so that relationships can be indicated. An album of photographs is different from a photograph of albums. The genus-species relationships so prevalent in hierarchically organized archival records pose particular problems for an archival indexing system.

The specificity of the indexing system is another important variable. Specificity is a measure of the extent to which the indexing language allows precision in labeling the subject. The greater the specificity, the greater the likelihood of relevance; that is, the records retrieved should be precisely those needed. On the other hand, if more general indexing terms are used, the larger the number of records retrieved but the lower the probability that they will be directly of interest.

The exhaustivity of the system measures the extent to which all the distinct subjects reflected in a particular record group are recognized and translated into the system. Deciding the number of terms to be assigned to any given record group, subgroup, series, or file is particu-

---

[24]Two good introductory texts to the ideas of information retrieval which follow are A.C. Foskett, *The Subject Approach to Information* (London: Bingley, 1977) and F. Wilfred Lancaster, *Information Retrieval Systems: Characteristics, Testing and Evaluation* (New York: Wiley, 1968).

larly difficult when dealing with archival record groups, since so many subjects may be present. Shall we index every committee, department, center, or other administrative subdivision reflected in the records of the College of Literature, Science, and the Arts of The University of Michigan?

An indexing system needs an address for the groups of documents located by the index. Indexing inventories and registers rather than records simplifies this problem. If the documents themselves are indexed, problems are compounded because archivists and users need either a relative location or a fixed location, both difficult to specify concisely.

Any archival system must be flexible, for the detail to which a collection or record group is processed depends on the importance of the material, anticipated use, and other administrative factors. Archivists need to be able to index at the record group level or at any of the subordinate levels.

In manual descriptive systems, indexing is pre-coordinate. Composite or complex subjects must be coordinated at the indexing or input stage and all possible uses of the indexes must be envisioned while assigning subject headings. Later manipulation of terms is not possible. In automated systems, sometimes called post-coordinate systems, the indexer can assign only simple terms during the input stage and the user can coordinate or manipulate complex subject terms during the output or use stage. It is this revolution that holds so much promise for the future.

In the final analysis, however, automated systems will be unable to solve our problems of subject access if we do not clearly identify the assumptions underlying our activities and specify our needs precisely and imaginatively. At the heart of any descriptive system lies careful and perceptive analysis of records. Good descriptive inventories coupled with an indexing system, whether manual or automated, are necessary if the reference archivist is to provide adequate service for users.

Chapter 8
Public Programs

As custodians of valuable historical materials, archivists work to ensure that their institutions' holdings are available to as wide an audience as possible. Public programs offer techniques for making archival documents and activities accessible and understood by a large segment of the public who may lack the training or time to undertake research.

In her article "Educational Programs: Outreach as an Administrative Function" (1978), Elsie Freeman argues that archives may serve the different needs of many publics. The goal of an archival institution, therefore, must be to identify its potential users and to match its service to their needs. Freeman notes that public programs permit institutions to respond to the interests of many individuals simultaneously; therefore, public programs are the most economical form of reference service. Such programs also provide an important means of building understanding and support for an archival institution throughout a community—a necessary foundation for a strong institution, whether public or private.

PUBLIC PROGRAMS

Joan Rabins focuses her attention on the most prominent element of public programs in archives in her article "Archival Exhibits: Considerations and Caveats" (1980). Rabins states that archives must examine their own priorities and resources to determine whether an exhibit program is appropriate. She concludes, however, that if such a program is undertaken and handled effectively, it can have significant benefits for an archival institution.

Education Programs:
Outreach as an Administrative Function

Elsie Freeman [Freivogel]

The *Washington Post*, commenting on the appointment of a new director of the National Endowment for the Humanities, reminds us of a forgotten truth, namely, that the health of humanistic studies is an important public value and that seeking to make cultural benefits widely available is neither to squander nor to vulgarize them. But the *Post* adds an unexpected twist:

> It is said that it is elitist of the Endowment to support certain fields of pure scholarship. We think the elitism exists on the part of those making the charge—people who assume that the general public is some part of a leaden mass unable to appreciate or make use of the fruits of a flourishing community of serious scholars.[1]

Scholarship, then, is one kind of educational enterprise, but not the only one. The possible products of scholarship comprise a continuum, and that continuum reflects the needs of a public comprised of many parts.

The *Post* editorial mirrors the thinking of those of us within the archival community who support archival education programs.[2] It is quoted to provide reassurance at the outset to other archivists who may feel that they are being pressured to abandon the scholarly community in the interests of popularization, or to view as somehow outmoded their talents as technical archivists. They are neither, by any means.

Gaining intellectual control of records remains the archivist's special work, without which no other activities proceed. We archivists are not,

---

Reprinted with permission from *The American Archivist* 41 (April 1978): 147-153.

[1]"The Politics of the Humanities," editorial in the *Washington Post*, 4 August 1963, p. A 18.

[2]We have used several terms in this paper which may confuse. The first, *archival education*, is used interchangeably with outreach, outreach programs, and education programs, terms in use in the United States, and subsumed in Canada under the rubric, diffusion. These programs are those which bring the products of archival research, the techniques of research in archives, or other aspects of humanist learning derived from primary sources to the user public, rather than to other archivists. The second term, *archives education* is here used to refer to the training of other archivists. So new is the concept of outreach that as yet we have no generally accepted term for it, as do our neighbors in the museum field who refer to their counterpart regularly as *museum education*, and who call the training of museum specialists, *museology*.

therefore, being asked to abandon technical archival work to open the doors to all comers.

Nor does it any longer seem necessary to persuade archivists to offer education programs. The numbers of these increase regularly, as a recent SAA survey indicates. The writer's impression, after many conversations with colleagues, is that many archivists are eager to extend their resources into wider communities, to make those resources available to publics they do not now reach. But behind these expressions of enthusiasm rests a dis-ease, a suspicion that these activities, however useful and laudatory, do not fit readily into the mainstream of activities we call archives administration, rendering them at the outset dubious. Why do these programs more often than not appear to be episodes or events, rather than programs in the ongoing administrative sense? What changes in our thinking will legitimize education programs within the larger administrative apparatus of an archives?

Outreach is first of all an extension of reference work, and as we use the word it generally describes any activity that brings the records or the means of using them closer to the public, multiplying in some way the effectiveness of the records or access to them. But that view—and the concept of outreach is still so new to our field that we can hardly refer to it as a definition—trips us up in two ways. First, to suggest *any activity* implies a randomness, a capriciousness, which immediately sets outreach programs apart from the more orderly stream of activity we call archives administration, rendering them decorative and therefore expendable. Frequently they are confused with public relations, an activity which has an entirely different thrust. Second, *the public* suggests a single, undifferentiated group, a notion which is equally misleading.

Our first job, then, is to recognize that we have many publics, ranging from institutionally connected researchers to general users, and across a spectrum that includes, among others, teachers at all levels of the educational system; elementary, secondary school, college and university students; genealogists, avocational historians, government employees, publicists, media professionals, and the merely curious. Next we must identify those potential publics in relation to our own mandates, depending on whether we represent, for example, a state archives, a county historical society, a state university, or a private institution. Finally, we must think in terms of providing service to the largest number of people within any of these publics in ways which fit the intellectual and logistical needs of its members. Only then can we begin to conceive of educational activities as programs rather than as scattershot episodes or events.

As archivists, we tend to think of our users as a monolith, a single body of clients who require uniform, detailed, scholarly reference service. But if we begin to recognize the differences among our users, to identify them as a series of publics, rather than as *the public*, we begin to see that they do not all need this uniform maximum service. We can begin to assess service in terms of content and logistics, and to fit it to need.

Outreach can range at the least from simple exhibits, tours, and curatorial talks to more sophisticated activity, including multilevel conferences, traveling exhibits, group instruction, teacher workshops, courses based on the archives using records as text and archivists as facilitators, or cycles of activities focused on a theme or a period. But in developing any of these educational services we must first decide for whom we are producing them, at what level of sophistication they need to be produced, and in what formats they can best be supplied to the maximum number of people. Such development removes from outreach its charity-basket connotations and turns it into an administrative device, one in which we make decisions about whom we serve and in what ways we serve them.

It is important to connect this proposition with two others, one historical and the other contemporary, which provide context and encouragement to the concept of the archives as an educational institution. The first added proposition is that only within the twentieth century in this country has adult education become the almost exclusive province of colleges and universities. Learning in nineteenth-century America, even as late as the early twentieth century, was conducted through public and informal institutions: chautauquas, workingmen's libraries, theaters and opera houses, museums, immigrant aid associations, and historical societies.

Today these institutions have changed their functions. Some have social welfare roles, others operate as service institutions, some serve a select public. They are run by professionals and, in the case of historical society-archives, by professionals trained in a European tradition with university and research orientation. Since the early twentieth century then, our training, reinforced by research directed standards bearing no necessary relation to the American experience, has isolated us from a function which once was ours, namely, that of serving as an educational institution, our staff being educators or organizers of educational activity.

The second proposition is corollary to the first, namely, that history is alive and well in this country everywhere but in the classroom. Look at the bulletin board of the public library, the adult services calendar of the community college, or the program of the garden club. Observe the interest in historic gardens, houses, architecture, interiors, costumes, and china. Count the number of tours of historical villages; the digs for amateur archaeologists; the films for admirers of the Hittites, the Medicis, or Indian mounds in Illinois. Consider, if the proposition is in question, genealogy, no longer the property of social climbers but the tool of teachers and the delight of students and avocationists. There is a fascination with the past in all its warty and populous beauty, a fascination undeniable in this nation of transients; and it is their right.

How do we begin to identify our users, and to fit service to need? A study of the users of the National Archives is useful as a model for this assessment.[3] That study found that more than five out of ten of our Washington users were genealogists; in some of our regional branches, that number is as high as eight out of ten. About one user in ten is a casual researcher, possibly an amateur historian, a film or television producer, an editor, lawyer, writer, or simply a passerby. Two out of ten users are connected with research institutions, and are likely to publish or otherwise disseminate their work through scholarly channels. The remaining two are students, working either for the doctoral, the master's, or, increasingly, the bachelor's degree.

If it is true that roughly eight out of ten users of our National Archives variously serve their own avocational needs or broad popular interests, how do we simultaneously serve them and the scholarly researchers who also have a claim on us? By providing systems which make the records more available to them in forms and through channels that serve their needs. There is no doubt that one-researcher to one-archivist service is necessary at a sophisticated, sustained level of research. But not every transaction requires it, and our dismay at the ideal of introducing more people to archives as sources of information may well arise from the assumption that this kind of service is the only kind.

More often, much information now transmitted in this expensive fashion can be transmitted in bulk. Such service can include audio and/or visual programs that orient fifty researchers at a time to an institution's facilities and to fundamental research information. It can include intensive classes that instruct genealogists and general researchers, because each group requires a different range of information, in how and when to approach records. Or it can include workshops for college classes or faculty, showing them either how to use documents in the classroom or how to do research. The variations are infinite, but the questions to be asked by the administrator are two. First, what are the specific publics we are mandated to serve? Second, given our administrative constraints, what services will convey our resources to the largest number of people in any one of those publics in forms most usable to them?

---

[3]A Study of Users of the Records of the National Archives. Prepared by staff of the National Archives and Records Service, October 1976, for administrative purposes. It is the writer's understanding that these figures have since changed but they serve the purpose of identifying publics.

Consider, for example, the needs of the secondary school teacher compared with those of the scholarly researcher. In general, teachers want to know two things before they will use records in the classroom. First, they must be able quickly to identify a record or a group of records that relates in a general way to a topic their class is studying. Second, they want to be comfortable with strategies for using those records in the classroom. Unless a teacher is also doing individual research, he or she does not need knowledge of that elaborate system for tracking records through a network of collections or record groups required of the scholar, nor does that teacher need a specific, unique document proving the point or justifying the argument. He does not need to track down all the sources, just the appropriate ones. He needs evaluations of internal and external validity in a document less than he needs to know that the document can be used in a classroom; that is, he must know that it is legible, has potential for building vocabulary, and is intrinsically interesting. And unlike the scholar, whose work ends in print to an unseen audience, he needs devices for using the material in the classroom. What that teacher needs, then, is not detailed reference service. What he needs is general familiarity with the existence of records appropriate to his topic, or even some boxes of records within that topic, plus a number of teaching strategies best shared with his peers. One answer to his needs is the teacher workshop, using peer teachers to share ideas, and an archivist, familiar enough with the topic and the institution's resources to point the teacher toward a general body of records, and otherwise serve as group facilitator. In this way we serve a number of people at once, who in turn expose many students and other teachers to records as sources of history, and serve them in ways particularly suited to their needs.

What we are producing here is a multiplier effect, an organizing principle that renders outreach programs far more efficient than we have previously seen them. First, by reaching more clients in less time we are multiplying the use of the records. Second, by providing service in bulk we are multiplying the number of potential clients within any given public. Finally, by interchanging parts of various programs or by combining several programs we provide multiple service to any single public. The scholarly researcher, for example, uses one-to-one reference service. But the researcher also views the exhibit, attends the lecture program, sends students to the introductory course on using records, and brings classes to sessions which engage students in the pedagogical uses of records.

In assessing our outreach programs, we need also to decide who will execute them and who will pay for them. With respect to personnel, we must first recognize that the professional skills and standards required for these programs may be different—not inferior, only different—from those with which, as archivists, we are familiar. We may well find that we need professional writers to prepare the press releases; education specialists to develop format and promote the lecture series, symposia, and institutes we will require; and audiovisual specialists to make our films and write our scripts. In a sense new to us, staffing our education programs requires an expansion of the concept of the archivist as professional to include the education archivist, just as we accept the concept of the documentary editor, administrator, or computer analyst as a comparable professional.

Some institutions should and do hire audiovisual experts, educational developers, secondary school curriculum specialists, designers, publication sales experts, and cultural administrators. But three other options are available and, for most institutions, far more accessible. The first two are immediate; the third is longer range.

The first option is an assessment of those talents already on our staffs. Inside every thin man, some wag said, is a fat man fighting to get out. The record seems to support the view that inside many archivists is a filmmaker, a lecturer, an impresario, or an exhibit designer fighting to get out. According to the survey done recently by the SAA Committee on Outreach, most education programs are organized at the outset around the talents of staff members presently on the job. Job descriptions will not necessarily reveal these skills. It may be necessary for the administrator to build an inventory of talents by personal conversations with staff members, by participating in pilot programs, or by other less traditional means of staff assessment.

The second option is the creation of networks of talent within a region. Just as we have devised research networks, so we can devise talent networks, and just as we accommodate joint teaching-archival appointments, we can accommodate joint archivist-educator appointments. Many models exist among community organizations, the performing arts, and other professions accustomed to sharing staff and resources; and the apparatus of joint appointments, released and reimbursed time, and outright moonlighting are negotiable within a region. What is needed is a sense of the larger profession of archivists, rather than the semi-imposed isolation to which we have adapted, combined with a keen appreciation of the fiscal advantages of shared time, staff, and talents. It may be in order to create a talent bank on which members of the profession can draw, with appropriate reimbursement to lending institutions, breaking the unyielding circle of technical chores which seem to deter us from reaching our larger clientele.

The third option is learning how to do it ourselves. To do this we must incorporate outreach techniques in our archives education programs where outreach training now has only a fingernail hold on the last hour of the last day in each session. At present, most of our archives education courses concentrate on basic technical skills—arrangement, description, and reference at one level and one only—and never associate education programs with the administrative apparatus of an archives. If we can agree that concentration on outreach will allow us to focus more sharply on reference services, and if we can agree that outreach is not the last priority of an archives but one that can help us define other priorities, then we can agree that archives education should include far more information on outreach than it now does. We can move beyond introductory courses in technical problems to thematic courses in education, designed to offer specialized instruction to staff of institutions ready to take hold of the concept.

We need not offer these courses in isolation. Museum educators have a ready literature and staff in this field, and they have long since fought the battle to legitimize outreach programs. Other professional groups are available to us, and the contribution of these would relate us to the larger universe of cultural and educational institutions. We need a midlevel archives education course dealing with problems of preservation, description, and reference from a client-centered point of view, identifying publics, offering options in the formats by which those publics are reached, and planning programs based on alternative methods of information dissemination. Ideally, such a course would be given in conjunction with a museum education program, since many of the techniques are similar. Dealing with the technical, informational, and managerial aspects of archives, this course is now within our reach.

Earlier, we noted the *Washington Post* on the relationship between humanistic and public values. Public values deserve public support, and archives, to the extent that records reflect public values, deserve public support. But archives deserve it only to the extent that they deliver their materials in ways that are comprehensible to the public. The public can be expected to pay for archival services if we give them the information they need in ways they can use. In other words, we can expect payment when we give good value for their money.

It is certainly the case that public endowments and private foundations are accessible to proposals for programs which reach wide publics. In fact, it is reasonable to expect that within the next several years public endowments will require in every proposal for public funds a component that makes the records available to a number of publics other than scholars.

In the meantime, we can charge for outreach programs. The National Archives Office of Educational Programs, whose activities range from public tours and lectures to scholarly conferences, and include short courses, exhibits, audiovisual productions, and numerous other client-directed programs, charges for many of them; and clients do not complain. Indeed, interest in these programs increases regularly.

287

PUBLIC PROGRAMS

But a persuasive example comes from the museum field, our most experienced allies in the pursuit of outreach programs. Daniel B. Reibel, curator of Old Economy Village, Ambridge, Pennsylvania, confirms the feasibility of client-supported services. Commenting on Old Economy's programs, Reibel says:

> Nothing in the world is free. . . .Although a museum staff with imagination and common sense can run programs at a very low cost, ultimately there is a bill. If the audience is divided into interest groups that pay fees commensurate with the program or services received, it is possible to cover all or most of the costs of the programs.[4]

Reibel suggests several other principles which reinforce the experience of the National Archives. Audience size tends to increase after a charge is levied. The quality of the clientele improves too, he says; and, as a corollary which has significant personnel implications, the staff delivers more. Staff performs better, program format improves. Finally, "an adequate charge is only a means to an end—more and better programs, tours, and other services. . . . Visitor financed programs offer a chance to give good programs suited to the need of both the museum and the visitor, regardless of the museum's budget."[5]

We have some choices in the next few years about the direction in which our archival programs will go; but these choices, like many we face, become clearer as we confront them. The clientele for expanded outreach programs is there; our job is to engage it. The engagement need not be sentimental. It can be analytical, cost-effective, and as useful to us as to our clients. We can choose the publics we serve, choose the means by which they are served, and organize much of our technical work around these choices. In this fashion, we generate public support by providing service—wide, but carefully considered and carefully developed public service.

---

[4]Daniel B. Reibel, "Visitor Financed Programs," *Museum News* 55 (July/August 1977): 27.

[5]Ibid., p. 30.

288

Archival Exhibits: Considerations and Caveats

Joan Rabins

One striking cultural development since World War II both here and abroad has been the steady growth in the popularity of what is often termed "exhibit-going." Museum visits are no longer dutiful and infrequent. Rather, museums are struggling to cope with ever-increasing crowds who attend exhibits as a normal part of their social activities.[1] Other institutions, including libraries, historical societies, businesses, and archives and manuscript libraries, find the public responsive even when rather recondite exhibit subjects are chosen. Because of this favorable climate, agencies for which exhibits are not a primary function must now decide whether or not to embark on such a program.

Archival institutions which face this question must constantly examine their priorities and resources to determine whether, and to what extent, they should venture into this area. This decision must take into account not only the relevance of a proposed exhibit to the institution's programs but also the degree to which the exhibition of archival materials may affect their safety and long-term physical condition. An agency which does begin an exhibit program must plan carefully not only for the display area and the exhibit itself but also for the scheduling and publicity which will maximize the exhibit's effectiveness.

Most archival administrators begin an exhibit program in order to publicize the institution's resources. Through exhibits an archives can dramatize the strong points of its particular collection and thus create a clear identity to which the general public as well as researchers can relate. Even in a university setting, according to Judith Cushman, it is not uncommon for scholars on the faculty to become aware of the research potential of an archival collection only as the result of an exhibit.[2]

Albert H. Leisinger, Jr., speaking in 1961, emphasized a different reason for undertaking an exhibit program: the obligation to make "our institutions centers of popular education,"[3] or, as the catchword of the

Reprinted with permission from *Georgia Archive* 8 (Fall, 1980): 29-40. *Georgia Archive*, the journal of the Society of Georgia Archivists, is now titled *Provenance*.

[1]The Belmont Report quoted in *Museums, Imagination and Education* (Paris: UNESCO, 1973), p. 91.

[2]Judith Cushman, "Creating and Managing an Exhibit Program," *The Midwestern Archivist* 1 (1975): 28.

[3]Albert H. Leisinger, Jr., "The Exhibit of Documents," *American Archivist* 26 (January 1963): 77.

time might have put it, "relevant." Since that time there has been increasing pressure on all institutions, both government and private, to open themselves as much as possible to the public and to relinquish any elitist pretensions. To the majority of the public, the word "archives" still has a vaguely dry and forbidding sound, and repositories can use exhibits to persuade the public to venture into the archives and to clarify the place of archives in the educational and intellectual structure. It is from such occasional impressions that the average citizen creates his image of the archives and its function in the community.[4]

In the same way, exhibits enable the archives to function as part of the broader intellectual and cultural community and of the university or cultural complex of which it is a part. It is fitting that the archives draw upon its own unique resources to contribute to the richness of the cultural experience available to the total community. One of the benefits for the archives is that such events provide natural opportunities for interaction with neighboring institutions or even those at some distance from which supplementary materials can be borrowed.

During the bicentennial year the Archives of Labor and Urban Affairs, a part of Wayne State University and located in a county named for Wayne, mounted an exhibit which exemplifed such interaction. This exhibit focused on Anthony Wayne's 1796 visit as a representative of the United States government to accept the transfer of Detroit and Michigan from British rule. A number of institutions in the area, including the Burton Historical Collection of the Detroit Public Library, the Michigan State Archives, the Clarke Historical Library at Central Michigan University, and the William L. Clements Library of the University of Michigan, contributed material to the exhibit, making it truly a community undertaking.[5] The broad public interest in the exhibit testified to the soundness of the choice of theme.

Even archivists who are wary of seeking publicity must confront the economic realities of the purely research institutions in today's world. No matter how well-endowed at the outset, there are few collections which have not been compelled to solicit funding merely to maintain their operations. Scholars' use of archives is increasing steadily, and this increased usage adds to the pressure on the archives to secure more funding.[6] Government or private support is essential to continued archival development, and a program of stimulating exhibitions which generates publicity and attention is an effective and relatively painless way to

---

[4]Kenneth W. Duckett, *Modern Manuscripts* (Nashville: American Association for State and Local History, 1975), pp. 257-58.

[5]Information on the exhibit furnished by Margery Long, Audio Visual Curator, who is also responsible for exhibits.

[6]"Publicity for Records," *Archives* 8 (April 1968): 113.

keep the presence and importance of the archives before an influential segment of the community.[7]

Archives must also appeal to potential donors of collections of papers and manuscripts. An attractive exhibit provides an opportunity to make a favorable impression on an individual who owns a valuable collection, one whose own personal papers would complement the holdings of the archives, or the decision-makers in organizations whose records the repository seeks. Exhibits are also occasionally used to announce recent acquisitions and give recognition to donors.

One of the side benefits of an exhibits program is that it provides an outlet for the research talents and creative impulses of the staff. Those familiar with the holdings of the archives are uniquely qualified to select and research topics which show the collection to advantage. Tracking down and securing suitable supplementary materials can be an interesting challenge to those creating the exhibit, and the opportunity for public recognition can contribute immeasurably to staff morale.

For these and other reasons many archives regard exhibitions as an extremely important part of their role. The National Archives, for example, feels an obligation "to place before the general public selected documents that have commemorative interest, exemplifying the traditions and ideals of the Nation, or serve . . . to dramatize or vivify important events and phases of its history."[8] Presidential libraries devote part of their space to permanent exhibits on the life of the president. These exhibits, which memorialize the president and educate the public about his career and the history of his time, attract a large audience and are often strong tourist attractions. Naturally, such exhibits contribute considerably to the nationwide reputation of the institution.

An article in 1978 by a member of the staff of the Folger Shakespeare Library raises some of the arguments against undertaking extensive exhibits.[9] These issues deserve serious consideration. The archivist's primary charge is to care for those materials worthy of preservation. It is surely a case of misplaced zeal if the materials are permanently damaged in the effort to enhance the prestige of the institution. Even with the precautions available today to protect papers and bindings from damage by light, improper humidity levels, and dust, the conditions of display cannot replicate the more ideal environment of the stacks or reading room; and there can be no question that the prolonged stress of exhibition takes its toll on original materials. Moreover, there is always the very

---

[7]L. A. Kenney, "Public Relations in the College Library," *College and Research Libraries* 25 (July 1964): 263.

[8]Leisinger, "Exhibit."

[9]Sandra Powers, "Why Exhibit?: The Risks Versus the Benefits," *American Archivist* 41 (July 1978): 297-306.

real danger of theft or vandalism during an exhibit even when security personnel are present.[10]

To avoid these pitfalls the imaginative curator can often convey the authentic flavor and impact of the original piece of paper without actually putting it on display. There are numerous processes available today to reproduce a document, possibly enlarging it and using color which can impart historic atmosphere. Blowups using such techniques often make excellent backdrops for exhibits of three-dimensional objects which are used to amplify the theme of the exhibit. Or, in some instances, a document can be selected of which the archives has more than one copy and which is therefore expendable.

There are situations in which substitution would vitiate the impact of the exhibit, and in these instances the archivist must weigh the advantages of exhibiting against the disadvantages, balancing responsibility to the researcher and the donor against the obligation to serve the public at large.[11] Naturally, the more rare and valuable the document, the more reluctant the archivist will be to use it for display for any prolonged time. If the decision is made to use originals for display, every precaution available through today's technology should be called upon to preserve the document in the condition it was before being shown.

The demand which exhibitions make on staff time and the cost involved might also dissuade an archives from beginning an exhibition program. If such a program would jeopardize the quality of service to users, an archives would be wise to forgo the ancillary benefits of exhibiting in favor of maintaining its standards as a repository.

Once the decision to exhibit has been made, the first practical consideration is the selection of the display area. Newer facilities generally include a specific exhibit space in their plans, but lack of a designated area for exhibits need not be a deterrent. It is often possible to convert an area into display space or have it serve a dual function.

The selection of appropriate themes for exhibits is of paramount importance. Topics should be selected on the basis of their timeliness, suitability to the particular collection, and overall appropriateness to the goals of the institution's exhibit policies as well as their attractiveness to the public. The more an institution can utilize its own resources, the more successful the exhibit will be in projecting the intrinsic character of that institution.

---

[10]Ibid. Very often the greatest danger of theft exists when an exhibit is being assembled and dismantled. For this reason most authorities advise completing these tasks outside public visiting hours so that control can be maintained over the number of people who have access to the objects on display. Duckett, *Manuscripts*, pp. 253-54.

[11]Powers, "Why Exhibit?," p. 303.

An intangible but vital factor in the success of an exhibit is its aesthetic impact. Though laudable in every other respect, an exhibit which does not appeal to the eye will not achieve its aim. The best exhibits have an aesthetic cohesiveness of color and style, often achieved by a well-designed overall motif, a signature identified in the viewer's mind with the theme. Exhibit information must be translated into forms which will capture the attention of the viewer, and the message must be imparted by visual symbols rather than long, detailed captions. Often it is wise to highlight only a small portion of a manuscript, that sentence or two which sums up the whole. Care also must be taken not to overtax the patience of the viewer. A few arresting, well-chosen objects are preferable to cases crowded with redundant examples.

Another major element in the success of a program of exhibits is careful and realistic scheduling based on the budget and staff size of an institution. It is better to aim for a few notable exhibitions rather than an overly busy schedule of mediocre or amateurish attempts. Not every exhibit on a schedule can be a magnum opus. For the sake of the staff as well as the public, it is advisable to alternate major efforts with smaller ones.

Sufficient lead time for each exhibit is vital.[12]Research, arrangements which must be made with cooperating institutions, printing, and construction require considerable time, and allowance also must be made for the inevitable delays which can wreak havoc with a tight schedule. Time must also be allotted in the schedule for dismantling each exhibit and returning borrowed items. Thus the time scheduled between shows must realistically reflect the capabilities of the staff.

An exhibit schedule should also be flexible enough to take advantage of unanticipated opportunities for staging exhibits—visits by dignitaries, local events, anniversaries. Nor should an archives be committed to taking down an exhibit before it has lost its public appeal. A good schedule also takes into account holidays and vacation seasons which, particularly in a university community, can have a marked effect on attendance and staffing.

Once a schedule is settled, the full benefit can be derived from each exhibit by planning as many events as possible to tie in with it. A reception for the exhibit opening, for example, creates excitement and often assures press coverage. An exhibit is also a natural opportunity to set up symposia and lectures on related topics. Or the archives can reverse the process, planning an exhibit to coincide with an anniversary or talks being given either at the archives or at a neighboring institution.

---

[12]Ideally, the exhibit should be in place one week before the official opening to permit those responsible to view it as a whole and make any alterations necessary to achieve its maximum effect.

The traffic flow through most archives is not so great that most repositories can rely on attracting exhibit viewers from among casual passersby as can a library or museum. Only by industriously generating publicity can an archives draw enough people to justify the effort and expense of an exhibit program. To interest the maximum number of people in an exhibit, it is essential to utilize the greatest variety of means available to reach the potential audience.

An effective publicity program begins with an up-to-date list of sources to be routinely informed of all events. Many newspapers and radio stations carry a weekly calendar of events, and concise, well-written press releases can sometimes lead to a mention in the columns of local papers. Media may also decide to provide coverage of newsworthy individuals who visit the exhibit, and this can reach an enormous audience. An archives newsletter is a natural vehicle for articles and photographs of exhibits and related events. An archives volunteer "friends" group can provide enthusiastic support and help to interest others. The archives which is part of a university complex can utilize the various official and student publications; and, when appropriate, notices should go out to academic and trade journals.

An attractive, well-written publication providing background information should accompany the exhibit. Such a pamphlet, designed with taste and imagination, contributes to the impact of the exhibit and provides a convenient way to acknowledge those who contributed work, funds, or materials for the show. Extra copies can be used in mailings to attract an audience and sent afterwards to those interested in the archives as evidence of its activities.

A more elaborate catalog providing information to supplement the captions in the cases, although more costly to write and print, has the virtue of being salable. In many instances such a catalog can be sold long after the exhibit has closed and frequently will even become a profit-maker for the institution.[13] This type of publication also has a certain prestige value and can be used to indicate the quality of an archives' exhibit program to a person or institution from which the archives seeks to borrow material for a future show. One historical society prepares carefully researched catalogs as a service to teachers who lead the numerous school groups to which the society's exhibits cater.[14]

Detailed record keeping during and after each exhibit provides a reservoir of expertise for the staff. Taking photographs of each case and recording all texts and captions facilitate the re-creation of the same

---

[13]P. William Filby, "Techniques of Exhibitions," *The 1968 A. B. Bookman's Yearbook, Part Two: The Old and the New* (Newark, N.J.: Bookman's Weekly, 1968), p. 9.

[14]Lucille Kane, "The Exhibition of Manuscripts at the Minnesota Historical Society," *American Archivist* 15 (January 1952): 40.

exhibit at some future date with a minimum of effort. Carefully itemized accounts help with future budgeting. Mailing lists should be kept current and samples should be kept of all press releases and publications. Detailed plans of any special construction should be kept in case a similar need arises in the future.

The final step in closing the book on an exhibit should be a detailed, critical report by the exhibit staff. Other members of the staff and selected viewers should be encouraged to contribute frank evaluations and suggestions on ways to improve the exhibit. This type of feedback is important to educate the staff and maintain a high standard for exhibits which will be a credit to the archives.

At this point many archives amortize the cost of an exhibit by sending their exhibits out on the road. Traveling exhibitions publicize the archives to a much wider audience and foster good relations with borrowing institutions. Preparing a touring exhibit requires considerable extra work and special staff expertise, however, and arranging for periodic transfer and supervising needed repairs consume additional staff time.[15]

The decision to tour an exhibit should be made before design and construction of the exhibit begin. Then display panels and cases can be used which can be packed into shipping crates without being disassembled. These insure greater safety in shipping and are economical both in terms of material cost and staff time. Once an exhibit is away from the supervision of those who designed it, there is an increased chance of damage or theft; and therefore only reproductions should be used for traveling exhibits.

Rather than originating traveling exhibits, most archival institutions would probably be more interested in using the traveling exhibits mounted by a great number of museums, government agencies, industrial firms, and other organizations. One of the largest and best-known collections is the SITES (Smithsonian Institution Traveling Exhibit Service) program which currently offers almost two hundred exhibits on a wide variety of subjects.[16] The fees charged vary and are based on the size and estimated value of the exhibit. SITES specifies the level of security which must be provided by the borrowing institution as part of the agreement and rules regarding shipping, damages, insurance, and cancellation penalities. In general, its regulations are fairly typical of those which would be imposed by any other supplier of traveling exhibits.

---

[15]Telephone interview with Betty Odle, Exhibit Designer, Cranbrook Academy, West Bloomfield, Michigan, October 17, 1978.

[16]Letter, November 4, 1978, from Mary Lou Cocker, Registrar for Scheduling, SITES, Washington, D.C.

Most archives draw upon traveling exhibits to fill out their exhibit schedules. This lightens the load on personnel who, in the typical archives, have duties other than those connected with exhibits. Most report favorably on their experiences with borrowed exhibits. The very fact that an exhibit emanates from another source means that it will be different in appearance and approach and will give variety to the archives exhibit program.

Any exhibit must be created with an eye to those factors which will insure success and bring prestige to the repository. An effective exhibit should be attractive to the prospective audience, done in a professional manner with a high level of visual appeal and aesthetic sophistication, and related to the noteworthy characteristics of the collection. Final success depends on the care which is given to publicity and scheduling and the extent to which the staff is able to build on past experience to steadily improve their offerings. If sufficient attention is devoted to these problems, an exhibit program can become the most effective means for an archives to promote its identity and mission.

There are many reasons which impel an archives or manuscript library to incorporate exhibits into its programs. Some institutions, because of the nature of their holdings or financial or staff limitations, will decline to enter this area. For those who do, the benefits which accrue to the institution are numerous and tangible.

Chapter 9
Establishing Priorities

Because resources of archival repositories are limited and potential work virtually limitless, archivists are confronted daily with difficult choices. Should the archivist's time be devoted to an aggressive acquisition program or to processing accessioned materials? Should more resources be allocated to conservation of a few items of high value or to development of an outreach program to stimulate greater interest in little used collections? An archivist's most important responsibility is establishing priorities among competing concerns.

James Worthy offers a framework to use in approaching difficult choices in archival management. In his article "Management Concepts and Archival Administration" (1979), Worthy reviews widely accepted management ideas and analyzes their application to archives administration. His observations provide sound guidance to archivists in the process of establishing priorities.

Megan Desnoyers examines the choices available to archivists within one function, the processing of personal papers, in her essay "When is a Collection Processed?" (1982). Desnoyers argues convincingly that archivists should evaluate the qualities of materials in order to establish appropriate processing goals for each collection. Although the author's conclusion relates to only one facet of archives administration, her approach and analysis offer a model that can be applied to other choices affecting basic archival functions.

F. Gerald Ham considers another aspect of priorities for archival institutions in his essay "The Archival Edge" (1975). Ham observes that archival repositories cannot preserve all available contemporary documentation and argues that archivists must establish priorities to document adequately the broad spectrum of human experience. Ham proposes a new degree of cooperation among archivists as the foundation for identifying and establishing these priorities. Though all archivists may not agree with Ham's conclusions, his discussion provides a vivid demonstration of the importance for archivists of examining their profession and balancing the complex of activities that must be interwoven for an effective archival program.

Management Concepts and Archival Administration

James C. Worthy

Your program chairperson has given me some rather broad instructions. Generally speaking, she wishes me to discuss "management principles and techniques applicable to archival administration, in particular personnel and organizational goals and objectives." More specifically, she has asked me to cover such topics as participatory management, communications, attitudes and motivation, measurement of managerial effectiveness, delegation of authority, the duties and responsibilities of leadership, and methods of planning and organizing. So that I might not feel too constricted, she has graciously allowed that I may want to add other topics, but she made it clear that my emphasis should be "management principles of personnel and goals in archival administration."

Now that is a rather large order. Many weighty tomes have been written on each of these subjects, and graduate students at schools of business across the country spend two years in earnest endeavor to earn advanced degrees by mastering them. Soberly assessed, however, my assignment is rendered practical by two considerations: its limitation to archival administration, and the over-complexity and superfluity of modern management literature.

The focus on archival administration allows me to eliminate or briefly dismiss a number of items that would require attention in a general discussion of management principles. Most archives are units within a larger institution: a university, a museum, a governmental bureau, a corporation, or some other body concerned with the preservation and utilization of historical documents. Under these circumstances, many aspects of management are "givens" for the archival administrator; they are matters to which the administrator must adapt but over which he or she has little or no control.

The host organization will have a body of personnel policies, including requirements for the selection, placement, compensation, and disciplining of personnel, whether in the archives or in its other constituent units. Budgetary and accounting procedures, as well as many other "givens," are usually matters to which the archivist must simply conform. Thus, with respect to a considerable portion of modern management

Reprinted with permission from *The Midwestern Archivist* 4 (2, 1979): 77-88. This essay is a slightly revised version of a plenary speech presented at the spring 1979 meeting of the Midwest Archives Conference.

theory, the task of the archivist is to learn, and learn to live with, the rules of its host organization. I do not counsel an attitude of "ours not to reason why." Rather, I urge upon you the importance of mastering the policies and procedures of your host organization in order to foster smooth relationships and enhance your ability to use those policies and procedures to the advantage of the operation for which you are responsible.

While they may be parts of large complex structures, most archives themselves are relatively small and simple. Your program chairperson informs me that while there are "great differences among budgets, resources, administrative organization, and work quarters," for the most part those in my audience today "will represent an archives with less than five professionals supported by clerical and student or volunteer staff and a budget of less than $50,000." Not only does this greatly simplify my task; in terms of management, it is exceedingly fortunate for you because it enables you to focus on essentials. In fact, if you are serious about wanting to improve your managerial skills, you will have to concentrate on a few central ideas and brush aside a great deal of what has come to be incorporated in modern management literature but what to my mind is not only superfluous but downright misleading. Let me illustrate with three examples: management by objectives, participatory management, and performance evaluation.

These ideas are among the most popular and most widely discussed in managerial circles today. There are few management conferences which deal in any way with personnel matters that do not include these subjects prominently on their agenda, and several five-foot shelves of books have been written on each. In each case, the underlying idea is simple. "Management by objectives" is based on the rather elementary notion that people will collaborate more effectively if each knows how his work contributes to the achievement of a common goal. "Participatory management" is based on the equally elementary thought that people will work better if they have some voice in setting the objectives of their own jobs and in determining how to reach them. "Performance evaluation" rests on the hardly exotic principle that people should be judged by their achievements.

All three precepts are fairly sensible. Peter Drucker, who gave the first specific formulation to the concept of management by objectives, states the matter succinctly: "Each member of the enterprise contributes something different, but all must contribute to a common goal. Their efforts must all pull in the same direction, and their contributions must fit together to produce a whole . . . ."

Peter F. Drucker, *Management Tasks, Responsibilities, Practices* (New York: Harper & Row, 1973), p. 430.

Douglas McGregor, an early exponent of the idea of participatory management, talks of the need for "creation of an environment which will encourage commitment to organizational objectives and which will provide opportunities for the maximum exercise of initiative, ingenuity, and self-direction in achieving them."

Marvin Bower, guru of professional management consultants, urges that people be judged "on the basis of their actions and achievements, not their personal qualities and skills . . . by what they do and how well they do it."

An amazingly voluminous body of literature has grown up on how to put these rather straightforward ideas into practice. In part this is a reflection of the fact that a fair number of people make a good living out of writing textbooks for students and "how to" books for practicing managers. In producing a book, they have to fill up a certain amount of space, and all too often this calls for tedious elaboration of detail, in the course of which the main thrust of the central idea may be lost.

A second and very practical influence is the administrator who wants to see a good idea widely adopted within his organization. Consider the company president who has read Drucker and wants to convert his executive staff to the use of management by objectives; or the general manager well schooled in McGregor who wants to encourage participatory management; or the personnel vice president seeking more equitable ways to recognize and reward accomplishment. How does one go about implementing even fairly simple ideas in large and complex structures (and here let it be noted that most of the literature deals with large and complex structures)? How does one change the behavior of a fairly large number of executive and supervisory staff who have been brought up in certain ways, who are accustomed to forms of behavior sanctioned by tradition, and who may in fact feel threatened by the prospect of forced imposition of new ideas? I assure you, the task is not easy.

Action may be taken along any of several lines, or along a combination of lines. One is by administrative fiat—usually not very effective. Another is through training courses, a time-consuming and often expensive process. Still another is by the installation of a "program," usually with someone made responsible for overseeing it and reporting on its progress. I imagine everyone in this audience has been exposed more than once to all three types of measures to promote the adoption of an administrative practice that someone higher up has wanted to introduce.

Douglas McGregor, *The Human Side of Enterprise* (New York: McGraw-Hill Book Company, 1960), p. 132.

Marvin Bower, *The Will To Manage*, (New York: McGraw-Hill Book Company, 1966), pp. 35, 37.

ESTABLISHING PRIORITIES

Common characteristics of all such attempts to change behavior are a set of forms and some kind of reporting system. But the heart of the problem is that the kinds of ideas we are talking about really involve attitudes. Attitudes are inherently difficult to change, and how is one to know whether a change has actually occurred? The purpose of forms is usually to provide leverage for enforcing changes in practice, but they are poor instruments for reaching or influencing the mental attitudes that underlie the practice. The purpose of reports is usually to assess the extent of change, but too often they distort and corrupt the entire endeavor.

These are very practical problems facing the administrator of a large and complex organization. They are major reasons for the seemingly endless elaboration of procedural detail, and for the voluminous body of literature that has grown up around these and other basically straightforward managerial concepts. Responsible professionals in organizations such as yours are fortunate indeed in that they are in positions that enable them to grasp and apply creative managerial ideas in their essentials and without the excessive detail that people in more complex organizations often feel it necessary to employ.

To put the matter directly, we are dealing with attitudes, and the important attitude you have to change is your own. That may not be easy, but you can change your own mind much more easily if you want to than if someone else wants you to do so. It is also a lot easier to change your own mind than to change the minds of a lot of other people you may want to persuade to your way of thought and practice.

I have dwelt at some length on what I consider to be the redundancy and over-elaboration of much of what currently passes for managerial theory. But I have done so with a dual purpose. On the negative side, I do not wish you to be discouraged or turned off by the sheer volume of stuff—I use the word deliberately—you find on library shelves or on reference lists. On the positive side, I want to emphasize that in modern management theory there are a number of creative and highly productive ideas that can be applied with particular effectiveness in archival administration. These ideas include: knowing the job, setting objectives, organizing to meet objectives, managing by objectives, managing by participation, and evaluating performance. In the course of discussing these subjects, I shall deal incidentally with such matters as communication, attitudes, motivation, and the working climate.

I want to begin by making a point that is seldom made in the standard literature of management: the importance of *knowing the job.* I am not being facetious. I mean simply that if you are going to be a successful manager, it is a great help to know what you are managing. This may seem rather obvious, but there is a widespread notion that management is management, and that if you know how to manage one thing you can manage almost anything. There is a germ of truth here, but not much more than a germ. Granted, it is by no means unusual for people to move between apparently quite different organizational environments. But those who do so successfully—and many do—are those who are able to grasp the essentials of their new jobs within a reasonable period of time.

I would therefore say that the first and most important qualification for the successful archival administrator is a firm grasp of archival functions and procedures. No amount of knowledge of human relations or principles of organization or techniques of planning will be of much avail unless the would-be administrator knows what archives are supposed to accomplish and how they function. These things, of course, can be learned; my point is that they *must* be learned, and here the experienced archivist is a far better guide than the most sophisticated management theorist. Professional meetings are probably the most important single means for raising the standards and improving the effectiveness of archival management.

The second requirement is *setting objectives*. Precious as its well-being may be to those responsible for its care, no archives exists for itself alone; its raison d'etre is to serve larger purposes. This is obviously true of archives that are parts of larger host organizations where they perform some function considered important enough to merit the investment of the resources required. But it is also true of free-standing archives, although here the larger purposes may not be so unambiguously discernible. A great presidential library exists not merely to preserve and protect the papers of a former president; that could be done perhaps more effectively in a sealed underground vault. Its purpose is also to organize these papers and make them accessible to scholars and others who may need them to serve the general society, both now and in the future.

Therefore, when we talk about setting objectives for archival administration we must begin by clearly defining the purposes for which the archives was established. This is obviously something that must be done in close collaboration with the host organization; or, in the case of a free-standing institution, with its board of trustees or other body that represents the larger community the archives is intended to serve. In a very real sense, of course, this larger community becomes the host organization.

An intimate reciprocal relationship exists between the archives administrator and the host organization. While the needs of the latter must be served, it may not clearly perceive what its real archival needs are. The archivist's duty as a professional is to assist in identifying and defining these needs. In this respect, the archivist's role is not essentially different from that of any other functional specialist in a larger organization. His first responsibility as a professional is to employ the conceptual resources at his command to assist the host organization in determining the specific means by which his specialty may best serve its purposes— whether the host is a manufacturing concern, a university library, or a scholarly community.

The key here is the purposes of the host. Anyone with a major in personnel management from a good school of business can recite all of the things a well-run and well-supported personnel department, for instance, "ought" to do; all one needs is access to any reasonably adequate (and reasonably recent) textbook on personnel administration. But the personnel department of a company does not exist to provide a stage upon which the well-trained personnel administrator can demonstrate his virtuosity; it exists to bring a specialized body of expert knowledge to the service of the larger needs of the company. The professional archivist has a comparable responsibility.

The first principle in setting objectives for archival administration is therefore close collaboration with the host to identify and define the ways in which the archival function can serve its particular needs. This is a task that requires the archivist's professional skills, but in which those skills must be related to the special characteristics of the host.

The second principle in setting objectives is selectivity. Resources are always limited. There is never enough money or enough people or enough space or enough time to do all of the things that would be well worth doing—or, indeed, all of the things there might well be an urgent need to do. Aside from the danger of failing to establish the archives' relevance to the host organization, the greatest menace to successful archival administration is failure to establish realistic priorities. It is so easy to try to cover too much ground, to try to do too many things. If anything significant is to be accomplished in any area—archival or other—there must be a concentration of resources on a few well-defined ends. Activities that do not contribute meaningfully to those ends must be forsworn, no matter how important or appealing they may be from a personal or professional viewpoint.

Here again, close collaboration with the host is essential. For resources to be concentrated, the central purpose of the archives must be identified, defined, and agreed upon. This central purpose must not only be relevant to the needs and interests of the host, but also achievable in terms of the resources it is able and willing to make available. And these resources must then be concentrated on the limited number of things most directly essential to the central archival purpose.

I would make only one more point under the general heading of establishing objectives: it is a good idea to put them in writing so they can be referred to as needed and can serve as guidelines for future action. The statement must be something more than a set of pious hopes or broad generalities; it must set forth objectives of sufficient precision to provide a workable frame of reference for both the archivist and the host.

Organizing to meet objectives is really not a complex matter and can be dealt with quickly. Once objectives have been clearly defined and agreed upon, and priorities to serve them have been established, the task of organization is easy. All that is necessary is to divide the tasks to be accomplished among the staff available for their accomplishment. This is greatly simplified by the fact that the great majority of archival operations are relatively small so far as numbers of people are concerned; beyond fairly broad allocations of responsibility, little detailed division of labor is necessary.

Actually, the key to effective organization is *management by objectives.* This is true in a general and rather abstract way for all organizations of whatever size, but it is specifically and concretely true for archival operations.

If objectives have been clearly defined and realistic priorities established, and if necessary tasks have been broadly allocated, the objectives themselves become the organizing principles that direct the application of human endeavor. If the objectives are clear, limited, and specific, each individual—because the staff is relatively small—can readily see how his or her work relates to the achievement of the objectives and how the work of each relates to and supplements that of the others. Problems of communication are minimal because relationships are direct and face-to-face; the communication process does not have to be mediated by impersonal means or distorted by passing through too many connecting links. And so long as all concerned understand the objectives toward which their combined efforts are directed, collaboration can be largely spontaneous and little specific coordination of individual efforts on the part of the administrator is required.

The habit of working together has been bred into human behavior by scores of millenia of biological and social evolution, and by and large people work well in small groups where they can relate to each other as individuals and where there is an understanding of common purposes. Problems arise, of course, as organizations grow larger and more complex, as relations between people become more tenuous and abstract, and as common purposes become obscured by parochial concerns. But these are not characteristics of organizations such as yours, and for that you may be thankful. I only urge that you capitalize on this inherent human capacity of people to work together. And this, I emphasize, is the essential meaning of that now fashionable term, "management by objectives."

Which brings me, quite logically, to *managing by participation.* Here again, the essential meaning of the concept is simple, although its application has been subject to incredible obfuscation. Shorn of the barnacles that have affixed themselves to it, the principle is simply that people work better—by which I mean more happily for themselves and more effectively for the organization—if they have some say in how the work is done.

In some interesting studies done years ago at Sears, Roebuck, two types of store managers were identified. One type we called "*means oriented*" because they not only set the sales and profit goals for each department but issued detailed instructions to the department managers as to the precise means by which these goals were to be achieved. The other type we called "*ends oriented*" because they set goals in consultation with the department managers and then left it largely up to them to figure out how to reach the goals. There were significant differences in the way the organizations run by the two types of managers worked. The ends oriented managers were less burdened by detail and thus able to concentrate their attention on really important matters. But the most striking difference was the much greater sense of responsibility evidenced by subordinates in the ends oriented organizations. Because the "tactical details" of their jobs were left largely to their judgment, the subordinates felt much more responsible for making them work. Their counterparts in the means oriented organizations felt much less personal responsibility because, after all, the boss had figured everything out and if things didn't work it was his responsibility, not theirs. Not surprisingly, morale was higher and results superior in the ends oriented stores.

Now, I do not mean to imply that people should be left wholly on their own, free to do their own thing in their own way and in their own good time. There must be a viable frame of policy within which people work, procedures that must be followed, and standards that must be maintained. Yet within these constraints, there is usually a fair amount of room for the exercise of individual discretion and judgment. Careful analysis of work to determine what elements are fixed and require strict adherence, and what elements can be modified without impairing results, is likely to disclose greater leeway for variation than might at first appear. The wise manager seeks means to enlarge rather than restrict room for the exercise of initiative. As long as the ends to be served by a particular activity, as well as the applicable constraints, are clearly understood by superior and subordinate alike, the ends oriented manager is likely to be more successful than his means oriented counterpart. This is one aspect of participatory management.

A second aspect has to do with the ends and constraints themselves. Just as employees will feel a greater sense of responsibility for work in whose design they have participated, so too will they feel more personally obligated to achieve goals they themselves have helped set. It is well to remember, too, that policies, procedures, and standards are not always rigidly predetermined. To the extent that employees can help shape constraints, they are likely to feel more committed to observe them— more likely to see them, in fact, as aids rather than as restrictions.

There is no neat formula for managing by participation. Basically, it is an attitude of mind, a recognition that all group effort is by definition team effort, which in turn depends upon a sense of personal responsibility on the part of each member of the team. It is an elementary axiom of human behavior that people feel more responsible for what they themselves have had a voice in determining. The means by which participation is achieved will vary widely from one type of work to another, from one manager to another, and even from one time to another, The common element is an attitude on the part of the manager that recognizes the importance of employee involvement and that seeks to create a work environment in which a sense of personal involvement can flourish.

This sense can never be a matter of administrative contrivance. It depends on the way the manager himself approaches his job and conceives of his relationships with his employees. If he sees himself as a team member—as a playing coach, if you will—and if he sees the members of his team as persons willing and able to take responsibility, participatory management will evolve spontaneously and take on a form compatible with the particular set of people and circumstances.

This brings me to the final item on my agenda: *evaluating performance*. Here again we are dealing with a subject around which an extensive literature has grown and on which weighty—if horribly dull—conferences are frequently held. And yet the underlying concept is one of extreme simplicity: people are best judged by what they actually accomplish. Its corollary is that people work better if they know how well they are doing.

As a very practical matter, those of you whose units are parts of larger organizations probably have a set of performance evaluation procedures that you are obliged to follow. Typically, you are required to rate your subordinates once or perhaps twice a year, using forms criteria that are specified by administrative fiat over which you have little control and in which you probably have little interest. These will appear in a number of different guises and exhibit varying degrees of complexity. The one characteristic most of them have in common is that they are not very effective. This is because too often performance evaluation is looked upon as a discrete function with little relationship to the vital processes of management; it is usually an add-on, something you are required to do because someone says so but extraneous to the real job of running a good archives.

Nothing could be further from the truth. There are no functions more central to managing—whether an archives or a steel mill—than making judgments about people and letting people know where they

307

stand. And the principles underlying these two functions are related in the most intimate and integral way to the central task of management.

Regardless of the format for performance evaluation established by your host organization and to which you must adhere, the process can be greatly facilitated and its usefulness for your administrative purposes greatly enhanced if the principles I have previously laid down have been conscientiously applied. If the archivist is professionally competent, if objectives have been clearly defined and realistically set, if the tasks necessary to accomplish the objectives have been rationally allocated among available staff, if the efforts of the group are coordinated toward achieving unambiguous goals, and if each member of the team has had some personal involvement in setting goals and determining how work is to be done, then it becomes a relatively natural and simple matter to reach an understanding as to what is expected of each individual. The central task of performance evaluation then becomes a matter of determining whether or not these expectations have been realized and, if not, the reasons for the deficiency. If these preconditions have been met, the individual probably knows how he or she is doing without being explicitly told. But this is something the good administrator never takes for granted and is at pains to make certain is explicitly understood.

The formal system of performance evaluation established by your host organization may be utilized for this purpose, but people should not have to wait for the semi-annual or annual evaluation cycle to be told how they are doing; rather, this should be a continuing process, and it can be if the principles previously enunciated are in continuing and effective operation. Prescribed formal procedures—usually so sterile—can take on life and vitality and be applied with striking effect if utilized in the spirit and within the context I have tried to set forth.

My thesis is that in spite of a formidable body of literature and an endless array of obfuscating detail, the important principles of management are essentially simple and straightforward and their application is largely a matter of common sense. But this thesis rests on an even more elementary foundation: the essential requirement that the manager have character and integrity, a genuine respect for fellow workers, and a commitment to fairness and justice in all relationships down, up, and across the line. Without these, the principles of management, even in their pristine form, are empty and sterile. With them, the relatively few central concepts can be the means for greatly improving the effectiveness of organizational effort and for materially enriching the quality of human life at work.

When is a Collection Processed?

Megan Floyd Desnoyers

Processing. The activities intended to facilitate the use of personal papers and manuscript collections generally comparable to arrangement, description, and preservation of archival material.[1] (To which the author would add the activity of screening or reviewing the material to insure that there are no legal or donor-imposed bars to opening it.)

W hen is a collection considered to be processed? When historically valuable material may be made available for research without violating any restrictions as to its use and without endangering its enduring physical state, and when that material is arranged and described so that a researcher may readily find what he/she is looking for in it.

Processing is done to meet the needs and interests of several different groups of people: donors, users, and archivists. Two of these groups—donors and users—often have mutually conflicting needs and interests.

Donors who have imposed restrictions on their materials want those restrictions applied before access is granted to any researcher to use any parts of their collections. To meet this need, archivists must review or screen each collection against restriction requirements and criteria as specified in deeds of gift, and must remove, for as long as necessary, those items embargoed by donors.

Users may be researchers, donors or their representatives, or archivists answering donors' or researchers' queries. Their common need is the ready retrieval of information, either facts or documents, from the material. Processing must result in adequate arrangement and description of the material to facilitate such retrieval.

The third constituency having needs and interests which processing must meet are the *archivists* or curators themselves. Archivists feel responsible for addressing the needs and interests of both the donor and the user, for enforcing legal restrictions on a collection's use, and for attending to the physical needs of the material itself. The archivists'

Reprinted with permission from *The Midwestern Archivist* 7 (1, 1982): 5-23.
[1]Frank B. Evans, Donald F. Harrison, Edwin A. Thompson, and William L. Rofes, "A Basic Glossary for Archivists, Manuscript Curators, and Records Managers," *The American Archivist* 37 (July 1974): 427.

needs and interests must also be met by adequate arrangement, preservation, description, and screening of each collection.

Archivists have accepted responsibility for applying donor restrictions to collections or parts of collections and for enforcing all other legal restrictions on the use of the material. We apply the provisions of the federal Privacy Act, of appropriate state laws, of legislation controlling the dissemination of national security classified information, and of any other relevant laws and regulations. This is a practical as well as an ethical responsibility. If we do not do the necessary screening, we run the risk of invading someone's privacy, compromising national security, angering a donor by violating his/her trust, and/or making ourselves liable for legal action on many different levels.

Archivists not only strive to meet users' needs for ready retrieval of information, but also have accepted responsibility for opening all collections as soon as possible after receipt and for supplying *all* researchers with as much information about a collection as possible, while giving the material adequate physical protection. Opening collections promptly requires speedy processing. Providing as much information as possible is accomplished through good description of the collection by the person who knows it best, the processor. The physical needs of the material are met by ensuring that appropriate preservation and conversation measures are applied to the papers.

To meet these complex and often conflicting requirements, archivists have accepted the responsibility of maintaining a certain level of processing that is professionally suitable, but we have not defined that level very well and, therefore, we strive for an ideal that may not always be practical or appropriate.

There are two problems with establishing a standard level of processing. The first is that it dictates what must be done to a collection whether or not the collection warrants it, and it limits what can be done to a collection that might need more work. We rarely ask the question: When is *this* collection processed? Instead, we process all collections to an ideal standard level. The second problem is that by processing all collections to the ideal standard level, we cannot keep up with the collections we have on hand or with the new collections coming in. The result tends to be a small number of beautifully processed collections available for use and an extensive backlog of collections that are closed while they wait to be processed.

This backlog is growing at an incredible rate because of two other fairly recent developments: the arrival of voluminous contemporary collections and the fact that more limited archival budgets are being spread over a greater variety of programs. The contemporary collections that institutions are now being swamped with are huge, and they differ from older holdings. They are collections "of great size and historical importance which contain few individual documents of specific research value or autograph interest in their own right."[2] At the same time, overall archival budgets are declining while services and demands are growing. Educational projects, professional meetings, and rising costs of staff, facilities, and materials stretch limited funds even further. There is not much money left for processing, and we are having to justify carefully how we spend the little that is available. We cannot afford to spend as much money to process a single collection as we might have in the past, now that we have more collections, less money, and bigger backlogs.

The backlog situation is especially serious because of its impact on the donors, researchers, and archivists. Donors may be annoyed when they discover that collections they deposited years ago remain unprocessed and inaccessible, and they may be even more unhappy when determined researchers approach them directly for access to their collections. Some donors understand and are patient; others become angry and testy. Researchers are frustrated and often angered by processing backlogs that keep collections unavailable. Their needs are certainly not being met. Archivists are equally frustrated because we would like to be opening these collections as soon as possible and to the greatest extent possible. We are apologetic to donors and researchers and genuinely concerned about the seeming impasse.

The author proposes that instead of trying to maintain an ideal standard level of processing, we look at processing as a *range of choices along a continuum* for each of the four essential processing activities: arrangement, preservation, description, and screening. The continuum runs from the found, or original, state of the material up to the highest possible level of each activity, e.g., a calendared collection where each item is individually filed in an acid neutral folder in an acid neutral box.

The archivist should evaluate each collection and decide how far that particular collection needs to be taken along the arrangement, preservation, description, and screening continua. In making these decisions, he/she would consider the found state of the collection and the requirements and interests of the donor, the users, the applicable legislation, and the material itself. These factors would determine the lowest level of each of the four activities with which the archivist could live comfortably while fulfilling all of those needs.

The archivist must also decide *when* each activity is to be done. This decision will depend on the nature of the papers, the level of each of the four activities to which they will be taken, and the processor's experience. The options range from doing the four activities as concurrently as possible to doing them completely sequentially. Concurrent processing is the most efficient in terms of time and money and sequential processing is

---

[2]Eleanor McKay, "Random Sampling Techniques," *The American Archivist* 41 (July 1978): 283.

the least efficient. An experienced processor might be charged with doing the arrangement, preservation, and screening on each box at one time while also taking all notes necessary for later description. But if any of the activities become complicated or if the processor lacks experience, it may be better to break the tasks apart and do them more sequentially. The four activities are treated separately here to avoid confusion.

> *Arrangement.* The process and results of organizing archives, records, and manuscripts in accordance with accepted archival principles, particularly provenance, at as many as necessary of the following levels: repository, record group or comparable control unit, subgroup(s), series, file unit, and document. The process usually includes packing, labeling, and shelving of archives, records, and manuscripts, and is intended to achieve physical or administrative control and basic identification of the holdings.[3]

Proper arrangement of the material in a collection is essential in order to retrieve information from that collection. Anticipating how users will approach the collection and how often they will use it, the archivist must decide on a scheme of arrangement and a work plan that is sufficient for the users' needs yet not too detailed to carry out with available budget and staff. The arrangement activity can be the most labor intensive, and therefore the most expensive, of the four processing activities, since rearrangement may be necessary on the series, folder, and document levels.

The archivist must first survey the entire collection, reviewing all folder, notebook, binder, or other container titles to answer the question: What is the found state of the collection? The found state can range along a spectrum from perfectly ordered, pre-existing series to total disorder. Most collections fall somewhere in the middle. The found state has a direct impact on the processing cost: the better the original order and the less arrangement the archivist has to do, the faster the processing can be accomplished and the lower the processing cost. The original order of a collection should be retained as much as possible, both because that order reveals how the papers were used and because of the practical consideration of cost. But the original order can be maintained only if it is usable and meets researcher needs. Cost factors do not outweigh usability.

The next question to ask is: Are there obvious series or major groupings of materials? These are frequently untitled but are readily apparent in the initial collection survey and are easily assigned a title. A common example is a correspondence file arranged either alphabetically by correspondent or chronologically by date of the letter. The materials may not be called "correspondence file," but a quick survey of the folder titles and

---

[3]Evans et al., "A Basic Glossary," p. 418.

a sampling of folder contents will show that that is what it is. Equally common are subject files where folders are titled by subject and arranged alphabetically, or a speech file which has a folder for each speech or for a chronological group of speeches. In each of these cases, a quick survey of the material will reveal the presence of the series.

Are the existing series usable for research? Evaluate them from a user's perspective. Often a minor change in the title of a series or in its arrangement will reconcile existing series with researchers' needs.

Are the existing series too general or too specific? Sometimes a great deal of material will be filed into one huge series when it really should be divided into several smaller, more specific series. At other times there are many small series which could conveniently be yoked together into a larger, more cohesive series. For example, there might be a modest sized subject file and several small files—such as civil rights, disarmament— which are also subjects. It makes sense to move the small units into the larger subject file.

Do the existing series need reordering among themselves? Are they filed consistently, either alphabetically, chronologically, or from general to specific or vice versa? Arranging the series in a logical order may be just a matter of renumbering boxes.

Unfortunately, the survey of the collection's arrangement may reveal that there are no series, either obvious or obscure. This will mean a lengthy, expensive sorting project, during which the processor will have to look carefully at all the materials, consider various arrangement schemes, settle on a final one, and put the material in that order. Maintaining original order is not important in this case, because the order reveals little of the way the materials were used and because the materials are unusable in the state they are in. Instead, we must settle on an arrangement that is determined by potential researcher use and by the ease of accomplishing the rearrangement. A sentence in the finding aid can explain what the original order was.

Once the series are determined, titled, and rearranged among themselves as necessary, the archivist must consider the internal arrangement of the units (folders, notebooks, binders, etc.) within the series. Each series should be reviewed and the following questions asked:

1. Are the units adequately titled?
2. Are they arranged in correct order?
3. Are they too large?
4. Are they too small?

An adequate title would include the series title and a unit description consisting of at least a name or word title for alphabetically arranged series or a date title for chronologically arranged series. Folders with word titles may also be given dates when the dates are significant or when there is so much material on a subject that it needs to be divided into thinner folders by date. Folder titles do not need to be absolutely consistent as long as their contents are clear and like materials are easily identifiable in a once-through of the finding aid. The author has recently finished processing a small collection of research materials where the donor's titles were accepted absolutely and this fact was explained in the finding aid. There are inconsistencies and repetitions and not every title is perfect, but all of the information is retrievable.

Correct order means that each folder is filed in the order set for that series, whether chronological or alphabetical. This is a minimum requirement in order for users to be able to locate folders.

Folders are too large when their bulk poses a preservation or retrieval problem. When there are more items in a folder than it will comfortably hold, for preservation reasons the materials should be divided into thinner folders. If the folder is thick and the titling is so general that researchers will waste time searching for a small unit of information, the folder should be broken into thinner, more specifically described folders.

Folders may be too thin or too specifically titled. The decision to correct this involves cost factors. If we are replacing existing folders with acid neutral folders and are listing each folder in the finding aid, we should consider consolidating items into folders with more general titles. Folders are rarely too specifically titled for researchers' needs, however. If the material is valuable and is finely foldered, it might also be wise to keep it that way for preservation considerations.

The final and most expensive level of arrangement is the document level. Whether it is necessary to arrange at the document level depends on the importance of the material, its retrievability, the frequency of its projected use, and its quantity.

Certain forms of arrangement and types of material necessitate arrangement at the item level. Chronological or alphabetical correspondence files must be correctly ordered to permit effective retrieval. If each item of the collection or series is extremely important or if researchers will be looking for specific items, then we must make sure those items are perfectly arranged; literary manuscript collections fall into this category. Subject files do not necessarily need such specific arrangement because there is no required and expected internal order and because the user will probably be reading the contents of an entire folder rather than searching for a specific item.

If the item can be pinpointed to a specific folder by an adequate finding aid, and if the item is not extremely important and/or will not be searched for often, we do not have to worry about the arrangement within the folder. We can expect the user to go through the entire folder

ARRANGEMENT CONTINUUM

Found State

SERIES
LEVEL

Consider the existing order; review all folder, notebook, binder, or container titles. Ask if there are any obvious groupings or series; if they are titled; if they are usable for research; if they are too general or too specific; if they are in correct order.

Review reveals no rearrangement or retitling needed at the series level.	Review reveals at least some rearrangement or retitling needed at the series level.
	Describe the rearrangement and retitling needed at the series level.

FOLDER
LEVEL

Review the units in the series (folders, notebooks, binders, etc.). Ask if they are adequately titled; if they are correctly arranged; if they are too thick or too thin.

Review reveals no rearrangement or retitling needed at the folder level.	Review reveals at least some rearrangement or retitling needed at the folder level.
	Describe the rearrangement and retitling needed at the folder level.

ITEM
LEVEL

Spot review the items in a few folders in each series. Ask if the folder titles accurately reflect the contents of the folders; if the items need to be in correct order; if they are already in correct order.

Review reveals no retitling of folders or rearrangement of items in folders needed.	Review reveals at least some retitling of folders or rearrangement of items in folders needed.
	Describe the retitling and rearrangement needed.
	Weigh the costs in time, staff and material expenses. Decide on the level and course of action.
	Apply the course of action.

to find the item, and the finding aid will tell him/her to expect to have to do that.

If the collection is massive, then regardless of the importance of the item or the frequency of its use, we probably cannot justify arranging the items within the folder.

In considering whether or not to arrange at the item level, spot review the folder contents within each series. The decision will vary from series to series. Important and/or valuable series may have the items arranged within the folder, while less important series in the same collection will not be given item level arrangement. When sampling the contents of scattered folders in each series, we should ask if the folder titles accurately reflect the contents, if the items need to be in a particular order, and if they are already in that order.

> *Preservation.* (1) The basic responsibility to provide adequate facilities for the protection, care, and maintenance of archives, records, and manuscripts. (2) Specific measures, individual and collective, undertaken for the repair, maintenance, restoration, or protection of documents.[4]

All collections should be evaluated to determine their need for protection from their containers, from self harm or destruction (such as from deteriorating chemicals or metal in, on, or near the documents), and from damage, destruction, or theft by users.

Preservation steps may either be taken at the time of processing, or scheduled for a later date if the materials will not be damaged by the delay. The major question to ask in determining how far to take the preservation activity and when to do so is: Is the danger, either from the environment or the users, immediate? If the answer is yes, the preservation steps must be taken immediately. Security preservation must be done prior to opening a collection. Steps to stop existing deterioration must also be taken immediately. Steps to prevent future deterioration may be scheduled for the future.

Preservation from containers is done at the box and folder levels. Looking at each box, we ask:

1. Is the box contributing to the deterioration of the material because of its:
   acidity,
   size (too large, too small),
   condition (torn, wet), or
   lack of strength?

2. Will it contribute to the deterioration of the material in the future?

---

[4]Ibid., p. 427.

3. What is the size of the items in the box? Do they fit comfortably in the box without folding or bending?

4. What will be the amount of future use of the items in the box? Will the box size and structure permit this degree of use without excessive wear on the contents?

At the folder level, we examine a sample of several folders from each series and ask the same questions. We also consider whether the folder is too thickly or thinly filled to protect its contents during storage or use.

Traditionally, archivists have routinely refoldered most personal papers or manuscript collections regardless of the found state of the folders. Custodians of massive holdings, such as the National Archives, have not done this and have instead retained the incoming folders wherever they existed. We need to begin questioning the need for refoldering instead of making it a standard requirement for finished processing.

Preservation from self harm or destruction takes place on the item level. The items in a few folders from each series are examined to identify existing or potential instances of rusted metal fasteners, acid transfer, and deteriorating copies. Recommendations are then made for preservation steps for each series and a timetable is given for each step. Series within a collection will have different recommendations depending on their natures: e.g., a clippings series comprised of acidic newsprint will eventually deteriorate unless deacidified or photocopied, while a general correspondence series might not need anything done to it. The archivist must then determine what he/she can afford to do.

Preservation at the item level is, of course, the most expensive, but there are choices as to how much we do and when. For example, for metal deterioration, we can choose to:

Least   Note deteriorating metal for future removal.
           Remove deteriorating metal.
           Note potentially deteriorating metal for future removal.

Most   Remove all metal and replace with non-rusting metal.

Security preservation steps to prevent intentional and unintentional harm from users are also taken at the item level. The contents of a few folders in each series are evaluated. To protect materials from honest user damage, we consider what level of use there might be. If the anticipated usage level will be extremely high, we might want to consider filling folders more thinly; numbering the pages of items that will frequently be photocopied instead of stapling them; or even closing the originals and making a microfilm or photocopy set available for use. To prevent dishonest damage or theft, we determine whether there are valuable items in the series. If there are, we can decide either to do nothing,

PRESERVATION CONTINUUM 1

Preservation from Containers

Found State

BOX
LEVEL

Consider the boxing; look at and open each box. Ask if the box contributes to the deterioration of the material because of its acidity, size, condition, or strength; if it will contribute to the material's deterioration in the future; if it is the correct size for its contents; if it is appropriate for the future use of its contents.

Review reveals no reboxing needed.	Review reveals at least some reboxing needed.
	Describe the reboxing needed.

FOLDER
LEVEL

Consider the foldering (or binding); make a sample exploration of several folders in each series. Ask if the folder contributes to the deterioration of the material because of its acidity, size, condition, or strength; if it has metal fasteners; if it will contribute to the material's deterioration in the future; if it is the correct size for its contents; if it is appropriate for the future use of its contents.

Review reveals no refoldering needed.	Review reveals at least some refoldering needed.
	Describe the refoldering needed.
	Weigh the costs in time, staff and material expenses against deterioration or damage potential. Decide on level and course of action for each series.
	Apply the course of action to each series.

PRESERVATION CONTINUUM 2

Preservation from Self

Found State

ITEM
LEVEL

*Consider the need for preservation from self; make a sample explora-
tion of several folders in each series and examine their contents.* Ask if
there is already deterioration from rusted metal, acid transfer,
fading images, deteriorating copies; if there is potential deterioration and when it can be expected to happen.

Examination reveals no preservation needed.	Examination reveals at least some preservation needed either now or in the future.
	Describe the level of preservation needed within each series.
	Weigh the costs in time, staff and material expense against deterioration potential. Decide on level of action and schedule for each series.
	Carry out the course of action decided on.

PRESERVATION CONTINUUM 3

Preservation from Use

Found State

Consider the potential for unintentional user harm; look at the contents of a few folders in each series. Ask what the level of use will be for each series.

Review reveals low use probable.	Review reveals medium to very high use probable.
	Consider the impact of use on the items; decide what preservation measures to take such as not stapling items, numbering items, placing fewer items in a folder, photocopying entire series, or microfilming the collection.
	Apply the measures decided on.

Consider the potential for intentional user harm; look at the contents of a few folders in each series. Ask if there are valuable materials in the series that might be stolen or defaced.

Review reveals no series have valuable materials.	Review reveals at least some series have valuable materials.
	Review each document and decide how to protect it (photocopy, ownership stamp).
	Apply the measures decided on.

to stamp each item on the back with the institution's name, or to replace the item with a photocopy.

There are, then, three continua for preservation:

Preservation from containers (continuum 1),

Preservation from self (continuum 2), and

Preservation from use (continuum 3).

Description. The process of establishing intellectual control over holdings through the preparation of finding aids.[5]

Description is necessary so that users will know where within a collection they can find information they want, and so that the processor can pass on to every researcher what he/she has learned about the collection.

The form of description for each collection is determined by the nature of the collection, its anticipated research use, and the rules and requirements of the institution. The nature of the collection and its research use are often closely interrelated. Important collections or series will probably be used heavily and thoroughly; their descriptions will have to be detailed to help serve their many users. Less important materials will probably be used less frequently, and the few users will be able to approach the collection with less detailed descriptions. Institutional requirements may influence the form and degree of description. For instance, the institution may have a card catalog of subject and title entries, requiring the processor to prepare entries for each collection processed.

Description may range from the least to the most detailed, but the minimum requirements for each collection are:

1. A citable title, so that researchers may ask for or cite that specific collection. Example: The Personal Papers of Jane Thomas.

2. The date span of the collection, to place it in time. Example: 1938-1945.

3. The quantity of the collection, to indicate the amount of material to be looked at. Examples: 5 linear feet, or 96,000 pages.

4. A summary of the collection's contents, describing the major record types, subjects, and correspondents or types of correspondents. Example: Diaries, draft manuscripts of Ms. Thomas's works, and original incoming correspondence and copies of outgoing correspondence with family members and academic associates in American social history. Subjects treated include American social history, 1850-1945, . . .

---

[5]Ibid., p. 421.

and perhaps:

5. When the material was received by the institution.

The lowest level of description is a container list of the material as received. Such a list sometimes comes with a collection, or it may be made by a staff member at the time of accessioning. If the archivist decides the material is useful in its receipt order and makes no changes in the arrangement, that list could serve as the basis for the final finding aid. The archivist would, at the least, add an introductory narrative including the minimum requirements listed above.

More often, the material needs some rearrangement, after which the archivist prepares a new list of the series and their folders as rearranged. This is the first element in an inventory or register, which consists of:

1. A list of the series and their folder titles,

2. Descriptions of each series,

3. A scope and content note for the collection,

4. A biographical note on the creator or an agency history, and

5. An introduction and provenance note.[6]

After an inventory/register is completed, the archivist may prepare catalog entries for the institution's catalog or guide to holdings and for outside sources (such as the National Union Catalog of Manuscript Collections). Notices of the collection's having been opened may also be sent to professional journals.

The most detailed forms of description are item listing and calendaring. A calendar is an item list, arranged chronologically, which includes a brief description of each item. These are very expensive and time consuming processes. They can only be justified when each item in the series or collection is extremely important or valuable, will be heavily used, and will be sought as an individual item. The manuscripts and correspondence of a famous writer might justifiably be described in this way.

Screen. To examine records or archives to determine the presence of restricted documents or information and to remove such documents from the files.[7]

---

[6]The Society of American Archivists' publication, *Inventories and Registers: A Handbook of Techniques and Examples* gives an excellent description and several examples of each element in an inventory/register.

[7]Evans et al., "A Basic Glossary," p. 430.

DESCRIPTION CONTINUUM

Found State

CONTAINER OR FOLDER LEVEL	*Consider the existing description.* Was any description provided by the donor? Is it accurate?

	Review reveals accurate container list exists.
	Review reveals no list or an inaccurate container list exists.
	Prepare an adequate list of the materials as received.

COLLECTION LEVEL	*Determine the final form of description.* Consider the nature of the material and its potential use.
COLLECTION LEVEL	Process the collection taking necessary notes.
FOLDER LEVEL	Write a folder title list of materials as processed.
SERIES LEVEL	Write descriptions of each series.
COLLECTION LEVEL	Write scope and content note for the collection.
COLLECTION LEVEL	Write biographical note for creator or agency history.
COLLECTION LEVEL	Write an introduction and provenance note.
COLLECTION LEVEL	Relate the collection to other holdings in the institution.
COLLECTION LEVEL	Relate the collection to other collections in other institutions.
COLLECTION LEVEL	Prepare catalog entries for the institution's catalog or guide to holdings.
COLLECTION LEVEL	Prepare catalog entries for outside sources.
ITEM LEVEL	List each item in the collection, if warranted.

Elements of an Inventory/ Register

The screening activity is probably the least flexible and most sensitive and immediate of the four activities. If a collection is going to be screened in part or in its entirety, it must be screened prior to opening, for there is no point in screening it once the material has been used by researchers. Screening has the greatest impact on the labor intensiveness of processing the collection, the length of time needed, and the resulting expense. Screening requirements drive us immediately down from the collection or series level to the document level.

Screening is done to meet the requirements of the donor and any applicable legislation. The first step is to review the donor's deed of gift to determine what restrictions the donor has imposed on the use of the collection. Next, the archivist needs to determine what other legislation applies to the collection. Once the pertinent restrictions are identified, the series titles are examined to determine which series might need to be screened. Within the identified series, the archivist then reviews the folder titles for folders whose contents have to be examined. Finally, he/she reviews each item in the identified folders.

Following this review, the archivist closes the items, folders, or series that the restrictions require be closed. The remainder of the collection is opened for research use.

When is a collection processed? When the archivist has selected from the processing continua and applied the appropriate degree of arrangement, preservation, description, and screening activities that will make that collection usable for the researcher while protecting the physical well-being of the material and honoring donor and legal restrictions on the collection. If this process is judiciously applied, many collections will be appropriately processed more quickly and at more reasonable expense than in the past, and processing backlogs will begin to disappear.

SCREENING CONTINUUM

Found State

COLLECTION LEVEL

Identify any restrictions on the use of the collection. Ask if there are any donor-imposed restrictions, Privacy Act restrictions, national security restrictions, or any applicable state laws.

Review reveals no restrictions on the use of the collection.	Review reveals some restrictions on the use of the collection.

SERIES LEVEL

Examine the series titles. Ask if any of the series are likely to contain sensitive materials that would be closed under the restrictions identified above.

Review reveals no series which are likely to contain restricted materials.	Review reveals some series which are likely to contain restricted materials.

FOLDER LEVEL

Examine the folder titles in the series identified as likely to contain restricted materials. Ask if any of the folders are likely to contain restricted materials.

Review reveals no folders which are likely to contain restricted materials.	Review reveals some folders which are likely to contain restricted materials.

ITEM LEVEL

Review the contents of the folders identified as likely to contain restricted materials. Ask if the items should be closed under the restrictions identified above.

Review reveals no items which need to be closed under the restrictions identified above.	Review reveals some items which need to be closed under the restrictions identified above.
	Close those items; open the remainder.

The Archival Edge

F. Gerald Ham

Our most important and intellectually demanding task as archivists is to make an informed selection of information that will provide the future with a representative record of human experience in our time. But why must we do it so badly? Is there any other field of information gathering that has such a broad mandate with a selection process so random, so fragmented, so uncoordinated, and even so often accidental? Some archivists will admit the process is a bit out of kilter. They say a simple formula of more cooperation, less competition, increased governmental largess, and bigger and better records surveys—a logistical device we often mistake for an acquisitions strategy—should be sufficient to produce a national mosaic that will bequeath to the future an eminently useable past.

A handful of critics, however, have suggested that something is fundamentally wrong: our methods are inadequate to achieve our objective, and our passivity and perceptions produce a biased and distorted archival record. In 1970, Howard Zinn told an SAA audience that the archival record in the United States is biased towards the rich and powerful elements in our society—government, business, and the military—while the poor and the impotent remain in archival obscurity. To correct this, the chief spokesman for history's new Left urged archivists "to compile a whole new world of documentary material about the lives, desires and needs of ordinary people."[1] How this task was to be done he shrewdly left to the archivists. In 1971 Sam Bass Warner, a noted historian of urban life, urged us to make our archives more useful. Like Zinn, Warner subscribed to Carl Becker's notion that history should help people to understand the world they live in. To do this Warner asked archivists "so far as it is humanly possible" to "abandon the pursuit of the classic subjects of American history" and turn instead to the collection of data that would yield a "historical explanation of the major issues of our own time."[2] Warner had specific notions of how this should be done which were dismissed as the half-baked product of an archivally uninformed mind.

Reprinted with permission from *The American Archivist* 38 (January 1975): 5-13.

[1]Howard Zinn, "The Archivist and Radical Reform," unpublished manuscript, pp. 12-13, 18.

[2]Sam Bass Warner, "The Shame of the Cities: Public Records of the Metropolis," unpublished manuscript, 1971, pp. 2, 3.

Even earlier there were rumblings in Columbus, Ohio, where a young and untamed archivist suggested that his colleagues' concern with quantity and competition inhibited discussion of advantages of quality and cooperation; that many, if not most, archival institutions operated "as introspective units justifying their existence solely on their own accomplishments rather than in terms of their role in the overall historical collection process"; and if this "egocentric attitude" was not abandoned competing archival programs would become so proliferated that the possibility of inter-institutional cooperation would be jeopardized.[3]

But the most sweeping indictment in what was emerging as a radical critique of the way archivists go about documenting history and culture came from the Cornell University historian and archivist, Gould P. Colman. Colman, in the *American Archivist* "Forum," charged that lack of concern about acquisition guidelines had produced possibly "the most serious problem facing archivists . . .; the politicalization of our profession," politicalization in the sense of "skewing the study of culture by the studied preservation of unrepresentative indicators of that culture." For example governments, particularly the one in Washington, preserved documents out of all proportion to government's impact on culture while other important institutions, such as the family, are poorly documented. Shouldn't archivists, Colman asked, have a responsibility to redress this balance? Documentation was biased further by our propensity to collect what is most easily accessible and by limiting oral history resources primarily to those relatively well-documented aspects of culture which could pay the expensive oral history piper.[4]

The empirical evidence—from published accession notes, from NUCMC, from recently issued guides, from anywhere an archivist keeps a record of what he collects—validates these charges. But the evidence reveals more than a biased record; it reveals incredible gaps in the documentation of even traditional concerns. Take the case of a midwestern state known both for its production and consumption of fermented beverages. Neither brewing nor the brewing industry is mentioned in any of the state's archival finding aids. It is possible that 1000 years from now some researcher will conclude that in a city known as Milwaukee the brewers art was unknown. The evidence also showed that many archivists waste time and space preserving random bits and pieces, as well as large accessions, of the most dubious value.

But the real cause for concern is that there doesn't seem to be any concern. With a few notable exceptions, there is no realization that our

---

[3]David R. Larson, "The Ohio Network of American History Research Centers," *Ohio History* (Winter 1970): 62.

[4]"The Forum: Communications From Members," *American Archivist* 35 (July/October 1972): 483-85.

present data gathering methods are inadequate or that our fundamental problem is the lack of imaginative acquisition guidelines or comprehensive collecting strategies at all levels of archival activity. You search archival literature in vain to find something more helpful than a "how we did it here" article on a particular collecting program or an essentially "nuts and bolts" piece on the mechanics of collecting. Equally barren are the annual reports of the SAA committees dealing with identification and acquisition of archives. Further, an examination of the works on historical methodology and social science research indicate that our clients do not think the matter deserves much attention either.[5] For the archivist, the area of acquisition strategies remains a vacuum.

These criticisms, even if correct, are irrelevant for some archivists. To them the archival endeavor is primarily a custodial one. And the so-called dean of Canadian bookmen, Bernard Amtmann, would agree with them. In the May issue of the *Canadian Archivist* he stated, "archivists are by definition custodians of the material in their possession and their professional training and qualifications do not exactly encompass the . . . historical evaluation of material." This evaluation, he said, "must surely be the responsibility of the historian."[6] Whether it was arrogance or ignorance, Bernard Amtmann was only echoing archivists. In 1969 as reported in the New York *Times* the archivist of New York City was asked what he saved. "Aside from the mayors' papers," he answered, "we try to keep only things which will protect the city against a suit or help it to document a suit against somebody else." He went on to suggest that "some of the historical societies" might be interested in examining the records he was destroying. "You never can tell," he said, "when you're going to come across something valuable."[7] And, in an uninformed way, he was only practicing what Hilary Jenkinson and others have preached.

Small wonder the custodial image is still widely held by our allies in the research community. Indeed, the persistence of the custodial tradition has not only been a major factor in the archivist's failure to deal with acquisition policy on a coherent and comprehensive basis, but has resulted in an obsession—with the "nuts and bolts" or craft aspects of our work.

---

[5]Examples of the historian's superficial approach to acquisition problems are the "Report of Ad Hoc Committee on Manuscripts Set Up by the American Historical Assoc. in December 1948," *American Archivist* 14 (July 1951): 233; and more recently, Walter Rundell, Jr., *In Pursuit of American History: Research and Training in the United States* (Norman: University of Oklahoma Press, 1970), pp. 104-07.

[6]An abbreviated version of this article by Amtmann, "Historical Manuscripts at Auction," was widely circulated in the United States in the July 22, 1974, issue of the *Antiquarian Bookman*, pp. 356-57.

[7]New York *Times*, November 23, 1969.

Reinforcing the custodial tradition is a parallel tradition, that of the researcher as data gatherer. We all know that many of the great manuscript collections—those of Belknap, Draper, and H. H. Bancroft come easily to mind—were brought together in this fashion. The American Historical Association through its committees on source material perpetuated this tradition and even today there are archival programs where the history faculty are the collectors while the archivists are the "keepers of the past."[8]

This tradition, of course, leaves the archivist too closely tied to the vogue of the academic marketplace. For example, only after historians rediscovered the importance of the city in American history did a few so-called urban archives come into existence. Similar efforts, often initiated by the action of concerned historians, were developed to meet the needs for documentation on the black community; on ethnic groups and immigrants; on social welfare; on architecture; on popular culture; the history of science; and so forth. These responses to changing patterns in the pursuit of history, and to the increase of other studies once considered outside the proper use of archives, are a temporary corrective. There is a dilemma here. Most researchers are caught in their own concerns and do not worry about all the history that needs to be written; yet in terms of documentary preservation this is precisely what the archivist must do. Small wonder, then, that archival holdings too often reflected narrow research interests rather than the broad spectrum of human experience. If we cannot transcend these obstacles, then the archivist will remain at best nothing more than a weathervane moved by the changing winds of historiography.

Turning from those traditions which have prevented the archivist from developing a larger acquisition design, let's consider five interrelated developments that are forcing him into a more active and perhaps more creative role.

The first is structural change in society. The process of institutionalizing and nationalizing decision-making, for example, has had a profound impact on documentation, making the archives of associations, pressure groups, protest organizations, and institutions of all sorts relatively more important than the papers of individuals and families. Accession data in the *American Archivist* reflects this change. Thirty years ago personal and family archives accounted for 38 percent of all reported accessions; but they account for only 14 percent today. In this same period, records of labor, of social and political protest, and of social welfare increased from less than 1 percent to nearly one-fourth of all accessions. Unlike family papers these archives usually do not fall unso-

---

[8]See William F. Birdsall, "The American Archivist's Search for Professional Identity, 1909-1936" (Ph.D. dissertation, University of Wisconsin-Madison, 1973), particularly ch. 5.

licited into the hands of a waiting archivist, and their percentage rise on the accession charts is partly the result of the sensitivity and hard work of many archivists. Further, as the government has become the primary instrument of social and economic policy the records of its dealings, especially with non-elite population groups, have become more important. But archival holdings do not reflect this change. One reason is the disorganization of state, county, and municipal records; another is the narrow appraisal criteria used by many public record archivists. The result has been the destruction of vast quantities of important social and economic data.

Closely related to institutionalized decision-making and increased governmental activity, is a second and more prosaic factor: bulk. With records increasing at an exponential rate, it is utopian to believe that society could ever afford the resources for us to preserve everything of possible value; for it to do so would be irresponsible. We must realize that when we preserve one body of data it probably means that something else won't be preserved. But I do not think we have adequate methodological tools to make these critical choices. In fact, we might be better off if we forget what we have been taught. It is irresponsible and unrealistic to argue for the integrity of a file of gubernatorial papers that fills up 1500 document cases of which 80 percent is either duplicate or of marginal worth.

If the volume of documentation has greatly increased, the quality of the information has greatly decreased. Arthur Schlesinger, commenting in the *Atlantic Monthly* on this third problem—missing data—wrote: "In the last three quarters of a century, the rise of the typewriter [and to this we should add modern quick copy machines of all sorts] has vastly increased the flow of paper, while the rise of the telephone has vastly reduced its importance. . . . If a contemporary statesman has something of significance to communicate, if speed and secrecy are of the essence, he will confide his message, not to a letter, but to the telephone."[9] An examination of files similar to the gubernatorial papers above is proof that there is much more bulk of much less usefulness.

If the archivist is going to fill in the gaps he will have to become, as Warner suggests, "a historical reporter for his own time." He can use any of several techniques: he can create oral history, he can generate a photographic record, and he can collect survey data. As a reporter he can produce oral history, not as a painstakingly edited source for written texts about the Presidents and their men, but rather as documentation of the day to day decisions of lower echelon leaders and of the activities and attitudes of ordinary men and women. He can use photography to sup-

---

[9]Arthur Schlesinger, Jr., "On the Writing of Contemporary History," *Atlantic Monthly* (March 1967), p. 71.

plement the written record and make it more meaningful. But today, though most archival institutions collect photographs, virtually none has an active field program. And he could, if he has the courage and energy, do as one archivist suggests and create his own mail questionnaires and use other survey techniques to establish a base line of social and economic data.

A fourth factor in the making of the active archivist is that of vulnerable records or what we might call "instant archives." It is documentation that has little chance of aging into vintage archives, that is destroyed nearly as fast as it is created, and which must be quickly gathered before it is lost or scattered. At my own institution, for instance, the collections which deal with the major 1960's movements on the left—civil rights, student activism, and the anti-Vietnam War protest—probably would not exist today if we had not initiated contacts before many of the organizations quietly dissolved.

Technology is a fifth development. We are all aware that electronic impulses easily and rapidly disappear from magnetic tape, that photographic images often fade beyond recognition, that files with quick copy documents are literally self-destructing, and that the program documentation to important EDP data sets often disappears long before the archivist is aware the set was ever created. Because of its short life-cycle, we must collect this material on a current basis or not at all.

Taken together, these five factors—institutionalization, bulk, missing data, vulnerable records, and technology—have expanded the universe of potential archival data, have given a contemporaneous character to archival acquisition, and have permanently altered the job of the archivist, forcing him to make choices that he never had to make before. I see three developments on the archival landscape which, in part, are responses to these conditions—the specialized archives, the state archival networks, and an emerging model for urban documentation.

The specialized archives, particularly those built around a subject area—the Archives of Social Welfare at the University of Minnesota is an example—have great appeal. They offer the possibility of well-defined parameters, and exhaustive documentation. They also allow the development of real staff expertise and may be easier to fund. The apotheosis of this type of program was the recent Eugene McCarthy Historical Project, described by its director as the most systematic attempt ever undertaken "to collect and organize all retrievable material of a political campaign for the presidential nomination." The records are voluminous and the project was expensive and the institutional competition for this prize was keen.[10]

---

[10]Werner Peters, "The McCarthy History Project," *American Archivist* 33 (April 1970): 155.

But these archives, especially those centered around the life and times of an individual, do not come to grips with acquisition problems. They side-step them. They contribute to the problem without adding to the solution. But they can contribute to the solution by plugging into larger conceptual frameworks, they can build the kind of inter-institutional linkages and coordination they now lack.

The need to link specialization with coordination was stressed by Sam Bass Warner. Speaking of the urban scene he argued that there is insufficient variation among American cities to justify the repetition everywhere of the same sort of collection. He urged historians and archivists to get together and divide up the archival turf. "San Francisco," he suggested, "might establish a business archive, Detroit, a labor archive, Los Angeles, a housing archive, . . . and so forth."[11] These specialized archives, in turn, would be *linked* with existing local, state, and federal programs. This was Warner's half-baked product that was dismissed out of hand.

But the concept of linkage is a key to the new state archival networks such as those in Ohio, Minnesota, Texas, and Wisconsin. The best of these have a coordinated acquisition program which seeks to be representative in subject coverage, inclusive in informational formats, and statewide in competence.[12] In these regards the Ohio network is one of the most advanced, conceptually if not operationally. The eight centers, most of which are part of a university, function as an integrated archives-library program for their assigned geographic area. Overall collection administration is provided by the Ohio Historical Society which supplies field service assistance in both the public and private sector and assumes responsibility for collections of statewide scope. Furthermore, interconnection assures that the activities of the centers are coordinative rather than competitive.[13] The network concept and structure offer not only a means to document society more systematically, but also to utilize better the limited resources of participating archival units.

In a similar fashion the Houston Metropolitan Archives Center hopes to do for one urban area what the networks have done for their states. Not only is the center the most ambitious urban archives program ever launched, it is also the most handsomely funded—a quarter of a million dollar grant from the National Endowment for the Humanities.

---

[11]Warner, "Shame of the Cities," p. 4.

[12]Richard A. Erney and F. Gerald Ham, "Wisconsin's Area Research Centers," *American Libraries* (February 1972): 135-40; James E. Fogerty, "Minnesota Regional Research Centers," *Minnesota History* (Spring 1974): 30-32; Marilyn von Kohl, "New Program Focuses Attention on Local Records," *Texas Libraries* (Summer 1972): 90-93.

[13]The Ohio Network of American History Research Centers: Charter; Agreement Number One, Administration of Local Ohio Government Records; Agreement Number Two, Ohio Newspapers; and Agreement Number Three, Ohio Manuscripts. Xerox copies.

The project is backed by a consortium of the three major urban universities and the Houston Public Library. In affiliation with the new statewide Regional Historical Research Depositories system, it serves as the public records depository for Houston and Harris County. Manuscript records, printed and non-text material, and oral history are part of its collecting program; and it will provide a fully automated bibliographic control system for all resources regardless of their location in Houston. And two historians—not archivists—using traditional archives-library components, created this comprehensive model for documenting urban life.[14] These approaches can be a beginning. But we must do much more.

First. We must change old habits and attitudes. The view, held by many in our profession that, in collecting, cooperation is synonymous with abdication, must become an anachronism. Given our limited resources, the competition which produces fragmentation and the idiosyncratic proprietary view of archives must yield to integrated cooperative programs which have easily available information on the location of their resources.

Second. We must commit a far greater proportion of our intellectual resources to developing guidelines and strategies for a nationwide system of archival data collecting. And let me say that I am talking about concepts and flexible programs, not rigid structures or uniform procedures. Let me suggest some beginnings. Our subject area committees must give as much attention to appraisal and acquisition criteria and methods as they do to the preparation of technical manuals and directories. Conceptualization must precede collection and, while this methodology is equally applicable to all subject areas, church archives provide a finely drawn example of how this process can be applied. Why couldn't archivists determine the documentation needed to study contemporary religious life, thought, and change and then advise denominations and congregations on how their records selection can contribute to this objective?

We must also develop empirical studies on data selection. For example, why don't college and university archivists compare the documentation produced by institutions of higher learning with the records universities usually preserve, to discover biases and distortions in the selection process and to provide an informed analysis on how archivists should document education and its institutions?

We need more seminars similar to the recent Midwest Archives Conference seminar on state networks to deal with collecting plans and strategies. One on labor documentation would be especially timely. The goal of that seminar might be a consortium of labor

---

[14]Proposal, "Houston Metropolitan Archives Center," National Endowment for the Humanities, Division of Research Grants.

archives. Such a cooperative effort would conserve and amplify rather than waste limited resources. Researchers would be better served if the consortium determined weaknesses in labor documentation and then did something about it. And the individual labor archival institutions *might* even find some workable way to decide who should knock on whose door.

We need to develop methodologies to cope with the important but vast time-series now produced by public and private agencies. Series such as case files of all sorts are so massive that wholesale preservation even on microfilm is impossible. The sample techniques of the various social sciences may offer a solution to the construction of a "representative" sample and suggest the limits and advantages of using one approach rather than another. Similarly, the conceptualization that went into the development of first economic and later social indicators may be transferrable to archival documentation. And the models built by anthropology, economics, sociology, and psychology may give clues to the direction of future research as well as a vision of what constitutes social relevance. The uneasy partnership of the archivist and the historian must be strengthened and expanded to include other students of society.

If our literature is an index to our profession's development, then we need a new body of writings because our old catechisms are either inadequate or irrelevant when they deal with contemporary archives and the theory and practice related to their acquisition. And without needed conceptual and empirical studies, archivists must continue to make their critical choices in intellectual solitary confinement.

Third. We need to reallocate our limited resources for collecting. The critics also present a strong case that far too much effort and money go to document the well documented. In addition, we need archival revenue sharing that will enable the states and localities to meet their archival responsibilities better. The passage of the National Historical Publications and Records Act would be a modest beginning by encouraging statewide planning and providing funds to implement these programs.

Finally, the archivist must realize that he can no longer abdicate his role in this demanding intellectual process of documenting culture. By his training and by his continuing intellectual growth, he must become the research community's Renaissance man. He must know that the scope, quality, and direction of research in an open-ended future depends upon the soundness of his judgment and the keenness of his perceptions about scholarly inquiry. But if he is passive, uninformed, with a limited view of what constitutes the archival record, the collections that he acquires will never hold up a mirror for mankind. And if we are not holding up that mirror, if we are not helping people understand the world they live in, and if this is not what archives is all about, then I do not know what it is we are doing that is all that important.

As archivists we must be in a more exposed position than we have been in the past, one that is more vulnerable. We might well heed the advice of one of Kurt Vonnegut's minor characters, Ed Finnerty, "a chronically malcontent boozer" and the real hero of the novel *Player Piano*. When someone suggested he should see a psychiatrist, Ed replied: "He'd pull me back into the center, and I want to stay as close to the edge as I can without going over. Out on the edge you see all kinds of things you can't see from the center. . . . Big, undreamed-of things—the people on the edge see them first."[15]

---

[15]Tim Hildenbrand, "Two or Three Things I know About Kurt Vonnegut's Imagination," in the *Vonnegut Statement*, Jerome Klinkowitz and John Somer (eds.) (New York: Delacorte, 1973), p. 121.

Appendix

Introduction to Archival Terminology

Maygene F. Daniels

Archival terminology is a flexible group of common words that have acquired specialized meanings for archivists. Since World War II, archivists worldwide have devoted considerable attention to the definition of these words. In 1964, an international lexicon of archival terminology was published.[1] This dictionary in 6 languages, the work of a committee of the International Council on Archives, provides a basis for international comparison of archival terms.

The Society of American Archivists published its own glossary of archival terms in 1974 after several years of debate, drafting, and review.[2] Definitions in the SAA glossary have been widely accepted as the basis for discussion of archival terminology in North America and have been the starting point for subsequent efforts to define American archival terms. Since publication of the SAA glossary, however, many archivists have concluded that some of its definitions require revision and that additional terms should be included. Teachers of archives administration and authors of basic archival texts, consequently, have developed their own glossaries that revise, update, or expand the 1974 work. At present, no single glossary of archival terms can be considered definitive.[3]

The most frequently used archival terms are those that describe documentary materials and archival institutions. Documentary materials can be characterized as "records," "personal papers," or "artificial collections" on the basis of who created and maintained the documents and for what purpose.[4] Records are documents in any form that are made or received and maintained by an organization, whether government

---

[1] *Elsevier's Lexicon of Archive Terminology*. Compiled in French, English, German, Spanish, Italian, and Dutch by a committee of the International Council on Archives. New York: Elsevier Publishing Company, 1964.

[2] "A Basic Glossary for Archivists, Manuscript Curators, and Records Managers," compiled by Frank B. Evans, Donald F. Harrison, and Edwin A. Thompson. Edited by William L. Rofes. *The American Archivist* 37 (July 1974): 415-433.

[3] The glossary included in this *Reader* was developed for the Modern Archives Institute. It is included here to provide assistance for readers who are unfamiliar with archival terminology.

[4] Documentary materials also may be characterized on the basis of their various physical forms: textual, audiovisual, machine-readable, cartographic, printed and others. The term "manuscript" is used for any handwritten or typed document, including press or carbon copy, or any document annotated in handwriting or typescript. In common usage, the term "manuscripts" also often is used as a synonym for "personal papers."

agency, church, business, university, or other institution. An organization's records typically might include copies of letters, memoranda, accounts, reports, photographs, and other materials produced by the organization as well as incoming letters, reports received, memoranda from other offices, and other documents maintained in the organization's files.

In contrast to records, personal papers are created or received and maintained by an individual or family in the process of living. Diaries, news clippings, personal financial records, photographs, correspondence received, and copies of letters written and sent by the individual or family are among the materials typically found in personal papers.

Traditionally, records and personal papers have been considered distinct entities, each with clearly definable characteristics. In the twentieth century, the physical qualities of records and personal papers have become more alike (see *Reader* introduction), however, and archivists increasingly have emphasized the similarities between these materials rather than their differences.[5] In particular, today's archivists recognize that both records and personal papers are bodies of interrelated materials that have been brought together because of their function or use. Archivists respect and seek to maintain the established relationships between individual items in groups of records and in personal papers.[6]

Artificial collections are fundamentally different both from records and from personal papers. Instead of being natural accumulations, artificial collections are composed of individual items purposefully assembled from a variety of sources. Because artificial collections comprise documents from many sources, archivists may elect to change established relationships in order to improve access or control.

Archival institutions can be termed either "archives" or "manuscript repositories" depending on the types of documentary material they contain and how it is acquired. "Archives" traditionally have been those institutions responsible for the long-term care of the historical records of the organization or institution of which they are a part.[7] Many archives are public institutions responsible for the records of continuing value of

---

[5]The term "records" now is even used occasionally as a general term for both records and personal papers. The Presidential Records Act of 1980 codified this usage by employing the term "personal records" to describe strictly personal and private or political papers of the President.

[6]Although some groups of personal papers and, less frequently, some series of records may have no perceptible order, if any order does exist it is likely to be meaningful and archivists seek to protect it. If no internal order is perceptible, the archivist's concern for protecting established relationships does not come into play.

[7]Records in an archival institution also are called "archives." A building in which an archival institution is located also is often referred to as an "archives." "Archives" is a collective noun.

a government or governmental body. The National Archives of the United States and the Public Archives of Canada are examples of public archives at the national level. Public archives also may be found at every other level of government, including state or province, county, and municipal levels. Nonpublic or nongovernmental archives care for the records of any other institution or organization of which they are a part. Church archives, for example, administer the historical records of a religious denomination or congregation. University archives are responsible for records of the university's administration. Archives acquire historical material through the action of law or through internal institutional regulation or policy.

"Manuscript repositories" are archival institutions primarily responsible for personal papers, artificial collections, and records of other organizations. Manuscript repositories purchase or seek donations of materials to which they have no necessary right. They therefore must document the transfer of materials by deed of gift or by other legal contract.

The distinctions between archives and manuscript repositories can be precisely stated, yet few archival institutions are simply "archives" or "manuscript repositories." Most archives hold some personal papers or records of other organizations. Even the National Archives of the United States is responsible for a small group of donated personal papers and nongovernment records. Similarly, many manuscript repositories serve as the archives of their own institutions. In recognition of this, the term "archives" gradually has acquired broader meaning for some archivists and is used by them in reference to any archival institution. This trend has been accelerated by the use of the word "archives" or "archive" in the names of some institutions that in the past might have been termed "manuscript repositories."[8]

Contemporary archival terminology provides a useful and necessary means of specialized communication within the archival profession. Its terms can be precise enough to preserve important distinctions among types of materials and archival institutions, and yet its usage also can be sufficiently flexible to reflect the changing nature of record materials and developments in the administration of archival institutions. As the archival profession grows and matures and as new technologies and records media affect the practice of archives administration, both the precision and flexibility of archival terminology will prove to be of continuing benefit to archivists.

---

[8]The Smithsonian Institution's Archives of American Art and the Dada Archive of the University of Iowa are both examples of this phenomenon.

Glossary

This glossary of commonly used archival terms is based in part on and draws several definitions from "A Basic Glossary for Archivists, Manuscript Curators, and Records Managers," compiled by Frank B. Evans, Donald F. Harrison, and Edwin A. Thompson (*The American Archivist* 37 [July 1974]: 415-433). The glossary includes most important archival terms with specialized meanings. Terms that are adequately described in dictionaries; technical manuscript, records management, and preservation terms; and terms relating to automated data processing are not included.

ACCESS. The archival term for authority to obtain information from or to perform research in archival materials.

ACCESSION. (v.) To transfer physical and legal custody of documentary materials to an archival institution. (n.) Materials transferred to an archival institution in a single accessioning action.

ACCRETION. An addition to an accession.

ACQUISITION. The process of identifying and acquiring, by donation or purchase, historical materials from sources outside the archival institution.

ADMINISTRATIVE VALUE. The value of records for the ongoing business of the agency of records creation or its successor in function.

APPRAISAL. The process of determining whether documentary materials have sufficient value to warrant acquisition by an archival institution.

ARCHIVAL INSTITUTION. An institution holding legal and physical custody of noncurrent documentary materials determined to have permanent or continuing value. Archives and manuscript repositories are archival institutions.

ARCHIVAL VALUE. The value of documentary materials for continuing preservation in an archival institution.

ARCHIVES. (1) The noncurrent records of an organization or institution preserved because of their continuing value. (2) The agency responsible for selecting, preserving, and making available records determined to have permanent or continuing value. (3) The building in which an archival institution is located.

ARCHIVES ADMINISTRATION. The professional management of an archival institution through application of archival principles and techniques.

ARCHIVIST. The professional staff member within an archival institution responsible for any aspect of the selection, preservation, or use of archival materials.

ARRANGEMENT. The archival process of organizing documentary materials in accordance with archival principles.

GLOSSARY

COLLECTING POLICY. A policy established by an archival institution concerning subject areas, time periods, and formats of materials to seek for donation or purchase.

COLLECTION. (1) An artificial accumulation of materials devoted to a single theme, person, event, or type of document acquired from a variety of sources. (2) In a manuscript repository, a body of historical materials relating to an individual, family, or organization.

COLLECTION DEVELOPMENT. The process of building an institution's holdings of historical materials through acquisition activities.

CONTINUOUS CUSTODY. (1) In contemporary U.S. usage, the archival principle that to guarantee archival integrity, archival materials should either be retained by the creating organization or transferred directly to an archival institution. (2) In British usage, the principle that noncurrent records must be retained by the creating organization or its successor in function to be considered archival.

CUBIC FEET (or METERS). A standard measure of the quantity of archival materials on the basis of the volume of space they occupy.

DEED OF GIFT. A legal document accomplishing donation of documentary materials to an archival institution through transfer of title.

DEPOSIT AGREEMENT. A legal document providing for deposit of historical materials in physical custody of an archival institution while legal title to the materials is retained by the donor.

DESCRIPTION. The process of establishing intellectual control over holdings of an archival institution through preparation of finding aids.

DISPOSITION. The final action that puts into effect the results of an appraisal decision for a series of records. Transfer to an archival institution, transfer to a records center, and destruction are among possible dispositions.

DISPOSITION SCHEDULE. Instructions governing retention and disposition of current and noncurrent recurring records series of an organization or agency. Also called a RECORDS CONTROL SCHEDULE.

DOCUMENT. Recorded information regardless of form or medium with three basic elements: base, impression, and message.

DONATED HISTORICAL MATERIALS. Historical materials transferred to an archival institution through a donor's gift rather than in accordance with law or regulation.

EVIDENTIAL VALUE. The value of records or papers as documentation of the operations and activities of the records-creating organization, institution, or individual.

FIELD WORK. The activity of identifying, negotiating for, and securing historical materials for an archival institution.

FINDING AID. A description from any source that provides information about the contents and nature of documentary materials.

HOLDINGS. All documentary materials in the custody of an archival institution including both accessioned and deposited materials.

INFORMATIONAL VALUE. The value of records or papers for information they contain on persons, places, subjects, and things other than the operation of the organization that created them or the activities of the individual or family that created them.

INTRINSIC VALUE. The archival term for those qualities and characteristics of permanently valuable records that make the records in their original physical form the only archivally acceptable form of the records.

LEGAL CUSTODY. Ownership of title to documentary materials.

LIFE CYCLE OF RECORDS. The concept that records pass through a continuum of identifiable phases from the point of their creation, through their active maintenance and use, to their final disposition by destruction or transfer to an archival institution or records center.

LINEAR FEET (or METERS). A standard measure of the quantity of archival materials on the basis of shelf space occupied or the length of drawers in vertical files or the thickness of horizontally filed materials.

MACHINE-READABLE RECORDS. Records created for processing by a computer.

MANUSCRIPT. A handwritten or typed document, including a letterpress or carbon copy, or any document annotated in handwriting or typescript.

MANUSCRIPT. See PERSONAL PAPERS.

MANUSCRIPT CURATOR. The professional staff member within a manuscript repository responsible for any aspect of the selection, preservation, or use of documentary materials.

MANUSCRIPT REPOSITORY. An archival institution primarily responsible for personal papers.

NONRECORD MATERIAL. Material that is not record in character because it comprises solely library or other reference items, because it duplicates records and provides no additional evidence or information, or because its qualities are nondocumentary.

ORIGINAL ORDER. The archival principle that records should be maintained in the order in which they were placed by the organization, individual, or family that created them.

PERSONAL PAPERS. A natural accumulation of documents created or accumulated by an individual or family belonging to him or her and subject to his or her disposition. Also referred to as MANUSCRIPTS.

PRIMARY VALUES. The values of records for the activities for which they were created or received.

PROCESSING. All steps taken in an archival repository to prepare documentary materials for access and reference use.

GLOSSARY

PROVENANCE. (1) The archival principle that records created or received by one recordskeeping unit should not be intermixed with those of any other. (2) Information on the chain of ownership and custody of particular records.

RECORD COPY. The copy of a document which is designated for official retention in files of the administrative unit that is principally responsible for production, implementation, or dissemination of the document.

RECORD GROUP. A body of organizationally related records established on the basis of provenance with particular regard for the complexity and volume of the records and the administrative history of the record-creating institution or organization.

RECORDS. All recorded information, regardless of media or characteristics, made or received and maintained by an organization or institution.

RECORDS CENTER. A records storage facility established to provide efficient storage of inactive records. Legal title to records deposited in a records center is retained by the originating agency.

RECORDS MANAGEMENT. The profession concerned with achieving economy and efficiency in the creation, use, and maintenance of current records.

REFERENCE MATERIALS. Nonaccessioned items maintained by an archival institution solely for reference use.

REFERENCE SERVICE. The archival function of providing information about or from holdings of an archival institution, making holdings available to researchers, and providing copies, reproductions, or loans of holdings.

RESPECT DES FONDS. See PROVENANCE.

REVIEW. The process of surveying documentary materials in an archival institution to determine whether the materials may be open for access by researchers or must be restricted in accordance with law, a donor's requirements, or an institution's regulations.

SANCTITY OF ORIGINAL ORDER. See ORIGINAL ORDER.

SCHEDULE. (v.) To establish retention periods for current records and provide for their proper disposition at the end of active use. (n.) See DISPOSITION SCHEDULE.

SECONDARY VALUES. The values of records to users other than the agency of record creation or its successors.

SERIES. A body of file units or documents arranged in accordance with a unified filing system or maintained by the records creator as a unit because of some relationship arising out of their creation, receipt, or use.

SUBGROUP. A body of related records within a record group, usually consisting of the records of a primary subordinate administrative unit or of records series related chronologically, functionally, or by subject.

Further Reading

General Works

Baumann, Roland, ed. *A Manual of Archival Techniques*. Harrisburg: Pennsylvania Historical and Museum Commission, 1982.

Bordin, Ruth B. and Robert M. Warner. *The Modern Manuscript Library*. New York: Scarecrow Press, 1966.

Brooks, Philip C. *Research in Archives: The Use of Unpublished Primary Sources*. Chicago: University of Chicago Press, 1969.

Clark, Robert L. *Archive-Library Relations*. New York: R.R. Bowker, 1976.

Duckett, Kenneth. *Modern Manuscripts: A Practical Manual for Their Management, Care, and Use*. Nashville: American Association for State and Local History, 1975.

Gracy, David B. II. *An Introduction to Archives and Manuscripts*. New York: Special Libraries Association, 1981.

Jones, H. G. *Local Government Records: An Introduction to Their Management, Preservation and Use*. Nashville: American Association for State and Local History, 1980.

Kane, Lucile M. *A Guide to the Care and Administration of Manuscripts*. 2d rev. ed. Nashville: American Association for State and Local History, 1966.

Lytle, Richard, ed. "Management of Archives and Manuscript Collections for Librarians." *Drexel Library Quarterly* 11 (January 1975).

Mitchell, Thornton W., ed. *Norton on Archives: The Writings of Margaret Cross Norton on Archival and Records Management*. Carbondale: Southern Illinois University Press, 1975.

Schellenberg, Theodore R. *The Management of Archives*. New York: Columbia University Press, 1965.

———. *Modern Archives: Principles and Techniques*. Chicago: University of Chicago Press, 1956.

Society of American Archivists. *College and University Archives: Selected Readings*. Chicago: Society of American Archivists, 1979.

The European Tradition

Jenkinson, Hilary. *A Manual of Archive Administration*. Edited by Roger H. Ellis. 2d rev. ed. London: Percy, Lund, Humphries and Co., 1966.

Muller, Samuel, J.A. Feith and R. Fruin. *Manual for the Arrangement and Description of Archives*. Translated by Arthur H. Leavitt. New York: H.W. Wilson, 1940.

Posner, Ernst. "Max Lehmann and the Genesis of the Principle of Provenance." In *Archives and the Public Interest: Selected Essays by Ernst Posner*, edited by Ken Munden, pp. 36-44. Washington: Public Affairs Press, 1967.

Schellenberg, Theodore R. "European Archival Practices in Arranging Records." National Archives Staff Information Circular 5. Washington: The National Archives, 1939.

FURTHER READING

Pre-Archival Functions: Records Management and Records Centers

Evans, Frank B. "Modern Concepts of Archives Administration and Records Management." *UNESCO Bulletin for Libraries* 24 (Sept.-Oct. 1970): 242-7.

Fleckner, John. *Archives and Manuscripts: Surveys.* Chicago: Society of American Archivists, 1977.

Lamb., W. Kaye. "The Fine Art of Destruction." In *Essays in Memory of Sir Hilary Jenkinson*, edited by Albert E.J. Hollaender, pp. 50-56. Chichester: Society of Archivists, 1962.

Leahy, Emmett J. "Modern Records Management." *The American Archivist* 12 (July 1949): 231-42.

Ricks, Artel. "Records Management as an Archival Function." *Records Management Quarterly* 11 (April 1977): 12-18, 20.

Appraisal and Disposition

Bauer, G. Philip. "The Appraisal of Current and Recent Records." National Archives Staff Information Circular 13. Washington: The National Archives, 1946.

Boles, Frank. "Sampling in Archives." *The American Archivist* 44 (Spring 1981): 125-130.

Brichford, Maynard J. *Archives and Manuscripts: Appraisal and Accessioning.* Chicago: Society of American Archivists, 1977.

Fishbein, Meyer H. "A Viewpoint on Appraisal of National Records." *The American Archivist* 33 (April 1970): 175-187.

Lewinson, Paul. "Archival Sampling." *The American Archivist* 20 (October 1957): 291-311.

Mitchell, Thornton W. "New Viewpoints on Establishing Permanent Values of State Archives." *The American Archivist* 33 (April 1970): 163-175.

Acquisition

Berkely, Edmund Jr. "The Archives and Appraisals." *Georgia Archive* 5 (Winter 1977): 51-63.

Duckett, Kenneth. "Acquisitions: The Mechanics and Ethics." *Modern Manuscripts: A Practical Manual for Their Management, Care, and Use*, pp. 56-85. Nashville: American Association for State and Local History, 1975.

Kemp, Edward C. *Manuscript Solicitation for Libraries, Special Collections, Museums and Archives.* Littleton: Libraries Unlimited, 1978.

Mason, Philip P. "The Ethics of Collecting." *Georgia Archive* 5 (Winter 1977): 36-50.

Taylor, R.J. "Field Appraisal of Manuscript Collections." *Archivaria* 1 (Summer 1976): 44-48.

Arrangement

Boles, Frank. "Disrespecting Original Order." *The American Archivist* 45 (Winter 1982): 26-32.

Brubacher, Robert L. "Archival Principles and the Curator of Manuscripts." *The American Archivist* 29 (October 1966): 505-14.

Evans, Frank B. "Modern Methods of Arrangement of Archives in the United States." *The American Archivist* 29 (April 1966): 241-63.

Gracy, David B., II. *Archives and Manuscripts: Arrangement and Description.* Chicago: Society of American Archivists, 1977.

Hurley, C. "Personal Papers and the Treatment of Archival Principles." *Archives and Manuscripts: The Journal of the Australian Society of Archivists* 7 (February 1977): 351-65.

Lathrop, Alan. "The Provenance and Preservation of Architectural Records." *The American Archivist* 43 (Summer 1980): 325-38.

Shaw, Renata. "Picture Organization: Practices and Procedures." *Special Libraries* 63 (October 1972, November 1972): 448-56, 502-06.

Vincent, Carl. "The Record Group: A Concept in Evolution." *Archivaria* 3 (Winter 1976-77): 3-16.

Description

Abraham, Terry. "Manuscripts: A Continuum of Description." *George Archive* 2 (Winter 1974): 20-27.

Berner, Richard C. "Arrangement and Description: Some Historical Observations." *The American Archivist* 41 (April 1978): 169-81.

——. "Manuscript Catalogs and Other Finding Aids: What Are Their Relationships?" *The American Archivist* 34 (October 1971): 367-72.

Gordon, Robert S. "Suggestions for the Organization and Description of Archival Holdings of Local Historical Societies." *The American Archivist* 26 (July 1963): 19-39.

Gracy, David B., II. *Archives and Manuscripts: Arrangement and Description.* Chicago: Society of American Archivists, 1977.

Papenfuse, Edward C. "The Retreat From Standardization." *The American Archivist* 36 (October 1973): 537-42.

Society of American Archivists. *Inventories and Registers: A Handbook of Techniques and Examples.* Chicago: Society of American Archivists, 1976.

Reference

Holbert, Sue E. *Archives and Manuscripts: Reference and Access.* Chicago: Society of American Archivists, 1977.

Kepley, Brenda Beasley. "Archives: Accessibility for the Disabled." *The American Archivist* 46 (Winter 1983): 135-47.

Lytle, Richard H. "Intellectual Access to Archives: I. Provenance and Content Indexing Methods of Subject Retrieval." *The American Archivist* 43 (Winter 1980): 64-75.

——. "Intellectual Access to Archives: II. Report of an Experiment Comparing Provenance and Content Indexing Methods of Subject Retrieval." *The American Archivist* 43 (Spring 1980): 191-205.

FURTHER READING

Rhoads, James B. "Alienation and Thievery: Archival Problems." *The American Archivist* 29 (April 1966): 197-208.

Rosenthal, Robert. "The User and the Used." *Drexel Library Quarterly* 11 (January 1975): 97-105.

Walch, Timothy. *Archives and Manuscripts: Security*. Chicago: Society of American Archivists, 1977.

Public Programs

Casterline, Gail Farr. *Archives and Manuscripts: Exhibits*. Chicago: Society of American Archivists, 1980.

Myres, Sandra. "Public Programs for Archives: Reaching Patrons, Officials, and the Public." *Georgia Archive* 7 (Spring 1979): 10-15.

Pederson, Ann and Gail Farr Casterline. *Archives and Manuscripts: Public Programs*. Chicago: Society of American Archivists, 1982.

Powers, Sandra. "Why Exhibit? The Risks Versus the Benefits." *The American Archivist* 41 (July 1978): 297-306.

Taylor, Hugh A. "Clio in the Raw: Archival Materials and the Teaching of History." *The American Archivist* 35 (July/October 1972): 317-30.

Establishing Priorities

Berner, Richard C. "Toward National Archival Priorities: A Suggested Basis for Discussion." *The American Archivist* 45 (Spring 1982): 164-74.

Burckel, Nicholas C. "Program Planning and Service Policies for a University Archives." *Georgia Archive* 6 (Spring 1978): 31-35.

Burke, Frank G. "Archival Cooperation." *The American Archivist* 46 (Summer 1983): 295-305.

Christian, John F. and Shonnie Finnegan. "On Planning an Archives." *The American Archivist* 37 (October 1974): 573-78.

Gracy, David B., II. "Starting an Archives." *Georgia Archive* 1 (Fall 1972): 20-29.

Ham, F. Gerald. "Archival Strategies for the Post-Custodial Era." *The American Archivist* 44 (Summer 1981): 207-16.

McCree, Mary Lynn and Timothy Walch, eds. "Setting Priorities for Historical Records: A Conference Report." *The American Archivist* 40 (July 1977): 291-347.

Miller, Frederick. "Social History and Archival Practice." *The American Archivist* 44 (Spring 1981): 113-24.

Society of American Archivists. *Evaluation of Archival Institutions: Services, Principles, and Guide to Self-Study*. Chicago, Society of American Archivists, 1982.

Contributors

HERBERT ANGEL retired from the National Archives and Records Service in 1972 after four years as deputy archivist of the United States and 36 years of federal service. He is a past president and fellow of the Society of American Archivists.

PATRICIA BARTKOWSKI is assistant university archivist for the Wayne State University Archives at the Walter P. Reuther Library of Labor and Urban Affairs. She is vice-president of the Midwest Archives Conference.

KATHARINE E. BRAND served in a variety of capacities in the Manuscript Division of the Library of Congress. At the time of her retirement in 1956, she was head of the Recent Manuscript Section.

GEORGE CHALOU is assistant branch chief of the Modern Military field branch of the National Archives and Records Service. From 1974 through 1978, he directed the National Archives staff training course for archivists.

MAYGENE F. DANIELS is special assistant to the deputy archivist of the United States and director of the Modern Archives Institute of the National Archives and Records Service.

MEGAN FLOYD DESNOYERS is a supervisory archivist at the John F. Kennedy Library in Boston, where she is responsible for paper and tape processing. She is also a frequent lecturer and workship director for the Society of American Archivists.

CHARLES M. DOLLAR is assistant director of the Archival Research and Evaluation Staff of the National Archives and Records Service. He also has served in many other capacities at the National Archives, including that of director of the Machine-Readable Archives Division.

RALPH E. EHRENBERG is assistant chief of the Geography and Map Division of the Library of Congress and former chief of the Cartographic Archives Division of the National Archives and Records Service. He is author of *Archives and Manuscripts: Maps and Architectural Drawings* (1982) and *The Mapping of America* (1980).

FRANK B. EVANS is on the staff of the National Archives and Records Service. He served as Program Specialist in Archives for the United Nations Educational, Scientific, and Cultural Organization (UNESCO) from 1977 to 1984. Prior to this appointment, he was on the staff of the National Archives and Records Service with responsibility for a variety of functions, including compilation of *The Guide to the National Archives of the United States* (1974). He also served as state archivist of Pennsylvania. He is a fellow of the Society of American Archivists, compiler of *Modern Archives and Manuscripts: A Select Bibliography* (1975), and a past director of the Modern Archives Institute.

ELSIE FREEMAN [FREIVOGEL] is the director of academic, professional, and public programs in the Office of Public Programs and Exhibits of the National Archives and Records Service. She is a fellow and former council member of the Society of American Archivists.

F. GERALD HAM is state archivist and assistant director for research services at the State Historical Society of Wisconsin. He is a fellow and past president of the Society of American Archivists.

EDWARD E. HILL is a senior records description specialist in the Military Archives Division of the National Archives and Records Service. He is a fellow of the Society of American Archivists and a two time winner of the Waldo Gifford Leland prize.

OLIVER W. HOLMES (1902-1982) joined the National Archives staff in 1935 and served in many capacities, including that of executive director of the National Historical Publications Commission. He retired from federal service in 1972. He was president and fellow of the Society of American Archivists.

HILARY JENKINSON (1882-1961) joined the staff of the British Public Record Office in 1906 and ended his service there in 1954. Jenkinson's volume, *A Manual of Archive Administration*, published in 1922 and revised in 1937, is the authoritative guide to archival practice in Great Britain. Jenkinson was knighted for his service in 1949.

RICHARD M. KESNER is manager of Office Systems and Services for the F. W. Faxon Company in Boston. He is the compiler of *Information Management, Machine Readable Records*, and *Administration: An Annotated Bibliography* (1983) and the author of two recent volumes: *Automating Archival and Records Administration* (1984) and *Micro-computer Applications in Libraries* (1984).

LYDIA LUCAS is the head of technical services in the Division of Archives and Manuscripts at the Minnesota Historical Society. She is the compiler of *Manuscript Collections of the Minnesota Historical Society, Guide No. 3* (1977).

NANCY E. MALAN produces audiovisual programs for the National Archives and Records Service. Her experience in the National Archives's Still Pictures Branch is reflected in her independent study course, *The Administration of Historical Photograph Collections* (1982), published by the American Association for State and Local History.

MARY LYNN MCCREE is the editor of the Jane Addams Papers and a frequent lecturer on archives management for the Society of American Archivists. She is a fellow and former officer of the SAA.

TRUDY HUSKAMP PETERSON has been a staff member of the National Archives and Records Service since 1968 and is a past director of the Modern Archives Institute. In 1983, she received a Fulbright grant to teach American studies in Finland. She is the author of *Basic Archival Workshop Exercises* (1982) and editor of the conference volume *Farmers, Bureaucrats and Middlemen*. She is a fellow of the SAA and winner of its Gondos Award.

CONTRIBUTORS

ERNST POSNER (1892-1980) was a professor of history and administrator at The American University in Washington, D.C., from 1939 to 1961. Among other achievements, Posner is remembered as founding director of the Modern Archives Institute and as the author of *American State Archives* (1964). Posner's life and importance to the archival profession are described in "Ernst Posner: The Bridge Between the Old World and the New," by Rodney A. Ross, *The American Archivist* 44 (Fall 1981): 304-312.

MARY JO PUGH is reference archivist at the Michigan Historical Collections, Bentley Historical Library, and lecturer in archives administration at the University of Michigan in Ann Arbor. Her essay "The Illusion of Omniscience: Subject Access and the Reference Archivist," included in this volume, is the winner of the first Ernst Posner Prize for the best article published in *The American Archivist* during the previous year.

VIRGINIA C. PURDY supervises development of subject guides for the Office of the National Archives of the National Archives and Records Service. She served as editor of *The American Archivist* from 1978-1981. She is a fellow and member of Council of the Society of American Archivists.

JOAN RABINS is responsible for finding aids, processing, and accessioning at Wayne State University's Archives of Labor and Urban Affairs. She also participates in the graduate education program of the Archives as a lecturer and supervisor of student projects.

LEONARD RAPPORT is an archivist in the Civil Archives Division of the National Archives and Records Service. He is a fellow of the Society of American Archivists. His essay, "No Grandfather Clause: Reappraising Accessioned Records," included in this volume, was awarded the Arline Custer Award of the Mid-Atlantic Regional Archives Conference.

T. R. SCHELLENBERG (1903-1970) joined the staff of the National Archives in 1935 and served in many capacities before his retirement in 1963. At the time of his retirement, he was assistant archivist of the United States. Schellenberg is best remembered as the author of two influential books: *Modern Archives: Principles and Techniques* (1956) and *The Management of Archives* (1965). Schellenberg's career and accomplishments are described in "Theodore R. Schellenberg: Americanizer and Popularizer," by Jane F. Smith, *The American Archivist* 44 (Fall 1981): 313-326.

VIRGINIA R. STEWART is the director of the Elmhurst Historical Museum in Elmhurst, Illinois, and also works as a consultant in archives and history. She is active in the Society of American Archivists and the Midwest Archives Conference and currently serves as vice-president of the Congress of Illinois Historical Societies and Museums.

TIMOTHY WALCH is editor of *Prologue: Journal of the National Archives* and codirector of the Modern Archives Institute of the National Archives and Records Service. He is the author of *Archives and Manuscripts: Security* (1977).

CONTRIBUTORS

JAMES C. WORTHY is a professor of management and Senior Austin Fellow of the J.L. Kellogg Graduate School of Management at Northwestern University. In addition, he serves as a consultant to a number of major American corporations.

Index

A

Access,
  definition of, 339
  in 19th-century Europe, 6, 8–9
  policy of equality of, 107, 142–143,
    260–262, 310
  See also Restrictions
Accessibility, 11–12, 45, 155, 156,
    159–161, 175
  in photo collections, 183, 185
  See also Usability
Accessioning, 85, 170, 207, 322, 339
Accretion,
  definition of, 339
Acquisitions, 101, 103–113, 114–123,
    124–138, 337–338
  definition of, 339
Administrative value,
  definition of, 339
Aerial photographs, 192
Aesthetic qualities,
  of records, 92–93, 187
African Studies Association, 253
Age,
  of records in appraisal, 64, 93
Agence Temporaire des Titres, 5
Alaska Historical Commission, 253
Algemeen Rijksarchief (Netherlands), 6
American Archivist, xii
American Association for State and Local
    History, 117
American Council of Learned Societies,
    Committee on Negro Studies, 248
American Historical Association, 329
American Records Management
    Association, 33, 38
Angel, Herbert E., 24, 46–53
Appraisal,
  and records management, 23–24
  costs of, 76–77
  definition of, 55, 339
  for evidential and informational value,
    57–70
  for intrinsic value, 91–99
  in manuscripts field work, 117–118,
    129–131
  of machine-readable records, 71–79
  reappraisal, 80–90
  role of records centers, 51

See also Tax appraisal
Archival institution,
  definition of, 337–338, 339
Archival profession,
  history of, xi, xiii–xiv
  records managers in, 25–37
Archival value,
  definition of, 339
Archives,
  definition of, 15, 18–19, 46, 339
Archives administration,
  definition of, 339
  dual nature of, xi
  in Europe, 3–14
  place of records centers in, 46–53
  principles of management in, 299–308
  public programs in, 282
  relation to records management, 25–37,
    38–45
Archives education, 286–287.
  See also Archivists, training of.
Archives Generales du Royaume
    (Belgium), 6
Archives Nationales (France), 5, 7, 10, 151
Archives of Appalachia, 115, 117,
    118–119, 121, 122
Archives of Labor and Urban Affairs, 290
Archives of Social Welfare, 331
Archivists,
  definition of, 339
  duties and qualifications of, 12–13, 15,
    17–18, 18–21, 31–32, 33–34, 67–70,
    81, 130–131, 136–138, 169–170, 286,
    290, 303–304
  training of, 12–13, 172, 281, 286–287
Arrangement,
  by subject, 10, 152
  definition of, 137, 275, 312, 339
  described in inventories, 221–224
  in 19th-century Europe, 11–12
  levels of, 162–180, 230–231
  of aural records, 197
  of graphic records, 188–190
  of photographs, 181–186, 192–193, 194
  of series, 230–233
  practice of, 162–180, 312–316
  principles of, 149–161, 265
  relation to reference service, 173, 175,
    267, 270
  See also Processing